UNDERSTANDING
LANGUAGE
THROUGH
SIGN LANGUAGE
RESEARCH

PERSPECTIVES IN
NEUROLINGUISTICS AND PSYCHOLINGUISTICS

Harry A. Whitaker, Series Editor
DEPARTMENT OF PSYCHOLOGY
THE UNIVERSITY OF ROCHESTER
ROCHESTER, NEW YORK

HAIGANOOSH WHITAKER and HARRY A. WHITAKER (Eds.).
Studies in Neurolinguistics, Volumes 1, 2, and 3
NORMAN J. LASS (Ed.). Contemporary Issues in Experimental Phonetics
JASON W. BROWN. Mind, Brain, and Consciousness: The Neuropsychology
of Cognition
SIDNEY J. SEGALOWITZ and FREDERIC A. GRUBER (Eds.). Language Devel-
opment and Neurological Theory
SUSAN CURTISS. Genie: A Psycholinguistic Study of a Modern-Day "Wild
Child"
JOHN MACNAMARA (Ed.). Language Learning and Thought
I. M. SCHLESINGER and LILA NAMIR (Eds.). Sign Language of the Deaf:
Psychological, Linguistic, and Sociological Perspectives
WILLIAM C. RITCHIE (Ed.). Second Language Acquisition Research: Issues
and Implications
PATRICIA SIPLE (Ed.). Understanding Language through Sign Language
Research

In preparation

MARTIN L. ALBERT and LORAINE K. OBLER. The Bilingual Brain: Neurophysiological and Neurolinguistic Aspects of Bilingualism
HAIGANOOSH WHITAKER and HARRY A. WHITAKER. Studies in Neurolinguistics, Volume 4

UNDERSTANDING LANGUAGE THROUGH SIGN LANGUAGE RESEARCH

Edited by
PATRICIA SIPLE

Department of Psychology
University of Rochester
Rochester, New York

ACADEMIC PRESS   New York   San Francisco   London   1978

A Subsidiary of Harcourt Brace Jovanovich, Publishers

ACADEMIC PRESS, INC.
111 Fifth Avenue, New York, New York 10003

United Kingdom Edition published by
ACADEMIC PRESS, INC. (LONDON) LTD.
24/28 Oval Road, London NW1 7DX

Library of Congress Cataloging in Publication Data

Main entry under title:

Understanding language through sign language
    research.

    (Perspectives in neurolinguistics and psycho—
linguistics)
    Based on the papers presented at the Conference
on Sign Language and Neurolinguistics, held in
Rochester, N. Y. in Sept. 1976.
    Includes bibliographies and index.
    1. Sign language——Addresses, essays, lectures.
2. Languages——Physiological aspects——Addresses,
essays, lectures. 3. Children——Language——Addresses,
essays, lectures. 4. Psycholinguistics——Addresses,
essays, lectures. I. Siple, Patricia. II. Con—
ference on Sign Language and Neurolinguistics,
Rochester, N. Y., 1976.
HV2474.U52   001.56   77—25631
ISBN 0—12—646550—9

Contents

III   NEUROLINGUISTIC STUDIES

IV   PSYCHOLINGUISTIC RESEARCH

V   HISTORICAL AND COMPARATIVE STUDIES

List of Contributors

Numbers in parentheses indicate the pages on which the authors' contributions begin.

CHARLOTTE BAKER* (27), Department of Linguistics, University of California, Berkeley, California 94720

URSULA BELLUGI (239), The Salk Institute for Biological Studies, San Diego, California 92112

JOHN D. BONVILLIAN (187), Department of Psychology, Vassar College, Poughkeepsie, New York 12601

RUTH ELLENBERGER (261), Research, Development, and Demonstration Center in Education of Handicapped Children, Pattee Hall, University of Minnesota, Minneapolis, Minnesota 55455

SUSAN D. FISCHER (309), Department of Linguistics, San Diego State University, San Diego, California 92182

ROGER FOUTS (163), Department of Psychology, University of Oklahoma, Norman, Oklahoma 73019

HARRY W. HOEMANN (289), Department of Psychology, Bowling Green State University, Bowling Green, Ohio 43403

M. M. KONSTANTAREAS (213), Clarke Institute of Psychiatry, Toronto M5T 1R8, Ontario, Canada

HARLAN LANE (271), Department of Psychology, Northeastern University, Boston, Massachusetts 02115

SCOTT K. LIDDELL† (59), University of California, San Diego, and The Salk Institute for Biological Studies, San Diego, California 92112

RACHEL I. MAYBERRY†† (349), School of Human Communication Disorders, McGill University, Montréal, Québec, Canada

* Present address: Linguistics Research Laboratory, Gallaudet College, Washington, D. C. 20002.

† Present address: Research Center for Language and Semiotic Studies, Indiana University, Bloomington, Indiana 47401.

†† Present address: Department of Communication Disorders, Northwestern University, Evanston, Illinois 60201.

KEITH E. NELSON (187), Department of Psychology, Pennsylvania State University, University Park, Pennsylvania 16802

HELEN J. NEVILLE (239), The Salk Institute for Biological Studies, San Diego, California 92112

ELISSA L. NEWPORT (91), Department of Psychology, University of California, San Diego, La Jolla, California 92093

CHARITY O'NEIL (163), Department of Psychology, University of Oklahoma, Norman, Oklahoma 73019

J. OXMAN (213), Clarke Institute of Psychiatry, Toronto M5T 1R8, Ontario, Canada

CAROL A. PADDEN (27), Linguistics Research Laboratory, Gallaudet College, Kendall Green, Washington, D. C. 20002

HOWARD POIZNER* (271), Department of Psychology, Northeastern University, Boston, Massachusetts 02115

GARY SHAPIRO (163), Department of Psychology, University of Oklahoma, Norman, Oklahoma 73019

PATRICIA SIPLE (3), Department of Psychology, University of Rochester, Rochester, New York 14627

MARCIA STEYAERT (261), Research, Development, and Demonstration Center in Education of Handicapped Children, Pattee Hall, University of Minnesota, Minneapolis, Minnesota 55455

TED SUPALLA (91), Psychology Department, University of California, San Diego, La Jolla, California 92037

KATHERINE NORTON WARREN (133), Office of Professional Development, National Technical Institute for the Deaf, Rochester Institute of Technology, Rochester, New York 14623

C. D. WEBSTER† (213), University of Victoria, B. C., Canada

JAMES WOODWARD (333), Linguistics Research Laboratory, Gallaudet College, Kendall Green, Washington, D. C. 20002

---

* Now at The Salk Institute for Biological Studies, San Diego, California 92112.

† Present address: Metfors, 999 Queen Street West, Toronto, M6J 1H4.

Preface

Each of the chapters in this volume explores some aspect of American Sign Language (ASL), a language used by most deaf adults in the United States and parts of Canada. Yet this volume is not just about American Sign Language. The contributors are linguists and psychologists who, first and foremost, want to understand language and language processing. Each has determined that the study of manual language communication provides a unique opportunity to broaden our knowledge of language and its use. At the same time, the study of sign language brings the researcher closer to the practitioner than is often the case. Thus, the chapters in this volume serve a dual function: They provide new approaches to contemporary issues in the study of language and, at the same time, shed light on topics of interest to educators, counselors, and those providing services for the deaf population.

In September, 1976, a Conference on Sign Language and Neurolinguistics was held in Rochester, New York. This conference was the first of its kind, bringing together researchers from several scientific fields to discuss the implications of sign language research. All but one of the chapters in this volume are based on presentations at that conference, but they are not the verbatim proceedings. A great deal of care has been taken to ensure that the chapters are accurate and readable. All the manuscripts were reviewed and many major revisions were undertaken in order to satisfy the needs of a book.

The sections of the book reflect the interdisciplinary nature of the meetings. Topics include discussions of the linguistic structure of ASL, implications of the study of ASL for neurolinguistics and psycholinguistics, and considerations of sociolinguistic and cultural aspects of ASL, both historically and comparatively.

The initial chapter provides an introduction to the language itself and an overview of sign language research. Each of the following 14 research chapters covers a particular aspect of ASL in depth. The introductory chapter provides background information for these chapters and serves to place them within the larger context of sign language research. For the reader who knows very little about ASL, this chapter should provide a satisfactory introduction to the remainder of the volume. Together, the contributors provide a comprehensive introduction to contemporary issues of language and language processing addressed by sign language research.

The final writing of the manuscripts could not have come about without the exceptional cooperation of each of the contributors. Many served as referees for other papers, knowing that their papers were undergoing the same kind of scrutiny from others. To each of the contributors, I owe a great deal of gratitude. The scope and depth of this volume were made possible by the National Science Foundation. The Conference on Sign Language and Neurolinguistics from which these papers were drawn was funded in large part by National Science Foundation Grant No. BNS76-10677. Harry Whitaker, as co-organizer of that conference and series editor for this book, deserves special thanks. Without him, the way would not have been so easy. A very special thank you goes to a group of women who have been a part of nearly every facet of this volume. They, as critics, proofreaders, and friends, have dedicated much of their time and effort over the past several months to this project. Thank you Carol Akamatsu, Laurie Brewer, Alinda Drury, Susan Garnsey, Melody Harrison, Nancy Hatfield, Betsy McDonald, Rachel Mayberry, and Kathy Warren.

I

INTRODUCTION

1

Linguistic and Psychological Properties of American Sign Language: An Overview

PATRICIA SIPLE

University of Rochester

American Sign Language (ASL) is the primary language used for communication among deaf people in the United States and parts of Canada. While it is the fourth most common language used in the United States (Mayberry, 1978), it has only recently been "discovered" by linguists and psychologists. The principal question underlying most investigations of ASL (and other sign languages) stems from the difference in modality of perception and production. American Sign Language is a visual–manual language rather than an auditory–spoken one. To what extent are proposed linguistic and cognitive structures and processes dependent on modality, or, stated differently, which of these posited structures and processes are modality independent? What follows is a general description of ASL and a review of the initial investigations into the question of modality specific and modality independent properties of language, language processing, and language acquisition.

The preparation of this paper was supported by National Science Foundation Grant No. GB–43913.

ORIENTATIONS

People approaching sign language research for the first time often come with many preconceptions. Some of these are based on incomplete information and lack of experience with deaf people. Others are the result of distinct cultural biases. In the United States, for example, a large amount of gesturing is often described negatively as being unsophisticated and crude. Before sign language research can be considered seriously, the preconceptions surrounding the use of gestural language must be put aside.

While 1% of the population of the United States is deaf, few hearing people have had anything more than minimal contact with a deaf person. Deaf people tend to interact with and socialize with one another, forming a distinct cultural group within the general population. The cohesiveness of this cultural group stems from the use of a common language—sign language—as the principal language, as well as the inability of many members of the deaf community to communicate well using the national language, English. In fact, deafness is often defined functionally as a "hearing loss of sufficient severity to prevent aural comprehension of speech [Furth, 1973, p. 7]," or as a "loss of hearing sufficiently severe to render an understanding of conversational speech impossible in most situations [Mindel & Vernon, 1971, p. x]." Thus, a major problem for the deaf community is one of communication, not *within* the community, where an appropriate language medium exists, but *outside* the community, where people depend on spoken language for communication.

Because of the way that signs, the lexical units of ASL, are used, sign language is often assumed to be a manual–gestural representation of English, with individual signs corresponding to English words. In ASL, the language used by the deaf community, this is definitely not the case. Often the meaning of a sign can only be approximated by an English word; the reverse is also true. Even when these differences are ignored and the best English gloss is assigned to each sign, a word-by-word translation of ASL discourse looks nothing like the same material in English sentences. For example,[1] the signed sequence:

FINISH TOUCH EUROPE?

[1]As is conventional, English glosses meant to represent signs will be indicated in capital letters to distinguish them from English words. This example is taken from Dennis Cokely's Foreword to Hoemann (1976).

is a perfectly acceptable ASL sentence, which can be translated into English as:

"Have you been to Europe?"

It must be quickly added that, whereas ASL, the language, differs from English, there are sign systems derived from oral language and used primarily as a vehicle to teach English to deaf students via signs (Mayberry, 1978). These systems generally borrow some lexical items from ASL and invent new ones. Fingerspelling, representing each English letter by a hand configuration, is also used, though it is only marginally a part of ASL. In all of these systems, English word order is maintained. Signed English uses ASL signs as they are, adding a few new signs that were created to represent English functions and inflectional endings. Two other systems, both called SEE—Seeing Essential English (Anthony, 1971) and Signing Exact English (Gustason, Pfetzing, & Zawalkow, 1972)—include rules for altering existing signs to make them correspond more closely to English words and new signs for English morphemes for which there are no existing signs. These sign systems are often used successfully in educational settings; however, they are generally abandoned outside the school environment because they are not as efficient as ASL.

If sign language is not a manual representation of a spoken language, then is sign language universal? The answer is no. There are as many different sign languages as there are distinct deaf communities. Often, but not always, these language communities are determined by national boundaries in the same way that spoken language communities are. The relationships among present-day sign languages are currently being established through historical and comparative studies of sign languages (e.g., Jordan & Battison, 1976; Woodward, 1976). For our purposes, an example will be sufficient. American Sign Language is a direct descendent of French Sign Language. Many cognates exist, and the two languages are to some extent mutually intelligible. The sign language of the deaf community in England is not directly related to ASL. Thus, it is difficult for a deaf person to engage in conversation with a visitor from England. It is difficult to set up the equivalent of "foreigner's talk" between two languages. In these situations, it is usual for the signers to resort to mime and gesture for basic communication (Battison & Jordan, 1976).

Perhaps the most striking aspect of sign language to the person seeing it for the first time is its picture-like quality. Because of this, signs are often described as "iconic," as copying elements of the thing signified. If indeed signs are iconic, how can one talk about things abstract? The belief that signs are iconic representations of concrete objects is pervasive among hearing people who are not acquainted with ASL. Such a belief questions the symbolic nature of ASL. That this notion is false can be readily demonstrated.

Sign language is regularly used to conduct religious services for deaf congregations; scientific papers have been presented in ASL, and the National Theater for the Deaf annually presents dramatic productions ranging from Homeric legends to contemporary drama. Signs exist for abstract concepts—*hope* and *wisdom*, for example.

Certain signs are iconic in origin. Some of these have retained their iconicity (Mayberry, personal communication, 1976). However, the study of historical change in ASL has indicated clearly that the trend is toward arbitrariness (Frishberg, 1975, 1976). When the formation of a sign changes, it changes systematically and regularly to a more arbitrary form that is characteristic of ASL. Like historical changes in spoken languages, the changes in ASL are governed primarily by ease of perception and production. For example, large, two-handed signs have tended to become symmetrical, making them easier to perceive (Siple, 1978). Evidence for an underlying arbitrary linguistic system for ASL exists in large quantity.

LINGUISTIC STRUCTURE

In *A Dictionary of American Sign Language*, Stokoe, Casterline, and Croneberg (1965) provided the first truly comprehensive description of the signs of ASL. Their linguistic description, based on the work of Stokoe (1960), and their accompanying transcription system have provided a firm base for later investigations of ASL. The new edition of this work (1976) provides the most thorough ASL–English dictionary available.

Stokoe (1960) provided evidence that a sign could generally be described by reference to three components, which he named tab, dez, and sig. The tab of a sign refers to the location where a sign is made with respect to the signer's body. The dez indicates the handshape (or handshapes) used to make the sign. The sig describes the movement involved in producing the sign. These components are roughly equivalent to the phonemes of a spoken language.[2] In order to

---

[2]The terms *phoneme, phonology,* and *phonological* will be used here to describe sign formation, even though these terms are derived from speech-related phenomena. It is

describe the more than 2000 signs in the dictionary, 55 phonemes were required: 12 places of articulation, 19 hand configurations, and 24 movements. Symbols were assigned to each of these, and conventions were established for providing an ordered written description for a sign. With this transcription system, usually called Stokoe notation, signs can be represented on paper. However, for general descriptions it is more usual to describe the three components in words because the special symbols required for Stokoe notation are not readily available to typesetters.

The handshapes used to form signs are similar to those used in fingerspelling. Thus, the A handshape looks like the manual-alphabet configuration for the letter A. However, as is noted in the dictionary, the manual alphabet S and T are acceptable variants of the A handshape in some signs; they are allophones. For descriptive purposes, all are assigned to the A handshape or dez class. The manual-alphabet chart shown in Figure 1.1 can be used to reproduce most of the handshapes of ASL. Thus the sign KNOW is formed by touching (the movement) the tips of the fingers of the B hand to the forehead (the location).

Phonology

Studies of ASL phonology since 1965 have focused on three major areas: The components or parameters of sign formation have been further described and delineated; investigators have asked how and why these parameters are combined to form signs; and attempts have been made to determine the feasibility of applying oral language linguistic techniques and principles to ASL. These studies point strongly toward underlying universal principles while at the same time emphasizing differences due to the modality of language perception and production.

Several investigators have argued that a fourth parameter, orientation, is necessary for a complete and efficient description of ASL signs (Battison, 1974; Friedman, 1975; Frishberg, 1975). It is argued that the parameter of orientation is necessary to distinguish between certain minimal pairs of signs—SHORT and TRAIN, for example. Both these signs are made in the open space in front of the body. The two hands in H handshape touch and move back and forth across each other. For

---

my opinion that it is easier to extend the meanings of these terms than to apply the new terms like *chereme* coined by Stokoe. This policy is also consistent with other writers in the field.

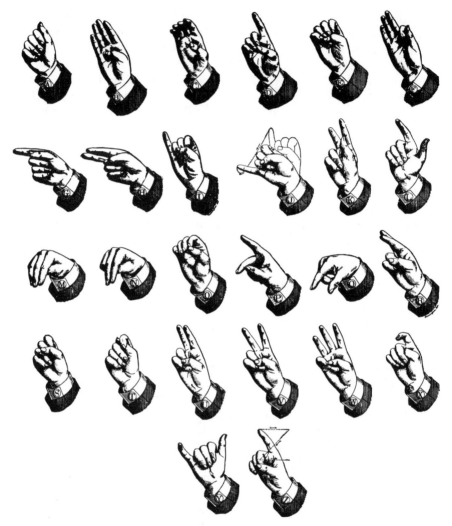

Figure 1.1. The American Manual Alphabet.

SHORT the hands are held in "shake hand" orientation, whereas for TRAIN the palm of each hand faces downward, and the two fingers of the dominant hand brush the backs of the fingers of the nondominant hand. Orientation does seem to be important in sign formation.

The number of possible signs, given the components described in the dictionary, is quite large. Several other aspects of sign construction, combined with these, permit nearly infinite variety. One or two hands may be used to make a sign, and movements may be combined together within the same sign. There are also compound signs (or "two syllable" signs), which had their origin in the concatenation of two simple signs joined with one sweeping motion (Frishberg, 1975, 1976). Given these possibilities for variety, what factors determine which combinations occur as actual signs in ASL?

Battison (1974) has described two conditions that constrain the formation of signs. The first of these, the Symmetry Condition, holds for two-handed signs in which both hands move. For these signs, handshape and movement specifications are identical and symmetrical. The second constraint, the Dominance Condition, states that when the two handshapes of a two-handed sign differ, only one hand, generally the dominant one, will move. In addition, only six handshapes can function in the nonmoving, or base, position in a sign. These are described as unmarked and maximally distinct. A third constraint is added by Frishberg (1976, citing Friedman & Battison, 1973). The movement involved in producing some signs requires two points of contact with the body. In such cases, constraints on the combinations of the two contact locations occur. If the body is divided into 4 major areas (head, trunk, arm, hand), only 8 of the 16 possible combinations occur. Of these, 4 involve contact in the same area.

Constraints such as those described provide redundancy in ASL in much the same way that similar constraints provide redundancy in spoken languages. Clearly, the mode of production shapes the form that these constraints will take. However, it should be noted that these constraints are not entirely physical ones. They have been arbitrarily selected from a larger group of possible constraints. Indeed, signs that once would have violated these conditions have evolved to a form that is consistent with the structural properties presented here (Frishberg, 1975, 1976). Counterparts to other oral language phonological mechanisms have also been described for ASL. These include assimilation, dissimilation, deletion, and insertion (Battison, 1974; Battison, Markowicz, & Woodward, 1973; Frishberg, 1975, 1976). These mechanisms of change generally provide for greater ease of articulation for both sign and spoken languages.

If the body dynamics of the signer influence the formation of signs, so too may the receptive characteristics of the receiver of the signed communication. Elsewhere (Siple, 1978) I have described constraints that may exist for sign languages due to limitations of the visual perceptual system. Visual acuity is at its best at the center of focus and rapidly drops off as the distance from that point increases. This means that a receiver could pick up finer discriminations between signs made near the point of focus than between others made farther away. Because signers tend to look at each other's faces to pick up nonmanual information about the message, we predict and find greater similarity among signs made in this area where finer discrimination is possible. In addition, we would expect to find redundancy rules just like those described by Battison (1974) for large, two-handed signs that occur in the periphery.

Several investigators (including S. D. Fischer, 1974a; Frishberg, 1975; Klima, 1975) have wondered on paper about a rather striking difference between ASL and spoken languages. In English and other spoken languages, the elements forming words occur sequentially in a linear order. The elements of a sign occur simultaneously, or at least are overlapping, and cannot be analyzed as temporal sequences. As Klima suggests, this may be just what you would expect when you make the visual system the primary language receiver.

The studies described to this point have been primarily concerned with the sign units equivalent to morphemes and phonemes in spoken languages. For example, Frishberg (1975) presents a typology of ASL morphemes. One set of investigators have moved in the other direction, seeking to define distinctive features for the hand configurations of ASL (Lane, Boyes-Braem, & Bellugi, 1976). Hand configurations embedded in visual noise were presented on videotape for recognition. Errors of recognition were analyzed using multidimensional scaling and cluster analysis techniques. These analyses yielded 11 distinctive features for the 16 ASL handshapes. Examples include spread and cross of the fingers. There is some evidence that these feature distinctions may differ for different sign languages (S. D. Fischer, 1974a; Bellugi & Klima, 1975).

Syntax and Semantics

The grammar of a language provides a set of mechanisms that can be used to convey the semantic relations among lexical units in an utterance necessary for the understanding of that utterance. It is easy to say that the grammar of ASL is uniquely its own; but it is more difficult to identify and describe the actual syntactic devices used. The change in language modality and the availability of three-dimensional space provide many opportunities for syntactic mechanisms that are unavailable for spoken languages.

Again, the dictionary (Stokoe et al., 1965, Appendix A) provides a starting place for a discussion of ASL structure. Sign language utterances, or sentences, are as clearly defined in ASL as they are in spoken languages. American Sign Language utterances occur within a space in front of the body consisting of an area bound by the waist and the top of the head and extending a few inches to each side of the body. The end of an ASL utterance is signaled by a pause as the hands return to a position of rest near the bottom of the signing space. This signal can be modified when a question is asked: At the end of the last sign in the utterance, the hands either remain in their final position or reach outward toward the addressee before returning to their rest position; at the same time, the face assumes a questioning look. Grosjean and Lane (1977) have demonstrated experimentally that pauses can be used not only to determine the end of an utterance but to ascertain major constituent boundaries within the utterance itself.

If is often remarked that ASL has free word order. While word order is freer in ASL than it is in English, order is used to show some syntactic relationships. Fischer (1974a, 1975) has concluded that modern ASL has a basic SVO (subject–verb–object) word order since this is the most common order used when subject and object are reversible. Word order is generally free when the verb is intransitive or when the verb is transitive and the subject and object nonreversible. When an auxiliary is added to the sign string, the number of permissible orders is greatly reduced from those possible, and order becomes relatively fixed within embedded sentences.

Given the relative freedom of word order in ASL, we should expect it to have a rich inflectional system. However, generally recognized inflections (separate morphemes concatenated with other morphemes) are rarely found in ASL. Instead, systematic modification of one or more of the parameters of a sign often serves the same function that an inflectional system or word-order constraint serves in a spoken language. The added grammatical information occurs contemporaneously with a sign. A motivation for this simultaneity is given by Bellugi and Fischer (1972). In a typical narrative situation, it takes longer to produce a sign than a spoken word: but propositions, or simple sentences, take about the same amount of time. This suggests that there is some underlying processing constraint on language perception (or production) that requires that the rate of information transfer must remain rather constant. ASL, then, must have mechanisms to compensate for the extended time necessary to produce signs.

Susan Fischer, in the Appendix of Bellugi and Fischer (1972), suggests three compensating mechanisms. One is simply to do without certain kinds of mechanisms. A second, incorporation, involves the above-mentioned modification of signs to convey grammatical relations. Incorporation is a productive mechanism in ASL. It is used to express location, number, manner, and size and shape, for example. Nonmanual signals, including body movements and facial expressions, compose the third category of compensating mechanisms. Both incorporation and nonmanual signals occur concurrently with a sign or signs, saving the time that would be necessary to add additional morphemes in spoken languages.

Certain grammatical mechanisms common to spoken languages occur in ASL but with the obvious change in modality. For example, reduplication, the repetition of a lexical item, is used with ASL verbs to express the concepts of durative and habitual (S. D. Fischer, 1973).

Other grammatical mechanisms are specific to the modality of ASL. Modification of the location of a sign in the signing space and of direction of movement are used to express grammatical relationships. Pronominalization is usually accomplished either by pointing to the person or object refered to or pointing to a location assigned to the person or object earlier in the narrative (S. D. Fischer, 1974; Friedman, 1975). A highly productive use of spatial referencing occurs with a large set of ASL verbs for which subject–object or subject–indirect object relationships are incorporated into the direction of movement of the sign (Fischer & Gough, 1978). For example, the verb MEET is signed in the open space in front of the body. Both hands held in G handshape, index fingers pointing upward and palms facing each other. In the citation form of the sign, the nondominant hand is held forward with the palm facing the signer. The dominant hand moves forward from just in front of the signer's chest, contacting the nondominant hand at the knuckles. In context, this sign would be glossed, "I meet you (or whoever is standing in front of the signer)." To say "You meet me," the locations of the hands would be interchanged, and the direction of movement of the dominant hand would be inward, toward the signer. If the signer has previously been talking about two people Bill and Sue, locating them in space, one on the right side and one on the left, the two hands would assume those two positions, and the direction of movement would indicate whether the signer intended "He met her" or "She met him." To sign "They met each other," both hands would move, contacting halfway between the two reference locations. Because direction of movement is used to indicate these relationships, there is no passive voice in ASL.

Verbs are not inflected for tense in ASL. Instead, time is indicated lexically. Most of the time signs are related morphologically; their locations fall along what has been called *the time line.* This line describes an arc beginning in front of the signer's dominant side, touching the cheek, and continuing behind the signer's head (Friedman, 1975; Frishberg & Gough, 1973). Present-tense time signs occur in a plane parallel to the signer's body and intersecting at the front of the face. Future signs are located on the time line in front of this plane; past signs, behind it.

It has been suggested by S. D. Fischer (1974a) and others that facial expression and body attitude may serve as grammatical mechanisms in ASL. There is no question that they correspond in many ways to intonation and stress in spoken languages (Covington, 1973). It has also been noted that certain nonmanual signals accompany manual indicators of grammatical relations. A questioning look or a headshake often accompany an ASL question, and head tilts and eye contact may indicate subordination. However, the actual role of these nonmanual signals is yet to be formulated for ASL.

While really very little is known about the grammatical mechanisms of ASL, it is of interest to note that the general form of language description used for spoken languages seems appropriate for ASL. General language processes may very well be universal and independent of modality. However, the mechanisms for carrying out the processes may be modality specific. Certain mechanisms in ASL are similar to those used in spoken languages, whereas others are dependent on the spatial nature of a manual language. Whether or not the form of linguistic description used for spoken languages will be sufficient for ASL is a question yet to be answered. It may be, as DeMatteo (1977) has suggested, that the discrete nature of this description will not capture some of the regularity in ASL and that, in addition to the traditional approach, a system based on visual analogues will be necessary for a complete description of ASL.

PSYCHOLOGICAL PROCESSING

Most of the research involving deaf persons has not been directed toward an understanding of the processing of ASL. The reasons for this fact are varied but certainly include the growing emphasis on oral education in the United States from the turn of the century to the 1960s. Also, most of the researchers were hearing, did not know ASL, and would have argued that ASL was not a "real" language. Only within the last decade have more than a handful of researchers come to understand the complexity, productivity, and arbitrariness of ASL. With this change in attitude, many recent studies have shown that the study of ASL can lead both to a greater understanding of manual language processing and to a better understanding of general psychological processes as well.

Language Acquisition

The general course of a child's acquisition of his or her native language has been studied for children learning a variety of different oral languages. Comparisons among these studies show a great deal of similarity, leading one to the conclusion that some universal capacity may underlie native language acquisition. The study of the acquisition of sign language is important for an understanding of this underlying capacity: Is it a general cognitive and linguistic capacity, or is it specific to the production and perception of speech and oral language? A comparison of the general course of ASL and oral language acquisition suggests that a general underlying capacity guides the course of all language acquisition.

In order to draw a comparison between ASL and oral language acquisition, the contexts of language learning must be comparable. In practice, this means that the child studied should be deaf and have deaf parents who use ASL in the home both with the child and with visitors to the home. Studies of this kind have led S. D. Fischer (1974b) and others to propose the following parallels between sign language acquisition and the acquisition of an oral language.

Hearing children begin to babble at approximately 6 months of age; deaf children do also—but with their hands. This gestural babbling has been reported by investigators attempting to study auditory babbling in deaf children as well as by deaf parents. At about 1 year, children begin to produce one-word utterances. At the same age, a deaf child in a sign environment begins to produce single signs. Two-word strings are formed by hearing children at about 18 to 24 months of age. Deaf children within the same age range begin to form two-sign strings.

The increase in mean length of utterance (counted in morphemes) with increasing age is often used to describe the rate of oral language acquisition (Brown, 1973). While the age at which a child begins to produce words varies a great deal, this rate of increase remains fairly constant from child to child. Figure 1.2 presents a similar count of mean length of utterance (MLU) for one deaf child, Pola, studied by Ursula Bellugi at the Salk Institute (Siple, 1973). The data from Pola are superimposed on the data from three children studied by Brown

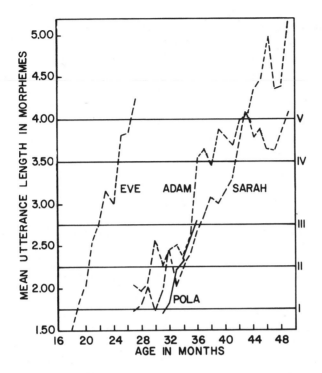

Figure 1.2. Mean length of utterance for Pola compared with that of three hearing children acquiring English. (Data for hearing children adapted with permission from Figure 2 in R. Brown, *A first language: The early stages*. Cambridge, Mass.: Harvard Univ. Press, 1973.)

and his colleagues. The rate of increase in MLU for Pola clearly parallels that of three children acquiring English as a native language.

That the rate of increase in MLU for sign language is the same as that for English is striking. Bellugi and Fischer (1972) have shown that it takes almost twice as long to produce a sign as to say a word; and, short-term memory studies (e.g., Bellugi & Siple, 1974) indicate that it also takes longer to rehearse a sign. If these processes were active in limiting utterance length in the young child, the rate of increase in MLU for sign language should be different from that for spoken language. The similarity apparent in Figure 1.2 suggests that production and rehearsal mechanisms are not limiting utterance length early in language acquisition. Instead, the limitations may be a product of the child's developing grammar.

Investigations of the acquisition of specific ASL constructions further support the contention that there are general cognitive or linguistic universals underlying language acquisition. As with comparisons among spoken languages, the complexity of the grammatical mechanism used to express a particular grammatical relationship will affect its acquisition. However, for ASL we have little knowledge of the complexity of mechanisms specific to the manual–visual modalities.

At the phonological level, Boyes (1973) and McIntire (1974) have investigated the acquisition of ASL handshapes developmentally. Hearing children acquire certain sounds before they do others. Jakobson (1968) has used the concept of markedness to argue that the order of acquisition of speech sounds corresponds to degree of markedness, with the least marked sounds acquired first. Boyes has used the notion of markedness to propose an order of acquisition for ASL handshapes. She argues from anatomical data that the A (or S) handshape is the first to be used by the child and thus corresponds to an unmarked form. A set of features corresponding roughly to those proposed by Lane *et al.*, (1976) are assumed to be acquired in a given order, first for the entire hand and then for individual fingers. In addition, a distinction is drawn between the thumb and index finger—the first two to be extended—and the three weaker fingers. Given these considerations, Boyes has grouped together the handshapes into four groups, ordered in difficulty and complexity.

Data examined by Boyes (1973) and by McIntire (1974) support this general outline of handshape acquisition. Just as there is "baby talk" in spoken language, there are "baby signs" in ASL. An examination of these baby signs shows that, in general, when an incorrect handshape is used for a sign, the substituted form is less marked. For example, one child used the G hand rather than the W hand to sign the concept *water*. Also, to the extent that it has been examined longitudinally, the more marked the handshape, the later it tends to be acquired by the child.

For the hearing child, the production of two-word utterances signals the operation of a grammar. The exact nature of this grammar may be language dependent. However, Brown (1973) has concluded that there is a universal principle underlying these first multiword utterances—the developmental level he calls Stage 1. Brown contends that, for all languages, the utterances in Stage 1 express a small set of semantic relations and that this set is ordered developmentally. Longitudinal studies of ASL acquisition support Brown's contention (Collins-Ahlgren, 1975; S. D. Fischer, 1974b; Klima & Bellugi, 1972; Nash, 1973; Schlesinger & Meadow, 1972). These investigators also report overgeneralizations in all the children studied. For example, Schlesinger and Meadow report that DOG was used to refer to other animals in addition to real dogs early in one child's signing.

The acquisition of specific syntactic mechanisms occurs in later stages of language acquisition and depends to some extent on the actual mechanisms involved. S. D. Fischer (1974b), Klima and Bellugi (1972), and Collins-Ahlgren (1975) have described three stages in the acquisition of negation. First, a sign for *no* occurs either before or after a sentence. In the next stage, other negatives come to replace NO, and often these are used internally within the sentence. Overgeneralization similar to that of hearing children has also been noted. These overgeneralizations are corrected in the third stage, and all lexical negatives are used correctly.

The acquisition of negation in ASL looks similar to that for English because the grammatical mechanisms used are similar. However, locative relations are expressed quite differently in the two languages and are more easily expressed in ASL because they use spatial reference points. Thus, we find locatives emerging earlier in ASL. Both yes–no and WH-questions occur in English and in ASL. However, the mechanisms differ greatly, and so do the stages of acquisition for questions (S. D. Fischer, 1974b).

The study of sign language acquisition has only just begun; problems faced by investigators are enormous. Following the tradition for spoken languages, free interaction sessions have been videotaped longitudinally for a few deaf children who are learning ASL from deaf parents in a native environment. The problems associated with the transcription of these tapes have stymied all but the hardiest. Investigators are now seeking to standardize their methods of study (Hoffmeister, Moores, & Ellenberger, 1975) so that the important aspects of sign language can be recorded and comparisons among children can be made.

Memory and Cognition

The processing of ASL by adults who are fluent in the language has been all but ignored. Instead, an emphasis has been placed on the deaf person's processing of spoken or written English. These studies, reviewed by Swisher (1976), point out the tremendous difficulties involved in learning an oral language without the ability to hear the spoken word. Several other studies have questioned the effect of early manual language acquisition on speech and oral language skills. Mindel and Vernon (1971) conclude from these studies that the effect is generally positive. However, the mechanisms involved in the use of ASL and their relationship to those used for spoken and written forms of oral languages have not been touched on in these studies. Research that has focused on the processing of ASL has generally fallen within the domain of the study of memory for ASL signs.

Experimental studies of memory for spoken and written language stimuli have led investigators to describe two types of memory: short-term and long-term. The primary distinction between the two is one of duration. Short-term memory is used to describe the maintenance of information for a few seconds after presentation. Information available after longer periods of time, or after other events have intervened, is said to be in long-term memory. Whether these two types of memory correspond to two separate memory systems (e.g., Atkinson & Shiffrin, 1971) or to two temporal regions along a continuum of processing (e.g., Craik & Lockhart, 1972) is currently under debate. However, the general distinction is useful, since the characteristics of the two types of memories differ.

One of the characteristic differences between short-term and long-term memory is a difference in encoding or in the format of representation of information in memory. Information in long-term memory is organized on the basis of semantic or conceptual relationships. Items that are meaningfully related are clustered together at recall, and interference is produced by conceptually similar items. Short-term memory for words is not conceptually organized. In fact, when a short list of words or letters are to be recalled, the evidence indicates that the representation of these items that are maintained in short-term memory is related to the names of the items even when they are presented in written form (Conrad, 1964). Errors in recall tend to be items whose names are similar to presented items. Items can be maintained in this form for some time through the process of rehearsal. The use of this name-based encoding strategy is pervasive. Congenitally deaf students who speak well use it to maintain English names in short-term memory (Conrad, 1970).

Short-term memory for ASL signs has been compared with results for spoken English words by Bellugi and Siple (1974), and Bellugi, Klima, and Siple (1975). We have shown that short-term processing characteristics are similar for oral and manual languages. When a list that exceeds the memory span is presented to either language group, both the first few items and the last few items are better recalled than the middle items of the list. These effects are often called primacy and recency, respectively. Atkinson and Shiffrin (1971) argue that the first few items receive more rehearsals and are thus better recalled, leading to the primacy effect. A similar effect for sign lists suggests a similar rehearsal mechanism. The last few words are better recalled, it is argued, because they are recalled first—directly from what has often been called an echo box. Again, a similar mechanism operates for sign lists, but the echo is not speech related, as it seems to be for words. Errors in recall for sign lists tend to be signs that are similar in formation. We conclude that the basis of encoding may be related to the parameters described for ASL signs. Some of the errors given differed from the presented sign by only one of the three parameters: handshape, location, and motion. Thus, the results of short-term memory studies suggest that the mode of representation differs for manual and oral languages. Manual language stimuli are represented in a manual–visual format, whereas oral language stimuli are represented in a name-based format. However, other short-term processes, such as rehearsal, seem to operate identically in both types of representation.

Long-term memory for signs has been investigated in a recognition paradigm (Siple, Fischer, & Bellugi, 1977). Both ASL signs and printed English words were presented randomly in a long list to deaf students who were fluent in ASL and English. Some time later, another list of signs and words were presented, and the student had to decide whether each item had been presented previously, and if so, in what mode. Results of this study indicated that ASL and English are treated as two separate languages in the same way that two oral languages are by fluent bilinguals (Saegert, Hamayan, & Ahmar, 1975). This study also suggests that signs are organized in long-term memory conceptually, just as oral language words are. Signs similar in formation to presented signs were not falsely recognized and, in a free-recall task following final recognition, signs similar in meaning tended to cluster together in recall. This study suggests that long-term memory for ASL signs is similar to long-term memory for words. A study reported by Bowe (1976) supports this conclusion. In a typical paired-associate learning task with hearing subjects and oral language stimuli, similar-sounding stimulus–response pairs produce faster learning. Bowe has shown that sign pairs similar in formation produce the same kind of facilitation for prelingually deaf subjects.

The primary difference reported thus far between memory for ASL signs and memory for English words involves the nature of early encoding processes. Other memory characteristics have been shown to be quite similar for the two languages. There is also a growing body of literature that suggests that English language stimuli are often translated into a manual-based code before they are stored in memory (Conlin & Paivio, 1975; Conrad, 1970; Locke & Locke, 1971; Odom, Blanton, & McIntyre, 1970). This strategy, while requiring a time-consuming translation operation early in processing, should be quite efficient thereafter, given the suggested similarities in further processing. Taken together, these studies suggest that the modality in which a language is produced and received may affect processing primarily in its early stages.

CONCLUSIONS

What is universal about language and language processing? While this question will not soon be answered, studies of American Sign Language and other manual languages will certainly bring the answer closer. The study of ASL has tended to broaden our concepts of linguistic and psychological processes. Many linguistic processes may indeed be universal; they do appear in ASL, a manual language. However, the mechanisms involved in carrying out these processes may not be universal. In this review, it has been suggested that several mechanisms may be modality dependent.

Consideration of psycholinguistic processes leads to the same generalization. The course of language acquisition is strikingly similar for both ASL and oral languages. However, the mechanisms of expression can be language and modality dependent. The same conclusion is reached from studies of memory for ASL. Early representation of linguistic information is affected by the language modality. However, general processing operations and later conceptual representations are unaffected. The studies reviewed here are only a beginning. Much work remains before we can again feel safe in positing linguistic and psychological universals.

REFERENCES

Anthony, D. *Seeing essential English*. Anaheim, California: Educational Services Division, Anaheim Union High School District, 1971.

Atkinson, R. C., & Shiffrin, R. M. The control of short-term memory. *Scientific American*, 1971, 225, 82–90.

Battison, R. Phonological deletion in American Sign Language. *Sign Language Studies*, 1974, 5, 1–19.

Battison, R., & Jordan, I. K. Cross-cultural communication with foreign signers: Fact and fancy. *Sign Language Studies*, 1976, *10*, 53–68.

Battison, R. M., Markowicz, H., & Woodward, J. C. A good rule of thumb: Variable phonology in American Sign Language. In R. Shuy & R. Fasold (Eds.), *New ways of analyzing variation in English* (Vol. 2). Washington, D.C.: Georgetown Univ. Press, 1973.

Bellugi, U., & Fischer, S. A comparison of sign language and spoken language. *Cognition: International Journal of Cognitive Psychology*, 1972, *1*, 173–200.

Bellugi, U., & Klima, E. Aspects of sign language and its structure. In J. F. Kavanagh & J. E. Cutting (Eds.), *The role of speech in language*. Cambridge, Massachusetts: The MIT Press, 1975.

Bellugi, U., Klima, E. S., & Siple, P. Remembering in signs. *Cognition, 1975, 3*, 93–125.

Bellugi, U., & Siple, P. Remembering with and without words. In *Current problems in psycholinguistics*. Paris: Centre National de la Recherche Scientifique, 1974.

Bowe, F. Sight, meaning, and sound: Coding of signs by deaf and hearing adults. Unpublished manuscript, Deafness Research and Training Center, New York Univ., 1976.

Boyes, P. An initial report: Work in progress on a developmental phonology of ASL. Working paper, Salk Institute, La Jolla, California, 1973.

Brown, R. *A first language: The early stages*. Cambridge, Massachusetts: Harvard Univ. Press, 1973.

Collins-Ahlgren, M. Language development of two deaf children. *American Annals of the Deaf*, 1975, *120*, 524–539.

Conlin, D., & Paivio, A. The associative learning of the deaf: The effects of word imagery and signability. *Memory & Cognition*, 1975, *3*, 335–340.

Conrad, R. Acostic confusions in immediate memory. *British Journal of Psychology*, 1964, *55*, 75–84.

Conrad, R. Short-term memory processes in the deaf. *British Journal of Psychology*, 1970, *61*, 179–195.

Covington, V. Features of stress in American Sign Language. *Sign Language Studies*, 1973, *2*, 39–50.

Craik, F. I. M., & Lockhart, R. S. Levels of processing: A framework for memory research. *Journal of Verbal Learning and Verbal Behavior*, 1972, *11*, 671–684.

DeMatteo, A. Visual imagery and visual analogues in American Sign Language. In L. A. Friedman (Ed.), *On the other hand: New perspectives on the American Sign Language*. New York: Academic Press, 1977.

Fischer, S. D. Two processes of reduplication in the American sign language. *Foundations of language*, 1973, *9*, 469–480.

Fischer, S. D. Sign language and linguistic universals. In C. Rohrer & N. Ruwet (Eds.), *Actes du colloque Franco-Allemand de grammaire transformationelle* (Vol. 2). Tubingen: Niemeyer, 1974. (a)

Fischer, S. D. The ontogenetic development of language. In E. W. Straus (Ed.), *Language and language disturbances: The Fifth Lexington Conference on Pure and Applied Phenomenology*. Pittsburgh: Duquesne Univ. Press, 1974. (b)

Fischer, S. D. Influences on word-order change in American Sign Language. In C. Li (Ed.), *Word order and word order change*. Austin: Univ. of Texas Press, 1975.

Fischer, S. D. & Gough, B. Verbs in American Sign Language. *Sign Language Studies*, 1978, *18*, 17–48.

Friedman, L. A. Space, time, and person reference in American Sign Language. *Language*, 1975, *51*, 940–961.

Friedman, L. A., & Battison, R. *Phonological structures in American Sign Language.* NEH Grant Report AY-8218-73-136, 1973.

Frishberg, N. Arbitrariness and iconicity: Historical change in American Sign Language, *Language*, 1975, *51*, 696–719.

Frishberg, N. Some aspects of the historical development of signs in American Sign Language. Doctoral dissertation, University of California, San Diego, 1976.

Frishberg, N., & Gough, B. Time on our hands. Paper presented at the 3rd Annual May California Linguistics Meeting, Stanford, California, 1973.

Furth, H. G. *Deafness and learning.* Belmont, California: Wadsworth, 1973.

Grosjean, F., & Lane, H. Pauses and syntax in American Sign Language. *Cognition*, 1977, *5*, 101–117.

Gustason, J., Pfetzing, D., & Zawalkow, E. *Signing Exact English.* Silver Spring, Maryland: Modern Signs Press, 1972.

Hoemann, H. W. *The American Sign Language: Lexical and Grammatical Notes with Translation Exercises.* Silver Spring, Maryland: National Association of the Deaf, 1976.

Hoffmeister, R. J., Moores, D. F., & Ellenberger, R. L. Some procedural guidelines for the study of the acquisition of sign language. *Sign Language Studies*, 1975, *7*, 121–137.

Jakobson, R. *Child aphasia and phonological universals.* The Hague: Mouton, 1968.

Jordan, I. K., & Battison, R. A referential communication experiment with foreign sign languages. *Sign Language Studies*, 1976, *10*, 69–80.

Klima, E. S. Sound and its absence in the linguistic symbol. In J. F. Kavanagh & J. E. Cutting (Eds.), *The role of speech in language.* Cambridge, Massachusetts: The MIT Press, 1975.

Klima, E. S., & Bellugi, U. The signs of language in child and chimpanzee. In T. Alloway (Ed.), *Communication and affect.* New York: Academic Press, 1972.

Lane, H., Boyes-Braem, P., & Bellugi, U. Preliminaries to a distinctive feature analysis of handshapes in American Sign Language. *Cognitive Psychology*, 1976, *8*, 263–289.

Locke, J. L., & Locke, V. L. Deaf children's phonetic, visual, and dactylic coding in a grapheme recall task. *Journal of Experimental Psychology*, 1971, *89*, 142–146.

McIntire, M. L. A modified model for the description of language acquisition in a deaf child. Masters thesis, California State University, Northridge, 1974.

Mayberry, R. I. Manual communication. In H. Davis & S. R. Silverman (Eds.), *Hearing and deafness* (4th ed.). New York: Holt, Rinehart and Winston, 1978.

Mindel, E. D., & Vernon, M. *They grow in silence.* Silver Springs, Maryland: National Association of the Deaf, 1971.

Nash, J. E. Cues or signs: A case study in language acquisition. *Sign Language Studies*, 1973, *3*, 79–92.

Odom, P. B., Blanton, R. L., & McIntyre, C. K. Coding medium and word recall by deaf and hearing subjects. *Journal of Speech and Hearing Research*, 1970, *13*, 54–58.

Saegert, J., Hamayan, E., & Ahmar, H. Memory for language of input in polyglots. *Journal of Experimental Psychology: Human Learning and Memory*, 1975, *1*, 607–613.

Schlesinger, H. S., & Meadow, K. P. *Sound and Sign: Childhood Deafness and Mental Health.* Berkeley: Univ. of California Press, 1972.

Siple, P. Language in a different mode and how it's learned. Paper presented at the Fifth Child Language Research Forum, Stanford, California, 1973.

Sipple, P. Visual constraints for sign language communication. *Sign Language Studies*, 1978, *19*.

Siple, P., Fischer, S., & Bellugi, U. Memory for nonsemantic attributes of American Sign Language signs and English words. *Journal of Verbal Learning and Verbal Behavior*, 1977, **16**, 561–574.

Stokoe, W. C. Sign Language structure: An outline of the visual communication systems of the American deaf. *Studies in Linguistics, Occasional Papers: No. 8*. Buffalo, New York: Univ. of Buffalo Press, 1960.

Stokoe, W., Casterline, D., & Croneberg, G. G. *A dictionary of American Sign Language on linguistic principles*, Washington, D.C.: Gallaudet College Press, 1965, 1976.

Swisher, L. The language performance of the oral deaf. In H. Whitaker & H. A. Whitaker (Eds.), *Studies in neurolinguistics* (Vol. 2). New York: Academic Press, 1976.

Woodward, J. C. Signs of change: Historical variation in American Sign Language. *Sign Language Studies*, 1976, *10*, 81–94.

II

LINGUISTIC
INVESTIGATIONS

2

Focusing on the Nonmanual Components of American Sign Language

CHARLOTTE BAKER

University of California, Berkeley

CAROL A. PADDEN

Gallaudet College

STUDYING AMERICAN SIGN LANGUAGE AS A MULTICHANNEL COMMUNICATION SYSTEM

The Importance of Nonmanual Behavior in American Sign Language

Studies (Bellugi & Fischer, 1972; Liddell, 1975; Woodward & Erting, 1975. Baker, 1976a, 1976b) have clearly revealed the fal-

The research reported in this paper was supported, in part, by NSF Grant SOC 7414724. We appreciate the generous assistance of Laura Grove-DeReitzes in transcribing the location of blinks in both oral and signing dyads. We are especially grateful for the energies of Kathy Burton in facilitating long-distance communications between the authors and for typing up the final product of our communications. We also would like to thank George Hung, Kathy Newman, James Woodward, and Dan Slobin for their differing roles as consultants or reviewers, and William Stokoe for his willingness to encourage our writing a paper of this nature. The errors belong to us.

UNDERSTANDING LANGUAGE
THROUGH
SIGN LANGUAGE RESEARCH

27

lacy of assuming the hands to be the only carriers of linguistic information in signed discourse. For example, we know that some lexical items are formed by facial movements (not hand movements) and that specific movements of the facial musculature are important in marking negatives, interrogatives, and relative clauses. We also know that, for example, a signer's gaze in the direction of a spatial referent can function as a pronominal reference or that tightly closing the eyes during a sign can serve to make that sign more emphatic.

Further illustrating this linguistic potential of nonmanual behaviors, Appendix A gives a brief summary of the known functions of the eyes and face that are reviewed and discussed in Baker 1976a, 1976b. Note that most of these regulatory and linguistic functions of the eyes and face in ASL discourse were not recognized by linguists until the last 2 years.[1] We expect, in the future, with more sophisticated tools (e.g., a standardized transcription system for the face), to add substantially to the number of items now shown in Appendix A.

To date, all discussions of the phonology of ASL have not formally taken into account the realization that the building blocks of sign language include more than manual configurations and movements. The obvious difficulty of devising a transcription system adequate for describing all these ASL components (or for just the hands alone for that matter) is clear. However, our work not only demonstrates that understanding the language will be much improved through the systematic description of these nonmanual components of Sign, but that understanding ASL will be *dependent* upon such an approach.

A Method for Studying Simultaneous Behaviors in American Sign Language

For the purpose of analysis, we distinguish the communicative behaviors observed during ASL discourse into five separate channels[2] on the basis of what body parts can move independently of other body parts and our intuitions about what would prove to be linguistically

---

[1] An incident which cued us for the linguistic potential of nonmanual behaviors occurred while Ms. Padden was looking at a videotape of a natural conversation dyad. The videotape was a split-screen of the two signers' faces and upper torsoes. Although a majority of the manual signs were not visible on the screen, Padden found she still could follow most of the conversation. She had to be getting the linguistic information from something on that screen.

[2] Weiner and Mehrabian (1968) define 'channel' as "any set of behaviors in a communication that has been systematically denoted by an observer, that is considered by that observer to have coding possibilities, and that can be studied (at least in principle) independently of any other co-occurring behaviors [p. 51]."

important (as outlined by Baker, 1976a). These channels are as follows: (*a*) the hands and arms; (*b*) the head; (*c*) the face; (*d*) the eyes; and (*e*) the total body orientation or posture. Individual behaviors within these channels are called *components*. For example, a component of the face channel might be a raised brow or a depressed lower lip. A component of the eyes channel might be a blink or a change in the direction of a signer's gaze.

Since these channels are always visible under normal signing conditions, we can record their simultaneous activity during discourse and begin to look for patterns in the context of specific components within a given channel. Thus, not only do we look at a wider variety of potentially linguistic behaviors but we are also exposed to the possibility that ASL can express a given meaning in a variety of different ways (that it has more alternatives than those provided by the hands alone) and that the occurrence of a given component might be systematically coordinated with other co-occurring components.

The data for our analysis using this multichannel approach come from several different sources. First, we have free-conversation videotapes of two same-sex dyads (two males, two females). The videotapes for each dyad include facial close-ups for each signer, a split screen of the two signers' faces and upper torsoes, and a full body shot of both signers together. All videotapes are synchronized with a digital clock reading (minute, second, tenth of second) on the bottom of each recording. As such, we are able to make detailed transcriptions of the nonmanual components of ASL and record when they occur in relation to one another and to the hand and arm movements of the signers. The practiced transcription of these simultaneous behaviors requires from 45 to 60 minutes per 1 second of videotaped conversation.

The tremendous advantage of analyzing free conversations is that we are discovering what signers *really do* when they converse with each other and not what they do out of context under informant or experimental conditions. The disadvantage of analyzing natural discourse is its incredible time requirement and the fact that a given behavior may not occur often enough to know if its occurrence is truly systematic or simply patternable for the few cases observed in the data. As a result, we use informant sessions to test out our observations from the free-conversation transcripts.

An Example of the Method

For example, after observing the frequent co-occurrence of certain nonmanual behaviors when conditional sentences arose in our free-conversation tapes, we decided to elicit different kinds of conditionals with several informants and see what patterns we could find. From our tapes we already knew that conditionals could occur with an overt manual marker, such as fingerspelled I-F, stylized flicking-F (Battison, 1976), or the sign SUPPOSE, or they could occur without such a manual marker—perhaps analogous to the Yiddish "You want fulfillment in life, eat bagels." Except in cases of emphasis, ASL usually has no manual equivalent to "then." In addition, ASL has no manual equivalent to "then" occurring after the *if* clause.[3]

For the elicitation, we varied the number of signs in each clause, and we included both conditional statements and conditional questions as well as negative conditionals. Informants were given a stack of cards, each with a different typed sentence on it. We explained that a Q on the card meant that the sentence was a question and the *Neg* meant the "first part of the sentence is negative. So if you see Neg ME WANT . . ., that means, "I don't want . . . ."" In these cases of negative conditionals, we wanted to determine the possible effect of the nonmanual Neg marker on the conditional sentences. Three examples of these elicitation sentences are seen below.

(on card)   THAT THOSE YOUR FRIEND JOIN ME BACK-OUT "If those people there, your 'friends,' are joining us, I'm backing out."

(on card)   Q TOMORROW RAIN YOU GO B-E-A-C-H "If it rains tomorrow, will you go to the beach?"

(on card)   Neg UNDERSTAND ME SAY ME HAPPY AGAIN "If you don't understand what I'm saying, I'll be happy to repeat it."

Forty signed sentences were elicited (using English glosses) from four deaf informants (three females, one male). Eighteen of these 40 sentences were nonconditionals, both statements and questions. The other were 22 conditionals and were arranged in random order with these sentences, so as not to fatigue the informant or encourage stereotyped responses. The English glosses used to elicit the conditionals

---

[3] It has been suggested that the sign (Ø 55a) may function as something like "then." However, WELL only seems to occur in contexts of great emphasis on the 'then' clause, as seen in the following example.

YOU DON'T-WANT GO, WELL STAY
"If you don't want to go, well then just *stay* here."

The sign WELL was not used in any of the conditional sentences we elicited and its use evidently would have resulted in a change of meaning.

did not contain any equivalent to *if* because we wanted to determine which nonmanual behaviors were able to mark the conditional (without a manual marker). Informants recognized these sentences as conditionals because the tester made the manual sign SUPPOSE before handing out each of these cards.

Prior analysis of the natural conversation data had revealed that brow movements and the location of eye blinks (see pages 35–48ff) would require special coding, so we added these two separate categories to our five channel distinctions. Components were transcribed along a horizontal time line, as illustrated in Figures 2.1 and 2.2. All behaviors transcribed within the same vertical column were synchronous. To facilitate reading the examples, we have translated our notation into English words whenever possible. In Appendix B, other examples are listed that will give the reader some idea of possible variance for each sentence.

Reading through Figure 2.1, we see (*a*) that the speaker blinked after he signed the first clause (TOMORROW RAIN); (*b*) that three behavioral changes occurred simultaneously with the signing of the first sign of the second clause (that is, Willy parted his lips, lowered his brows back to normal position, and changed his gaze from looking to the right of the addressee to looking directly at the addressee); and (*c*) that two other behavioral changes (change in head position and beginning of headshake) began slightly *after* the first sign of the second

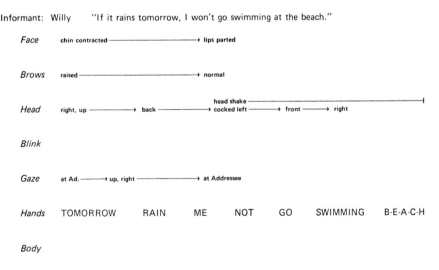

Figure 2.1.

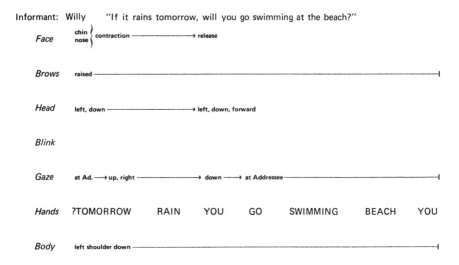

Informant: Willy   "If it rains tomorrow, will you go swimming at the beach?"

Figure 2.2.

clause. One interpretation concerning the slightly different timing of the changes in head movement is that the headshake is a redundant marker of the negated second clause, where such nonmanual signals tend to precede the manual signals slightly (Baker, 1976a), and that the occurrence of the headshake has slightly retarded the timing of the change in head position (since both occur in the same channel). Otherwise, the change in head position (to "cocked left") might have occurred simultaneously with the other three behavioral changes.

In Figure 2.2, we see behavioral changes in the signer's chin and nose contractions, head position, and gaze direction occurring simultaneously after the signing of the first clause. No blink occurs during the entire conditional question, and the raised brows and leftward leaning of the shoulders are maintained throughout the sentence.

Analysis of these 22 conditionals (or a total of 88 for four informants) revealed the following general pattern of nonmanual activity as shown in Table 2.1.

Note that this is a *general pattern*. Although these are the most frequently occurring behaviors, none of them are invariable. In fact, it does not appear that *any* given nonmanual behavior is absolutely critical in signaling the initiation of a conditional or the termination of its first clause. Rather, it seems that a signer may have a preference for certain nonmanual behaviors and will use those systematically,

TABLE 2.1

General Pattern of Nonmanual Activity during Conditionals

	'If' clause	Juncture	'Then' clause
Conditional statements	brow raise	———————→ eyeblink	normal position (unless negative) change in gaze direction change in head orientation
Conditional questions	brow raise	——————————— no eyeblink	gaze at addressee (Ad) head forward/cocked to one side

whereas another signer may prefer a different configuration of be-haviors to serve the same function. For example, one signer, Lisa, does not display as much brow movement as the other signers. How-ever, Lisa uses more lip movement (some speech associated, some not), and she does follow the general pattern for head and gaze move-ment. Another signer, M. J., displays more head nodding and shaking where these occur systematically with respect to clause boundaries within the conditional. These and other examples of variation in co-occurring nonmanual behaviors suggest that it is the *configuration* or pattern of co-occurring behaviors that serves a given function rather than any *specific* behavior.

In all of the conditional statements reviewed, there were at least four behavioral changes (e.g., eye blinks, release of nasolabial contrac-tion, brow lowering, initiation of head nodding) occurring at the point of juncture between the two clauses. For the conditional questions, there were at least two such behavioral changes. Noting this potential for variation across channels, we expect in the future to be able to talk about different *weightings in context* for each channel component. For example, if A and B are present, then C and D are optional. But if B is not used, then C and D are required. In this way, we can begin to talk about *channel interaction*. We also want to know whether the function or weightedness of a given channel or component is physio-logically determined. Or is it determined by its visibility to the ad-dressee?

Some Implications of Research on Multichannel Behaviors
in American Sign Language

Another question raised anew by this channel approach is that of redundancy. American Sign Language has previously been characterized as an 'only the meat' language, with either little redundancy (Bellugi & Fischer, 1972) or some manual redundancy in low-acuity areas (Siple, 1972).

However, because of the several channels at its disposal that we know are capable of serving linguistic functions, ASL appears to have considerable potential for redundancy. We have seen this in the case of conditional sentences when a signer raises his/her brow and then fingerspells I-F. The aforementioned conditional sentences without the manual markers also suggest that some of the nonmanual behaviors are redundant.

Another case of cross-channel redundancy is revealed in the observation that movements of the face, eyes, head, and body posture can function as adjectives and adverbs occurring simultaneously with the manual noun or verb signs they modify (Baker, 1976a). Since these nonmanual movements often occur during the manual signing of the modifier as well, they and/or the manual modifier are carrying redundant information.

For example, Baker reports that puffing out the cheeks, looking up, retracting the eyelids, raising the shoulders, and tilting the head back are ways of showing that something is big. One signer did these things to express the concept 'big tree' where only TREE was signed manually. When the adjective 'big' was also signed manually, the signer still tilted her head back, raised her shoulders, and puffed out her cheeks. Some of this must be redundant information.

Summary

In summary, we are saying that there is now reasonable evidence demonstrating that research on sign language structure that only looks at what the signer's hands are doing is severely limiting itself. Because of this, we need a way of systematically looking at nonmanual behaviors co-occurring with manual signs in discourse. You have seen a sample of how we are trying to understand the nonmanual components of ASL. Initial analysis of these multichannel behaviors during the signing of conditional sentences suggests a great deal of synchronous behavior, in which configurations of behaviors rather than any specific behavior is important as the carrier of a meaning.[4] When viewed as a language transmitted through several different channels simultaneously, the question of redundancy in ASL takes on a new meaning and suggests a very different structure than has been attributed to it up until now.

EYE-BLINKING BEHAVIOR IN A VISUALLY MONITORED LANGUAGE[5]

The Need for a Tool for Discerning American Sign Language Constituents

We do not yet have a grammar of American Sign Language. One major obstacle toward our devising such a grammar is that we do not really know what to call a sentence in ASL or what constitutes a grammatical unit. This is particularly true of those signed sequences that involve mechanisms not found in oral languages—such as the signer's use of space to indicate grammatical relationships. We want to be wary of imposing English or oral-language-based structure on the sign. What we need is a tool for understanding what deaf signers perceive to be grammatical units in their language.

It should be made clear from the outset that when we talk about "grammatical units" or "constituent boundaries," we are, in part, begging the question. If we cannot presently specify the formula for a grammatical unit in ASL, then we cannot be sure what the tools we will propose (gaze shifts and blinks) are marking, if anything. However, we *are* able to determine if they are internally consistent and if their occurrence agrees with our intuitions concerning unit boundaries and with those of native users of ASL. We are also able to observe whether they co-occur with other behavioral changes (such as those described for conditional sentences on pages 30–35.). If their occurrence does match our combined intuitions and the other clues we have relating to the grammatical structure of ASL, then we can begin to use these eye behaviors as a tool, either to support our previous decisions or to suggest different analyses, as well as to help us understand those uniquely ASL (or Sign) structures that have most evaded our linguistic deciphering.

---

[4] However specific nonmanual behaviors in other contexts are associated with specific meanings, such as in the example of lexical items made on the face.

[5] The following discussion was presented as a separate paper, now conjoined for publication.

Possible Uses of Gaze Shifts

As was just mentioned—but is still surprising—one possible tool for identifying these signed grammatical units may be the eye movements and blinking behavior of deaf interactants. Baker (1975) has observed that, like speakers of oral languages (Kendon, 1967),[6] signers tend to look away from their addressees while initiating a turn and then look back at what seem to be constituent boundaries to check on their addressee's decoding.

However, more recent study (Baker, 1976b) has shown that the frequency of occurrence of this kind of shift in the speaker's gaze direction seems to be much influenced by the context of the interaction and individual discourse styles. Frequent shifting takes place in competitive turn exchanges, where the use of −GAZE (not looking at the other interactant) is an important means of holding the floor. For example, during a competitive signed sequence (five separate turns, 40 seconds) between two males, Baker found the ratio of speaker time spent looking/not looking at the addressee to be approximately 50:50. Thirty-two speaker gaze shifts from the addressee to the nonaddressee were recorded during this period.

Example (1) illustrates how grammatical boundaries are marked by the speaker's gaze shift away from the addressee. This example comprises the first turn in the male dyad mentioned earlier.[7]

(1) CONNECT-WITH KEEP MEMBER U-N-I-O-N or $\overset{+}{\text{FRIEND}}$
    $\overset{+}{\text{TRUE SILLY}}$
    "In relation to either my keeping my membership in the union or my friends, it's really silly."

   $\overset{+}{\text{KNOW}}$ I-F
    "I know if"

---

[6] Kendon (1967) found that speakers in oral dyads generally spend more than half of their speaking time *not* looking at their addressee. However, this approximation varies considerably across individuals and seems to be a function of utterance length and (semantic) complexity. That is, longer and more complex sentences may require more concentration or "advance planning [p. 31]" which may necessitate the speaker's cutting off visual stimulation from the addressee.

[7] Words in capital letters are English glosses for ASL signs, which are written left-to-right on a horizontal time line. Words separated by hyphens are signs that require more than one English word as their gloss. In Example (1), each new line was begun with a gaze shift away from the addressee. A return to +GAZE (looking at the addressee) is shown on the transcript by a small "+" at the point of its occurrence along the time line.

$\overset{+}{\text{ME MAYBE HAVE TRUE SEVERAL TRUE FRIEND}}$

ME MAYBE HAVE TRUE SEVERAL TRUE FRIEND
"I had, let's say, several true friends,"

INDEX W-D REMAIN FRIEND WITH ME I-F ME TEAR-CARD
"They would remain friends with me even if I left the union."
("tear up my union card.")

INDEX U-N DOESN'T-MATTER
"Even if they were unionists, it wouldn't matter to them."

WELL MY WORK
"After all, it's my business."

Problems Encountered in Using Gaze Shifts

In long-turn sequences where there is less competition for the floor, less shifting of gaze takes place. For example, a long turn (40 seconds) by one member of a female–female dyad revealed a 96:04 looking/not looking ratio. Only 6 gaze shifts (addressee to nonaddressee) were recorded during this period. The other member, however, during another long turn (42 seconds) in the discourse, spent 20% of her speaking time not looking at the addressee-suggesting considerable individual differences between the two female interactants. Thus, although the gaze shifts found in these long turns do seem to occur at constituent boundaries, many other similar grammatical boundaries are not so marked.

It follows that the analysis of competitive turn exchanges might be better suited to the purpose of discerning grammatical boundaries since more gaze shifting occurs in these contexts. However, such analysis is complicated by the frequent occurrence in these contexts of discourse overlap and simultaneous turns[8]—both of which require mutual +GAZE (both interactants looking at each other). This means that there are factors other than the need to check on addressee

---

[8] Discourse overlap occurs either when interactant B begins a turn shortly before interactant A has completed his/her turn or when interactant B demonstrates decoding and response (during A's turn) by copying a few of the speaker's signs, by signing agreement (e.g., YES, RIGHT, TRUE) or with any of the numerous other types of back-channel responses which do not constitute a claim for the speaking turn (Baker, 1977). Simultaneous turns occur when two interactants are claiming the floor (the turn) at the same time.

decoding at constituent boundaries that can also influence the gaze-shifting behavior of the speaker. In addition, in all these contexts there remains the problem of separating out when the gaze shift is lexically determined[9] (Baker, 1976a, 1976b) as opposed to when the shifts were regulated by grammatical relationships.

As such, looking at the location of gaze shifts may be helpful in pointing to the location of grammatical boundaries but cannot by itself provide sufficient information for this analysis because gaze-shifting behavior is a function of several different regulatory and linguistic concerns.

Blinking Behavior—Is It Systematic?

Increasingly detailed transcription of signers' eye behaviors during free conversation has resulted in the recent surprise observation that the locations of both speaker and addressee eye blinks[10] seem to be systematic with respect to constituent boundaries. Contrary to our naïve assumption that people blink simply to keep their eyes from becoming dry,[11] we have observed that the time period between blinks during signed discourse is often quite irregular, with considerable individual variation. Similar to that found for speaker gaze shifts, signers do not always blink at what we would expect to call a major constituent boundary, but when they do blink, it usually is at such a boundary.

---

[9] The movement and direction of the speaker's gaze seems to be predictable for a certain group of signs. In the first group (e.g., FIELD, MOUNTAIN, RIVER), the eyes visually index the area shaped by the hands. When the sign refers to an activity which in some way involves the eyes, the signer's eyes will imitate their real-world movements (e.g., SEARCH, LOOK-AT, DREAM).

[10] The term, *blinking*, as discussed in this paper, refers to the involuntary, usually unconscious, quick eye closures known otherwise as *periodic blinking* (as opposed to *reflex blinking* which occurs, for example, when an object is suddenly thrust toward someone's face). Periodic blinking may be absent or infrequent in infants, but has an average frequency of 15–16 per minute in relaxed adults, with a wide range of 3–28 per minute (Drew, 1951).

[11] Until Ponder and Kennedy's 1927 series of experiments on the subject, periodic blinking was generally considered to be a reflex to external conditions, such as the degree of moisture and/or light present. However, the authors found no difference in the interblink interval under different conditions of humidity and light intensity or when the eyes were anesthetized to block out sensations at the cornea and conjunctiva. They did find differences due to mental tension (which will be discussed in following sections).

Evidence from Free Conversations

Example (2) is typical of the majority of transcripts we now have of blinking behavior during free conversations. The break between lines 2 and 3 demonstrates that by "constituent boundary" we mean a unit that may be smaller than what in English would be a complete sentence. It is not unusual to find a blink occurring between (what in English would be) subject and predicate, or setting off a direct object, or what Fant (1972) calls a "time indicator" (e.g., YESTERDAY, LONG-TIME-AGO, NEXT-FEW-DAYS).[12]

(2) THAT ME START HOW PRINT (blink)
    "You want to know how I started printing?"

    ME ME-WANT (blink)
    "Well, I wanted"

    DEAF BORROW-ME (blink)
    "a deaf friend to lend me (his ITU card)."

    ME TAKE (blink)
    "I took it"

    ME GO WASHINGTON P-O-S-T ME (blink)
    "and I went to the Washington Post."

    SHOW-CARD LOOK-AT-CARD (blink)
    "I showed the card to the manager and he looked at it."

    COME-ON LABOR (blink)
    "He said, 'Come on in and work.' "

Evidence from elicited conditional sentences

Examples (3)–(5) illustrate the usual result obtained for the location of blinks during elicited conditional sentences, as discussed on pages 31–33.

(3) a. "If it snows, I can go skiing."

          SNOW (blink)
          ME GO SKI

   b. "If it snows, will you go skiing?"

         ? SNOW YOU GO SKI

[12] Examples of how time indicators may be set off by a blink are (a) TOMORROW (blink) SUPPOSE RAIN (blink) ME CAN'T TAKE-OFF B-E-A-C-H ME; and (b) LONG-TIME-AGO (blink) GIRL SMALL LIVE WITH GRANDMOTHER (blink).

(4) a. "If I don't buy a house, I'll buy a car."

   DISMISS BUY HOUSE (blink)
   BUY CAR

   b. "If you didn't buy a house, would you buy a car?"

   ? DISMISS BUY HOUSE BUY CAR

(5) "If those people there, your 'friends,' are joining us, I'm backing
    out."

   THAT THOSE YOUR FRIEND JOIN (blink)
   ME BACK-OUT

Table 2.2 summarizes the blinking behavior (between the *if* and
then clauses) for four informants, each signing the same 18 conditional
statements and 4 conditional questions.

As indicated here, the informants usually blinked between the two
clauses of conditional statements but did not blink at this juncture
while signing conditional questions. At present, we do not know why
this difference exists but suspect it is related to the observation that
speakers generally maintain continuous eye gaze on the addressee
during the signing of questions, as opposed to statements (Baker,
1975). Our concern here, however, is to demonstrate that blinking
behavior is systematic in conditionals with respect to utterance type
and to the interclause juncture in the conditional statements.

TABLE 2.2

Presence–Absence of Eye Blinks (EB) during Juncture: Conditionals

Statements (18)	+EB	−EB
Cinnie	16	2
MJ	17	1
Lisa	18	0
Willy	18	0
Totals	69	3
Questions (4)		
Cinnie	1	3
MJ	0	4
Lisa	0	4
Willy	0	4
Totals	1	15

Using Speaker and Addressee Blinks to Understand American Sign Language Constituents

Returning to the free-conversation videotapes, we were especially intrigued by the observation that although addressees blinked only about half as often as speakers, their blinks were usually at grammatical junctures in the speaker's turn. We wondered if speakers were somehow cuing the addressee about the presence of a constituent boundary and if that was how the addressee then knew to blink there in harmony with the speaker. However, after observing that about an equal number of the addressee blinks occurred slightly (e.g., .1 second) *before* the speaker blinks as those that occurred slightly *after* the speaker blinks, we surmised that addressee blinks were not dependent upon speaker blinks.[13] We also noted a few cases where the addressee blinked at a major constituent boundary in the absence of a speaker blink.

Thus, we hypothesized that our addressees were aiding their own decoding by *anticipating* grammatical boundaries in the speaker's turn. Evidence supporting this hypothesis is seen in Examples (6) and (7). In Example (6), the addressee blinked after what could have been a sentence boundary, but the speaker added another argument before blinking.

(6) INDEX ACT SAME TEACH AGENT (addressee blink)
     SPEECH + T-H-E-R-A-P-I-S-T (speaker blink)
     "She was acting like a teacher, a speech therapist."

[13] We also wanted to know, in general, if a blink was a perceptible unit (consciously or not) and if it could have some kind of signaling function. Two unsuccessful experiments were performed to try to test out this possibility. Both used conditional statements which, in our elicitations, were always signed with a blink occurring between the *if* and *then* clauses. In the first experiment, a videotape was made of a deaf, native ASL user signing each of 10 conditionals twice—once with a blink in the expected place and once without. The order of the ± blink renditions was randomized. The model was rehearsed to vary only the blink in signing behavior. Deaf, native ASL informants watched the 2 renditions of each sentence and then chose (check A or B) the one they preferred (for whatever reason or lack thereof). Analysis of the first 5 informants demonstrated that (*a*) they preferred the sentences with the blink present, but (*b*) they were consciously making their decision on the basis of which sentence had "more facial expression." It appears that the model was unable to make herself not blink in the appropriate place without constraining other appropriate facial behaviors. In the second experiment, a 16 millimeter film was made of a rehearsed model signing 20 conditionals with the between-clause blink present. A copy of this film was made for the purpose of editing out the blink on one rendition, and then making a videotape of the resulting spliced-

If addressee blinks do occur at what addressees expect will be constituent boundaries, then a comparison of speaker–addressee blink discrepancies might reveal what *could* be a grammatical juncture and how the speaker can deviate grammatically from that unit. In regard to Example (7), if the addressee has correctly anticipated a possible grammatical boundary, then the final index (referring to the two children) must be optional. According to native informant intuitions about the passage, this index here is indeed optional.

(7) THAT INDEX MEET TWO CHILDREN (addressee blink)
INDEX (speaker blink)
"Later, she met two children."[14]

Another way the analysis of speaker blinking behavior could be helpful is in the translation of signed discourse. For example, in Example (8), there are two different possible English translations of the same ASL sequence: ME WORK O-T O-T FINISH ME MONEY ME (which was elicited with the conditional sentences discussed on pages 30–35.).

(8) a. ME WORK O-T O-T (blink) FINISH ME MONEY ME
"If I'd work overtime a lot, I'd really get a lot of money."

b. ME WORK O-T O-T FINISH (blink) ME MONEY ME
"If I had worked overtime a lot, I'd have a lot of money now."

Three of our informants blinked after the second fingerspelled O-T ("overtime"), as seen in Example (8a). Using the location of the

---

together film having 2 renditions (± blink) of each of the 20 sentences. To make a long story short, the editing process was unsuccessful. And we still don't know if the addressee gets any cues from the speaker blinks.

[14] The signed sequence which immediately follows this example is especially intriguing.

INDEX WELL WANT HELP (blink)
"They (the children) decided they wanted to help"
H-E-R INDEX AROUND (blink)
"her. The story goes on."

Although we have seen other instances of a blink occurring before a direct object, we suspect the blink found before H-E-R is due to an intrusion from Signed English (a system which uses many ASL signs, but English syntax). ASL does not have fingerspelled pronouns. Since it is clear from context that the deaf girl is the one who will be helped, the signed proposition should have ended with HELP—which is where the addressee also blinked. However, a recent trend has been observed among certain groups of ASL users schooled in English in which fingerspelled pronouns are added on as a means of (supposedly) favorably enhancing the level of the communication.

speaker blink as a tool for grouping signs into units, we deduced that the next sign, FINISH, must belong to the second "clause" and interpreted the sequence as "If I'd work overtime a lot, I'd *really* get a lot of money."

One informant, however, blinked *after* FINISH Example (8b). We interpreted this to mean, "If I *had* worked overtime a lot, I'd have a lot of money now." In this case, FINISH belongs to the first "clause." When FINISH follows the verb, as it does here, it usually marks the verb as an action occurring in the past (Fischer & Gough, 1972). A deaf bilingual reviewing the videotape of these sentences reported that the two different interpretations as judged by the location of eye blinks matched her own intuitions about the separate meanings. In addition, the raised brow marker of the *if* clause was maintained by all four signers until right after they blinked, hence lending support to the above interpretations.

The Relationship between Gaze Shifts and Eye Blinks

How blinks relate to the gaze shifts discussed earlier is a question we still know little about. We do notice that some signers blink more often than others and that some signers engage in more frequent gaze shifting. It may be that individual signers have a preference for one particular eye behavior over the other. However, it is not unusual to find *both* occurring at a grammatical juncture. Similar to that found for speaker gaze shifts, signers do not always blink at what we would expect to call a major constituent boundary. However, when they do blink, it usually is at such a boundary.

The Relationship between Blinking and Stress

Exceptions to the above statement seem to be predictable on the basis of what is known about the relationship between blinking and stress (Meyer, Bahrick, & Fitts, 1953; Kanfer, 1960; Harris *et al.* 1966). Although ophthalmologists do not yet know what actually causes periodic blinking, they do have considerable evidence that it increases in frequency during periods of stress.

In our signed free-conversation data, we have found two cases of blinks occurring within a fingerspelled word. One occurred after the *a* in "therapist," where the signer then looked at her hand after she blinked. Signers often look at the hand that is doing the fingerspelling when the word is unusual or difficult to spell (Baker, 1976b). Earlier in the same text, the speaker had misspelled *affair* as A-I-F-A-I-R and had tried to correct her spelling A-F (blink) -F-A-I-R. Since blinks occurred word-internally in these two cases but not during any of the other (and easier) fingerspelled words (such as K-I-D-S, T-V, A-B-L-E, H-E-R), we believe that the blinks here were the result of some kind of performance stress. Hall (1945) similarly found that (hearing) readers would blink when a word was "unusual or unexpected [p. 452]."

Is Blinking a Sign of Language Processing?

Ophthalmologists have noted that lid closure is a way of controlling the flow of sensory information to the brain (Kennard & Glaser, 1964). Quoting from a classic neuro-ophthalmology text (Walsh & Hoyt, 1969):

> Correspondence between lid closures and the reduction of visual attention would thus signify a change in brain activity. Such lid activity may be considered to indicate varying functions of the brain with a fluctuating level of sensory operation taking place. . . . Placed at the portal of entry of visual sensation, the eyelids may regulate dominant patterns of brain activity [p. 321].

Since this control of visual information was occurring at grammatical boundaries, we wondered if periodic blinks could be a response of the autonomic nervous system to language processing in grammatical chunks.

Comparative Evidence from English-Speaking Dyads

To examine this possibility, we needed to know if similarly systematic blinking behavior occurred while conversing in other languages. Condon and Ogston (1971) had looked at where speakers blink with respect to word boundaries in English. They reported that the majority of blinks occur either at the beginning of a word or right after its completion, where co-occurrence of the blink with word initiation–termination was precisely timed to at least the same 1/24 second. In some cases, blinking was found word-internally and then seemed to occur at exactly those points of articulatory change, such as the onset of voicing or aspiration. Condon and Ogston did not look at the relationship between blinking and English sentence structure, nor has anyone else to our knowledge.

Our initial analysis of videotaped conversation between same-sex hearing dyads in English showed that although the rate of blinking per minute was similar between the deaf and hearing conversants, the location of blinks seemed to be different. First of all, blinks during speech quite often occurred during the production of a word but rarely occurred during a sign. Second, hearing blinkers seemed to be more affected by sentence or topic stress as well as by hesitations, false starts, and filled pauses, than by grammatical boundaries. However, they always blinked at the end of their turn.

Example (9), though semantically strange, is a good illustration of the results we obtained for two dyads of female speakers. Underlined words, syllables, or spaces indicate where the speaker blinked. A check mark above one of these units indicates where the addressee blinked. We did not have the advantage of a video recorder that retains its audio portion during slow-motion playback, so our analysis is necessarily informal and much less precise than the work of Condon and Ogston.

(9) 'An interpreter I you know I I believe it would be____ah what a person is going to interpret. If it's an interpreter for a for a class I'm he would also have to go through the ah___ extension of learning the ah___ subject itself (addressee: um-hum) like an interpreter for English ____ or an interpreter for law ____ I'm sure he would have to learn the English ah__ ____ ____ the basic concepts of English an' also a lawyer would have to probably go to law school (addressee: um-hum). We have one here on campus Richard White who's an interpreter for ah____ for ____ going to I think he just goes to court with the students if they have to go (addressee: ooh) an' he interprets ____ you know to the lawyers (addressee: hmm) which is good.

The Possible Effect of Sign Language Communication on Blinking Behavior

If blinking does not so systematically occur at grammatical junctures in other languages, then is there something about communicating in a visually received and monitored language that brings about the systematicity of blinking behavior we observe only in sign language discourse?[15]

The Effect of Rate of Signing

Addressing ourselves to this new question, we wondered if rate of signing might be an important consideration. Perhaps addressees

[15] We need, of course, to check other sign languages and other oral languages to be sure that this difference in blinking behavior is modality-specific.

must blink at grammatical junctures (where it is more likely pauses
will occur, see Grosjean & Lane, 1976) so as not to miss any of the
message, since unlike oral discourse, here the entire message is visually received.

Our figures on rate of signing during rapid turn-taking showed 3.12
signs per second for the male dyads and 3.00 signs per second for the
females. Long turns for the females were 2.4 and 2.6 signs per second.
No long, less competitive turns for the males could be found.

For the purpose of comparing average length of sign (calculated
from the signs-per-second figure) with average length of blink, we
chose the females' 3.00 signs per second, or 333 milliseconds per sign.
The average blink for both females (whether speaker or addressee)
lasted between 9 and 12 VTR fields, or 150–200 milliseconds. These
figures tell us that rarely would a whole sign be missed by blinking
during its production. If a sign is not seen, there is probably enough
redundancy in the system to make up for that miss anyway. However,
the fact remains that lid closure does cut off the possibility of receiving visual information. It seems reasonable to assume that if blinks
were to occur at syntactic junctures, the communication system would
be more efficient.

Other Evidence for the Effect of Context on Visual Behaviors

Evidence supporting the claim that monitoring communication in a
sign language could affect the blinking behavior of the interactants is
seen in Hall's (1945) observation that (hearing) readers usually blink
at punctuation marks and that those who more consistently blink at
these junctures are better readers.

There is also evidence to support the underlying claim that the
actual mechanisms of vision may be shaped by the environment of the
see-er and that vision is a learned, developmental process. Recent
study by an anthropologist and an optometrist (Carr & Francke, 1976)
gives strong evidence that Chinese and Americans actually "see"
differently as measured by such tests as point of convergence to
double vision, habitual phoria at a distance, and static retinoscopy.
They compared the results of the optometric tests with predictions
concerning different visual traits of the two cultures they had made on
the basis of such environmental factors as table height, writing posture, number and height of house windows, and clothing tightness.
Finding significant differences between the two cultures on these
tests, Carr and Francke concluded that "an individual's visual

physiology is significantly affected by the culture in which he (she) lives [p. 28]."

Thus, we see that blinking at constituent boundaries could be something *learned* by deaf interactants as a result of their communication context. At least this is a reasonable assumption when considering the needs of the addressee. For the speaker, our suggestions are much more speculative. Hall (1945) observed that blinks, in general, occur at points of relaxation. It makes sense, then, that signers would maintain a level of tension during performance with intermittent "rest breaks" at grammatical boundaries—where blinks would then occur. But why, then, would speakers of oral languages be different from signers? That is, why don't oral speaker blinks occur more consistently at syntactic junctures?

The Effect of Other, Concomitant Behaviors

An observation especially relevant to why *signers* blink at constituent boundaries is that these are the places of "release" of many other kinds of muscular tension. Signed communication is composed of continuous, and often synchronous, behavioral changes across several different channels—the hands and arms, head, face, eyes, and body posture (Baker, 1976a). Looking at the blink between the *if* and *then* clauses in conditional statements, we note (see Examples 1, 3, 5 in Appendix 2B) that it occurs immediately prior to a major change of activity in other channels. This change often means lowering the brows to normal (relaxed) position, returning to upright body posture from a forward lean, and/or a release of muscular tension on the face (e.g., chin, upper lip, nose). So, it appears that perhaps the signer's blink can be seen as both a concomitant and a product of a more generalized release of muscular tension at syntactic junctures. Evidence supporting this hypothesis is seen in the fact that no interclause blink occurs in conditional questions—where the muscular tension of the raised brow, etc., is maintained until the end of the sentence. However, the signer usually does blink after the conclusion of the conditional question.

Summary

We have observed that the periodic blinking of both speakers and addressees during ASL discourse is surprisingly consistent in its occurrence at what we consider to be constituent boundaries. As such, the location of blinks may be a useful tool for grouping signs into grammatical units, thus telling us something about the relationships between signs.

We hypothesize that addressees aid their own decoding by anticipating syntactic boundaries in the speaker's turn. Because addressees blink at these anticipated boundaries, we suggest that analyzing discrepancies in the location of speaker–addressee blinks may reveal (a) what could be a grammatical unit; and (b) how the speaker can deviate grammatically from that unit.

Exploring the possibility that periodic blinking is an indication of human language processing in grammatical chunks, we observed its occurrence among English-speaking dyads. Results of this informal analysis suggest that the blinking behavior of English speakers is different from that of ASL signers. We hypothesize that because ASL is a visually received and monitored language, it has fostered the systematicity of blinking behavior described in this chapter. Evidence supporting this hypothesis considers the needs of an efficient, visual communication system and the possible influence of other concomitant, muscular changes.

APPENDIX 2A

Some Functions of Eye Movements and Facial Movements in American Sign Language Discourse

---

Functions of eye movements[1]	
Regulatory	
Speaker (Spk)	−GAZE controls interruptions, maintains own turn.
	+GAZE signals turn-yielding at grammatical juncture.
Addressee (Ad)	+GAZE signals Spk may initiate/continue a turn.
	−GAZE signals impending inter-
Linguistic	ruption.
I. GAZE-direction	
a. Lexically determined	For example, SEARCH requires "searching" movements of eyes. Spk can't look directly at Ad.
	For example, FIELD, MOUNTAIN, RIVER usually receive a visual index (gaze) toward the area shaped by the hands.
b. Part of modifier	For example, look up to show something is big, retract eyelids.

APPENDIX 2A (Continued)

	Eyes closely follow hands as they outline road in *short* ROAD, but are constantly ahead of hands during *long* ROAD as if to demonstrate that the road continues out into the distance.
c. Pronominal reference	A gaze in the direction of a spatial referent can function similarly to manual indexing (pointing with the index finger).
d. Direct quotation	For example, look up to show that the child is the speaker and that what follows is in quotes.
e. Evidence of constituent boundary	Speakers tend to check on Ads' decoding by looking back at them at grammatical junctures (and then looking away again as a new constituent is initiated).
II. Lengthy eye closure	
a. Emphasis	Occurs atop manual signs (esp. noun/verb modifiers).
III. Blinking	
a. Marking constituent boundaries	(See preceding discussion, pages 41–43.)

Functions of facial movements

Regulatory	
Speaker	Signals forthcoming initiation (eg. mouth open).
	Signals forthcoming continuation (concomitant with other behaviors showing 'thinking').
	Signals forthcoming shift in role to that of Ad (eg. via question signaling).
Addressee	Signals decoding
	Signals desire to speak
Linguistic	
a. Small class(es) of lexical items	For example, nose twitching = YEAH; puffed cheek = MENSTRUAL PERIOD.
b. Required concomitants of manual signs[2]	For example, NOT-YET (vs. LATE) ACCIDENTALLY (vs. WRONG)
c. Modifier	Occurs atop manual noun/verb (Briefly discussed in chapter.) For example, "Big tree" can be

APPENDIX 2A (Continued)

	signed with only the manual sign TREE and several nonmanual behaviors occurring concomitantly.
d̂. Negation	Frown, lowering brows, wrinkling nose, sticking out tongue.
e. Question signaling	Raised brows, retracted eyelids, head and posture forward, etc.
f. Conditionals	(See preceding discussion).
g. Relative clauses	Signaled by specific facial movements and head position (Liddell, 1975).
h. Expect that a shift (synchronous change in facial behaviors) is important in signaling constituent boundaries.	Change in facial movements occurring at medial points in conditionals (see preceding discussion).

[1] +GAZE indicates looking at other interactant; −GAZE indicates not looking at other interactant.

[2] Sometimes these are capable of distinguishing minimal pairs, although we expect manual movements to be slightly different.

Additional Examples of Conditional Sentences

EXAMPLE 1.

Informant: MJ   "If it rains tomorrow, I won't go to the beach."

Face   nose contraction ——————→
                lips ⎫
                chin ⎬ contraction ——————→ only chin contraction ——————
                tongue extended ——————→

Brows   raised ——————————————————————————→ normal

Head   cocked right ——→ right down —————————→ headshake ——————
                                                  up, right ——————

Blink   ∨

Gaze   up ——→ up, left ———————————————→ down ————→ right

Hands   TOMORROW   RAIN   ME   NOT   GO   B-E-A-C-H

Body

51

APPENDIX 2B (*Continued*)

EXAMPLE 2.

Informant: MJ   "If it rains tomorrow, are you going to the beach?"

	?RAIN	TOMORROW	YOU	GO	B-E-A-C-H
Face	upper lip contraction ————→ closed lips			lip / nose / chin contraction ————→ lips parted	
Brows	raised ———————————				
Head	back, right ——→ right ——→ cocked right ——→ forward				
Blink					
Gaze	up, left ——→ slight left ——→ at Addressee ——→ up, left ——→ at Ad.				
Hands	?RAIN	TOMORROW	YOU	GO	B-E-A-C-H
Body					

EXAMPLE 3.

Informant: Lisa   "If it rains tomorrow, I'm not going to the beach."

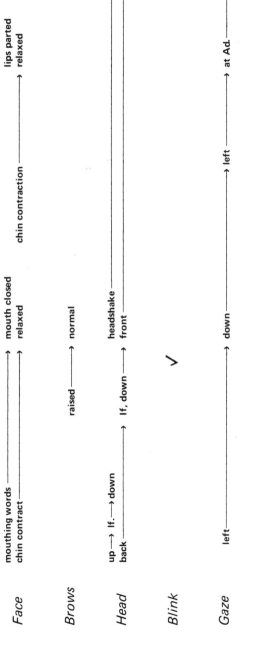

Face   mouthing words ——→ mouth closed ——→ lips parted
         chin contract ——→ relaxed   chin contraction ——→ relaxed

Brows raised ——→ normal

Head   up—→ If.—→ down   headshake
         back ——————→ If, down —→ front

Blink ∨

Gaze   left ——————→ down ——————→ left ——————→ at Ad.

Hands TOMORROW   RAIN   ME   NOT   GO   B-E-A-C-H

Body

APPENDIX 2B (*Continued*)

EXAMPLE 4.

Informant: Lisa   "If it rains tomorrow, are you going to the beach?"

Face	mouthing words ——→	mouth closed	chin contract ————————		upper lip contr. ——	
Brows	normal ———					
Head	forward ———		nodding ———————→ slight headshake			
Blink						
Gaze	at Addressee ————————→ right ————————→ at Addressee ————————					
Hands	?TOMORROW	RAIN	YOU	GO	B-E-A-C-H	
Body			lean right forward ——————————————→ normal			

EXAMPLE 5.

Informant: Cinnie   "If it rains tomorrow, I'm not going to the beach."

Face   lips parted   lips parted ⎱ lips   contraction   closed ——→ parted
                                                         ⎰ nose   chin contraction

Brows raised ————→ squint

Head   down, cocked left ————→ front   headshake
                                           front ————→ cocked left

Blink   ✓

Gaze   up, right   at Addressee

Hands TOMORROW   RAIN   ME   NOT   GO   B-E-A-C-H   ME

Body   left shoulder down ————→ normal

APPENDIX 2B (*Continued*)

EXAMPLE 6.

Informant: Cinnie   "If it rains tomorrow, are you going to the beach?"

Face   lips } contraction
           chin

Brows   raised ——————————————————————————

                                                    slight nod
Head   right ——————————————→ left, forward

Blink

Gaze   right ——————————————————————————→ at Addressee

Hands   ?TOMORROW   RAIN   GO   B-E-A-C-H   YOU

Body

REFERENCES

Baker, C. Regulators and turn-taking in American Sign Language discourse. In L. Friedman (Ed.), *On the other hand: New perspectives on American Sign Language.* New York: Academic Press, 1977, 215–236.

Baker, C. What's not on the other hand in American Sign Language. In *Papers from the twelfth regional meeting of the Chicago linguistic society.* Univ. of Chicago, 1976a.

Baker, C. Eye-openers in ASL. In *CLAC proceedings.* San Diego State Univ. 1976b.

Battison, R. Lexical borrowing in American Sign Language: Phonological amd morphological restructuring. Working paper. Psychology Dept., Northeastern Univ. 1976.

Bellugi, U., & Fischer, S. A comparison of sign language and spoken language. *Cognition,* 1972, *1,* 173–200.

Carr, W., & Francke, A. Culture and the development of vision. *Journal of the American Optometric Association 47,* 1976, *1,* 14–41.

Condon, W., & Ogston, W. Speech and body motion synchrony of the speaker-hearer. In Horton & Jenkins (Eds.), *The perception of language.* Columbus, Ohio: Charles E. Merrill, 1971.

Drew, G. C. Variations in reflex blink-rate during visual motor tasks. *Quarterly Journal of Experimental Psychology,* 1951, *Vol. 3,* 73–88.

Fant, L. *Ameslan: An introduction to American Sign Language.* Northridge, California: Joyce Motion Picture Co., 1972.

Fischer, S. D., & Gough, B. Some unfinished thoughts on Finish. The Salk Institute for Biological Studies (working paper), 1972.

Hall, A. The origin and purpose of blinking. *British Journal of Ophthalmology,* 1945, *29,* 445–467.

Harris, C. S. *et al.* Blink rate as a function of induced muscular tension and manifest anxiety. *Perceptual Motor Skills,* 1966, *29,* 155–160.

Kanfer, F. Verbal rate, eyeblink, and content in structured psychiatric interview. *Journal of Abnormal Social Psychology,* 1960, *61, 3,* 341–347.

Kendon, A. Some functions of gaze direction in social interaction. *Acta Psychologica,* 1967, *26,* 22–63.

Kennard, D., & Glaser, G. An analysis of eyelid movements. *Journal of Nervous Mental Disorders,* 1964, *139,* 31–48.

Liddell, S. Restrictive relative clauses in American Sign Language. Salk Institute, San Diego, California, 1975.

Meyer, D., Bahrick, H., & Fitts, P. Incentives, anxiety and human eyeblink. *J. Exp. Psychol.,* 1953, *43, 3.*

Ponder, E., & Kennedy, W. On the act of blinking. *Quarterly Journal of Experimental Psychology,* 1927, *18,* 89–110.

Siple, P. *Constraints for a sign language from visual perception data.* Unpublished manuscript, 1977.

Walsh, F., & Hoyt, W., *Clinical neuro-ophthalmology* (Vol. 1). Baltimore: Williams & Williams, 1969. Pp. 318–330.

Wiener, M., & Mehrabian, A. *Language within language: Immediacy, a channel in verbal communication.* New York: Appleton-Century-Crofts, 1968.

Woodward, J., & Erting, C. Synchronic Variation and Historical Change in American Sign Language. *Language Sciences,* 1975, *37,* 9–12.

3

Nonmanual Signals and Relative Clauses in American Sign Language

SCOTT K. LIDDELL

University of California, San Diego and The Salk Institute for
Biological Studies

People seeing ASL for the first time are immediately struck by the signer's seemingly continuous use and rapid change of facial expression. Ordinarily this is assumed to be a personal expression on the part of the signer. Yet when individual signers' use of facial expression in ASL is compared with their use in another gesture language they know well, Signed English, the difference is striking: When signing ASL, the signer's face is much more active. This suggests that the "heavy" use of facial activity is not characteristic of sign language in general, or specific to individual signers, but may play a special role in ASL itself.

It goes without saying that ASL carries out communicative functions similar to those of spoken language, however, these functions are often accomplished in a form very different from those we are familiar with in spoken language. For example, there is a large category of

This research was supported, in part, by National Institutes of Health Grant No. NS-09811 and by National Science Foundation Grant BNS-76-12866 to Dr. Ursula Bellugi at the Salk Institute for Biological Studies.

facial expressions in ASL that, together with the posture, movement, and orientation of the body, serve important grammatical or other linguistic functions in ASL sentences. In fact, without attending to nonmanual signals, it is possible for the analyst to miss entirely significant linguistic processes in the language. While it has been claimed that ASL exhibits no syntactic subordination of any kind (Thompson, 1977), I will argue here that the grammar of ASL includes a major form of subordination—relative clauses—and that such clauses are marked by a specific nonmanual signal.

NONMANUAL SIGNALS AND GRAMMATICAL FUNCTIONS

Though a signer's emotions can be communicated through posture and facial expression, this alone cannot account for the expressions produced. Nonnative signers' guesses concerning the emotional content of a sign sequence are often wrong; in most cases a nonnative signer wrongly interprets facial expression as a reflection of the emotional state of the signer. Stokoe and Battison (in press) showed deaf native and hearing nonnative signers the sentence EUROPE IM-PRESS [X: 'me'][1] (the two signs carry the meaning "Europe impressed me"). The native signers properly interpreted the facial signal that accompanied the sentence as indicating emphasis (i.e., "Europe really impressed me"), but nonnative signers interpreted the expression to mean that there was something sad or unfortunate about the experience. Similar informal experiments I have conducted have had the same results: Facial expressions are mistaken as a reflection of the

---

[1]The following conventions will be used for the English translation gloss of ASL utterances. Individual signs are written in all capital letters (e.g., EUROPE). When more than one word is required to translate a single sign, the words are connected by hyphens (e.g., LOOK-AT). Free English translations of ASL sentences are written in quotes with standard English capitalization. Reference to indexical signs is made by writing an appropriate English gloss in capital letters and enclosing it in single quotation marks, 'ME', 'YOURSELF', 'HIS'. These are all indexical markers. When the pronoun is "incorporated" in the verb, this will be indicated in superscript notation, using X to mean indexical incorporation and single quotes for meaning:

    'ME' GIVE[X: 'you'] PIE
    "I gave you a pie."

To indicate modulation or inflection of a sign, without specifically identifying it, I will use the superscript +. If a nonmanual signal "y" occurs throughout a sign sequence such as, DOG CHASE CAT, this will be symbolized by $\overline{\text{DOG CHASE CAT.}}^{\text{y}}$

signer's emotional state and, as a result, are misunderstood. A facial expression may reflect the emotional state of the signer, the emotional content of a sentence, or a signer's feeling about the subject, etc; but it does not necessarily reflect any of these.

Nonmanual Signals with Lexical Scope

Certain nonmanual signals are associated specifically with particular lexical items; the expression occurs only while the sign it accompanies is being made. BITE is often accompanied by a biting motion of the mouth, BEG by a pleading expression, RELIEVED by a rapid exhaling of a burst of air through pursed lips (almost like "phew!"). These movements appear to serve only the function of acting out the meaning of the sign in some way, though this is not always the case.[2] Whether or not this type of movement should be regarded as part of the citation form of the sign as a lexical unit or as a usual addition to it is a difficult question; of the signs above, Stokoe, Casterline, and Croneberg (1965) list only RELIEVED as being made optionally with a sigh. However, since some signers consistently use nonmanual signals when asked to produce the signs in citation form, the question remains open.

In studying the difference between some current ASL signs and their previous forms, Frishberg (1975) found signs that previously required facial expression, environmental contact, or body movement and now only require movement of the hands. She views this as a historical tendency to concentrate lexical information in the hands in the citation form of individual signs. This is interpreted by her as part of a general shift in ASL from iconicity in signs to arbitrariness. The following example is typical.

> COMPARE is one of the few signs for which we have information from OFSL [Old French Sign Language], as well as from Long and Stokoe, et al. The original form of this sign had two flat hands facing the signer, separated. The eyes moved from one to the other, and then the hands moved together, eyes focused on both at once. Long describes an intermediate stage in which the hands have begun moving "inward and up before you side by side as if looking at them and comparing palms [99]." The modern form simply rocks the two hands, either in alternation (which can be related to the older eye movements) or in unison—an arbitrary, but symmetrical change [p. 711].

[2] There are mouth–jaw movements, which may or may not include vocalization, such as [ba], that sometimes accompany certain signs (i.e., GIVE-IN) (personal communication, Battison). These do not appear to be pantomimic, the way that the examples listed in the text do.

While the historical tendency toward concentration of lexical content in the hands (and away from body or facial involvement) in the citation form of signs noted by Frishberg may well continue to operate, for the present there are still many individual signs often accompanied by a specific nonmanual signal, though the factors that control this use are not known.

Nonmanual Signals with Phrasal Scope

Certain nonmanual signals are associated specifically with certain kinds of phrases and, in fact, are a part of the grammar of those phrases.

There is a specific facial expression and body posture that is part of a modulation of certain time adverbs in ASL. In its citation form, RECENTLY, for example, is signed as shown in Figure 3.1a (note the facial expression associated with the sign RECENTLY); when recency is being contrasted with a much greater period of time (e.g., "not last week—just recently"), the signer's head leans and turns

(a) RECENTLY
    "recently"

(b) RECENTLY⁺
    "just recently"

Figure 3.1. When recency is being stressed, the head turns toward the shoulder, which is raised. Also note the special facial expressions.

toward the side of the body on which RECENTLY is being made, and the shoulder on that side (or on both sides) is pulled forward and raised; the facial expression is also made more intense by a greater contraction of the same facial muscles used with RECENTLY (see Figure 3.1b). Variation in the intensity of these movements is possible depending on how much contrast the signer wants to provide.

Other past-tense adverbials, such as PAST TUESDAY, YESTER-DAY NIGHT, and LAST-YEAR (see Figure 3.2), undergo the same modulations. NOW undergoes a similar modulation, as do such future adverbials as NEXT-YEAR, NEXT-WEEK, and TOMORROW MORNING.

When such adverbial phrases consist of two signs (e.g., YESTER-DAY NIGHT), they are signed as a compound and both signs are accompanied by the nonmanual signal. In all cases the sign is made closer to the shoulder. In addition, if the adverbial sign has a path of movement rather than a local movement, the length of the path of movement is reduced.

For evidence that this particular nonmanual signal is itself syntacti-cally an adverb, see Liddell (in press), where this and other non-manual adverbs are analyzed.

(a) LAST-YEAR   (b) LAST-YEAR⁺
    "last year"   "just last year"

Figure 3.2. LAST-YEAR undergoes the same process (stressing recency) illustrated in Figure 3.1 with the sign RECENTLY. Notice that when recency is stressed, the sign is made closer to the shoulder. While LAST-YEAR is made with a neutral facial expres-sion, LAST-YEAR⁺ will have the same facial expression as RECENTLY.⁺

NONMANUAL SIGNALS WITH CLAUSAL SCOPE:
YES–NO QUESTIONS, NEGATION

Nonmanual signals can occur with entire clauses and perform grammatical functions.

Yes–No Questions

It has often been observed that nonmanual activity is used in forming yes–no questions in ASL. This has been discussed in Stokoe *et al.* (1965), Bellugi and Fischer (1972), Baker (1976), and others. All these agree that a particular facial expression, head position, and body position signals the yes–no question. If throughout the signing of a sentence the head and shoulders are leaned forward, the chin is forward far enough to keep the face vertical, and the eyebrows are raised, the sentence will be interpreted as a yes–no question.

ASL can also mark yes–no questions lexically, by using the index finger to draw a question mark and adding a dot with a stab (Stokoe, Casterline, & Croneberg, 1976). This sign does not replace the nonmanual signal but is used in conjunction with it. The same sign may be used to express doubt or disagreement.

> This same sign and a variant [an index finger erect at the base but bending repeatedly at the first two joints, the palm oriented toward the addressee] have another use, as a one-sign utterance expressing slight skepticism, doubt, or polite but complete disagreement about another's statement. Curiously the "question mark" sign *with appropriate facial expression* works at either end of the range: "Oh, do you think so?" and "I question that very much [p. 65; italics added]."

It appears to be the case that facial expression and body movement play the determining role in the identification of yes–no questions in ASL since (*a*) the facial expression and body attitude alone can signal a yes–no question but generally signs alone will not; and (*b*) the interpretation of the two question signs depends on facial expression and body movement.

Negation

Another function of nonmanual signals that has been described (Stokoe, 1960; Bellugi & Fischer, 1972 ; and Baker, 1976) is negation. The signal I will describe here consists of a side-to-side headshake accompanied by a nonneutral facial expression that, without any manual help, negates a sentence. This will not negate an otherwise negative sentence such as 'ME' NOT BUY DOG, "I didn't buy a dog," though it will negate 'ME' BUY DOG, "I bought a dog." Although the most common way to negate a sentence is lexically (i.e., with the sign NOT), even when the sign NOT is present in a sentence, the sentence is often accompanied by the negative headshake.

RESTRICTIVE RELATIVE CLAUSES

Certain clauses in ASL are also accompanied by a specific nonmanual signal "r," illustrated in Figure 3.3. They function like restrictive relative clauses, and I will argue that, in fact, syntactically they are relative clauses. Both the position of the head and the expression

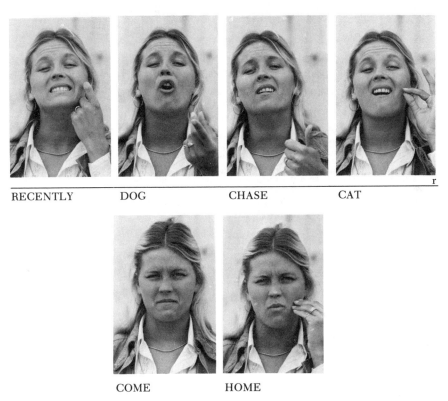

| RECENTLY | DOG | CHASE | CAT |

| COME | HOME |

Figure 3.3.   "The dog that recently chased the cat came home."
"The cat that the dog recently chased came home."

on the face are significant, as Figure 3.3 illustrates with regard to the sentence:

_____ r
RECENTLY DOG CHASE[+] CAT COME HOME
"The dog that recently chased the cat came home."
"The cat that the dog recently chased came home."

The ambiguity of the ASL relative clauses will be discussed later.

Although the six photographs each show a different facial expression, some aspects of the facial expression and head position remain constant throughout the relative clause. First, the head is tilted back for the signs RECENTLY, DOG, CHASE, and CAT, but it is lowered for the signs COME and HOME. Second, the eyebrows are raised during the relative clause and lowered for the rest of the sentence. Third, the muscles that raise the upper lip are tensed during the relative clause. This gives a characteristic shape to the nasolabial fold (the crease in the skin that runs from the sides of the mouth to the sides of the nose). Taken together, these three independent features of the facial expression and head position form a nonmanual signal that distinguishes a relative clause from a simple sentence.[3] This way of marking the relative clause is clearly not determined by the individual signs in the clause.

If a single lexical item that is ordinarily accompanied by a characteristic facial expression occurs inside a relative clause, the one type of nonmanual signal does not suppress the other. Rather, the effect is similar to adding the two signals together. Lexical and clausal nonmanual signals seem to be independent and additive (cf. RECENTLY, Figure 3.3).

The nonmanual signal marking relative clauses was by no means obvious upon first examination of the videotapes containing them. Only when photographs taken from the TV screen as the individual signs in the sentences were being made were placed side by side did it become clear that the signs within the relative clauses have those special features in common.[4]

_____

[3] Invaluable assistance in identifying the specific muscle groups responsible for producing the nonmanual signal "r" was provided by Paul Ekman of the Langley Porter Neuropsychiatric Institute in San Francisco. The muscle groups, which could be identified on our videotapes that produced the expression, are muscle groups 1, 2, and 10. The reader is referred to Ekman and Friesen (in press).

[4] Birgitte Bendixen, of University of California, San Diego (personal communication)

Signers consistently interpret this nonmanual signal as being used to identify one of the noun phrases inside the clause. This is not to say that a signer will always choose the relative clause construction where an English speaker would use a relative clause; there is, of course, more than one way to say the same thing. A signer could easily convey the same information using two sentences instead of one complex one.

There is also evidence that this construction is widespread. The backgrounds of the native signers who were informants for this research are quite varied. The deaf researchers at the Salk Institute are from Texas, California, and Oregon. I was also able to consult some of the faculty and staff (hearing and deaf) at California State University, Northridge, who learned ASL as a native language, and they were in agreement as to the function of the relative clause as well as the form of the relative clause. This work was also discussed with a research group from the Research Development and Demonstration Center in Education of Handicapped Children, which is located in Minneapolis, Minnesota, who have subsequently found results identical to those presented here (personal communication).

Sentences containing ASL relative clauses had been elicited by asking native signers to translate into ASL a list of English sentences containing restrictive relative clauses. To minimize the possibility that the translation might be somehow biased by the fact that the English sentences contained relative clauses, the informants were not asked for on-the-spot translations but were given a few days. Relative clauses were not always produced; sometimes a signer introduced information in one sentence and referred to it in the next. This seems to occur naturally if the speaker assumes that the addressee is unfamiliar with the subject. For instance, for one native signer, not involved in the above translation, a hypothetical situation was established in

---

and Harry W. Hoemann, Bowling Green State University (personal communication) suggested independently that they had the impression that the signing space is reduced during the signing of a relative clause. This may be true in some cases, but there are also cases where the signing space is not reduced. If the reduction of the signing space takes place, it occurs in addition to, not instead of the nonmanual signal discussed in this chapter. That is, reduction of the signing space, by itself, does not appear to be able to signal a relative clause.

In addition, when this reduction takes place, the signing is often done to one side of the body rather than in the center of the neutral signing space. One signer (who learned ASL from peers at a school for the deaf) placed the signing space to the side while also leaning to that side. This was during the narration of a story and may fall into the category of style. Such extreme use of space in ordinary conversation has not occurred in my experience.

which there had recently been two men in the room with us, one of whom knew ASL and one of whom knew nothing about ASL, with locations established for each one. When asked to explain that the man who knew nothing about ASL knew her mother (a relative clause was not used in the request), the signer repeated the description of the situation, including establishing a location for each man, and referred to the man by referring to "his" location.

However, when asked to omit the explanation of the backgrounds of the two men and simply indicate which man knew her mother, the signer immediately produced a sentence containing a relative clause:

------------------------------ r

ONE CAN'T SIGN KNOW 'MY' MOTHER
"The one who can't sign knows my mother."

In this case there was no translation involved; the relative clause occurred naturally and only after it was established that the previous situation was already known by the signer's addressee (i.e., two men, one who could sign and one who could not, had been in the room). I also attempted to see if these relative clauses occurred naturally in stories. In one short story the amount of information concerning the three characters was carefully limited; they were not given names but were introduced as "one man," "another man," etc. Later in the story these characters needed to be referred to, and the most convenient way to do this in English was by using a relative clause construction. The story was given to signers to read, and, after they were familiar with the story, each signer was asked to tell the story in ASL. In their videotaped signed stories, the signers used two main ways of identifying characters. One was to assign a "number" to each character as he was introduced; that is, the first man introduced in the story was called "the first," which the signer indicated by pointing to the thumb and then signing MAN. The second man was referred to on the index finger, etc.

The other way used to refer to the characters in the story was to identify them by what they had done. This involved the use of relative clauses. For example, to identify the man who had made a beet pie, one signer said,

------------------------------ r

MAN MAKE RED PIE FLIRT⁺ FINISH
"The man who made the 'beet' pie stopped flirting."

Two separate studies bear upon the arbitrariness and the salience of facial expression as a grammatical signal for relative clauses. Part of the first study (Liddell, in preparation) involved showing sentences containing relative clauses to hearing people studying ASL and asking them for a written translation of what they saw. There were more than 100 subjects from beginning to advanced classes. Where facial expression was the only signal for relativization, there was not one single translation that contained a relative clause.

This demonstrates the arbitrariness of the nonmanual signal. The students did not have a complete knowledge of the grammar of ASL and did not understand the role of the nonmanual signal that marks relative clauses. A group of deaf signers was involved in another study (to be described) that demonstrates the salience of the signal.

Tweney and Liddell (in preparation) conducted a sentence perception experiment involving the perception of ASL sentences masked with visual "noise." This "noise" made the task of even recognizing individual signs difficult, which in turn made the task of understanding the sentences difficult. Some of the sentences used in this experiment contained relative clause constructions. Relative clauses in ASL do not use relative pronouns like *who* in English. Though many signers will use WHO as a relative pronoun, the deaf researchers here at the Salk Institute regard this as an intrusion of English. None of the sentences used in the sentence perception experiment contained the sign WHO, yet two of the subjects reported seeing the sign—in each case, in response to a sentence containing a clause marked by the "r" nonmanual signal. One of the cases was especially interesting. The signer correctly identified every sign in the main clause but incorrectly identified every sign in the subordinate clause. In spite of this, the signer knew there was a relative clause present and actually reported seeing the sign WHO.

So far, no justification has been provided for the claim that what is being described is really a relative clause in terms of syntactic structure and not a separate independent clause. That is, why not assume

$$\overline{\qquad\qquad\qquad^{r}\qquad\qquad\qquad}$$

that RECENTLY DOG CHASE CAT COME HOME is simply a case of adjacent sentences, with the subject of the second sentence deleted because it is understood, as in the following diagram of conjoined sentences.[5]

---

[5]The symbol [∅]x will be used to point out the previous location of the deleted element *x* in a string of signs.

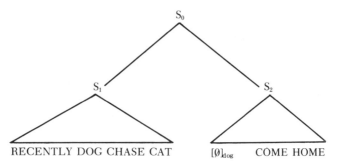

Whereas this illustrates a very common phenomenon in ASL, it is distinct from the relative clauses described here. Figure 3.4 illustrates the same sequence of signs signed as two sentences.

It can be clearly seen by comparing Figure 3.3 and Figure 3.4 that there is a formational difference between the two. The relative clause has a special facial expression and head position associated with it. Connected with this difference in form is a difference in what the two mean and how they behave syntactically. The two-sentence version involves two assertions. In the case of Figure 3.4, it is asserted that the dog chased the cat and also that the dog came home. In the case of the sentence containing the relative clause, there is only one assertion— that the dog came home; it is assumed as already known that the dog chased the cat. As a result, the two-sentence version is interpreted as describing a sequence of events, whereas the sentence containing the relative clause is interpreted as describing a single event.

The sentence containing the relative clause and the corresponding two sentences also differ with respect to continuity. A break in the signing may quite naturally occur between separate sentences. By this I mean a brief relaxation of the hands other than a normal transition from one sign to the next. I have found no such lack of continuity between the relative clause and the main clause on the videotapes I have examined. What I have found is that the duration of the final sign in the relative clause is generally longer than if the same sign were to occur in medial position within the relative clause. Associated with this extension in the signing time is a continuation of the nonmanual signal "r." When the nonmanual signal "r" ends, there is an immediate transition to the following sign, with no pause in between.

The relationship between the following times for the sign CAT are typical of the changes in duration of other signs I have timed. A sign like CAT, when viewed on videotape field by field, has a fairly clear "beginning." That is, the hand approaching the head slows down so that there is no longer a blur on the frame, and the F handshape is also

RECENTLY DOG CHASE CAT

COME HOME

Figure 3.4. The signing of two independent clauses: "The dog recently chased the cat and then he came home."

definite before the hand makes contact with the head. I take this to be the beginning of the sign. I count any change away from the F hand-shape to mean that the sign is over.

I found the duration of the sign CAT to be shortest when it was neither initial nor final in the relative clause. There the average duration of the sign was 14 VTR fields, or .23 second. When CAT appears in final position, the average is 24 fields, or .4 second. In initial position the average is 20 fields, or .33 second. In all cases where CAT appeared in initial position in the relative clause, it was the logical object of a transitive verb and preceded both the subject and the verb. Not only did I find differences in duration based on position in relative clauses, but there were also differences based on whether or not a given sign was the "head" of the relative clause (methods for distinguishing the head of a relative clause are discussed later). When the sign DOG (logical subject of a transitive verb) appeared in initial position in a relative clause and was the head of the relative clause, I found an average duration of 27 fields (.45 second), but if it was not the head of the relative clause, the duration was 17 fields (.28 second). Similarly, in medial position, if DOG was the head of the relative clause, the duration was 22 fields (.37 second), as opposed to 14 fields (.23 second) if DOG was not the head.

The duration of a sign in a relative clause is obviously a very complicated matter that appears to be affected by at least two separate factors: the position and the syntactic function of the sign.

I have found similar results where relative clauses were not involved. In comparison with medial position, signs that were topics were held roughly 22 fields (.37 second) longer, initial nontopics were held 11 fields (.18 second) longer, and final signs roughly 17 fields (.28 second) longer.[6]

Both sets of figures were derived from limited data samples. For example, the relative clause averages for CAT and DOG were based on 35 occurrences of the sign CAT and 31 occurrences of the sign DOG. In addition, there was considerable variation within groups that were averaged. As a result, it seems reasonable to view the figures presented in the text as no more than tendencies.

There are further grammatical differences between conjoined sentences and a sentence containing an "r" clause. Adjacent sentences may be conjoined with a sign like BUT, but an "r"-marked clause and a sentence cannot be conjoined in this way:

[RECENTLY DOG CHASE CAT] BUT [NOT-YET COME HOME]
"The dog recently chased the cat but hasn't come home."

$$\overline{\hspace{5cm}}^{\text{r}}$$
*[RECENTLY DOG CHASE CAT]$_{\text{NP}}$ BUT [NOT-YET COME HOME]$_\text{S}$[7]
"[The dog which recently chased the cat] but hasn't come home."

Whereas there are several possible explanations for the ungrammaticality, the fact that the second sentence—with the special posture and muscular action of the face discussed earlier—is ungrammatical is predicted by the relative clause analysis. It would be ungrammatical

---

[6] For a discussion of the distinction between initial nontopics and topics, the reader is referred to Liddell (in press).

[7] The symbol * will precede a grammatically unacceptable sentence. A ? will precede sentences that are somewhere between fully acceptable and unacceptable.

for the same reason that a sentence with a simple noun-phrase subject would be ungrammatical if it were followed by BUT:

*[DOG]$_{NP}$ BUT NOT-YET COME HOME
"The dog but hasn't yet come home."

Relative clauses may also be introduced by signs like REMEMBER.

<pre>   r   </pre>
[REMEMBER CAT DOG BITE]$_S$]$_{NP}$ RUN-AWAY[8]
"(Remember) the cat the dog bit, (it) ran away."

The translation looks like a question followed by a statement, but the ASL will not be analyzed in this way for the following reasons.

<pre>   r</pre>
First, the string REMEMBER CAT DOG BITE is not the same as a question about whether or not someone remembers the incident. A question about the incident would have subject–verb–object order, not object–subject–verb order.

<pre>   q</pre>
REMEMBER DOG BITE CAT
"Do you remember that the dog bit the cat?"

Second, a question in ASL has its own special nonmanual signal, "q," illustrated in Figure 3.5.

Third, as was mentioned earlier, a question in ASL may optionally be followed by the question marker (the finger drawing a question mark and adding a dot with a stab). It is significant that whereas the

<pre>   q</pre>
question REMEMBER DOG BITE CAT can be followed by the question marker, the relative clause cannot.

Fourth, a question in ASL can be preceded with the sign NOT. This forms a negative question.

<pre>   q</pre>
NOT REMEMBER DOG BITE CAT
"Don't you remember that the dog bit the cat?"

However, the relative clause may not begin with NOT RE-MEMBER. This would be completely ungrammatical.

---

[8] Friedman (1976) has claimed that word order is not signficant in ASL, yet there is only one interpretation of the grammatical relations in this example. It is unambiguously object–subject–verb. This is not because dogs bite cats and not the other way around. It would still be interpreted as object–subject–verb if it were

<pre>   r</pre>
REMEMBER DOG CAT BITE.

q

REMEMBER   DOG   CHASE   CAT

Figure 3.5. "Do you remember that the dog chased the cat?" The nonmanual signal used for a yes–no question consists of shifting the body forward and raising the eyebrows.

Thus, there are formational, semantic, and syntactic differences in ASL between relative clauses and simple sentences or questions.

r

I am also assuming that the string REMEMBER DOG CHASE CAT is itself a relative clause rather than a sentence containing the main

r

clause verb REMEMBER, with a relative clause, DOG CHASE CAT, as its object. This assumption was made because of the presence of the "r" signal during the sign REMEMBER. If REMEMBER were not part of the relative clause, it should not be accompanied by the nonmanual signal "r."

If this assumption is correct, this automatically explains why the relative clause may not begin with the signs NOT REMEMBER. If REMEMBER were functioning as a main clause verb in a sentence with a relative clause object, then it should be possible to negate that verb with the sign NOT. If REMEMBER is part of the relative clause, there is no reason to expect NOT to be able to precede it.

There is one final difference that distinguishes relative clauses from simple sentences and/or questions. Relative clauses optionally contain the sign THATa between the subject and the verb.[9]

[9] During the research that led to this chapter, it became clear to me that distinctions needed to be made between the various signs that I was glossing as THAT. This chapter includes four such signs:

    1. THATa (a demonstrative and relativizer)

Figure 3.6. THATa, a demonstrative and relativizer.

$$\overline{\text{r}}$$
THATa

To make this sign, the forearm is elevated roughly 60 degrees above horizontal, and the sign is made with a single short forward motion of the hand by bending the wrist. This may be accompanied by some forward and downward forearm motion. The following example illustrates its use.

$$\overline{\text{r}}$$
[[RECENTLY DOG THATa CHASE CAT]$_{S_1}$]$_{NP}$ COME HOME
"The dog that recently chased the cat came home."
"The cat that the dog recently chased came home."

THATa, in addition to the nonmanual signal, seems to mark the entire clause S_1 as subordinate, not just the signs after DOG. Thus this is not just a copy of the English relative clause structure. As further evidence of this, the adverb RECENTLY is interpreted as part of the relative clause, not the main clause. In other words, DOG, as the bracketing in the example indicates, is part of the relative clause. Thus THATa appears to be functioning as a relative conjunction.

The fact that the relative clause is ambiguous provides further evidence for this analysis. There could be no ambiguity if DOG were

2. THAT (cf. Stokoe *et al.*, 1976, p. 65)
3. THATb (see the text for an explanation)
4. THATc ("that's the one")

No significance should be attached to the lowercase a, b or c, other than their function as a naming device.

an external head, as it is in the translation "The dog that recently chased the cat. . . ."

Another sign generally glossed as THAT, discussed in Stokoe *et al.* (1965), is illustrated in Figure 3.7. This sign is associated with forms of signed English. It also occurs in what appear to be borrowings from English, such as

THAT RIGHT   and   THAT ALL (A-L-L)
"that's right"   "that's all."

But this sign is completely rejected as unacceptable when it is presented to native signers as a substitute for THATa in relative clauses.

Two other signs generally glossed as "THAT" play an important role in the relative clauses of ASL. They are the signs THATb and THATc, and their use is illustrated in the following example:

$$\overline{\overset{\overline{}^{\,i}}{_{\,r}}}$$

'ME' FEED [[DOG BITE CAT THATb]$_S$ THATc]$_{NP}$
"I fed the dog that bit the cat."
"I fed the cat that the dog bit."

The notation ____^{i} above the sign THATb refers to an intensification of the signal "r" during that sign. This is discussed in more detail later. Based on the criterion of co-occurrence with the nonmanual signal "r," THATc is not part of the relative clause, though THATb is.

Figure 3.7. THAT cannot be grammatically used as a substitute for THATa in relative clauses.

THAT

Both signs differ in form and function from the other "THAT"s discussed in this chapter. These two signs are illustrated in Figure 3.8.

To make the sign THATb, the forearm remains nearly vertical, with the wrist cocked back slightly. Often there is no motion at all in this sign. However, there may be a fast but very slight shaking motion of the forearm. I have also occasionally seen this sign made by uncocking the wrist. The sign itself does not translate well. It is a sign that is made and held to give the addressee a chance to signal to the signer that he knows which person or thing the relative clause is describing. When the speaker receives such a signal (i.e., a head nod), he signs THATc.

In a context where two people have been looking for something they saw advertised, upon finding that thing, one person could point it out to the other and then sign THATc. Its meaning is very much like "That's the one." THATc performs the same function in the above example. Both signers know that a dog bit a cat. THATc makes it clear that "that's the one I'm talking about." THATc is optional if the relative clause appears in nonfinal position. However, a relative clause may not be left hanging. If the relative clause appears in final position, either the sign THATc follows it or there is some kind of affirmative head nod that serves the same function.

THATa and THATc are similar in form but not identical. There are two significant differences: THATc begins with a backward motion, whereas THATa begins with a forward motion. THATc is also made with a more clear-cut end to the arm motion. (Cf. Supalla & Newport [this volume] for the distinction between the "continuous" and the "hold" manners of movement.)

There is one other aspect of the last example that is of interest. It

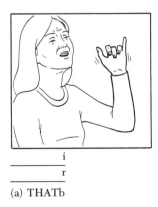

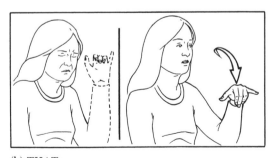

(b) THATc

(a) THATb

Figure 3.8.

also provides evidence against a conjoined sentence analysis of the data.

Suppose that the following conjoined sentences underlie (at some level) the surface form (2):

(1)   ['ME' FEED DOG]$_S$ [DOG BITE CAT]$_S$
       "I fed the dog." "The dog bit the cat."

                                                          r
                                              _____

(2)   'ME' FEED [[DOG BITE CAT]$_S$ THATc]$_{NP}$

In order to derive (2) from the conjoined sentence source, it would be necessary to delete *backward* into an adjacent sentence.[10] Not only is there no independent evidence from ASL to support such a rule, but this would violate what is believed to be a universal of human languages (Langacker, 1969). Finally, one might ask what the object of FEED is in (2). A supporter of the conjoined sentence analysis would have to say that there is no object of FEED in surface structure.[11]

In the relative clause analysis the answers to both of these questions are completely straightforward. The underlying structure would look like the figure on page 79.

_____

[10] Consider the following conjoined English sentences: "Mother gave me some cookies and gave me some money." This is a perfectly grammatical English construction, which presumably comes from joining the two sentences, "Mother gave me some cookies" and "Mother gave me some money." Notice that in the conjoined sentences *mother* is present with the first occurrence of the verb *give* but has been deleted from the second occurrence of *give*. This is an example of forward deletion. The first instance of a noun is unaffected, but the second is deleted. Notice that ungrammaticality is a result of deleting backward, i.e., deleting the first and keeping the second. (*"Gave me some cookies and Mother gave me some money.") This type of backward deletion would be necessary in order to derive (2) from (1) in the text. This is just one aspect of a larger phenomenon in language that is dealt with at length in Langacker (1969).

[11] In order to avoid the backward deletion and still maintain a coordinate analysis, someone might argue that it was really the second occurrence of DOG that was deleted. This would also involve a change in the surface bracketing:

    ['ME' FEED DOG]$_S$ [DOG BITE CAT]
    ['ME' FEED DOG]$_S$ [∅ BITE CAT]

                                           r
                   _____

    ['ME' FEED   [DOG BITE CAT]

Unfortunately this argument will not work because, as was mentioned earlier, these relative clauses are ambiguous. That is, there is one more reading to (2).

    ['ME' FEED [DOG BITE CAT]$_S$ THATc]$_{NP}$
    "I fed the cat that the dog bit."

It is clear that it would be necessary to delete backward.

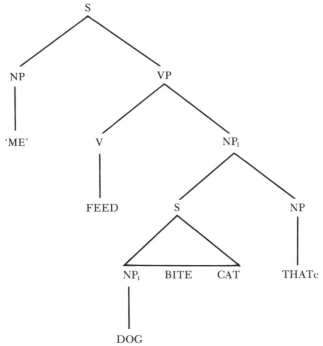

This schematic figure shows the proposed structure of the sentence containing a relative clause: 'ME' FEED $\overline{\text{DOG BITE CAT}}^{\text{r}}$ THATc, where DOG is the head of the relative clause. Notice that now there is no problem with deletion, and there is no embarrassment about identifying the object of FEED. The object of FEED is the relative clause, and nothing has been deleted.

The following sentences are ungrammatical:

$$\overline{\text{*DOG BITE CAT}}^{\text{r}} \left\{ \begin{array}{l} \text{ANYWAY} \\ \text{'ME' THINK} \end{array} \right\} \text{THATc BRING HOSPITAL}$$

"The cat the dog bit— $\left\{ \begin{array}{l} \text{anyway} \\ \text{I think} \end{array} \right\}$ that's the one that was brought to the hospital."

They are ungrammatical because THATc has been separated from the relative clause.

The ungrammaticality of these examples provides good support that THATc is not structurally equivalent to "that's the one" in the following English sentence: "You know the cat the dog bit—well that's the one that ran away."

In ASL the type of relative clause described here is really ambiguous. The following relative clause for instance, may be interpreted in two ways:

r
_____

RECENTLY DOG CHASE CAT COME HOME
1. "The dog that recently chased the cat came home."
2. "The cat that the dog recently chased came home."

The fact that it is ambiguous should not be surprising considering the form of the relative clause in ASL. Since the sentence forming the relative clause is intact in surface structure and does not follow an external head noun, it is not obvious what the relative clause is describing. Contrast this with the English translation, where the relative clause, *that recently chased the cat*, apparently has had its subject, *the dog*, replaced by the pronoun *that*. As a result, the relative clause is interpreted as being about the dog. Again, notice that this is not the case with the ASL relative clause. The relative clause maintains the sentence intact and could be about either the dog or the cat. This type of relative clause is called an internal head relative clause and has been reported in a number of different languages, such as Bambara (Bird, 1968), Navajo (Hale & Platero, 1974), Diegueño (Gorbet, 1974), and Wappo (Li & Thompson, 1976).

The context is usually sufficient to let the addressee know which noun phrase is functioning as the head of the relative clause. Further help is provided by semantic plausibility (i.e., in the following example DOG is a more likely subject of BARK than CAT).

r
_____

$[[\text{DOG CHASE CAT}]_S]_{NP}$ BARK
The dog that chased the cat barked."

Another ASL syntactic device, spatial indexing, also can be used to identify the head of the relative clause. This is discussed in Friedman (1976) and Fischer (1975), among others, and will not be elaborated on here. The important point is that a location in space is referred to in conjunction with a sign. This serves to establish that location as a reference point. Later reference to that point is functionally equivalent to pronominal reference in spoken language. This type of indexic reference is not ambiguous the way *he* is in the Enghish sentence "When John looked at Bill, he was surprised."

This sentence is ambiguous because it is not clear who was surprised—John, Bill, or someone else. There is no such ambiguity in the following ASL sentence:

JOHN	LOOK- AT [X: 'him']	BILL	'HE'	SURPRISE
-sign is made to the right of the body by the right hand-	-made with the right hand, palm down, extended fingers pointing left-	-made with the left hand on the left side of the body-	left index finger points left	two hands

"John looked at Bill and   he [=Bill] was surprised."

Alternatively, if 'HE' had pointed to the right rather than to the left, it would have referred to John. This same process of spatial indexing can be used in the relative clauses.

<u>   r   </u>

[[DOG BITE CAT]$_S$]$_{NP}$	COME	HOME
-left- -left to right- -right-	-starts on right and moves toward the center-	

"The cat that the dog bit came home."

Note that the relative clause is still ambiguous (by itself it does not indicate its head) but that the ambiguity is resolved by the spatial reference that follows. That is, by signing COME on the right, the subject is interpreted as that noun phrases that was established on the right (i.e., CAT).

In addition to the examples above, in which the head of the relative clause was not marked, ASL has three ways of explicitly marking the head of the relative clause. The first consists of intensifying the nonmanual signal "r" by contracting the same muscle groups more severely and either (a) thrusting the head forward (slightly); or (b) nodding the head quickly; or (c) both, while the head of the relative clause is signed. This is the intensification of the signal "r" referred to earlier.

<u>   i   </u>
<u>   r   </u>

[DOG BITE CAT] COME HOME
"The cat that the dog bit came home."

The above example is not ambiguous. The only reading is the one shown. There is a striking parallel in the formal means used to disambiguate ASL and Diegueño relative clauses.

Diegueño is a Yuman language spoken in San Diego County, California. It also has internal head relative clauses. For example:

[[xatkcok wi: +m tuc]$_S$ pu c]$_{NP}$ n^{y}iL^y
dog rock + COMIT I-hit DEM SUBJ black
"The rock I hit the dog with was black."
"The dog I hit with the rock was black."

As the preceding example (from Gorbet, 1974) illustrates, these internal head relative clauses are also ambiguous. COMIT in this example stands for the comitative case marker, m, which indicates that the rock was used to hit the dog. DEM represents the demonstrative morpheme pu, and SUBJ stands for the subject marker c. Notice that the subject marker is not attached to either "dog" or "rock" but marks the entire relative clause as subject of the verb n^{y}iL^y (black). The Imperial Valley dialect of Diegueño can disambiguate a relative clause by placing a demonstrative pronoun after the head.[12]

[i:pac   ['wa: n^{y}i+k]   wyiw]   pu   c]   n^{y}imšap
man [house that + ABL(case marker)]   come   white
"The house that the man came from was white."

The above example is interpreted as shown since the demonstrative (n^{y}i) follows house ('wa:). In both cases, ASL and Diegueño, the disambiguation is accomplished without changing the basic structure of the relative clause. However, the head of the relative clause is specially marked.

The second way of disambiguating an ASL relative clause consists of rearranging the constituents so that the relative clause actually takes on the shape of a noun phrase: demonstrative–modifier–noun. In addition, the intensification of the "r" signal also accompanies the head noun.

$$\overline{\phantom{\rule{6cm}{0pt}}}\,\overset{\textstyle i}{}$$

$$\overline{\phantom{\rule{6cm}{0pt}}}\,\underset{\textstyle r}{}$$

THATa CHASE CAT DOG RUN-AWAY[13]
"The dog that chased the cat ran away."

---

[12] Margaret Langdon (personal communication) informs me that even in this dialect this process is limited to very specific grammatical contexts. As a result, this process will not necessarily be possible in any given relative clause in this dialect.

[13] This example is not ambiguous as to who did the chasing and who was chased. The only reading is one in which the dog chased the cat. In other words, it is the order of the signs that indicates the grammatical relations in this case. Again, this is contradictory to Friedman's (1976) claim that the order of signs does not indicate grammatical relations in ASL.

This example also provides evidence against a conjoined sentence analysis of relative clauses, since the relative clause in this case does not have the form of a sentence but that of a noun phrase— that is THATa also has a demonstrative function; [THATa BROWN DOG]$_{NP}$ RUN-AWAY. In an earlier paper I reported that one of the three informants who provided the data for this research found

$$\overline{\rule{3cm}{0pt}}^{\;i}_{\;r}$$

THAT CHASE CAT DOG to be unacceptable. However, I have since had a chance to check with several other informants. They agree with the first two. They characterize such relative clauses as informal ASL signing.

ASL can also move the object to initial position as in:

$$\overline{\rule{3cm}{0pt}}^{\;r}$$

[CAT DOG BITE]$_{NP}$ COME HOME
"The cat that the dog bit came home."

However, this topicalization process does not have the same disambiguating force as the example just shown, where the subject appears in final position. That is, though the interpretation shown is the most likely interpretation, the relative clause is still ambiguous.

Gorbet analyzes the Mesa Grande dialect of Diegueño as having a rule that moves the head of the relative clause to initial position within the clause, leaving a pronoun behind that is appropriately marked for case. This eliminates the ambiguity. This will be made clear by comparing the sentence

```
'xat       'wil^y +m          'tu:
dog        rock+COMIT         I-hit
"I hit the dog with the rock."
```

with the following relative clause, in which those changes have been made.

```
[['wil^y  'xat   n^yi +m      'tu:]_s  pu    c]_NP              n^yiL^ycis
  rock    dog    that+COMIT   I-hit    DEM   SUBJ    black-indeed
```

"The rock I hit the dog with was black."

The parallel between ASL and Diegueño is obvious. The order of constituents is changed and results in an unambiguous structure.

In ASL the relative clauses are also unambiguous if the head noun appears again at the end of the relative clause preceded by THATa.

$$\frac{\quad\quad\quad\text{i}\quad}{\quad\quad\quad\quad\quad\text{r}\quad}$$

[[[DOG BITE CAT]$_\text{S}$]$_\text{NP}$ THATa CAT]$_\text{NP}$ 'ME' FEED
"I fed the cat that the dog bit."

In addition, the final phrase containing the repeated noun is accompanied by the nonmanual "intense" signal.

Once again there is a parallel between ASL and Diegueño. Gorbet has argued that Diegueño has a rule that copies the head at the end of the relative clause, producing a string very similar to the ASL string.

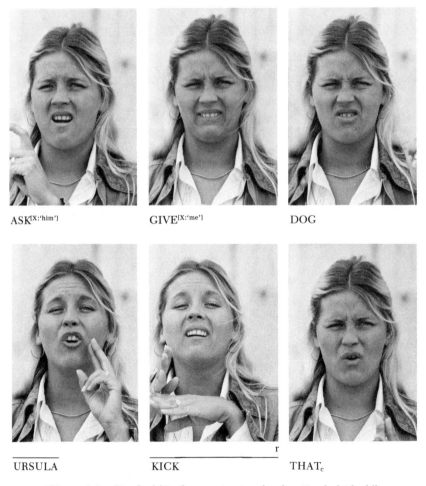

ASK$^{\text{[X:'him']}}$ GIVE$^{\text{[X:'me']}}$ DOG

URSULA   KICK   THAT$_\text{c}$

Figure 3.9. "I asked him/her to give me the dog Ursula kicked."

[[[i:pac a:k wi:+m   tuc$k$ pu]$_{NP}$ a:k pu]$_{NP}$ si:n^y+c w^{y}aw
man   bone rock+COMIT hit DEM   bone   DEM
                                         woman+SUBJ found
"The woman found the bone that the man hit with the rock."

The three means of disambiguating relative clauses discussed here are strikingly similar in ASL and Diegueño. Both have ways of marking the head without any order change. Both have order changes that eliminate the ambiguity, and both have structures in which the head is identified by appearing for a second time at the end of the relative clause.

In addition to this type of internal head relative clause, ASL also has the external head relative clause. Figure 3.9 illustrates this kind of clause in the sentence:

$$\overline{\qquad\qquad\qquad\qquad}^{\;r}$$

ASK$^{[X:'him']}$ GIVE$^{[X:'me']}$ [DOG [URSULA KICK]$_S$ THATc]$_{NP}$
"I asked him/her to give me the dog that Ursula kicked."

(The subject of ASK is assumed to be the signer.)

In this construction, according to the criterion of co-occurrence of the nonmanual signal "r," the head of the relative clause is outside the relative clause. The sign DOG receives the same expression it would normally be signed with if no relative clause were present. Relative clauses of this type are not ambiguous; the head of the relative clause is interpreted as the noun that precedes the relative clause (in this case DOG).

The use of the internal versus the external head relative clause appears to be optional. Naturally, the formal means for disambiguating relative clauses do not apply with the external head relative clauses.

COMPLEX RELATIVE CLAUSES

Up to this point only relative clauses involving one S (sentence) node beneath a noun phrase node have been considered. American Sign Language also allows more complicated structures, though signers tend to use simpler structures in everyday conversation. The following example contains one such relative clause.

$$\overline{\qquad\qquad\qquad\qquad\qquad}^{\;r}$$

[CAT WATCH [DOG EAT HAMBURGER]] 'ME' BUY
"I bought the cat that watched the dog eat the hamburger."
"I bought the dog that the cat watched eat the hamburger."
"I bought the hamburger that the cat watched the dog eat."

As the transcription indicates, the nonmanual signal "r" accompanies the entire complex string. The above example has three possible readings depending on which of the three possible internal heads is interpreted as the head of the relative clause. The syntactic processes that disambiguate simple relative clauses can also be used in these complex relative clauses.

UNDERLYING STRUCTURES FOR AMERICAN SIGN LANGUAGE RELATIVE CLAUSES

It is clear that there are basically two types of relative clauses to be derived: internal head and external head.

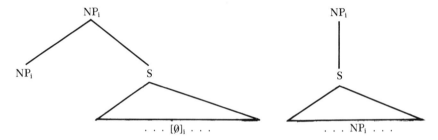

If one attempts to derive both types from the same source, an internal head source is superior to an external head source. Deriving the internal head relative clause from an external head source would involve a rule that deletes the external head:

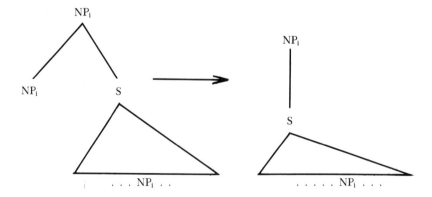

But the external NP bears all the primacy conditions (it both precedes and commands the internal NP) and should not be deletable on the

basis of identity with the internal NP.[14] The deletion of the external
NP would violate what is believed to be a universal property of human
languages. That is, the controller of the deletion must bear at least one
of the primacy conditions, and since the lower NP bears none of
primacy conditions, it may not control the deletion of the external NP.

On the other hand, an underlying structure like Fauconnier's (1971)
would not involve this problem.

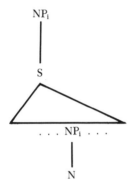

Given an underlying structure such as this, there would be no
problem with the derivation of an internal head relative clause because it is basically the structure to be derived. That is, there would be
no "derivation" since the underlying structure and the surface structure are basically the same.

The derivation of the external head relative clauses would involve a
rule that promotes the internal head.

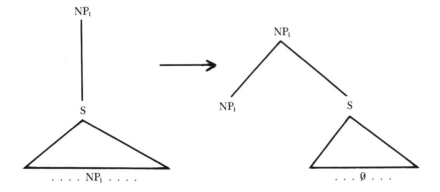

[14] For details the reader is referred to Langacker (1969).

This would not have the undesirable consequences associated with the deletion of the external head. When the rule is applied, the result is an unambiguous surface structure.

Naturally, evidence against one solution does not count as evidence in favor of an alternate solution. This would be true only if there were exactly two possibilities. However, the ASL data *can* be used to compare competing theories of relativization. It is then possible to say that one handles the data better than the other. From this point of view the internal head analysis is far superior to the external head analysis.[15]

The superior performance of the promotion analysis in this case provides independent support for those who have argued for similar processes in other languages (Schachter, 1973; Hale & Platero, 1974; and Gorbet, 1974). At the same time, the fact that there is evidence for such an analysis in other unrelated languages indicates that the fact that ASL is produced manually rather than orally has not had any significant effect on the kind of relative clause structures used— though the difference in mode reveals some interesting differences in the *formal* means of marking relative clauses.

CONCLUSION

There can be no doubt that in ASL the hands carry only part of the language signal. In addition to the hands, the signer's facial expression, posture, and movement of the head and body are all significant. Further, a specific combination of head position and facial expression forms a grammatical signal of subordination and marks relative clauses in ASL.

[15]Naturally, it is also possible that, as Fauconnier suggests, languages may simply choose to expand either NP_i in the following structure:

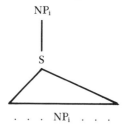

Expanding the top NP_i results in an external head, and expanding the lower NP_i results in an internal head. From this point of view, one type of relative clause structure is not derived from the other.

The existence of the ASL relative clause structures was only noted because of the special head position and muscular activity of the face that accompanies the relative clauses. Without these nonmanual features, these structures (with the exception of those with the relative conjunction THATa) would be indistinguishable from corresponding ASL sentences.

The internal head relative clause structures (a distinction based on nonmanual signals) were shown to be very similar to Diegueño internal head relative clauses, and the formal means that the two languages have that disambiguate the relative clauses were strikingly similar.

I also hope that I have shown that the fact that ASL is produced manually rather than orally has had no significant effect on the existence and nature of the relative clause structures used in the language. Of course, ASL also has processes, such as spatial indexing, that are unique to a manually produced language. The specific uses of the muscles of the face and body, such as those needed to produce the nonmanual signal that accompanies a relative clause, and the intense expression that identifies the head of a relative clause are apparently unique to ASL, though, of course, the use of facial expression and body movement in communication is not restricted to a manually produced language.

ACKNOWLEDGMENTS

Edward S. Klima provided guidance, insight, and criticism throughout the periods of research and writing which resulted in this paper. His assistance and encouragement has played a major role in this research.

Ursula Bellugi, Elissa Newport, Robbin Battison, and Cheri Adrian provided helpful comments and suggestions. The American Sign Language data were provided by Bonnie Gough, Carlene Canady Pedersen, and Ted Supalla; my thanks go to them all. The drawings included in this chapter were done by Frank Paul.

REFERENCES

Baker, C. What's not on the other hand in American Sign Language. In *Papers from the twelfth regional meeting of the Chicago Linguistic Society*. Univ. of Chicago, 1976.

Bellugi, U. & Fischer, S. A comparison of sign language and spoken language. *Cognition*, 1972, *1*, 173–200.

Bird, C. S. Relative clauses in Bambara. *Journal of West African Languages*, 1968, 5, 35–47.

Ekman, P., & Friesen, W. V. *Unmasking the face*. Englewood Cliffs, New Jersey: Prentice-Hall, 1975.

Ekman, P., & Friesen, W. V. *Facial Action Coding System.* Palo Alto, California: Consulting Psychologists Press, in press.

Fauconnier, G. Theoretical implications of some global phenomena in syntax. Unpublished Ph.D. dissertation, Univ. of California, San Diego, 1971.

Fischer, S. Influences on word order change in American Sign Language. In Li (Ed.), *Word order and word order change.* Austin, Texas: Univ. of Texas Press, 1975.

Friedman, L. The manifestation of subject, object, and topic in the American Sign Language. In Charles N. Li (Ed.), *Subject and topic.* New York: Academic Press, 1976.

Frishberg, N. Arbitrariness and iconicity: Historical change in American Sign Language. *Language,* 1975, *51.3,* 696–719.

Gorbet, L. Relativization and complementation in Diegueño: Noun phrases as nouns. Unpublished Ph.D. dissertation, Univ. of California, San Diego, 1974.

Hale, K., & Platero, P. Aspects of Navajo anaphora: Relativization and pronominalization. *Diné Bizaad Náníl'įįh (Navajo Language Review),* 1974, *1,* 9–28.

Klima, E. S., & Bellugi, U. *The signs of language.* Cambridge, Massachusetts: Harvard Univ. Press, to appear.

Langacker, R. W. On pronominalization and the chain of command. In D. A. Reibel & S. A. Schane (Eds.), *Modern studies in English.* Englewood Cliffs, New Jersey: Prentice Hall, 1969.

Li, C. N., & Thompson, S. A. Strategies for signalling grammatical relations in wappo. *Papers from the twelfth regional meeting of the Chicago Linguistics Society.* Univ. of Chicago, 1976.

Liddell, S. K. An investigation into the syntactic structure of American Sign Language. Unpublished Ph.D. dissertation, Univ. of California, San Diego, 1977.

Liddell, S. K. Nonmanual signals in American Sign Language. In *Proceedings of the First National Symposium in Sign Language Research and Teaching,* in press.

Liddell, S. K. The acquisition of some American Sign Language grammatical processes. Univ. of California, San Diego, and The Salk Institute, La Jolla, California. Manuscript in preparation.

Schachter, P. Focus and relativization. *Language,* 1973, *49*(1), 19–46.

Stokoe, W. *Sign language structure: An outline of the visual communication of the American deaf. Studies in linguistics, Occasional Papers 8,* Buffalo, 1960.

Stokoe, W. C., & Battison, R. Sign language, mental health and satisfying interaction. *Proceedings of the First National Symposium on the Mental Health Needs of Deaf Adults and Children (June, 1975),* in press.

Stokoe, W. C., Casterline, D. C. & Croneberg, C. G. *A dictionary of American Sign Language.* Washington, D. C.: Gallaudet College Press, 1965.

Stokoe, W. C., Casterline, D. C., & Croneberg, C. G. *A dictionary of American Sign Language* (revised edition). Silver Spring, Maryland: Linstock Press, 1976.

Thompson, H. The lack of subordination in American Sign Language. In L. Friedman (Ed.), *On the other hand.* New York: Academic Press, 1977.

Tweney, R. D., & Liddell, S. K. Bowling Green State University, Bowling Green, Ohio and The Salk Institute, La Jolla, California. Manuscript in preparation.

4

How Many Seats in a Chair?
The Derivation of Nouns and
Verbs in American Sign Language

TED SUPALLA

University of California, San Diego and
The Salk Institute for Biological Studies

ELISSA L. NEWPORT

University of California, San Diego

INTRODUCTION

A number of recent studies of American Sign Language leave no doubt that this manual system is highly elaborated and fully expressive (see, for example, Klima, Bellugi *et al.*, in press, and the chapters in this volume), and to this extent closely approximates spoken languages. For example, individuals proficient in both American Sign Language (ASL) and English experience no special difficulties in translation different from those of an individual proficient in, say,

This research was supported in part by NIH Grant No. NS09811 and NSF Grant No. BNS-76-12866 to the Salk Institute for Biological Studies, by PHS Training Grant No. MH 14268 to the Department of Psychology, and by PHS Grant No. MH 15828 to the Center for Human Information Processing, University of California, San Diego.

UNDERSTANDING LANGUAGE
THROUGH
SIGN LANGUAGE RESEARCH

91

English and German. However, despite these manifest similarities in the messages that can be computed in the vocal and manual modes, it is quite possible to suppose that spoken languages and sign languages differ in the formal means by which they achieve the same expressive ends. After all, there is good evidence to suggest that human communication, in hearing populations, has evolved over many millennia in connection with the auditory–vocal channels (cf. Lenneberg, 1967; Lieberman, 1973; Liberman, 1970). Possibly, demands of these modalities impose formal constraints on what a language must be like, if people are to learn and use it. The constraints imposed by a visual–manual modality, and therefore the structure of a sign language, might be quite different. For example, although spoken languages universally use word order or case marking to express grammatical relations (e.g., subject vs. object), there is some question about the existence of such formal devices in sign languages (Schlesinger, 1970; Fischer, 1974). Wasow (1973) and Osherson and Wasow (1976) have used this evidence to argue for the task-specificity of at least some linguistic universals.

On the other hand, since spoken and sign languages serve the same communicative purposes, we might expect them to be quite similar in formal structure. In fact, more recent evidence on grammatical relations in ASL demonstrates that word order, along with grammatically functioning facial expressions, operates quite systematically in ASL to mark subject versus object (Liddell, 1977). This new evidence thus suggests that the formal marking of grammatical relations may, after all, arise not from the specific constraints of the spoken language medium but rather from the more general cognitive functions of human communication. Similar evidence exists for the generality of compounding devices (Bellugi & Klima, in press; Newport & Bellugi, in press) and relative clause structure (Liddell, Chapter 3 this volume).

In the present chapter, we consider the formal relations between nouns and verbs in American Sign Language, for in our opinion this topic has special relevance to the question of modality-specific versus language-general forms. Hockett (1963) has postulated that a major form-class distinction between nouns and verbs is universal to spoken languages. Similarly, Slobin (1975) has suggested that a formal distinction between noun and verb may be a minimal requirement if a language is to be fully expressive, and he has shown that this minimal formal apparatus exists even in quite primitive contact vernaculars. In contrast, such a distinction has not been previously noted in American Sign Language; rather, it has been claimed that nouns and verbs in ASL are formally identical (Stokoe, Casterline, & Croneberg, 1965). This claim raises the possibility that a noun–verb distinction, and perhaps the attendant morphophonological processes, are specific to the auditory linguistic processing system. However, as we shall see, our findings are that noun and verb are structurally distinct in ASL, and that the morphophonological rules needed to describe this distinction in ASL bear some striking resemblances to those required for the description of spoken languages. For this case at least, vocal and manual systems seem to be similar, as though it were the functions that must be computed, rather than the modalities in which they are expressed, that determine what is to be "universal" in a human communication system.

In most spoken languages, nouns and verbs are systematically distinguished by means of inflection, reduplication, or tone. A few languages, most notably those that lack inflectional morphology, distinguish nouns and verbs only by syntactic environment. In English, a language with little inflectional apparatus, nouns and verbs are often morphologically identical, for example, *hammer/hammer, paint/paint;* however, in many instances related nouns and verbs are distinguished by a wide variety of semiproductive derivational affixes: *staple/stapler, erase/eraser,* but *sing/song/singer, prove/proof, laugh/laughter, refuse/refusal.* In ASL, the distinction between nouns and verbs, and much of the inflectional apparatus of the language, appears in the nature of movement in the sign. We will argue that many apparent formal differences between ASL and spoken languages derive from the fact that the analysis of movement has been incomplete. First, in Section 2, we will propose a set of parameters of movement in signs; these parameters will be relevant for describing the formal differences between nouns and verbs. We then proceed to discuss nouns and verbs, and their inflected forms. These descriptive facts will suggest a derivational relationship between surface nouns and verbs which is mediated by abstract *movement units.* Finally, we will return to the implications of these findings for the more general issue of modality-specific versus language-general forms.

CATEGORIES OF MOVEMENT

Stokoe (1960) and Stokoe, Casterline, and Croneberg (1965) first described the sign (the individual lexical item in ASL) as a configuration composed of (a) a place of articulation; (b) a handshape; and (c) a movement.[1] Bellugi and Klima (1975) have presented evidence that

---

[1] Stokoe's analysis does not explicitly include orientation as a "chereme," but his notational system does specify orientation for each sign by a subscript on handshape.

these aspects of the sign, along with orientation, are internal formational parameters on which signs may be classified.

Stokoe (1960) and Stokoe *et al.* (1965) have described movement as
either upward, downward, side to side, rotating, circular, etc. Friedman (1974) has reanalyzed movement in terms of a set of features:
±straight, ±contact, ±toward and away from the body, ±up and down,
±right and left, etc. These descriptions cover the *shape* of movement
in ASL; there are, however, other aspects of movement that these
descriptions omit. In this section we describe three further dimensions of movement in signs: directionality, manner, and frequency.
These dimensions are not intended to provide an exhaustive description of movement in ASL. They will, however, provide us with a
vocabulary for examining the derivational and modulation processes
of interest in this chapter. As will be detailed in the following discussion, related nouns and verbs (and the modulated forms of each) share
handshape, place of articulation, and shape of movement but differ
from one another by systematic changes in directionality, manner, and
frequency of movement.

Directionality of Movement

The dimension of directionality can be divided into two values:
unidirectional and bidirectional. *Unidirectional* movement, as the
name suggests, consists of moving the hand(s) in only one direction, in
any orientation (e.g., up or down) with respect to the signer's body.
Unidirectional movement within a sign can occur either once (as in
the sign COVER-UP[2]) or repeatedly (as in the sign PAPER). These
signs are represented in Figures 4.1a and b. For both COVER-UP and
PAPER, the form of movement is the same: the right hand, palm
down, brushes to the left over the stationary upturned palm of the left
hand. The signs differ in that this movement is performed once in
COVER-UP but is repeated in PAPER. Even with repetition, however, the primary movement is made in only one direction, with a
transition movement in the opposite direction occurring between the
repetitions to return the hands to their initial positions. *Bidirectional*
movement, in contrast, consists of moving the hand(s) in two directions, back and forth, as in the sign MOVIE[3] (see Figure 4.1c). With

---

[2] In this chapter, signs will be represented by an English gloss in capital letters.
Where more than one English word is required to gloss a sign, the words are connected
by hyphens.

[3] There are at least two forms of the sign MOVIE in free variation, one in which the

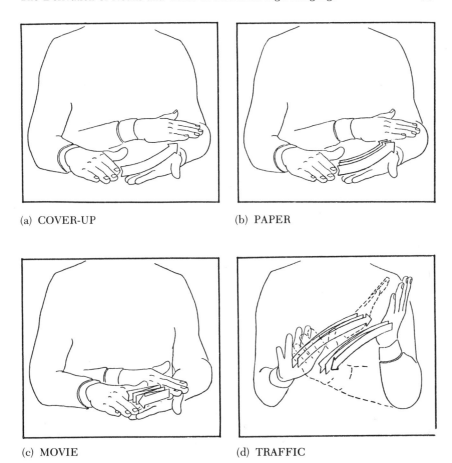

(a) COVER-UP   (b) PAPER

(c) MOVIE   (d) TRAFFIC

Figure 4.1. Examples of unidirectional and bidirectional movement.

bidirectional movement, no transition occurs between repetitions. The movement is primary in both directions. Also included as bidirectional is the movement of the two hands in alternation, as in the sign TRAFFIC: First, one hand moves in one direction while the other hand moves in the opposite direction, and then the directions switch (see Figure 4.1d).

---

active hand brushes back and forth across the base hand (as in Figure 4.1c) and the other in which the hands are in contact throughout the sign with only the fingers waving back and forth. While both involve bidirectional movement, only the former is a true minimal pair with the unidirectional signs discussed in the text.

Manner of Movement

There are three distinctive manners of movement[4] in ASL: continuous, hold, and restrained. While all three are possible manners for unidirectional movement, only two appear in bidirectional movement.

In *continuous* manner, the hands move across the signing space with no interruption. Movement is smooth and loose. The loci of movement (e.g., elbow or wrist) are in free variation and often combine with one another, thus contributing to the grossness of the movement. For example, consider the sign THAT'S-THE-ONE, which can occur in three different forms, all of which involve a "Y"-handshape moving downward with continuous manner. These forms are presented in Figures 4.2a, b, and c. (Continuous manner is graphically represented by a full arrow.) In the first, only the elbow is bent during continuous movement with the wrist held firm. In the second, also continuous movement, only the wrist is bent, while the elbow is maintained in a steady position throughout the sign. In the third form, both elbow and wrist are bent during the sign.

Hold manner occurs in signs that begin with a loose movement of the arms and hands, as in continuous manner, but end with an abrupt stop, in which the arms and hands become stiff and are held stationary for a short time. Hold manner often occurs in signs with one active hand moving to a contact point on a base hand, as in the sign THAT (see Figure 4.2d, in which hold manner is represented by a flat-headed arrow). Note that this sign differs from THAT'S-THE-ONE in two ways: The manner is hold rather than continuous, and a base hand is used. However, contact is not required for the hold manner; some signs involve a hold in midair. For example, the sign STAY (Figure 4.2e) is identical to the signs described above, but with a hold manner and no base hand or contact.

The third manner of movement is *restrained* manner. Restrained manner differs from the other manners of movement in that there is no looseness in the hands and arms. Because the muscles are tightened,

---

[4]One can talk about manner of movement at the beginning, middle, and end of the sign. For example, the sign EXPAND begins with a hold manner but ends with a continuous manner. The sign BIG is formationally similar but with a continuous manner at the beginning and a hold manner at the end. This suggests that signs may have sequential internal segments, contrary to the predominant view that signs are simultaneous bundles of features. This important issue is, however, well outside the scope of the present chapter. For present purposes, we will discuss manner of the *end* of signs only.

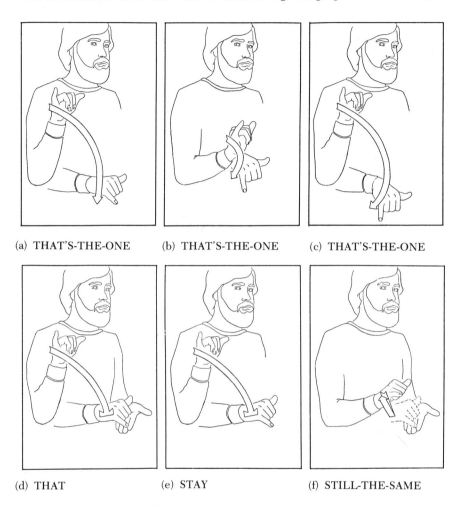

(a) THAT'S-THE-ONE   (b) THAT'S-THE-ONE   (c) THAT'S-THE-ONE

(d) THAT   (e) STAY   (f) STILL-THE-SAME

Figure 4.2. Examples of continuous, hold, and restrained manner of movement.

movement is small, quick, and stiff, and the hand may bounce back to its initial position. Furthermore, locus of movement is restricted to one joint; for example, movement may occur at either the wrist or the elbow, as in the other manners of movement, but, unlike the others, may not occur at *both* wrist and elbow. Figure 4.2f shows the sign STILL-THE-SAME, which is formationally similar to THAT but uses restrained manner. (Restrained manner is graphically represented by an arrow which doubles back on itself.) Restrained manner tends to

occur almost exclusively in citation-form[5] signs with repeated movement; single movement signs with restrained manner (e.g., STILL-
THE-SAME) are typically marked, emphatic forms.

Thus far, all of the examples presented for the various manners of
movement have been unidirectional signs. Predominantly two manners of movement occur in bidirectional signs: continuous (as in the
sign FLAG) and restrained (as in the sign FISH). See Figures 4.3a and
b for illustrations of these two signs. Bidirectional movement occurs
only very rarely with a hold manner; PUT-ON-GLOVES and TYPE
(pp. 104–105) are the only citation-form signs we have been able to
find.

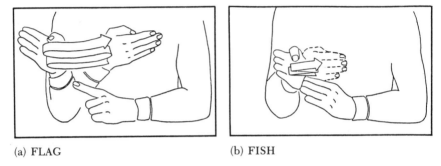

(a) FLAG   (b) FISH

Figure 4.3. Examples of continuous and restrained manner of movement in bidirectional signs.

Frequency of Movement

In addition to varying in directionality and manner of movement,
signs can vary in frequency of movement; as Stokoe (1960) and Stokoe
et al. (1965) have noted, signs may consist of either *single* movement
or *repeated* movement. Examples of two signs differing only in frequency of movement (COVER-UP and PAPER) were discussed on
pages 94–95.

Thus far, with two types of directionality, three manners and two
types of frequency, we might expect 12 categories of movement in
signs. Table 4.1 presents the 12 possible categories of movement in
ASL, indicating which of these in fact occur productively. We have
already seen that bidirectional hold movements occur very rarely in
ASL. Similarly, not all types of movement discussed thus far occur in
both single and repeated forms. Table 4.1 shows that bidirectional

---

[5] Citation form is the form of the sign a native speaker will produce when asked
"What is the sign for ——?"

TABLE 4.1

Combinations of Movement Characteristics that Predominate in Citation-Form Signs of American Sign Language

	Single	Repeated
Continuous		
Unidirectional	X	X
Bidirectional		X
Hold		
Unidirectional	X	X
Bidirectional		
Restrained		
Unidirectional		X
Bidirectional		X

signs, regardless of manner of movement, are always repeated (see all the examples of bidirectional movement discussed above).[6] For unidirectional signs, all three manners of movement may occur with single movement (see THAT'S-THE-ONE, STAY, and STILL-THE-SAME above) as well as with repeated movement. However, as noted above, restrained manner occurs with single movement only in marked, emphatic forms of verbs and is therefore omitted from Table 4.1.

In sum, as shown in Table 1, there are seven combinations of movement characteristics that predominate in citation-form signs of ASL. Having described these basic movement categories, we are prepared to consider the distinctions between nouns and verbs, and the operation of modulation processes on these two classes.

DISTINCTIONS BETWEEN CONCRETE NOUNS AND VERBS IN AMERICAN SIGN LANGUAGE

Spoken languages very often distinguish phonologically between nouns and verbs. Perhaps the most common marking of nouns versus

[6]Once again, there are a very few counterexamples: PUT-ON-GLOVES and TYPE have already been discussed; the signs HAND and STORY are rare instances of bidirectional single-movement signs with continuous manner. We have found no examples whatsoever of bidirectional single-movement signs with restrained manner.

verbs is with inflectional endings: nouns are marked with one set of inflections, while verbs are marked with another. In some parts of English, and in other spoken languages as well, related nouns and verbs are distinguished by stress, for example, *tórment* versus *tor-mént*, *cómmune* versus *commúne*. Yet other languages distinguish related nouns and verbs by distinctions in tone or in internal vowels.

Is there a formal distinction between nouns and verbs in American Sign Language? We will concentrate here on concrete object nouns and action verbs.[7] To answer this question, we must first separate two kinds of concrete nouns and verbs. In the first type, nouns and verbs occur as unrelated lexical entries. A noun (e.g., ELEPHANT) may occur in the language where there is no conceptually related action verb. The reverse, a verb without a conceptually related noun (e.g., YELL), may of course occur as well. However, even when conceptually related verbs and nouns exist, the two may be entirely unrelated signs. For example, the verb FISH and the noun FISH, although formally related in English, are unrelated signs in ASL. In these cases where noun and verb occur as unrelated lexical entries, there is no apparent distinction between the two classes in form. Using the movement categories described above, one finds that both nouns and verbs occur in all possible categories. Table 4.2 presents five common nouns and five common verbs in each of these categories.

There is, however, a second type of noun and verb in ASL, where the noun referring to an object is quite obviously related in form to the verb for the action performed with this object. In this case, it has been assumed that the signs for noun and verb are identical and that context alone may serve to distinguish reference to the object from reference to the action performed with this object. For example, Stokoe *et al.*'s (1965) dictionary lists CHAIR and SIT as the same sign; in the context "two____," the sign presumably refers to "chair."

In this section we will examine this second type—nouns and verbs that are related in form and meaning. Using the movement character-istics outlined earlier, we will argue that, in this special group of noun–verb pairs, nouns and verbs are not identical in form. Rather, there is a consistent formal distinction between noun and verb.

Defining Noun–Verb Pairs

Noun–verb pairs are defined by two criteria: First, the noun and verb are related in meaning, in that the verb expresses the activity

---

[7] This does not imply, of course, that only actions may be expressed as verbs or that only concrete objects may be expressed as nouns in ASL. For example, there are nonconcrete noun–verb pairs like IDEA-IMAGINE, and nonconcrete verbs and their nominalizations like LEARN-LEARNING. However, the regularities described here seem to apply primarily to concrete nouns and action verbs.

TABLE 4.2

Examples of Unrelated Verbs and Nouns in Each Movement Category

	Common verb		Common noun	
	Single	Repeated	Single	Repeated
Continuous				
Unidirectional	ESCAPE	FEEL	COLLEGE	GIRL
	FINISH	LAUGH	EGG	GREASE
	LET	PITY	ELEPHANT	SAND
	MELT	PLAY	GHOST	SOAP
	SLEEP	TEASE	WEEK	SPAGHETTI
Bidirectional		ACT		BUSINESS
		DANCE		DRAMA
		DECORATE		EARTH
		FLATTER		STAR
		WALK		WAR
Hold				
Unidirectional	ARRIVE	ARGUE	BOWL	BOY
	BUY	COUGH	FLOWER	EYEGLASSES
	JOIN	HOARD	FRIEND	SHOWER
	START	RAIN	HOUSE	SOLDIER
	STOP	WORK	YEAR	TIME
Bidirectional				
Restrained				
Unidirectional		DO		BUG
		KNOCK		FLOOR
		PATRONIZE		PEPPER
		PREACH		PIG
		URGE		SPIDER
Bidirectional		INTERPRET		APPLE
		SHAKE-HEAD		CHEESE
		SHIVER		MEAT
		VIBRATE		MEDICINE
		WRESTLE		TREE

performed with or on the object named by the noun. For example, the verb SIT expresses the activity performed on the object CHAIR. The verb GO-BY-AIRPLANE (i.e., FLY) expresses the activity performed with the object AIRPLANE. Second, the noun and verb share formational characteristics. The signs SIT and CHAIR are depicted in Figures 4.4a and b. As the figures show, these signs have the same handshape, orientation, and place of articulation. Furthermore, they have the same shape of movement: In both, the active hand moves downward to contact the base hand.

In fact, if one attempts to examine signs that are related on these criteria, one finds that the notion of a noun–verb "pair" is oversimplified: In some cases, there is a whole family of verbs related to a particular noun. Variation in verbal forms is of two sorts. First, there are related forms of the verb that differ from one another in standardized ways. For example, related to a particular noun (e.g., LAWNMOWER) there may be a verb with punctual meaning (e.g., GIVE-THE-LAWNMOWER-A-PUSH) as well as a verb with durative meaning (e.g., MOW). (See section "Movement in Verbs" (pp. 103–104) for definitions of these semantic oppositions.) In such cases we have listed in the Appendix only one of these verbs (e.g., MOW) with

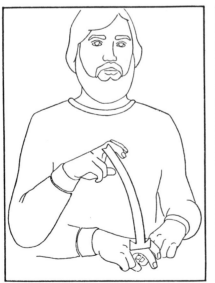 

(a) SIT   (b) CHAIR

Figure 4.4.   One noun–verb pair.

the related noun; however, in the text we discuss the families of related forms. In all cases the verbal relatives follow the semantic and formal regularities of noun–verb pairs discussed below. Second, verbs often allow a less standardized, pantomimic type of variation. For example, one can change the form of the verb GIVE-THE-LAWNMOWER-A-PUSH to depict pushing the lawnmower in a figure-8, in a circle, or up and down small bumpy hills. We will not consider such "mimetic depiction" here; see Newport and Supalla (forthcoming) and Newport and Bellugi (in press).

For purposes of this study 100 noun–verb pairs were collected and analyzed (see the Appendix for a full listing). As will be detailed in the following discussion, such nouns and verbs are in fact not identical in form; rather, nouns differ consistently from verbs in both frequency and manner of movement. First, nouns are always repeated, while verbs are either single or repeated. Second, nouns are always restrained in manner, while verbs are either hold or continuous.

Movement in Verbs

Here we will examine the movement characteristics in the verbs represented in the 100 noun–verb pairs. These pairs are presented in the Appendix as categorized by movement in the verb. Table 3 presents the frequencies of verbs in each movement category. Overall, these verbs appear primarily in only five of the seven possible movement categories in ASL; with only two exceptions, verbs do not occur with restrained manner of movement.

Furthermore, there are consistent relations between the meaning of verbs and the particular values of manner and frequency of movement of which they are formed.[8] In spoken languages, some verbs are durative; that is, they refer to an activity which inherently lasts for some time. In contrast, other verbs are punctual; that is, they refer to actions that do not last in time but rather take place momentarily. Similarly, verbs may be perfective, i.e., they may view an event as though it were momentary, without internal temporal structure, regardless of the objective temporal character of the event. Such distinctions in the inherent meanings of verbs are often marked in spoken languages by distinctions in form. The same is true in ASL.

In general, *single* movement in the sign corresponds to single, punctual or perfective action. *Repeated* movement, in contrast, refers

---

[8] Such relations might be described as *iconic*. That is, aspects of the form of the verb are related in some transparent way to the features of action it represents. Similar kinds of iconicity occur in spoken languages and will be mentioned where appropriate.

TABLE 4.3

Frequency of Related Verbs and Nouns in Each Movement Category
(100 Noun–Verb Pairs)

	Verb		Noun	
	Single	Repeated	Single	Repeated
Continuous				
Unidirectional	9	12		
Bidirectional		19		
Hold				
Unidirectional	51	5	2	
Bidirectional	1	1	1	
Restrained				
Unidirectional	2			74
Bidirectional				23

to durative or iterative activity which is made of repeated punctual actions (e.g., SMOKE is composed of iterative actions of bringing a cigarette to the mouth).[9] Further, while the *hold* manner corresponds to an action with specified spatial end-points, the *continuous* manner is used for actions with unspecified spatial end-points.

Most verbs in the collection (63 out of 100) are formed with a *single* movement. All of these refer to single punctual or perfective actions. For example, the verbs SIT, PUT-ON-HAT, TURN-JAR-LID, and OPEN-DOOR all refer to single, momentary actions. Some of these verbs (e.g., STRIKE-MATCH) have a related repeated form that has an iterative or durative meaning, for example, STRIKE-MATCH-SEVERAL-TIMES. Of these single verbs, 51 are made with a unidirectional *hold* manner. One (PUT-ON-GLOVES) is made with a bidirectional (alternating) *hold* manner. In all 52 cases, the hold manner corresponds to an action with clear spatial end-points. For example, OPEN-DOOR in its citation form, with a hold manner, refers to the action of opening the door to its conventional "open" position. A related form with continuous manner corresponds to opening the door "all the way." Nine verbs are made with continuous manner. These

---

[9] The relationship between repetition and durative meaning in ASL has been noted by Fischer (1973).

nine make up a special class of "GO-BY" verbs: GO-BY-AIRPLANE (i.e., FLY), GO-BY-TRAIN, etc. Although these single movement verbs are not strictly punctual, momentary actions, they are actions viewed as single events (i.e., perfective). Again, the continuous manner refers to the event without specifying start and end locations (e.g., FLY), while related forms with hold manner in both the initial and final parts of the sign movement specify start and end-points. For example, FLY with a hold manner at the end of the sign means "fly there," while FLY with a hold manner at the beginning of the sign means "fly from here." With the hold manner in both the initial and final parts, the sign would mean "fly from here to there." The remaining two single-movement verbs are unidirectional *restrained* movements, whose corresponding single actions are rare instances where the referent action in the world is itself a restrained movement, for example, STAPLE.[10]

Thirty-seven of the verbs are formed with a *repeated* movement. In contrast to the single-movement–single-action verbs, these correspond to activities that have duration and/or that are composed of a series of repeated punctual actions. For example, the verb EAT, a repeated verb, refers to an activity that extends over time. A related form, EAT-UP, is a single-movement verb that refers to eating as a punctual-perfective act. Twelve of these verbs are unidirectional with *continuous* manner; 19 are bidirectional with continuous manner. As in single-movement verbs, the continuous manner does not specify spatial end-points. The sign EAT is an example. In contrast (again, as in single-movement verbs), the *hold* manner does specify spatial end-points—for example, HAMMER. (The sign EAT also has a single hold relative, PUT-IN-MOUTH, which follows the same principle.) Five verbs in the collection have a repeated unidirectional hold. The remaining 1 verb is a bidirectional repeated sign with hold manner.

In sum, most verbs are either unidirectional hold or continuous, or bidirectional repeated continuous. Some of the less frequent categories of verbs (bidirectional holds, bidirectional single movements) are rare (or prohibited) in the language as a whole; however, there is a more striking absence of signs with restrained manner, an absence that appears to be characteristic only of verbs within the

---

[10] Restrained movement in verbs is exceedingly rare and therefore will be treated throughout this chapter as a nonproductive category that occurs exceptionally only where, as above, the referent action is restrained. We have been able to find only two restrained verbs—STAPLE and SNAP-PHOTOGRAPH—in all the noun–verb pairs we have examined.

noun–verb pairs. As we will see, restrained manner of movement in noun–verb pairs is apparently reserved for nouns.[11]

Movement in Nouns

As we have seen, verbs may be either unidirectional or bidirectional, single or repeated, continuous or hold. The only movement characteristic that does not occur in verbs is restrained manner. In contrast, there is much less variance in types of movement among the nouns in the collection. In fact, a consistent pattern appears across all the nouns, regardless of how their paired verbs are made. Although the noun's directionality of movement is always as in the paired verb,[12] the manner and frequency of movement do not follow those of the verb. For all the nouns, the manner of movement is restrained, and movement is always repeated.[13] Because of the restrained manner, nouns are also made with smaller movements than are verbs. Table 4.4 presents the movement categories of verbs and their associated nouns. Figure 4.5 depicts one noun–verb pair for each of these categories:

1. FLY (a single unidirectional sign with continuous manner) and its noun AIRPLANE
2. SWEEP (a repeated unidirectional sign with continuous manner) and its noun BROOM

[11] We have already mentioned two exceptional verbs with restrained manner. There are two additional circumstances in which we have found restrained manner in verbs of noun–verb pairs. First, the signs EAT and DRIVE, which we treat as signs with continuous manner, each have a variant with restrained manner that is sometimes produced as the citation form. However, these restrained forms do not participate in the productive regularities of the language: Inflected forms of the signs EAT and DRIVE (see pp. 111–118) occur only with continuous manner and have no variant with restrained manner. The restrained citation forms thus appear to be isolated frozen forms that have developed for a few very common verbs of the language. We therefore concentrate on the more regular forms with continuous manner. Second, there are certain inflectional processes that result in restrained manner in verbs: With the addition of super-fast reduplication, manner of verbs becomes restrained. See footnote 18 for further discussion of changes of manner with inflection.

[12] There are a few counterexamples to this consistency of directionality from noun to verb. In the sign TRAIN, movement is bidirectional, whereas movement in the paired verb, GO-BY-TRAIN, is unidirectional. The reverse is true of the pair MILK and MILK-COW; while MILK-COW is bidirectional, with two hands alternating, MILK is one-handed and thus unidirectional. Nevertheless, in both these counterexamples, the distinction between noun and verb in manner is retained.

[13] There are three exceptions to this generalization: The nouns COAT, SCARF, and GLOVES are single movements with hold manner.

3. IRON (a repeated bidirectional sign with continuous manner) and its noun IRON
4. SIT (a single unidirectional sign with hold manner) and its noun CHAIR
5. HAMMER (a repeated unidirectional sign with hold manner) and its noun HAMMER

As can be seen, there is no relationship between manner and frequency of movement in the noun and those of its paired verb: All the nouns have the same manner and frequency, regardless of those of the verb.

TABLE 4.4

The Movement Categories of Verbs and Their Related Nouns

	Verb		Noun	
	Single	Repeated	Single	Repeated
Continuous				
Unidirectional	X	X		
Bidirectional		X		
Hold				
Unidirectional	X	X		
Bidirectional				
Restrained				
Unidirectional				X
Bidirectional				X

Derivation of Noun and Verb

We have demonstrated that, contrary to previous formulations, paired nouns and verbs in ASL are in fact not phonologically identical; rather, there are systematic differences in movement between noun and verb. We now consider how to represent these facts in a description of ASL.

The regularity of formational features of nouns and verbs makes clear that nouns and verbs should not be listed as independent items in the lexicon. Rather, we will argue on the basis of parsimony that one need posit only one lexical entry for each noun–verb pair; forma-

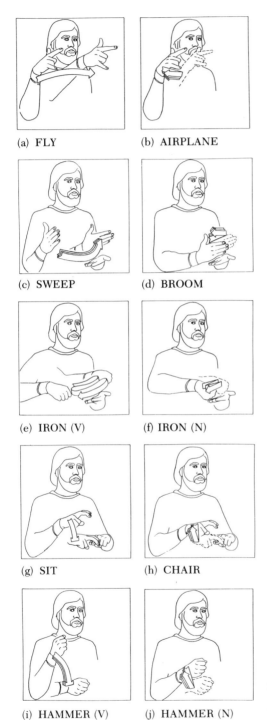

(a) FLY   (b) AIRPLANE

(c) SWEEP   (d) BROOM

(e) IRON (V)   (f) IRON (N)

(g) SIT   (h) CHAIR

(i) HAMMER (V)   (j) HAMMER (N)

Figure 4.5. One noun–verb pair in each movement category for related verbs and nouns.

108

tional rules will then derive the members of the pair. How might one characterize this derivational process?

One possibility is that there is a direct derivational relationship between surface forms: either the noun is derived from the verb, or the verb is derived from the noun. We first consider deriving verbs from nouns. On this alternative, only the noun would be listed in the lexicon; the verb would be derived from it by a series of rules. There is substantial indication in the data that verbs should not be derived from nouns. First, such a derivational process is impossible without a specification in the lexicon of the inherent semantic features of the related verb. Since all the nouns are restrained in manner, one could not predict the manner of the verb (i.e., continuous or hold) from that of the paired noun; likewise, since all the nouns are repeated, one could not predict the frequency of the verb (i.e., single or repeated) from that of the noun. However, since there are semantic correlates to the phonological features of the verb, we could of course solve these problems by listing the semantic features of the verb in the lexicon along with the noun, and by referring to these semantic features in the derivational rules. That is, we could derive verbs from nouns with the following rules:[14]

$$\begin{bmatrix} +V \\ \alpha\text{durative} \end{bmatrix} \rightarrow [\alpha\text{Repeated}]$$

$$\begin{bmatrix} +V \\ +\text{spatial end-point} \end{bmatrix} \rightarrow [\text{Hold}]$$

$$\begin{bmatrix} +V \\ -\text{spatial end-point} \end{bmatrix} \rightarrow [\text{Continuous}]$$

These rules will rather neatly derive appropriate verb forms, and in fact will derive the whole set of regular related verb forms (e.g., EAT, PUT-IN-MOUTH, and EAT-UP) from a given noun where semantically appropriate. However, deriving verbs from surface nouns has one major flaw: Such a derivation completely fails to capture the

---

[14] In our rules, semantic features are written in lowercase; formational features are written with the first letter in uppercase. The rules operate to replace semantic features, on the left, with formational features, on the right. α is a variable which can be either + or −. However, when it takes the value + on the left side of the arrow, it must likewise be + on the right; and when − on the left, it must be − on the right.

Although it is conventional to represent all formational characteristics in terms of binary features, we represent manner of movement as a three-valued feature: continuous, hold, and restrained. It is possible to represent manner by various combinations of binary features, but our data do not indicate which of these ways is preferable.

generalization that all the nouns are repeated and restrained. We therefore consider such a solution undesirable and will consider it no further.

On the other hand, we could list the verb in the lexicon and derive the noun from the verb with the following rules:

$$[+N] \rightarrow [\text{Restrained}]$$

$$[+N] \rightarrow [+\text{Repeated}]$$

This solution succeeds in capturing the regularity of nouns; but it requires either additional verb modification rules or a rather large number of lexical entries for those verbs with regular related forms (e.g., EAT, PUT-IN-MOUTH, and EAT-UP).

Another, rather different possibility neither derives nouns from verbs nor verbs from nouns; instead, both are derived from a common underlying form. In this case, location, handshape, orientation, and shape of movement are specified in the underlying form for both noun and verb. Manner and frequency of movement are then introduced by rule to derive surface nouns and verbs:

$$[+N] \qquad\qquad\qquad \rightarrow [\text{Restrained}]$$

$$[+N] \qquad\qquad\qquad \rightarrow [+\text{Repeated}]$$

$$\begin{bmatrix} +V \\ +\text{spatial end-point} \end{bmatrix} \rightarrow [\text{Hold}]$$

$$\begin{bmatrix} +V \\ -\text{spatial end-point} \end{bmatrix} \rightarrow [\text{Continuous}]$$

$$\begin{bmatrix} +V \\ \alpha\,\text{durative} \end{bmatrix} \qquad \rightarrow [\alpha\text{Repeated}]$$

This solution requires more rules for deriving nouns and verbs than does the previous solution; however, these rules will generate regular related forms of the verb, along with the more common citation forms, with no additional rules or lexical entries.

We will not attempt at this point to choose between these latter two solutions. In the next section we will examine the inflectional processes that apply to nouns and verbs. As we will see, these further regularities begin to suggest that the proper solution involves hypothesizing a shared underlying form for nouns and verbs.

THE BASIC MOVEMENT UNIT

So far we have seen that nouns and verbs may be distinguished by consistent differences in frequency and manner of movement. In this section we will examine the operations of inflectional (modulation) processes on nouns and verbs. While some modulation processes apply to only one of these grammatical classes, others apparently apply to both nouns and verbs (Supalla, 1977). Here we consider the effect of the same modulation on the two formally distinct classes. As we will see, even similarly modulated nouns and verbs retain their distinctive manners of movement. However, the distinction between nouns and verbs in frequency of movement is lost in the modulation process. For both nouns and verbs, modulations appear to operate on a single movement. This will lead us to hypothesize an abstract *movement unit* that underlies nouns and verbs.

The Basic Unit in Inflectional Processes

As in spoken languages, there are in ASL a variety of ways in which nouns and verbs can be inflected to express changes in meaning. In spoken languages, inflections may take the form of suffixes, prefixes, reduplications, or changes in vowels, stresses, or tones (Matthews, 1974). In ASL, inflections operate primarily on the movement parameter of signs. Fischer and Gough (1973) and Fischer (1973) have described a set of inflectional processes that operate on verbs in ASL: verbs can be modulated in form to indicate, for example, number and person of their arguments; in addition, verbs can be modulated for continuous and habitual aspect. Supalla (1977) has examined inflectional processes of nouns in ASL. In fact, some of the inflectional processes described for verbs appear to apply to nouns as well, with related changes of meaning. Two of these processes will be described here: (*a*) slow reduplication and (*b*) dual inflection. The details of how these processes influence the movement of the signs to which they are applied will impose some constraints on formulating derivational rules.

Slow Reduplication

Many spoken languages inflect nouns and verbs for such things as pluralization or iteration by reduplicating part or all of the base form of the word. Similarly, reduplications of various kinds occur in ASL.

As Fischer and Gough (1973) have described, slow reduplication in

ASL superimposes, roughly, a slow circular motion on the formation of the verb. This process inflects the verb for continuous aspect. When applied to a punctual-perfective verb (e.g., PUT-IN-MOUTH, EAT-UP), the meaning is *iteration;* when applied to a durative verb (e.g., EAT), the meaning is *elongation.* This process of reduplication is at least roughly similar to reduplicated constructions in English: "The psychopath killed and killed and killed." versus "I waited and waited and waited for the train." With the punctual verb *kill,* the meaning is iteration, while with the durative verb *wait,* the meaning is elongation (from Fischer, 1973).

For present purposes we must examine the form of this ASL modulation in some detail. The verb PUT-IN-MOUTH is presented in its base form in Figure 4.6a and in its reduplicated form in Figure 4.6b. In the base form there is a straight path of movement that occurs just once toward the mouth, ending with a hold manner. In the modulated form, this path of movement is reduplicated several times. In detail, with reduplication the sign consists of repeated cycles, each of which are made up of the straight path of movement, ending with a hold and followed by a transition. We will call the first part of the movement cycle the *sign unit*. Note that this sign unit resembles the single, hold movement in the base form. The transition phase begins after the hand reaches the mouth. In this transition phase, the hand moves slowly back to the initial position, in an arc rather than a straight line. At the initial position the cycle begins again. Two or three cycles complete the modulated form. This modulated form means "put something in the mouth over and over and over." The same slow reduplication process can be applied to the verb EAT-UP (see Figure 4.7a for the base form and 4.7b for the reduplicated form). This sign in its base form is a single movement with continuous manner. When slow reduplication is applied, the result is similar to that of the reduplicated PUT-IN-MOUTH, with one exception: The reduplicated cycles are now missing the hold at the mouth and instead have a more continuous elliptical path.[15] This is apparently due to the fact that the base form, and therefore the sign unit, of EAT-UP has a continuous rather than a hold manner.

In short, for single movements, slow reduplication involves cyclic reduplications of a sign unit that retains the manner of movement of

---

[15] Nevertheless, one can still speak of a sign unit followed by a transition in each cycle. In the case where manner is continuous, one still sees different rates of movement in the two components: The sign unit is performed at the normal rate, while the arc-like transition, as before, is slow.

the base sign. When the base form has a hold manner, so does the reduplicated form; when the base form has a continuous manner, so does the reduplicated form.[16]

Now consider the effect of this same modulation applied to another related form, EAT. In contrast to PUT-IN-MOUTH and EAT-UP, EAT is performed with continuous manner and repetition. The sign is shown in Figure 4.8a. In this case, where the base form itself includes repetition, how is slow reduplication applied? One possibility is that slow reduplication will be performed on the entire sign. That is, the reduplicated cycles will each include a sign unit that itself has repetition. If true, this would suggest a simple model of modulation processes: Modulations are applied to the surface forms of base signs. However, this is *not* the form of EAT with slow reduplication.[17] Figure 4.8b presents the sign EAT with slow reduplication. In fact, repetition is not present in the sign unit of the reduplicated form. The sign unit of EAT, like that of PUT-IN-MOUTH and EAT-UP, includes only a single movement. Recall that the path of the movement cycle is different for the modulated forms of PUT-IN-MOUTH and EAT-UP: PUT-IN-MOUTH has the hold manner in its sign unit, and, thus, the modulated form retains this hold at the mouth before entering the transition phase for the next reduplication. No such pause is found in the modulated form of EAT-UP. Rather, the continuous manner of the base form EAT-UP is maintained in the sign unit of the modulated form. Likewise, the continuous manner of the base form EAT is maintained in the sign unit of the modulated form. As a result, while the base forms of EAT and EAT-UP differ in frequency of movement, their modulated forms are identical.

In short, slow reduplication retains the manner but not the frequency of movement of the base form. Regardless of frequency of movement in the base form of the sign, slow reduplication is performed on a *single*-movement sign unit.

The slow reduplication process can also be applied to nouns

---

[16] In fact slow reduplication can be used as a diagnostic for determining manner of movement in difficult cases. For example, in base signs with repetition, determination of manner is sometimes problematic, since one might argue that manner of movement is assimilated to repetition. Slow reduplication clearly separates sign units from one another and thus permits easy assessment of manner.

[17] There is a modulation of EAT that does have the form described above: reduplicated cycles, each consisting of a repeated sign unit. The form is not, however, the simple form of continuous aspect. Rather, it is a complex of two modulations, with a correspondingly complex meaning. See page 126 for discussion of this form.

(Supalla, 1977). The resultant meaning—"serial pluralization"—is also related to that of the modulated verb. In this case it means the object again and again, for example, "food after food after food." Slow reduplication affects the form of the noun in a way similar to that of the verb. Consider the sign FOOD, which is depicted in Figure 4.9a. In its base form, the noun FOOD has repetition and restrained manner of movement. Figure 4.9b presents the reduplicated form of FOOD. When this noun is inflected with slow reduplication, the restrained manner is retained in the sign unit: In the modulated form, the hand bounces slightly back after reaching the mouth. This sign unit is then followed by the transition arc back to the initial position for the next reduplication. As with verbs undergoing slow reduplication, the sign unit consists of a single movement rather than the repeated movement of the base form.

Comparison of the four modulated forms (Figures 4.6b, 4.7b, 4.8b, and 4.9b) indicates that slow reduplication applies similarly to nouns and verbs. In particular, there are two consistent attributes of the sign unit for the slow-reduplication process. First, the frequency of movement is limited to a single movement, regardless of whether there is repetition in the base form (e.g., EAT and FOOD have repetition in the base forms, but their sign units for reduplication are limited to a single movement). Second, there is consistency in manner of movement for the base form and the modulated form of a particular sign. When base forms (e.g., PUT-IN-MOUTH, EAT/EAT-UP, and FOOD) are distinct in manner, their modulated forms are also distinct, since the sign units preserve the same manner found in the base forms. When base forms (e.g., EAT and EAT-UP) are the same in manner, the modulated forms are also the same. These two attributes appear not only in the examples discussed but more generally across all reduplicated nouns and verbs.

So far we have considered the effects of modulation processes only on signs with unidirectional movement. Figures 4.10a and 4.11a illustrate the noun–verb pair CAR and DRIVE, two signs with repeated bidirectional movement. As is typical for nouns and verbs, the noun CAR has restrained manner, while the verb DRIVE has continuous manner. Once again, the slow reduplication process affects these base forms in the ways already discussed. Figures 4.10b and 4.11b show the slow reduplicated forms of CAR and DRIVE. These modulated forms of CAR and DRIVE each consist of cycles of a sign unit. As with unidirectional signs, the sign unit retains the manner of the base form of the sign: The sign unit of CAR has restrained manner of movement,

(a) PUT-IN-MOUTH   (b) SLOW REDUP. FORM (c) DUAL FORM

Figure 4.6. PUT-IN-MOUTH: base form and two inflected forms.

(a) EAT UP   (b) SLOW REDUP. FORM (c) DUAL FORM

Figure 4.7. EAT-UP: base form and two inflected forms.

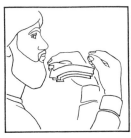  

(a) EAT   (b) SLOW REDUP. FORM (c) DUAL FORM

Figure 4.8. EAT: base form and two inflected forms.

 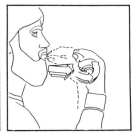 

(a) FOOD   (b) SLOW REDUP. FORM (c) DUAL FORM

Figure 4.9. FOOD: base form and two inflected forms.

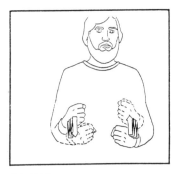

(a) CAR

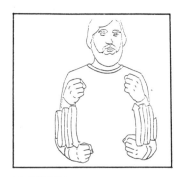

(a) DRIVE

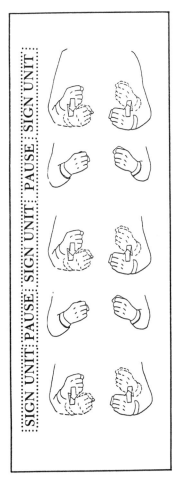

(b) SLOW REDUPLICATED FORM

(b) SLOW REDUPLICATED FORM

Figure 4.10. CAR: Base form and slow reduplicated form.

Figure 4.11. DRIVE: Base form and slow reduplicated form.

116

while the sign unit of DRIVE has continuous manner of movement. Thus the first attribute of the sign unit applies to bidirectional as well as unidirectional signs. The second attribute of the sign unit is that frequency of movement is always single. This attribute is true of bidirectional signs as well, despite the fact that repetition is required for the base forms of bidirectional signs. When CAR and DRIVE are modulated for slow reduplication, the sign units of each include only one complete bidirectional, or alternating, movement.

We should note one interesting fact about the effect of slow reduplication on bidirectional movement. Fischer (1973) has described the slow reduplication process as one which superimposes a circular movement on the movement of the base sign. For unidirectional signs, we have described this instead as an arc-like transition inserted between sign units. Unlike the modulated forms of unidirectional signs, with modulated bidirectional signs there is no arc-like transition between cycles of the sign unit; instead, the hands simply remain motionless for a short time after each sign unit. (This pause is not present in the base form of bidirectional signs.) The transition movement is absent in reduplicated bidirectional signs apparently because the completion of the sign unit itself has returned the hands to the appropriate position for starting the next cycle. This pattern suggests that the primary effect of slow reduplication is not the superimposition of a circular movement, but rather the introduction of extra *temporal* spacing between reduplicated sign units. If the sign unit is unidirectional, this temporal spacing will manifest itself on the surface as a slow (therefore arc-like) transition back to the starting point for the next sign unit; in contrast, if the sign unit is bidirectional (so that no further movement to the starting point is necessary), this temporal spacing will appear on the surface simply as a pause.

Dual Inflection

The two attributes of the sign unit are not unique to the slow reduplication process but are true of the sign unit in other types of modulation processes as well. Here we will examine the dual inflection, which, like slow reduplication, applies to both nouns and verbs (Supalla, 1977).

A variety of spoken languages inflect nouns and verbs for a dual, as well as a multiple, plural. American Sign Language, unlike English, similarly distinguishes dual from multiple plural forms of the noun and verb. In the dual inflection in ASL the sign unit is, roughly, performed once in each of two locations in space. When the base sign is made in neutral space, the dual form is made on the right and then the left. In contrast, when the base sign is made in contact with the head or body (as in the examples below), the dual form is made with both components in their usual places of contact but with the head or body facing right during the first component and then left during the second component. When applied to the verb, the dual form refers to performing the action twice; when applied to the noun, it refers to two objects. Here again we must examine the form of the modulation process in some detail. Figures 4.6c, 4.7c, 4.8c and 4.9c show the dual forms of the verbs PUT-IN-MOUTH, EAT-UP, and EAT, and the noun FOOD. As in slow reduplication, the dual forms of these signs have the same manner of movement as the base sign: The dual PUT-IN-MOUTH has a hold manner, dual EAT-UP and EAT have continuous manner, and dual FOOD has restrained manner. Furthermore, as in slow reduplication, the two components of the dual form are always each *single* movements, regardless of whether the movement in the base form is single or repeated. Therefore, as before, when base forms (PUT-IN-MOUTH, EAT/EAT-UP, and FOOD) are distinct in manner, the modulated forms are also distinct. When the base forms (EAT and EAT-UP) are the same in manner, the modulated forms are also the same. These descriptive facts confirm the generality of the two attributes of the sign unit across different modulation processes.[18]

THE DERIVATIONAL PROCESS FOR NOUNS, VERBS, AND THEIR INFLECTED FORMS

So far, we have seen the following:

1. For concrete nouns and verbs, the base form of the noun and verb may differ from one another in both manner and frequency

[18] There are some modulation processes that themselves change the manner of movement of verbs. For example, adding an intense, super-fast reduplication to the sign unit (the inflection for "mental preoccupation") results in restrained manner on the verb. Adding stress to the sign unit (Friedman, 1974) results in hold or restrained manner on the verb. We suspect that these changes in manner of movement are merely surface phonetic reflexes of rapid or stressed movement (see Friedman for a similar argument). Like Friedman, we consider such an argument highly tentative at this time. At any rate, the model we will propose on pages 119–121 does not depend crucially on the generality of the two attributes of the sign unit across *all* modulations.

of movement: while verbs are either continuous or hold in manner, nouns are restrained in manner; while verbs are either repeated or single, nouns are always repeated.

2. For inflected forms of nouns and verbs, modulations are applied to a basic movement unit (the sign unit) rather than to the base form of the sign. The sign unit of such modulated forms is always a single movement, regardless of whether the corresponding base form is single or repeated. However, the manner of the sign unit is the same as that of the corresponding base form: continuous or hold for the modulated verb, and restrained for the modulated noun.

In this section we will present a derivational system and an informally stated set of rules that represent these descriptive facts.

Derivation of Noun–Verb Pairs from an Underlying Form

The preceding facts are most naturally captured by the rule system diagrammed in Figure 4.12. As Figure 4.12 shows, the derivational process begins with a common underlying representation for nouns, verbs, and their modulated forms. Such an underlying representation

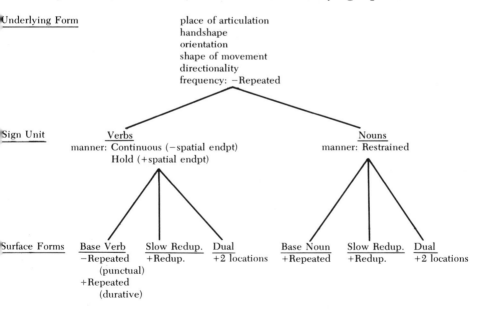

Figure 4.12. The derivational system for related nouns and verbs.

captures the fact that the various forms of the noun–verb pair share some, but not all, formational features. This common underlying representation includes such features as the place of articulation, handshape, orientation, shape of movement, and directionality for the noun–verb pair. Values on these features are specified in the lexicon for each noun–verb pair. The frequency of movement at the underlying level is always single. (Of course, syntactic and semantic features for the noun–verb pair are also specified in the lexical entry; the rules below operate to convert these syntactic and semantic specifications to further phonological features.)

As has already been noted, manner of movement is distinct for base forms in the noun–verb pair (i.e., noun versus verb) but is shared by any given base form and its related modulated form (i.e., noun and modulated noun versus verb and modulated verb). This fact suggests that manner of movement is introduced by an early rule that distinguishes nouns and verbs before repetition or inflections are added.[19] The output of this early rule is what we have thus far called the sign unit.

RULE 1:

A. *Verb manner rules:*

$$\begin{bmatrix} +V \\ -\text{spatial end-point} \end{bmatrix} \rightarrow [\text{Continuous}]$$

$$\begin{bmatrix} +V \\ +\text{spatial end-point} \end{bmatrix} \rightarrow [\text{Hold}]$$

B. *Noun manner rule:* $[+N] \rightarrow [\text{Restrained}]$

Finally, repetition, slow reduplication, or the dual inflection are added to the sign unit and result in surface verb, noun, or inflected forms.

RULE 2:

A. *Slow reduplicated*
       noun or verb: $[+\text{iteration/elongation}] \rightarrow [+\text{Redup}]$

B. *Dual noun or verb:* $[+\text{dual}] \rightarrow [+2 \text{ locations}]$

---

[19] Manner of movement could of course be specified as a neutral value (e.g., continuous) for all lexical entries and then altered by rule for verbs with spatial end-points and for nouns. It is more conventional to alter, rather than introduce, features by rule; however, since our data do not distingish between these alternatives, we have chosen the more straightforward alternative of adding manner when it is needed.

If neither A nor B apply,

C. *Noun or durative verb:* $\left\{\begin{matrix}[+N]\\[+V\\+durative]\end{matrix}\right\} \rightarrow [+\text{Repeated}]$

D. *Punctual verb:*   No further rules apply

Rules 2A and 2B (slow reduplication and dual inflection) may apply to any sign unit and result in a noun or a verb form, depending on the manner of movement specified by the application of Rule 1. Rules 2C and 2D are ordered after 2A and 2B; that is, surface single or repeated movement in the noun or verb appear only when inflections do not apply.

We are therefore claiming that the most natural account of the descriptive facts for nouns, verbs, and their modulations derives all related forms from a common underlying representation, with an intermediate level of representation (the sign unit) that distinguishes noun forms from verb forms in terms of manner of movement. It is, of course, possible to account for these facts in other ways, for example, (a) by listing surface nouns and verbs separately in the lexicon and deriving inflected forms from these directly; or (b) by deriving nouns from surface verbs and deriving inflected forms from each of these directly. However, as we will show, each of these alternatives is more complex than the solution just proposed and in addition misses significant generalizations that the preceding solution captures by positing underlying levels of representation.

Alternative 1: Independent Noun and Verb Derivations

On this account, nouns and verbs that have been described above as related members of a pair would be listed as separate items in the lexicon. This account clearly adds complexity to the lexicon by increasing the number of independent lexical items. In addition, it fails to represent the regular formal relationships between nouns and verbs that were described on pages 99–101. From the start, it is therefore an undesirable way of representing (i.e., failing to represent) the facts. Moreover, this alternative requires rather clumsy ways of deriving inflected forms of the noun and verb. This alternative clearly requires that inflections be added to the surface noun or verb, since these are the only representations available for modulating. Let us first consider the rules that would be required for inflecting verbs. If the verb is single in movement (e.g., PUT-IN-MOUTH, EAT-UP), inflecting the verb for continuous aspect (i.e., slow reduplication) or duality (i.e., dual inflection) is no problem: The surface verb is simply reduplicated or performed in two locations appropriately. In fact, the inflection of single verbs is simpler on this account than on the account which hypothesizes an underlying representation. If, however, the verb is repeated in movement (e.g., EAT), inflecting it for either continuous aspect or duality would require two steps: (1) deletion of repetition, and (2) addition of the inflection to this unrepeated form. Inflecting the noun (e.g., FOOD) would require the same two steps. This is clearly an unparsimonious account of the inflection process. First, it requires an additional step (deletion of repetition) in the inflection of both the repeated verb and the noun. Second, it misses the generalization that, for all forms of the verb and noun, the basic unit in the inflectional process is a single movement. Although a single movement appears in the derivations of single verbs, repeated verbs, and nouns, this fact is on this account merely a coincidence.

Alternative 2: Deriving Nouns from Surface Verbs

In this solution, no underlying form for nouns and verbs is hypothesized. Instead, only the verb (e.g., EAT) is listed in the lexicon; nouns are then derived from verbs by a series of rules:

Noun manner rule: [+N] → [Restrained]

Noun frequency rule: [+N] → [+Repeated]

This possibility was discussed on page 110 and at that point seemed to be the simplest way of describing the noun–verb relation. However, this solution becomes much more complex when one attempts to include the derivation of inflected forms of the noun and verb. As in Alternative 1, this solution requires adding inflections to the surface noun or verb, since these are the only representations hypothesized. Therefore, as in Alternative 1, the inflection of both repeated verbs and nouns requires (1) deletion of repetition, and (2) addition of the inflection to this unrepeated form. Once again, this solution requires the additional step of deleting repetition; and it misses the generalization that, for all forms of the verb and noun, the basic unit in the inflectional process is a single movement.

One variant of this solution would be to derive all nouns and verbs from the punctual-perfective, single-movement form of the verb. For example, PUT-IN-MOUTH, EAT, and FOOD might all be derived from EAT-UP. In this case, since the root form is always single in movement, no additional rules, such as "deletion of repetition," would be required. In fact, this solution is rather similar to hypothesizing an abstract underlying form that is single in movement. There are, however, two arguments that make the underlying form more desirable. First, not all verbs have a punctual single-movement form. For example, the durative verbs DISCUSS, FUCK, WALK, WRESTLE (and many others), all repeated in movement, have no single-movement relative that is a permissible surface form. Therefore, for these verbs, an underlying form must be hypothesized. Since underlying forms are required for some verbs, it seems more parsimonious overall to speak of abstract forms throughout the lexicon. Second, even for those verbs that have a permissible punctual form, there are difficulties in representing this form as the unmarked form. For many verbs (e.g., ROCK-BABY, BICYCLE, SWEEP) signers feel strongly that the single form is a very unusual, marked form.

In short, the simplest account of the relation between nouns, verbs, and their inflected forms involves hypothesizing a shared underlying representation for noun and verb, followed by: (1) a pair of manner rules, one of which adds continuous or hold manner to produce the verb sign unit, the other of which adds restrained movement to produce the noun sign unit; and (2) a set of alternative frequency rules, which either leave frequency unchanged or add repetition, slow reduplication, or the dual inflection. These rules generate all possible forms of the noun and verb discussed here. In addition, they capture several significant generalizations:

1. The various base and inflected forms of related nouns and verbs share a set of formational properties with one another. This fact is captured here by deriving all related noun and verb forms from a common underlying representation.
2. All the noun forms are distinguished from all the verb forms by manner of movement. This fact is captured here by deriving surface forms of the noun from one sign unit and surface forms of the verb from another sign unit; these sign units differ from the underlying form only in manner of movement.
3. All the inflected forms, for both noun and verb, involve modulations applied to single, rather than a repeated, movement unit. This is captured by having inflections apply to the sign unit rather than to the surface noun or verb, since the latter may be either single or repeated.

Derivation of Unrelated Nouns or Verbs

Thus far we have concentrated our discussion on noun–verb pairs, where the noun refers to the concrete object involved in the action referred to by the verb. As mentioned in Section 3, most nouns and verbs in ASL, like most nouns and verbs in English, are simply unrelated lexical items. In this case there are no apparent differences between the forms of nouns and the forms of verbs: Such nouns and verbs may be either single or repeated, and may be continuous, hold, or restrained in manner (see Table 4.2 for examples). One might speculate that a formal distinction between nouns and verbs arises only where there is a possibility of ambiguity; where there is no possibility of ambiguity (i.e., where either no concrete object or no action exists), no formal distinction between noun and verb is needed.

In such cases of individual nouns or individual verbs, clearly no noun–verb derivation is appropriate. Nevertheless, some portions of the noun–verb derivational system are applicable and are in fact required for explaining the distributional facts. In particular, inflected forms of individual nouns and verbs are like inflected forms of noun–verb pairs, in that the modulation is always applied to a *single* movement unit, even when the surface noun or verb is repeated. For example, consider the sign PAPER, which is illustrated in Figure 4.1b and described on page 94. This is a noun that occurs without a related verb in the ASL lexicon.[20] The sign PAPER is a unidirectional sign with continuous manner and repeated movement in the base form. However, in the slow reduplicated or the dual inflected form, the typical modulation is performed on a *single* movement unit. For example, in the slow reduplicated form, the active hand performs its unidirectional movement *once,* then goes through a slow arc-like transition, etc. The same pattern is true for other verbs and nouns as well. In short, even for unrelated nouns or verbs, inflections are applied to a sign unit that is a single movement. Figure 4.13 shows the derivational system for modulating these individual nouns or verbs.

In sum, lexical items in ASL, whether noun–verb pairs or unrelated lexical items, are uniformly represented in the lexicon in an abstract form rather than a surface form. In all cases, frequency of movement in this abstract form is single. For each noun–verb pair, only one entry,

[20] There is a formally related sign, COVER-UP, which is illustrated in Figure 4.1a. The sign COVER-UP is similar to PAPER in handshape, location, etc., and differs from PAPER only in frequency of movement: PAPER is repeated in movement, whereas COVER-UP is single. However, these two signs are merely a minimal pair in formational features, like *bat* and *pat* in English; like *bat* and *pat,* they are lexically (i.e., semantically) unrelated and do not form a noun–verb pair.

Underlying Form (= Sign Unit)

place of articulation
handshape
orientation
shape of movement
directionality
manner
frequency: −Repeated

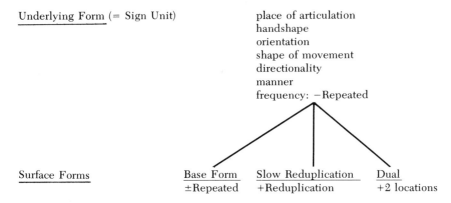

Surface Forms

Base Form   Slow Reduplication   Dual
±Repeated   +Reduplication   +2 locations

Figure 4.13. The derivational system for unrelated nouns or verbs.

specifying place of articulation, handshape, etc., is needed; manner and frequency of movement (which distinguish noun from verb and base from inflected forms) are introduced or altered by a series of rules. For each individual item without a paired noun or verb, this lexical entry will include manner of movement; frequency of movement is then altered by the same rules used for noun–verb pairs (Rule 2).[21]

Complex Inflections

The derivational process we have hypothesized will account rather neatly for one additional phenomenon. It is permissible in ASL to modulate nouns or verbs for more than one inflection. For example, one can form the dual of a slow-reduplicated noun or verb. With this complex inflection applied to the verb EAT, the sign unit would be slowly reduplicated first on one side and then on the other. We will represent this sign as: $[[STEM]_{Redup}]_{Dual}$.[22] This complex form means

[21] Actually, Rule 2 must be modified slightly to apply to individual lexical items. As we have stated it above, 2D (no further change) will occur only for punctual verb. In the case of unrelated lexical items, some nouns, in addition to punctual verbs, may be single in surface form. Therefore, these lexical entries must be marked to block the application of Rule 2C (N→+Repeated).

For unrelated lexical items, any derivation in which 2D applies has a surface form identical to the underlying form. In such cases it is vacuous to hypothesize an underlying form; one could just as well claim that inflections are added to the surface sign itself. Nevertheless, since underlying forms are required in all cases where the surface noun or verb is repeated, it seems more parsimonious overall to speak of abstract forms throughout the lexicon.

[22] In this notation, the underlying form = ROOT; the sign unit (i.e., ROOT + manner) = STEM.

"eating continuously in two different instances." One can also form a slow-reduplicated dual noun or verb: $[[\text{STEM}]_{\text{Dual}}]_{\text{Redup}}$. In this form, the sign unit is made first on one side and then on the other, followed by a transitional arc, and then reduplicated. This form means "eating twice over and over again."

In addition, one can combine repetition with either the dual inflection or slow reduplication: $[[\text{STEM}]_{\text{Repeated}}]_{\text{Dual}}$ or $[[\text{STEM}]_{\text{Repeated}}]_{\text{Redup}}$. Whereas the simple dual inflection means "eating twice without stopping in between," the dual repeated means "eating once, stopping, and then eating again." For example,

> LAST CHRISTMAS, HAVE DINNER NOON EVENING. ME
> FINISH $[[\text{EAT}]_{\text{Repeated}}]_{\text{Dual}}$.
> "Last Christmas we had dinner at noon and evening. I ate, and then ate again."

Similarly, while the simple slow reduplication means "eating continuously," the slow reduplicated repeated means "continually eating, then stopping, then eating."

> DICK $[[\text{EAT}]_{\text{Repeated}}]_{\text{Redup}}$. BETTER INTERRUPT WHILE HE
> NOT EAT.
> "Dick is continually eating and eating again. Better catch him while he's not eating."

Such complex forms can easily be generated by allowing our rules of pages 120–121 to apply cyclically. For example, the dual slow reduplicated is generated by applying slow reduplication on the first (inner) cycle and dual on the second; in contrast, the slow reduplicated dual is generated by applying the dual on the first cycle and the slow reduplication on the second. Such cyclic rule application accounts not only for the surface forms of such complex modulations; it accounts in addition for the semantic scope relations among these modulations. Finally, ordering Rule 2C

$$\left\{\begin{array}{l}[+\text{N}]\\ \left[\begin{array}{l}+\text{V}\\ +\text{durative}\end{array}\right]\end{array}\right\} \rightarrow [+\text{Repeated}]$$

disjunctively with the dual inflection and slow reduplication on each cycle accounts for the acceptability of $[[\text{STEM}]_{\text{Repeated}}]_{\text{Dual or Redup}}$ but the unacceptability of $[[\text{STEM}]_{\text{Dual or Redup}}]_{\text{Repeated}}$.

CONCLUSION

As we have seen, ASL, like spoken languages, distinguishes systematically between nouns and verbs. In addition, like many spoken languages, ASL distinguishes punctual verbs from durative verbs, and inflects noun and verb for various kinds of plurality and aspect.[23] In short, the semantic distinctions made in nouns and verbs of ASL are those commonly made in other natural languages. Only one semantic distinction we have considered—presence/absence of spatial endpoint—seems unique to a language in the visual–gestural modality.

American Sign Language is also similar to many spoken languages in the form by which these distinctions are marked. Spoken languages often derive nouns from verbs by reduplicating part or all of the verb form (as in African languages; Eulenberg, 1971). Spoken languages also inflect nouns or verbs for plurality, iteration, duration, and continuation by reduplication of the root form (Eulenberg, 1971; Key, 1965). As we have seen, ASL marks all of these distinctions by various kinds of reduplication—what we have called here "repetition," "dual," and "slow reduplication." Although for each of these functions one can find a spoken language that uses reduplication, we know of no spoken language that uses distinct types of reduplication to mark all of these semantic functions.[24] In this sense, sign languages may be unique. We speculate that the availability of space and movement, as well as time, in the phonology of gestural languages makes this richness of reduplicated forms possible.

Finally, we have considered the phonological process by which these forms are derived in ASL. As we have seen, the derivation of noun and verb forms in ASL requires hypothesizing an abstract underlying representation for lexical items. Likewise, in spoken languages, it has been hypothesized that the underlying phonological forms of roots are abstract (Chomsky and Halle, 1968). That is, the underlying forms of roots may be items which do not occur as surface phonetic forms in the language. In spoken languages, as in ASL, the abstract nature of root forms is justified by the savings that accrue in the rules which operate on these representations (cf. Anderson, 1974, Chapter 3). Moreover, in spoken languages as in ASL, the rules for deriving surface forms are ordered, and they may apply cyclically to generate complex expressions.

[23] See Fischer (1973), Fischer and Gough (1973), and Klima, Bellugi et al. (in press) for a description of other forms of plurality and aspect in ASL.

[24] We are grateful to Sandy Chung and Alan Timberlake for pointing this out to us.

In a variety of ways, then, the formal description of ASL is similar to that of spoken languages. These similarities suggest that, at least in these cases, language structure is determined more by the general cognitive demands of communication than by the specific constraints of the input and output channels over which this communication is accomplished.

Discussions of ASL have often centered on iconicity, with the implication that the possibility of iconicity in the visual–manual mode must make sign languages radically different in character from spoken languages. In the concrete nouns and verbs we have considered, there is some obvious iconicity between the form of the sign and the form of the action to which it refers. We have also seen iconicity in the form of inflections (e.g., reduplication) and the semantic values these inflections represent (e.g., iteration), an iconicity which is also found in spoken languages.[25] Such gross relations between form and meaning in natural language should not be surprising, particularly in a gestural mode where the means for representing actions in space is rather directly available. What *is* surprising is the degree to which natural languages, even gestural languages, are abstract. As we have seen, the sorts of abstract rule systems that are needed in the description of spoken languages are also needed in the description of ASL.

APPENDIX 4A

One Hundred Noun–Verb Pairs Categorized by Frequency, Manner, and Directionality of Movement in the Verb

For the noun, directionality is the same as that for the verb; manner is always restrained; and frequency is always repeated. Note: * indicates violation of these patterns in the noun.

Place of articulation, handshape, orientation, directionality, and shape of movement for each noun–verb pair are represented in Stokoe *et al.* (1965) notation. We do not represent in this notation manner or frequency of movement. Our use of this notation thus represents the underlying form for noun–verb pairs.

FREQUENCY:	SINGLE
MANNER:	CONTINUOUS
DIRECTIONALITY:	UNIDIRECTIONAL

1. AIRPLANE .... GO BY AIRPLANE (i.e., FLY) .... $\checkmark Y_D{}^\perp$
2. BOAT .... GO BY BOAT .... $B_a{}'B_a{}^\perp$
3. FLYING SAUCER .... GO BY FLYING SAUCER .... $\checkmark \ddot{L}_<{}^\perp$
4. ROCKET .... GO BY ROCKET .... $B_D\,R^\wedge$

---

[25] See Eulenberg (1971) and Cassirer (1965) for a discussion of the iconic character of reduplication in spoken languages.

5. SHIP .... GO BY SHIP .... Ḃₐ ろ ꜀ₓ
6. SKIS .... GO BY SKIS(i.e., SKI) .... ḦₐḦₐ ꜀
7. SUBMARINE .... GO BY SUBMARINE .... Ḃₐ ろ ⊥
8. SURFBOARD .... GO BY SURFBOARD(i.e., SURF) ..... Hᴅᵼʜᵥ ⊥
9. TRAIN* .... GO BY TRAIN .... Hᴅᵼ Hᴅ ꜀ₓ

FREQUENCY: SINGLE
MANNER: HOLD
DIRECTIONALITY: UNIDIRECTIONAL

1. BACKPACK .... PUT ON BACKPACK .... []AᴛAᴛ ˣ
2. BED .... GO TO BED .... }B ˣ
3. BLANKET .... COVER WITH BLANKET .... []B>ᴅB<ᴅ ᵀˣ
4. BOOK .... OPEN BOOK .... B>'B< ᵃ
5. BRACELET .... PUT ON BRACELET .... DL̈ ᵡ
6. BROOCH .... PUT ON BROOCH .... []G ˣ#
7. CHAIR .... SIT .... Hᴅ Ḧᴅ ˣ
8. CLIPPER .... CLIP FINGERNAIL .... G X̣ᴛ #[A]
9. CLOTHESPIN .... PUT ON CLOTHESPIN .... G̃ Ḣᵥ ᵡ
10. COAT* .... PUT ON COAT .... []ÅᴅÅᴅ ᵧˣ
11. DOOR .... OPEN DOOR .... B⊥' B⊥ ᵃ
12. DOORBELL .... PRESS DOORBELL .... B> Å ˣ
13. DOORKNOB .... TURN DOORKNOB .... Ö̈ ᵃ
14. DRAWER .... PULL DRAWER .... AₐAₐ ᵀ
15. DRESS .... PUT ON DRESS .... []5>5< ꜀ₓ
16. EARPHONES .... PUT ON EARPHONES .... CC>C< ˣ
17. EARRING .... PUT ON EARRING .... }F ᵡ
18. GAS MASK .... PUT ON GAS MASK............... ⌣5̈ᴛ ˣ
19. GASOLINE .... FILL UP WITH GASOLINE .... O Å ꞯ̣
20. GATE .... CLOSE GATE .... B>' B< ꞯ̥
21. GEARSHIFT* .... SHIFT .... A ᵀᵥ
22. GIRDLE .... PUT ON GIRDLE .... []A>A< ꜀ᶜ
23. GOGGLES .... PUT ON GOGGLES .... ⌐C>C< ˣ
24. GUN .... SHOOT .... G⊥ ᵑ
25. HANGER .... HANG UP .... Ḡᴅ × ᵡ
26. HAT .... PUT ON HAT .... ⌐Bᴅ ˣ
27. HEARING AID .... PUT ON HEARING AID .... }× ꞯ̥ₓ
28. JARLID .... SCREW ON JARLID............... C> Cᴅ ᵃꞯ
29. KEY* .... LOCK UP .... ꞯ Aᴅ ᵃꞯ
30. LATCH .... LATCH UP .... O Xᴅ ⊚
31. LIGHTER .... FLICK LIGHTER .... Å ᵑ
32. MATCH .... STRIKE MATCH .... B' × X̂ₓ
33. MELON .... THUMP MELON .... D ꓯ X̌
34. PILL .... TAKE PILL .... ⌣X⊥ ꞯ̥[G]
35. PLIERS .... SQUEEZE PLIERS .... Cₐ #
36. PLUG .... PLUG IN .... V V ⊚
37. RING .... PUT ON RING .... 5ᴅ Fᴅ ᵀ꜀ₓ
38. SCARF* .... PUT ON SCARF .... ⌣X>X< ⊚⁺
39. SCISSORS .... CUT .... V⊥ #
40. SCREWDRIVER .... TURN SCREW .... Bₐ Hᵥ ꞯ꜀ₓ
41. SOCK .... PUT ON SOCK .... Bᴅ> Cᴅ ꜀ₓ
42. SUSPENDERS .... PUT ON SUSPENDERS .... []3ᵥ3ᵥ ꜀#[Oᴅ]ₓ

43. TAPE .... PUT ON TAPE .... H$_D$$^{\pm}$ H$_D$ $_X^T$
44. TELEPHONE .... TELEPHONE ....)Y$_T$ ^{X}
45. THONGS .... PUT ON THONG .... 5$_D$$^{\odot}$ G$_V$ $^{<X}$
46. UMBRELLA .... OPEN UMBRELLA .... Ā A $^\wedge$
47. WALLET .... OPEN WALLET .... B$_>$'B$_<$ ^{D}
48. WHISTLE .... BLOW WHISTLE .... ↄḦ ^{X}
49. WINDOW .... CLOSE WINDOW .... B̄$_>$ B$_<$ ^{X}
50. WRENCH .... TURN NUT .... G$_D$ H $_X^D$
51. ZIPPER* .... ZIP UP .... [ ]A$_T$ $^\wedge$

FREQUENCY: SINGLE
MANNER: HOLD
DIRECTIONALITY: BIDIRECTIONAL

1. GLOVES* .... PUT ON GLOVES .... B̄$_D$ B$_D$ $_X^{Tↄ}$

FREQUENCY: SINGLE
MANNER: RESTRAINED
DIRECTIONALITY: UNIDIRECTIONAL

1. CAMERA .... SNAP PHOTOGRAPH .... ɔC G ^{L}
2. STAPLER .... STAPLE .... B̄$_a$ B$_D$ $^{VX\wedge}$

FREQUENCY: REPEATED
MANNER: CONTINUOUS
DIRECTIONALITY: UNIDIRECTIONAL

1. BROOM .... SWEEP .... B$_a$ B $_X^{\langle}$
2. COMB .... COMB .... ⌒C̈$_D$ ^{V}
3. FOOD .... EAT .... ↄO$_T$ ^{ɔC}
4. GUITAR .... STRUM .... C$_a$ C̈ ^{V}
5. ICE CREAM .... LICK ICE CREAM .... ↄA$_D$ ^{V}
6. LAWNMOWER .... MOW .... A$_D$A$_D$ $^\perp$
7. MOP .... MOP .... A$_{a9}$A$_D$ $^\perp$
8. MOVIE CAMERA .... CRANK MOVIE CAMERA .... ɔB A $_X^D$
9. RAKE .... RAKE .... B$_a$ C$_D$ ^{T}
10. SEWING MACHINE ..... SEW BY MACHINE .... Ḡ X$_D$ $_X^\perp$
11. SHOVEL .... DIG .... B$_a$ B$_V$ $_D^{X\langle}$
12. VACUUM CLEANER .... VACUUM .... B$_a$ 5̈ $_X^\perp$

FREQUENCY: REPEATED
MANNER: CONTINUOUS
DIRECTIONALITY: BIDIRECTIONAL

1. BABY .... ROCK BABY IN ARMS .... ✓B̄$_a$✓B$_a$ ^{Z}
2. BICYCLE .... BICYCLE .... A$_D$A$_D$ $^{\rho\sim}$
3. BLACKBOARD ERASER . ERASE BLACKBOARD .... A ^{N}
4. CAR .... DRIVE .... AA ^{NN}
5. ERASER .... ERASE .... B̄$_a$ A$_<$ $_X^{\mathsf{Z}}$
6. FILE .... FILE FINGERNAIL .... G$_D$ H $_X^{\mathsf{Z}}$
7. HAIRSPRAY .... SPRAY HAIR ....)X$_<$ ^{I}
8. IRON .... IRON CLOTHES .... B̄$_a$ ✓A$_D$ ^{Z}

9.	LIPSTICK	.....	PUT ON LIPSTICK	.....	ᴗX_T ²
10.	MILK*	.....	MILK COW	.....	CC ⁞∿
11.	PAINT	.....	PAINT	.....	B_T B_D ⁱ₂
12.	PIANO	.....	PLAY PIANO	.....	5_D5_D ⁞
13.	SAW	.....	CUT WITH SAW	.....	B_D ✓A ¹
14.	SKATES	.....	SKATE	.....	✓V̈_a✓V̈_a ²∿
15.	SWING	.....	SWING	.....	H_D*H ¹
16.	TOOTHBRUSH	.....	BRUSH TEETH	.....	ᴗG_< ²
17.	TOWEL	.....	RUB BACK WITH TOWEL	.....	[]A_V✓A_< ¹
18.	TOY CAR	.....	ROLL CAR BACK AND FORTH	.....	B_a ✓A ²
19.	VIOLIN	.....	PLAY VIOLIN	.....	✓A_a ✓A_D ²

FREQUENCY: REPEATED
MANNER: HOLD
DIRECTIONALITY: UNIDIRECTIONAL

1.	AIR PUMP	.....	PUMP AIR	.....	A_VA_V ᵛ
2.	CIGARETTE	.....	SMOKE	.....	ᴗH_T ¹
3.	HAMMER	.....	HAMMER	.....	✓A ᵀ
4.	HOE	.....	HOE	.....	✓A_ǫ✓A ᵛ
5.	PLAYING CARDS	.....	DEAL CARDS	.....	O_⟩ ẋ ⁞[A]

FREQUENCY: REPEATED
MANNER: HOLD
DIRECTIONALITY: BIDIRECTIONAL

1.	TYPEWRITER	.....	TYPE	.....	C_D C_D ∿∿

ACKNOWLEDGMENTS

We would like to thank Ursula Bellugi, Heidi Feldman, Susan Fischer, Susan Goldin-Meadow, Ella Lentz, Jay McClelland, and Carlene Canady Pedersen for extremely helpful discussion throughout this work. Our special thanks to Sandy Chung, Ed Klima, and Alan Timberlake for their advice on linguistic matters, and to Lila Gleitman for her suggestions in countless conversations about earlier drafts of this paper.

REFERENCES

Anderson, S. R. *The organization of phonology.* New York: Academic Press, 1974.
Bellugi, U., & Klima, E. S. Aspects of sign language and its structure. In J. F. Kavanagh & J. E. Cutting (Eds.), *The role of speech in language.* Cambridge, Massachusetts: M.I.T. Press, 1975.
Bellugi, U., and Klima, E. S. On the creation of new lexical items by compounding. In E. S. Klima, U. Bellugi *et al.* (in press).
Cassirer, E. *The philosophy of symbolic forms* (Vol. I: Language). New Haven, Connecticut: Yale University Press, 1965.

Chomsky, N., & Halle, M. *The sound pattern of English.* New York: Harper, 1968.

Eulenberg, J. B. Conjunction reduction and reduplication in African languages. In Chin-Wu Kim & H. Stahlke (Eds.), *Papers in African linguistics.* Edmonton, Canada: Linguistic Research, 1971.

Fischer, S. Two processes of reduplication in the American Sign Language. *Foundations of Language,* 1973, 9, 469–480.

Fischer, S. Sign language and linguistic universals. In C. Rohrer and N. Ruwet (Eds.), *Actes du colloque Franco-Allemand de grammaire transformationelle, Band II: Etudes de semantique et autres.* Tubingen: Max Niemeyer Verlag, 1974.

Fischer, S., & Gough, B. *Verbs in American Sign Language.* Salk Institute working paper, 1973.

Friedman, L. A. On the physical manifestation of stress in the ASL. University of California, Berkeley, manuscript, 1974.

Hockett, C. F. The problem of universals in language. In J. H. Greenberg (Ed.), *Universals of language.* Cambridge, Massachusetts: M.I.T. Press, 1963.

Key, H. Some semantic functions of reduplication in various languages. *Anthropological Linguistics,* 1965, 7, 88–102.

Klima, E. S., Bellugi, U. *et al. The signs of language.* Cambridge, Massachusetts: Harvard Univ. Press, in press.

Lenneberg, E. H. *Biological foundations of language.* New York: Wiley & Sons, 1967.

Liberman, A. M. The grammars of speech and language. *Cognitive Psychology,* 1970, 1, 301–323.

Liddell, S. *An investigation into the syntactic structure of American Sign Language.* Unpublished doctoral dissertation, University of California, San Diego, 1977.

Lieberman, P. On the evolution of language: A unified view. *Cognition,* 1973, 2, 59–94.

Matthews, P. H. *Morphology: An introduction to the theory of word structure.* Cambridge, England: Cambridge Univ. Press, 1974.

Newport, E. L., & Bellugi, U. Linguistic expression of category levels in a visual–gestural language: A flower is a flower is a flower. In E. Rosch & B. B. Lloyd (Eds.), *Cognition and categorization.* Hillsdale, New Jersey: Lawrence Erlbaum, in press.

Osherson, D. N., & Wasow, T. Task-specificity and species-specificity in the study of language: A methodological note. *Cognition,* 1976, 4, 203–214.

Schlesinger, I. M. The grammar of sign language and the problems of language universals. In J. Morton (Ed.), *Biological and social factors in psycholinguistics.* Urbana, Illinois: University of Illinois Press, 1970.

Slobin, D. I. The more it changes . . . : On understanding language by watching it move through time. *Papers and Reports on Child Language Development,* 1975, 10, 1–30.

Stokoe, W. C., Jr. Sign language structure: An outline of the visual communication system of the American deaf. *Studies in linguistics,* Occasional Papers 8, 1960.

Stokoe, W. C., Jr., Casterline, D., & Croneberg, C. G. *A dictionary of American Sign Language on linguistic principles.* Washington, D. C.: Gallaudet College Press, 1965.

Supalla, T. *Modulation of nouns in American Sign Language.* Salk Institute working paper, 1977.

Wasow, T. The innateness hypothesis and grammatical relations. *Synthese,* 1973, 26, 38–56.

5

Aspect Marking in
American Sign Language

KATHERINE NORTON WARREN

Office of Professional Development, National Technical Institute for the Deaf, Rochester Institute of Technology

INTRODUCTION

Description of the linguistic structure of ASL, the visual–manual language of the deaf population in the United States, has been long in coming. First efforts to identify its various features began in the early 1960s, when researchers (Stokoe, 1960; Stokoe, Casterline, & Croneberg, 1965) described gross parameters of the phonological repertoire of ASL. Even more recently, researchers (Fischer & Gough, forthcoming[1]; Woodward, 1973; Friedman, 1975) have tackled the description of syntactical features of ASL, specifically those related to negation, person, tense, and aspect.

It is the purpose of this chapter to focus primarily on the feature of aspect as it manifests itself through adverbial modification of verb forms in ASL. Fowler (1974) describes aspect as that which "characterizes the manner, duration, repetition, . . . of an action or state relative to the temporal base-line set by the time of utterance [p. 114]." Hirtle (1975) refers to aspect as the designation of event time as opposed to universe time, which is designated by tense. Much confusion exists between tense and aspect in English because they are

---

[1] All further mention of the work by Fischer and Gough refers to this paper.

UNDERSTANDING LANGUAGE
THROUGH
SIGN LANGUAGE RESEARCH

133

often overtly marked in the same ways. However, tense is strictly related to time per se, while aspect is related to the status of an activity with respect to its beginning, frequency, duration, manner, or completion.

The examples:

(1)   *He ate*
(2)   *He has eaten*

are both in the past tense (in universe time), but they differ in the way event time is viewed. Thus, the distinction between the two is one of aspect rather than tense.

In English, aspect is present in all utterances but is most obvious when it has morphological manifestation, such as:

(3)   *We are going to the library*

Here, aspect (specifically, duration) is specified by the auxiliary *be* and the present participle (base + -ing) form of the verb.

Even though this particular example has the overt marking of aspect, it is still ambiguous in its surface structure for denoting aspect that is future action or continuing action in the present. It is with the help of adverbials that such ambiguity disappears, where a continuing action in the present could be designated as follows:

(4)   *We are going to the library every Friday*

Thus, in English, adverbials are separate lexical items that help to clarify aspect. Rules for the order of insertion or selectional restriction of adverbials have yet to be written. However, their significance for deriving tense and aspect is beginning to be explored (see Hirtle, 1967, 1975; Macauley, 1971). Adverbials appear to be more reliable in specifying time. Hausmann (1972) uses the example:

(5)   *John comes home tomorrow*

to demonstrate the fact that the use of the present tense here rather than the future auxiliary *will* is irrelevant in specifying the actual event time. Therefore, the marking of aspect occurs through the time adverbial *tomorrow*.

Still, there is little question that adverbials are not the primary agents for marking aspect in English, and their influence over tense and aspect is relatively small.[2] However, the relationship between

---

[2] For a complete discussion of aspect in English see Macauley (1971) and Hirtle (1967). Hausmann (1972) discusses at length the derivational relationship between tense and time adverbs with some reference to aspect.

verbs and adverbs in ASL appears to be of a different order.[3] In the next section, this relationship will be discussed briefly, with attention to adverbial modifiers for intensity, duration, and frequency.

Verbs and Adverbs in American Sign Language

Verbs (hence, tense and aspect) and adverbials are intrinsically linked in ASL. Bellugi and Fischer (1972) and Fischer and Gough report that ASL verbs can incorporate information regarding the manner, frequency, and duration of an activity. Fischer and Gough (in press) use MEET as an example of manner incorporation: "The sign MEET, if performed quickly and intensely such that the hands come apart slightly, seemingly as a result of the impact, means 'run into by accident', or 'bump into' (chance to meet). If it is performed quite slowly, it means something like approach [p. 30]." This example indicates how a variation in the production of a sign can alter its meaning. Although the example makes its point with an idiomatic verb phrase of English (*run into*), the same example can illustrate the relationship between a verb and a manner adverbial in ASL. Presumably a signer, given the English sentence to translate into ASL "I met him accidentally," would produce MEET in the first way just described.

In their discussion of frequency and duration aspect markers, Fischer and Gough focus on one end of the continuum in both cases, that is, activities that are habitual and continuous (as opposed to those that are sporadic, or short-lived). An example they cite of frequency aspect marking for habitual action is READ, which is modulated by repeating the sign quickly and with a horizontal sweep and is glossed as "always read" or "read all the time." Duration aspect markers of continuous action are formed by a slow, drawn-out repetition of the sign and translate in the case of TELEPHONE as "telephone for a long time."

The authors cite examples of verbs in ASL that cannot modulate for either frequency or duration because of the semantic restriction of stativity. They point out that even though one can convey the idea of "fearing something for a long time" in English, the fact that *fear* is a stative verb precludes the possibility of repetition as the means of

[3] Smeltz (1975) has rightly criticized researchers of ASL for their overemphasis on comparison between ASL and oral languages. The mere fact that ASL is a visual–manual language rather than an oral language requires a somewhat different research perspective, particularly one that will not preclude investigation of spatial features of ASL.

marking "a long time" or "all the time" in ASL. The authors do not discuss how these ideas would be conveyed in ASL.

Friedman (1975) explores means for designating tense in ASL. Here, adverbials play a major role with respect to time and in fact serve as the primary tense markers. When discussing past tense, Friedman notes: "The adverbial referring to previous time is sufficient to mark the 'tense' of a sentence as past. After one adverbial reference to past time, all discourse refers to that period until new time reference is made [p. 951]."

The adverbials discussed here are specific time indicators such as YESTERDAY, RECENTLY, or NEXT-WEEK. The author stresses the unique link between verbs and adverbials in ASL with respect to tense but does not discuss aspect per se. In reference to iconicity and the effect of a visual modality on ASL, however, she cites the capability of the language to convey nuances of meaning through an alteration of the base sign. A manner aspect marker is cited as an example in the case of WALK, where WALK-FOR-MILES-AND-MILES is conveyed by producing the base sign WALK more slowly and longer in duration.

' These studies point out the unique relationship between adverbials and verbs in ASL. However, this relationship can best be seen in the actual manifestation of adverbial influence on ASL verbs in the surface structure. The various processes available for adverbs to influence verbs overtly in ASL will be discussed in the next section.

Processes of Modulation in American Sign Language

In the example used earlier

(6)   *We are going to the library every Friday*

clarity of aspect in English is accomplished by the addition of separate lexical items, that is "every Friday." Information regarding aspect, specifically manner, duration, or frequency, of an activity is usually conveyed in this way rather than through some sort of internal change to the verb itself.

In ASL, on the other hand, the signer can actually alter the production of the verb (its base form) to arrive at a new form. Using the same example

(7)   *We are going to the library every Friday*

the base or citation form[4] of "go" changes to a new form where "go" is signed GO-GO-GO-GO. In this case, the location, handshape, and orientation of the citation form remain the same, but the movement changes from one that is circular and singularly executed to one that is straight and repeatedly executed. The gloss of the new form then becomes "go regularly." This change is the key difference between English and ASL with respect to aspect marking. In ASL, the signer can incorporate new information by changing the production of the verb itself as opposed to adding new lexical items or agglutinating some sort of affix to the verb.

Change in the verb is accomplished by various processes. Such changes are generally referred to as modulations of the citation form. In the case of durative verbs, Fischer and Gough state that marking for habitual action occurs through fast repetition (reduplication) of the citation form. Elsewhere, Fischer (1973) states that fast reduplication must be accompanied by a horizontal sweep. The horizontal sweep denotes additional information regarding the plurality of either subject or object. The author cites a few exceptions to this rule, that is, durative verbs that can reduplicate without an accompanying horizontal sweep, in the cases of COME and KNOW. However, she finds that those verbs that regularly permit reduplication without horizontal sweep seem to be restricted to point-action verbs.

As has already been noted, Fischer and Gough discuss marking for continuous action as occurring through slow repetition (reduplication) of the citation form of the verb. In her 1973 paper, Fischer states that both point-action verbs and durative verbs can be reduplicated slowly; however, the interpretation varies. Point-action verbs that are reduplicated slowly are interpreted as actions that are repeatedly performed, whereas durative verbs when reduplicated slowly are interpreted as elongated actions. Thus, with slow reduplication, FIND becomes "keep on finding things" and DRINK becomes "drink for a long time [p. 474]."

Throughout all of her discussion of reduplication, Fischer assumes that the real distinction between marking for habitual action versus marking for continuous action is the rate of reduplication. That such a qualitative distinction actually exists is questionable, however. In general, slow reduplication might be interpreted merely as negative affect toward the given action, whether it is habitual or continuous. Con-

---

[4]*Citation form* is the form of the sign commonly described in dictionaries of sign language. It is also the usual form produced when a signer is asked, "What is the sign for———?

versely, fast reduplication may imply merely a general acceptance of the given action, regardless of habituality or length. If this is the case, then, reduplication alone is the process by which both types of aspect are marked for durative verbs, and the rate of reduplication will simply add information regarding the signer's attitude.

Aspect marking for manner appears to be accomplished by some change in the speed, size, or strength of the citation form of the verb. Frishberg (1972) has discussed categories for such change in her description of "sharp" and "soft" features of movement in ASL. She describes "sharp" as movement that is intense and therefore denotes "intensity of meaning, emphasis, rapid onset of action and total satisfaction of criterion [p. 1]." "Soft" movement, on the other hand, is a "gentler motion [that] indicates uncertainty, gradual onset of action or partial satisfaction of criterion [p. 2]."

The semantic distinctions resulting from such variations in movement have implication for understanding the total lexicon of ASL. The citation sign for STUDY when performed with a sharp plus rapid movement can be glossed as "cram." The sign RUN when performed with either sharp or soft movement can be glossed respectively as "sprint" or "jog." On a superficial level, a comparison between ASL and English leads one to think that ASL has a rather meager lexicon. However, upon closer investigation of such regular changes to ASL's citation forms, the lexicon appears to be considerably more extensive.

Supalla and Newport (Chapter 4, this volume) have also investigated the parameters of movement, specifically describing the nature of directionality and frequency in sign production. Their discussion of manner of movement (i.e., continuous, hold, or restrained) is most interesting as it relates to Fischer and Gough's and to Frishberg's (1972) broader description of modulation through changes in speed, size, or strength of the citation form. Care should be taken here to distinguish uses of the terms *manner* and *continuous*. Fischer and Gough use both terms in reference to semantic categories. *Manner* and *continuous*, in this case, are categories of information that can be incorporated into the verb to mark aspect. When Supalla and Newport use *manner,* they are referring only to the phonological feature of movement. In this case, *manner* is composed of three separate types: continuous, which is free movement across the signing space with no interruption; hold, which is the same, except that the sign comes to an abrupt stop; and restrained, which is quick, stiff movement where the hand often bounces back to the initial position.[5]

[5] For purposes of clarity, the term *intensity* will be used in place of *manner* when referring to the semantic category to mark aspect.

Progress to Date

At this point, it is necessary to summarize progress to date with respect to which aspect markers have been described in other studies and which processes of modulation have been identified.

Marking for aspect in ASL can occur by incorporating information about the intensity, duration, or frequency of an activity. Intensity, in this case, usually denotes the relative degree or amount of a given activity. Thus, an intensity adverbial normally answers the question of "how" or sometimes "how much" with a quantifiable verb. Intensity is an antonymous category in which gradations of degree or amount can occur. Both extremes of the intensity continuum have been discussed by Fischer and Gough in their example of MEET.

A duration adverbial is also an antonymous category, in which infinite gradations of time can be conveyed. Fischer and Gough discuss only one end of the duration continuum, that is, marking for "long time" (which they call continuous aspect). No studies of which this author is aware deal with marking for "short time."

Frequency, as well, is an antonymous feature that answers the question of how often an activity occurred. Again, Fischer and Gough are the only authors who have investigated frequency in any depth. In this case, they describe habitual aspect or marking for activities that occur "all the time." No discussion has dealt with the opposite end of the frequency continuum for the marking of sporadic, relatively infrequent occurrence of an activity.

A schema of analysis to date, and the respective processes identified for each feature, is shown in Figure 5.1.

A variety of questions yet to be answered will be discussed in the next section. Foremost in the discussion are questions regarding usage within the deaf population, variability with respect to specific

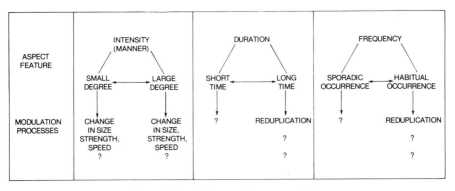

Figure 5.1. Schema of aspect marking.

aspect feature, and other modulation processes in use among fluent
signers.

THE PROBLEM

The primary question to be answered is the extent of interaction
between verbs and aspect adverbials in ASL. If marking for aspect is a
possibility, what is the nature and circumstance of adverbial influence
over the verb?

Usage

Previous investigations of modulations of ASL verbs have not discussed at any length the actual usage of modulated forms within the
deaf population. One exception is Woodward's (1973) study of dialectical variation in ASL as evidenced in usage of negative incorporation,
directional verbs, and reduplicated verbs. However "usage" here is
derived from questionnaire responses; therefore, little information is
provided on semantic restrictions of usage for the various categories of
adverbials.

Assuming that modulations occur, to what extent are they really used
by fluent signers? One can ask whether marking (therefore modulation) is variable according to relative influence of the English language. In other words, do deaf native signers mark for aspect more
frequently through modulation than do hearing native signers? Would
all native signers prefer to keep adverbials of intensity, duration, or
frequency present without incorporating them into the verb? For both
groups, the question of option versus rule pertains. Depending upon
the restrictions on the verb, will marking through modulation be so
extensive as to suggest it as a rule of ASL?

Restrictions

A large category for investigation of marking is that of restrictions on
the verb. Fischer and Gough suggest semantic restrictions concerning
stativity of verbs for marking of habitual frequency and long duration.
Woodward suggests phonological restrictions concerning the location
of a sign for reduplication of verbs. Presumably, these are not exhaustive categories of restrictions on marking. Structures of complementation are presumed to have some influence on marking. One could
posit, for example, that intransitive verbs would be marked more

frequently than transitive verbs because the verb is contiguous to the adverbial. So, too, iconic and pantomimic signs might lend themselves more readily to marking.

Variability by Aspect Feature

A straightforward question can be asked as to variation in usage according to specific aspect feature. For example, might frequency and duration be marked more readily than intensity because of the availability of a fairly stylized process of modulation, that is, reduplication?

A more interesting question can be asked regarding variation in marking depending upon which end of the feature continuum is being conveyed. By aspect feature, might the greater end (i.e., large degree, long time, habitual occurrence) be modulated more frequently than the lesser end (i.e., small degree, short time, sporadic occurrence)? The answer to this question would have implications for the semantic content carried by the citation form of a sign. If a continuum really exists for aspect features, one would presume that the citation form of a sign falls somewhere in the middle. If, for example, "short time" were to be marked much less frequently than "long time," this result could imply that the semantic content of the citation form of the sign is closer to "short time" in the signer's mind.

Processes of Modulation

Reduplication and alteration of size, strength, and speed of the movement of a sign have already been identified as processes through which modulation occurs. Questions remain as to what other processes are available to signers. For example, under what conditions might a modulation involve the use of a new sign or a pantomime of the activity?

Here, too, the question of incorporation arises. Throughout this chapter, as well as other works, the assumption has been that real modulation meant collapsing the verb sign and adverb sign together to form a new modulated verb–adverb sign. Is this, in fact, the case? When signers are given the choice, do adverbs disappear altogether if the verb is modulated to add the meaning of the adverb? Or is the adverb retained? Presumably, if the adverb is retained, there are again two possibilities for its production—either citation form or a modulated form much like that of the verb. When discussing incorporation of manner, Fischer and Gough use examples other than verbs. Modulations on the sign LARGE, for instance, can be glossed as "pretty large," "very large," "enormous." Therefore, the option of modulating the adverb, with or without modulation of the verb, is certainly available in ASL.

These questions will be dealt with in the following study.

EXPERIMENTAL METHOD

Twenty verbs were chosen from the first 100 listed in an English word frequency list (Kucera & Francis, 1967). Ten were designated as transitive and 10 as intransitive.[6] Criteria for selection were (a) approximate equivalence of high frequency in ASL; (b) limit of one sign equivalent in ASL; (c) capability (in English and ASL) of adverbial modification for intensity, duration, frequency. Many stative verbs can be modified for duration; however, as Fischer and Gough note, reduplication is probably not the process by which this is conveyed in ASL. Also, an attempt was made to choose a fair sample of highly iconic verbs, though this was not done systematically.

Verbs chosen were:

Intransitive	Transitive
CHANGE	CONTROL
PLAY	HELP
RUN	LIKE
SIT	LOOK-FOR
STAND	PLAN
STUDY	REMEMBER
TALK	READ
WALK	SHOW
WORK	USE
WRITE	WANT

For each verb, seven sentences were constructed. All sentences were in simple past tense, and almost all with first-person singular *I* in the subject position. Use of the first-person singular avoided any possible interference by modulations for plurality or directionality.

The first sentence for each verb was a noun-plus-verb construction with no adverbial modifiers for intensity, duration, or frequency. This sentence was used to establish subjects' citation forms for each verb tested. Each subsequent sentence included an adverbial modifier, one for each of the aspect features, that is, small degree, large degree, short

---

[6] Many of the verbs chosen can be either transitive or intransitive. However, the test materials constructed designate 10 verbs in each category.

time, long time, sporadic occurrence, and habitual occurrence. Using RUN as an example, the following seven sentences were used:

(8)   *I ran yesterday* (citation form)

(9)   *I ran slowly yesterday* (small degree)

(10)   *I ran quickly yesterday* (large degree)

(11)   *I ran for a short time yesterday* (short time)

(12)   *I ran for a long time yesterday* (long time)

(13)   *I sometimes ran to school* (sporadic occurrence)

(14)   *I always ran to school* (habitual occurrence)

The adverbials *for a short time* and *for a long time* were used in all test verbs for marking duration. The adverbials *sometimes* and *always* were used in all test verbs for marking frequency. Adverbials of intensity, on the other hand, are dependent upon the semantic content of the verb. Therefore, they vary throughout the test cases from *a little bit* versus *a lot* for the verbs CHANGE, PLAY, WORK, among others, to *slowly* versus *quickly* for such action verbs as SHOW, WALK, RUN. Although *quickly* and *slowly* can denote length of time, in the case of action verbs they are more indicative of the intensity with which the action occurred.

The first sentences (unmodified) for each verb ($N = 20$) were randomly ordered, followed by the remaining 6 sentences (modified) for each verb ($N = 120$) randomly ordered, for a total of 140 sentences.

Procedure

Ten subjects were chosen—five hearing and five deaf, all of whom were native signers. They ranged in age from 19 to 31 years, and the average age was 24.7 years.

A brief interview was held with each subject to determine age, state in which ASL was learned, and any dialectical differences in lexicon from that of the author, as well as to derive the subject's citation forms for all adverbials used in the test sentences. Each subject was then given a script of the 140 sentences printed in English and asked to translate all into ASL.[7] All subjects were videotaped during the exercise.

---

[7] The advantages and disadvantages of the "back translation" method of investigation for ASL have already been well documented (Tweney & Hoemann, 1973; Stokoe, 1973;

The author then analyzed the videotapes to identify variations from the subjects' citation forms of each verb and adverb tested. Variations were categorized in terms of (a) the use of a modulated form as opposed to the citation form; (b) the use of a new lexical item to convey the same information (e.g., the use of REALLY to convey "a lot" in the translation of "I liked him a lot"); (c) the use of pantomime to convey the same information (e.g., in the translation of "I showed him the picture for a short time"). The criteria for determination of modulation included any reduplication of the citation form; any change in the speed of production, size of production, and strength of production; or any combination of these.

RESULTS—USAGE

In this study, the 10 subjects were given a total of 1200 opportunities (10 subjects × 120 adverbially modified test sentences) to demonstrate the relationship between verbs and aspect adverbials. The analysis shows that of these 1200 opportunities, 694 cases demonstrate the interaction between the verb and aspect adverb to be so high that the combination results in a new sign production. As just mentioned, the new sign production occurred through modulation of either verb or adverbial, new lexical items added, pantomime, or omissions. See Figure 5.2.

The other 506 cases resulted in no change of any kind to the citation forms of the verbs and adverbs tested. For example, the test sentence

(15)   *I sometimes ran to school*

was translated by subjects in 8 out of 10 cases as ME-RUN-SCHOOL-SOMETIMES,[8] where RUN and SOMETIMES were both in citation form. The interaction of RUN and SOMETIMES did not influence the production of either sign. However, in the other two cases, subjects modulated RUN to incorporate information about sporadic occurrence (i.e., "sometimes") by changing the movement from one that was continuous to one that was restrained, signing:

Smeltz, 1975). Clearly, free discourse is the optimal method for studying real performance of native signers. One could posit that the results in a study using the back translation method, then, are probably quite conservative with respect to actual usage of ASL.

[8] The sign order often varied from this sample according to what seemed to be the subject's arbitrary choice of emphasis. While some interesting data regarding sign order were inadvertently collected in this study, no analysis will be undertaken here.

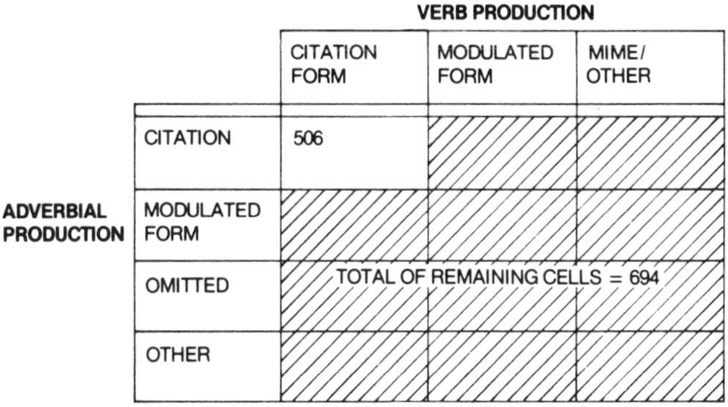

VERB PRODUCTION

		CITATION FORM	MODULATED FORM	MIME / OTHER
ADVERBIAL PRODUCTION	CITATION	506		
	MODULATED FORM			
	OMITTED	TOTAL OF REMAINING CELLS = 694		
	OTHER			

Figure 5.2. Summary of verb–adverbial sign production.

(16)   ME RUN [+ sporadic occurrence] SCHOOL SOMETIMES

The large number of cases where new sign production occurs is indicative of the extent to which overt aspect marking is possible in ASL. It appears that the question of option versus rule can best be answered by an analysis of type of verb and specific aspect feature. Here, marking of verbs was analyzed only, with no attention to performance of the adverbial.

Intransitive verbs were marked much more frequently than were transitive verbs [$F(1, 8) = 41.60, p < .0001$]. Additionally, hearing and deaf subjects did not differ in performance in any significant way for this category (see Table 5.1).

Significant differences in marking occurred according to the type of adverbial modifier [$F(2,16) = 23.05, p < .0001$]. Intensity and duration were marked in the verb much more often than frequency. Addition-

TABLE 5.1

Frequency of Aspect Marking for Verbs
by Deaf and Hearing Subjects

	Verbs	
Subjects	Intransitive	Transitive
Deaf	163	107
Hearing	160	100
Total	323	207

ally, little difference in performance between intensity adverbs and duration adverbs resulted (see Table 5.2).

TABLE 5.2

Frequency of Aspect Marking of Verbs by Adverbial

	Number of times verb marked
Adverbials	
Intensity	207
Duration	209
Frequency	114

The interaction between type of verb and type of adverbial was also significant [$F(2, 16) = 7.84, p < .004$]. In this case, the difference in marking for duration was most conspicuous (see Table 5.3).

TABLE 5.3

Frequency of Aspect Marking according to Verb and Adverbial Type

	Verbs	
	Intransitive	Transitive
Adverbials		
Intensity	119	88
Duration	134	75
Frequency	70	44

It is interesting to note that overall frequency of marking is almost exactly the same for intensity and duration, whereas in the analysis by verb type, duration is marked more frequently with intransitive verbs than is intensity.

Earlier, the question was asked as to which end of the aspect feature continuum might be more frequently marked. Other studies had not mentioned possibilities of marking for "short time" or for sporadic occurrence. In the schema shown in Figure 5.1, each end of the marker continuum was labeled as a theoretical feature of ASL (e.g., small degree and large degree for the aspect feature intensity). For purposes of clarity, the generic term *extent* will be used here to denote the continua that exist for all three aspect features. *Extent* can in turn be broken down into its polar features small (S) and large (L) (see Figure 5.3). These terms will be used in the following analysis.

The S and L features for each aspect feature were analyzed to

EXTENT CONTINUUM	
SMALL (S)	LARGE (L)

ASPECT FEATURE	
INTENSITY	SMALL DEGREE ←——————→ LARGE DEGREE
DURATION	SHORT TIME ←——————→ LONG TIME
FREQUENCY	SPORADIC OCCURRENCE ←——————→ HABITUAL OCCURRENCE

Figure 5.3. Extent continuum.

determine any differences in frequency. The results show that L is marked much more frequently than is S regardless of verb type or adverbial type [$F(1, 8) = 69.77$, $p < .0001$] (see Table 5.4).

Frequency by verb type indicates that again L is marked more often than S for each type of verb and that intransitives are marked more frequently generally. The specific difference by verb type is not as impressive as some of the above categories, but it is still significant [$F(1, 8) = 6.14$, $p < .038$].

Finally, frequency by adverbial type points out some interesting differences. The interaction is significant [$F(2, 16) = 6.02$, $p < .011$] and the figures show that L-Duration is most frequently marked, followed by L-Intensity and then S-Intensity and L-Frequency (see Table 5.5).

In all of the above categories, analysis of variance showed no difference in performance between deaf and hearing subjects. Also, all analyses concentrated on marking that occurred within the verb rather than the adverbial.

Table 5.6 shows a breakdown of the specific interaction of verb and

TABLE 5.4

Frequency of Aspect Marking according to Verb Type and Extent Feature

	Verbs	
	Intransitive	Transitive
Extent feature		
S	115	77
L	208	130

TABLE 5.5

Frequency of Aspect Marking according to Extent Feature
and Adverbial Type

	Adverbial type		
	Intensity	Duration	Frequency
Extent feature			
S	90	77	25
L	117	132	89

TABLE 5.6

Marking Frequency by Interaction of Verb Production with Adverbial Production[a]

	Verb production		
	Citation form	Modulated form	Pantomime or other lexical item
Adverbial production			
Citation form	506 (1)	315 (2)	18 (3)
Modulated form	108 (4)	90 (5)	2 (6)
Omitted	16 (7)	98 (8)	12 (9)
Other lexical item	27 (10)	7 (11)	1 (12)

[a] Numbers in parentheses refer to the cell. These numbers are referred to in the
discussion.

adverbial production. As noted above, verb citation with adverbial
citation (Cell 1) most frequently occurs. As approximately ⅔ of the
cases with transitive verbs received no overt marking, it is again
transitive verbs that comprise the majority of cases in Cell 1. The next
highest frequency is that of verb modulated with adverbial citation
(Cell 2). Earlier the question was asked as to what would happen to
the adverbial in cases where the verb was modulated to incorporate
aspect information. The large difference between Cells 2 and 8 tells
us that the adverbial rarely disappears completely, therefore modulation does not seem to mean a real collapsing of verb and adverbial into
an altogether new sign. When the verb is modulated, the adverbial is
most commonly retained in citation form (Cell 2, $N = 315$), and
sometimes it is modulated as well (Cell 5, $N = 90$). This result has
interesting implications for how redundancy occurs in ASL. Cell 11
($N = 7$) shows the rarity of occurrence of adding a new lexical item
in place of the adverbial.

There appear to be very few occasions when pantomime or use of a
new lexical item is necessary for the verb production. Use of pan-

tomime in place of the sign SHOW comprises most of the cases in Cells 3 and 9, particularly for marking of intensity (i.e., "I showed him the picture quickly," "I showed him the picture slowly") and for S-Duration (i.e., "I showed him the picture for a short time").

It also appears that modulation of the adverbial with verb production in citation form (Cell 4) is often preferable to modulation of both adverbial and verb (Cell 5). When deaf and hearing subjects were compared, there appeared to be much more adverbial marking done by deaf subjects than by hearing subjects (deaf = 69, hearing = 39). Particularly in cases of verbs where modulation almost never occurred (e.g., LIKE, USE, REMEMBER), more deaf subjects tended to modulate the adverbial for effect. Cases of adverbial omissions or replacement with new lexical items were rare with citation form verbs (Cells 7 and 10). An instance where omission was possible seemed to be with the adverbial SOMETIMES. In this case, subjects might tentatively (as opposed to definitively) nod their heads for the same effect. It should be noted here that extensive analysis of changes in facial expression might shed additional light on marking of aspect.

The few cases where test adverbials were replaced by new adverbials were A-LOT and FOR-A-LONG-TIME, which changed to VERY-MUCH and SINCE, respectively.

Restrictions and Processes

Figure 5.4 shows the relative frequencies of marking for each verb.

In general, categorizing by transitive versus intransitive verb does elicit some information about adverbial influence over verbs. Intransitives are clearly marked more frequently than transitives. However, the results are inconclusive for generalizing until further study is done with those verbs that can function as either transitive or intransitive— for example, READ, WRITE, or CHANGE. Special attention should be given to the verb SHOW. Because of its pantomimic nature, it appears that SHOW functions as an intransitive verb. This might account for its high frequency of marking. In most cases for marking L-Duration, S-Duration, L-Intensity, and S-Intensity with SHOW, subjects resorted to pantomime. A pantomime in each case consisted of incorporation of the object (i.e., PICTURE). Additionally, SHOW was the only point-action verb tested and as such lends itself to easy marking for L-Frequency through reduplication.

As Fischer and Gough note, durative action verbs could be reduplicated, but stative verbs could not. This distinction is certainly a good starting point for analysis of marking. Figure 5.4 shows that all verbs with a marking frequency above 30 are, in fact, durative action verbs.

VERB TYPE

NO. OF VARIATIONS	INTRANSITIVE	TRANSITIVE
60		
45	PLAY CHANGE RUN	SHOW READ
30	SIT TALK WORK STUDY WRITE WALK STAND	LOOK-FOR WANT
15		HELP PLAN CONTROL REMEMBER USE
1		LIKE

Figure 5.4. Frequencies of marking for individual verbs. (Note that number of variations refers to the number of times each verb was marked for aspect, whether by pantomime, modulation, or an additional lexical item.)

Those below 30 are mostly stative. The exceptions (WALK, STAND, USE) must be analyzed differently.

Perhaps the most productive category for analysis is the type of movement used for each verb. Earlier, mention was made of the Supalla and Newport paradigm for frequency, manner, and direction of movement. Manner was divided into the categories of hold, restrained, and continuous. With the exceptions of SHOW and SIT all verbs with a marking frequency above 30 in Figure 5.4 are produced with either a continuous manner or have repeated frequency. Those below 30 in Figure 5.4 are for the most part produced with a hold manner and have single frequency. Direction (either unidirectional or bidirectional) does not appear to be a workable category for analysis, since examples of both appear equally above and below a marking frequency of 30.

In terms of the processes of modulation, categories of movement are certainly the most workable. While quantitative analysis was not undertaken for processes of modulation, some general trends are evident. In marking for L-Duration and L-Frequency, those verbs having continuous manner or repeated frequency were most often reduplicated (e.g., PLAY, CHANGE, RUN, TALK, READ, LOOK-FOR, WRITE, WORK, TALK). Those verbs having hold manner or single frequency were most often modulated by a change in speed of the sign. For example, WANT, LIKE, and REMEMBER were modulated for these features by slowing down the production. In all cases, additional and radical change in facial expression occurred—squinting of the eyes being the most notable.

Marking for S-Frequency and S-Duration did not occur nearly as often as for their L counterparts. However, when modulation occurred, an interesting change in the manner of movement resulted. For those verbs having continuous manner, subjects most commonly used a restrained manner in modulation. The example of RUN has already been mentioned. Others include TALK, PLAY, WRITE, and READ. This finding is interesting in light of Supalla and Newport's finding of only one verb in their lexicon that is produced with restrained manner in citation form. Perhaps restrained manner is then reserved for those cases where modulation for S-Frequency and S-Duration can occur.

Modulation for both features was virtually nonexistent for verbs having hold manner. In these cases (e.g., STAND, LIKE, REMEMBER) one must look to the adverbial. Quite often, the adverbial (i.e., SOMETIMES, FOR-A-SHORT-TIME) is modulated by an increase in speed.

One notable exception in this analysis is the verb WORK. Supalla and Newport classify WORK as having hold manner but repeated frequency. However, it appears that WORK behaves much like verbs having continuous manner. Perhaps this discrepancy is due to a difference in citation form production between that of the subjects and Supalla and Newport. Regardless, the frequency of the movement is probably a more important factor here. In all cases of continuous manner, those verbs that are repeated in their citation form (e.g., TALK, PLAY, READ, LOOK-FOR, WORK, WALK) changed to a single movement when modulated for S-Duration and S-Frequency. Thus, although frequency in movement does not appear to be a determining factor in marking, it is changed in the results of marking.

Marking for intensity (either S or L) appears to occur only through a change in size or strength of a given sign. Speed does not appear to play any role here. As could be expected, marking for S-Intensity results in a decrease in strength and size of the sign. Apparently, verbs having continuous manner and those having hold manner do not differ in this respect. Also, marking for L-Intensity results in an increase in strength and size of the given sign. For both features (S and L), a difference in the size of the sign is possible, but modulation is more readily evident in a difference in the strength of the sign, corresponding to Frishberg's (1972) two movement categories of "sharp" and "soft."

Therefore, in order to understand marking by feature and the resulting modulation, a new category, that is, manner of movement, needs to be added to the original paradigm shown in Figure 5.1. Figure 5.5 is an expanded paradigm of the features and processes of modulation. In general, it can be stated that when marking occurs the following unordered rules are at work:

A. *L-Duration, L-Frequency*
    RULE 1: *If manner is* **continuous,** *change to* **repeated** *frequency (reduplication).*[9]
    RULE 2: *If manner is* **hold,** *change to slow speed of production.*
B. *S-Duration, S-Frequency*
    RULE 1: *If manner is* **continuous** *and frequency is* **repeated,** *change to* **restrained** *manner and* **single** *frequency.*[10]
    RULE 2: *If manner is* **hold,** *do not modulate.*

    [9] This rule implies that verbs that are repeated in citation form are also repeated in modulation form and that the number of repetitions increases.
    [10] This rule implies that verbs that have single frequency in citation form also have single frequency in modulation form.

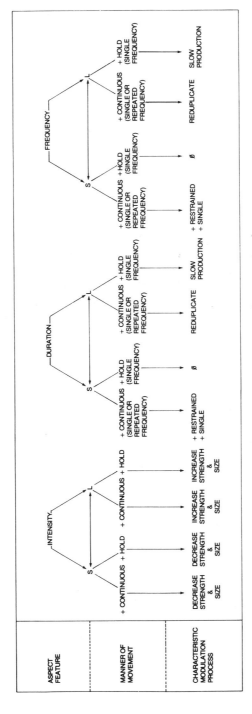

Figure 5.5. Modulation paradigm for aspect marking.

C. *L-Intensity*
     RULE 1: *If manner is* **continuous** *or* **hold,** *increase strength of sign.*
D. *S-Intensity*
     RULE 1: *If manner is* **continuous** *or* **hold,** *decrease strength of sign.*

Earlier it was noted that in almost all cases, the adverbial was retained regardless of production form of the verb. Also when the verb was in citation form and the adverbial was modulated, the majority of the cases were transitive verbs. The opposite alternative—that is, when verb is modulated and adverbial is in citation form—occurred most frequently with intransitive verbs. Figure 5.6 shows the overall frequency of corresponding adverbial modulation for each verb. In general, it appears that where verbs are frequently modulated, the corresponding adverbials are relatively infrequently modulated. The most striking example is that of PLAY. This verb has a high frequency of modulation, whereas its corresponding adverbials, taking all features together, have the lowest frequency of modulation. The same tendency is evident for the verbs RUN, CHANGE, READ, and SHOW.

The converse, verbs with low frequency of modulation while corresponding adverbials have relatively high frequency of modulation, is also evident. For example, LIKE, USE, and REMEMBER are rarely modulated. However, the adverbials matched with these verbs are more often modulated.

Further study may elicit more information with respect to the behavior of the adverbial in the light of aspect feature variability. On the surface, it appears that the combinations of L-Duration and L-Frequency often result in verb modulation with adverbial citation. Also, S- and L-Intensity often results in verb citation with adverbial modulation.

The two features of L-Duration and L-Intensity are quite variable, however, and often appear to be in the category verb modulation with adverbial modulation as well. Figure 5.7 shows a very tentative paradigm with respect to general trends in aspect marking. The data from this study indicate differences in the verb–adverbial relationship based upon specific aspect feature. However, a larger sample of both verbs and subjects should result in more conclusive findings. It is important to note here that the interaction of verb and adverbial by aspect feature resulted in productions in each of the four possible

VERB TYPE

NO. OF VARIATIONS	INTRANSITIVE		TRANSITIVE	
	VERB MODULATION	ADVERBIAL MODULATION	VERB MODULATION	ADVERBIAL MODULATION
60				
45			SHOW	
	PLAY CHANGE			
	RUN SIT TALK WORK STUDY	WORK	READ	
30	WRITE WALK		LOOK-FOR	
			WANT	
	STAND	TALK, WALK WRITE, STUDY RUN, CHANGE STAND, SIT	HELP PLAN	WANT, CONTROL LOOK-FOR USE, PLAN, REMEMBER SHOW
15		PLAY		HELP READ
			CONTROL	LIKE
			REMEMBER USE	
1			LIKE	

Figure 5.6. Verb and corresponding adverbial modulation frequencies.

VERB PRODUCTION

		CITATION	MODULATION
ADVERBIAL PRODUCTION	CITATION	S-FREQUENCY S-DURATION (1)	L-DURATION L-FREQUENCY (2)
	MODULATION	S + L−INTENSITY (3)	L-DURATION L-INTENSITY (4)

Figure 5.7. Interaction in production by aspect feature.

categories above (Cells 1–4), however *tendencies* of production are reflected in Figure 5.7.

Examination of the polar features, S and L, for each aspect adverbial showed that large extent (L) was more frequently marked than small extent (S). Analysis by specific feature indicates a scale of "choosiness" for marking. In general, marking for L-Duration can occur for all verbs tested. However, the features become increasingly more "choosy" as to which verbs are satisfactory for marking. L-Duration is less "choosy" than is L-Intensity, which in turn is less "choosy" than S-Intensity, L-Frequency, S-Duration, and finally S-Frequency. The order of aspect features by frequency is the same regardless of verb type.

Reasons for this ordering are unclear. The spatial nature of ASL lends itself to much greater specificity with respect to representations of time than does an oral language. It is feasible as well that "long time" representation is more visually discriminable than is "short time." Testing for production time of S-Duration might elicit more refined modulations of citation forms than were discernible to the author. As noted in the introduction, reduplication, the modulation process by which L-Duration is shown, is a more stylized, more easily defined process. The other processes of modulation in the cases of S- and L-Intensity are considerably more ambiguous visually. Differences in strength or size of a sign must be dramatic in order to characterize them as modulations.

In the case of S-Frequency, modulations were so rare as to suggest a rule of nonmarking. It is feasible that sporadic occurrence of any one activity is more often the norm than is habitual occurrence, therefore the interaction of a verb and the adverbial SOMETIMES comes closest to the citation form of the sign.

SUMMARY

Analysis of the results showed that the interaction between verbs and aspect adverbials commonly brought about new sign production. The new sign production was most frequently in the form of a modulation to the citation form of either the verb or adverbial. Modulations were executed by way of reduplication, change in manner of movement, size, speed, or strength of movement.

General marking for aspect did not appear to be so extensive as to suggest a rule in ASL; however, fairly conservative results could be expected given the use of a back translation method and the limited context provided in the test sentences, that is, the fact that test items were not in discourse.

Analysis by verb type and by specific aspect feature sheds more light on the question of rule versus option. Nine out of 10 intransitive verbs tested were modulated more than 50% of the time. Results were significant in demonstrating a higher frequency of modulation for intransitive verbs than for transitive verbs. The interaction of verb type with adverbial type was also significant: intransitive duration was most frequently marked, followed by intransitive intensity, transitive intensity, transitive duration, intrasitive frequency, and transitive frequency. In general, duration and intensity were marked equally often, whereas frequency was much less often marked.

No differences in performance between deaf and hearing subjects for any of the above categories resulted. This finding is significant in light of the fact that more extensive exposure to English syntax in the case of hearing subjects had no influence whatsoever on aspect marking in ASL.

In terms of semantic or phonological restrictions on marking, it appears that stative verbs are much less frequently marked than are durative action verbs. However, the phonological restriction of manner of movement is more fruitful in predicting marking differences. In almost all cases, the stative verbs chosen are executed with hold manner. Conversely, the durative action verbs are executed with continuous manner or are repeated. Analysis of the modulation process used for each aspect feature suggested a set of rules for marking. Marking for S-Intensity and L-Intensity occurred through a decrease and increase, respectively, in the strength of the sign. Size differences appeared to be a second option in each case.

Marking for S-Duration occurred in general for verbs executed with continuous manner. When marking occurred, the manner changed to restrained. Marking for L-Duration occurred through reduplication for verbs executed with continuous manner and through slow speed of production for verbs executed with hold manner.

Finally, marking for S-Frequency, though very rare, did occur with verbs executed with continuous manner. In this case, modulation was brought about through a change to restrained manner. Hold manner verbs were not modulated. L-Frequency was marked by reduplication for continuous manner verbs and by slow speed of production for hold manner verbs.

It is noteworthy that the original analysis by Fischer and Gough distinguished between slow and fast reduplication when discussing continuous aspect and habitual aspect, respectively. The data from this study did not suggest any syntactical distinction whatsoever between the two processes of modulation. Instead, the rate of reduplication appeared to be more dependent upon the subject's imagined context and his or her attitude toward it. If RUN-FOR-A-LONG-TIME was slowly reduplicated, the subject imagined the activity as a boring one. In other words, the results were so variable that the speed of reduplication seems to be an attitudinal factor only.

Iconicity does not seem to play a role in analysis of marking. It happened that the most iconic verbs (STAND, SIT, READ) received relatively infrequent marking. Manner of movement again appears to be the determining factor. SHOW was the most pantomimic verb chosen and received the highest frequency of marking. It appeared that SHOW functioned as an intransitive verb in the cases where it was pantomimed. This result suggests the need for further study of other highly pantomimic verbs. It is feasible that the high frequency of marking that occurred with SHOW is indicative that other point action and pantomimic verbs satisfy conditions for marking in general.

The adverbial rarely disappears when marking of the verb occurs. It is often retained in citation form for the features of L-Duration and L-Frequency. It is often modulated for the features of S- and L-Intensity, even when the verb is most commonly in citation form. Also, "double" marking often occurs for the features of L-Duration and L-Intensity where both the verb and adverbial are modulated. The results led to a tentative paradigm for predicting adverbial and verb production based upon specific aspect feature. Further quantitative analysis is needed to determine more precise interaction between the two for production. However, these general tendencies indicate that redundancy is a consideration in ASL when marking aspect.

Also, overall frequencies for marking of verbs and corresponding adverbials suggest general rules of production. Verbs most easily modulated will have corresponding adverbials in citation form, and conversely, verbs least easily modulated will require corresponding adverbials in modulation form where possible. Again, in the majority of cases, the co-occurrence of verb and adverbial in citation form is apparently not sufficient for marking aspect. Some other and redundant marking seems necessary.

In sum, marking for aspect in ASL is not only possible but probable. Rather than clarifying aspect as separate lexical items, as in English, ASL adverbials influence verb production overtly through a series of fairly systematic processes of modulation. In turn, the adverbial is influenced by the type of verb in its own production—whether in citation or modulation form. Investigation of the specific aspect features—that is, intensity, duration, and frequency—indicates wide variability in marking in ASL, extensive enough to suggest grammatical regularities, although such regularities are dependent upon polar feature and type of verb.

REFERENCES

Bellugi, U., Fischer, S. A comparison of sign language and spoken language: Rate and grammatical mechanisms, *Cognition*, 1972, *1*, 173–200.

Fischer, S. D. Two processes of reduplication in the American Sign Language. In *Foundations of Language*, 9, March, 1973.

Fischer, S. D., & Gough, B. *Verbs in American Sign Language*, in press.

Fowler, Roger *Understanding Language*, Routledge and Kregan Paul Ltd., London, 1974.

Friedman, Lynn On the semantics of space, time, and person reference in American Sign Language, *Language*, 1975. *51*, 940–961.

Frishberg, Nancy Sharp and soft: Two aspects of movement in sign, working paper, 1972.

Hausmann, R. B. A transformational analysis of English tense and time adverbs, Unpublished Ph.D. dissertation, Univ. of Wisconsin, 1972.

Hirtle, W. H. *The simple and the progressive forms: An analytical approach*, Presses de l'Université, Laval, Quebec, 1967.

Hirtle, W. H. Time aspect and the verb, Presses de l'Université. Laval, Quebec, 1975.

Kucera, Henry, & Francis, W. Nelson *Computational analysis of present-day American English*, Brown Univ. Press, Providence, 1967.

Macaulay, R. K. S. Aspect in English, Unpublished Ph.D. dissertation, Univ. of California, Los Angeles, 1971.

Smeltz, Johnny K. Some sociological-linguistic aspects of the American Sign Language of the deaf, Unpublished Ph.D. dissertation, Georgetown Univ., Washington, D. C., 1975.

Stokoe, William C., Jr. Sign language structure: An outline of the visual communication systems of the American deaf. In *Studies in linguistics, occasional papers, 8*, Buffalo, New York, 1960.

Stokoe, William C., Jr.,Casterline, D.,& Cronenberg, C. *A dictionary of American Sign Language on linguistic principles*, Gallaudet College Press, Washington, D. C., 1965.

Stokoe, William C., Jr. Comments on back translation, *Sign Language Studies, 1973, 2*, 73–76.

Tweney, Ryan D., & Hoemann, Harry Back translation: A method for the analysis of manual languages, *Sign Language Studies*, 1973, 2, 51–72.

Woodward, James C. Implicational lects on the deaf diglossic continuum, Unpublished Ph.D. dissertation, Georgetown Univ., Washington, D. C., 1973.

III

NEUROLINGUISTIC
STUDIES

6

Studies of Linguistic Behavior in Apes and Children

ROGER FOUTS
GARY SHAPIRO
CHARITY O'NEIL[1]

University of Oklahoma

INTRODUCTION

This chapter will review much of the recent experimentation involving human–chimpanzee conmunication as well as some similar studies involving other higher primates. Other reviews of this sort (Fouts, 1975a,b; Fouts & Rigby, 1975) have covered the historical aspects prior to the successful attempts to promote two-way communication between apes and man. Rather than recapitulate the historical details, we will concentrate our discussion on the work that has not been reviewed extensively as well as current and proposed research.

We will start our discussion with the work of the Hayeses, which was certainly the most successful experimental attempt to train a chimpanzee to speak. Their success was relatively insignificant, however, when compared with the achievements of the Gardners, who decided to abandon the vocal–auditory modality of communication in favor of a visual one.

The main emphasis of the chapter will involve the research that has

---

[1] Order of authorship determined by toss of coin.

UNDERSTANDING LANGUAGE
THROUGH
SIGN LANGUAGE RESEARCH

163

recently been completed at the Institute for Primate Studies. The experiments to be covered will fall under the headings of psycholinguistics, sociolinguistics, and cultural linguistics. The last section of the chapter will discuss additional chimpanzee linguistic research, ongoing and proposed studies, as well as work with other higher primates including human children.

HISTORICAL PERSPECTIVE

During the first half of this century, several respected scientists struggled vainly to evoke human speech from chimpanzees (Kellogg & Kellogg, 1967). The final and most exhaustive project of this nature was conducted by Keith and Catherine Hayes (1951, 1952; C. Hayes, 1951; K. Hayes & Nissen, 1971), who reared a female chimpanzee, Viki, in their home for more than 6 years. Viki learned to produce only four spoken words, *mama*, *papa*, *cup*, and *up*, and her pronunciation of these words was largely voiceless. The common conclusion of the scientific world was that the chimpanzee was incapable of language. Lack of speech was thus equated with lack of language abilities.

In the 1960s, Lieberman undertook a comparative morphological scrutiny of the vocal apparatus of chimpanzees and humans (Lieberman, 1968; Lieberman, Crelin, & Klatt, 1972). He discovered that the chimpanzee is incapable of human speech for anatomical reasons. The supralaryngeal vocal tract of *Pan troglodytes* is quite different from that of *Homo sapiens*, both in position and in configuration. Furthermore, the chimpanzee tongue lacks the mobility of the human tongue and is incapable of changing the shape of the vocal tract to produce certain human speech sounds. Interestingly enough, the supralaryngeal vocal tract of the human neonate appears comparable to that of the adult chimpanzee; it, too, is incapable of producing the vowel sounds that mark the first stage toward production of human speech. Spectrographic analysis indicates that the cries of the human neonate are strikingly similar to those of other young primates.

The problem of attempting to teach chimpanzees to vocalize in the same fashion as humans do becomes even more obvious after prolonged observation of chimpanzee vocal behavior. Chimpanzees are, for the most part, quiet. They vocalize in rather specific situations (eating, greeting, etc.) and in highly stereotyped sound patterns. Vocalizations are largely emotive in nature and subject to environmental control.

Robert Yerkes demonstrated great foresight with regard to language abilities in chimpanzees. In *Almost Human* (1927) he stated: "I am inclined to conclude from the various evidences that the great apes have plenty to talk about, but no gift for the use of sounds to represent individual, as contrasted to racial, feelings or ideas. Perhaps they can be taught to use their fingers, somewhat as does the deaf and dumb person, and helped to acquire a simple, nonvocal 'sign language' [p. 180]." Drs. Beatrice and Allan Gardner of the University of Nevada were the first to take seriously the approach that Yerkes had long since suggested. They had viewed the films of Viki and had been struck by the highly gesticulative nature of Viki's behavior as she attempted to utter each word. In fact, they seemed to understand her much better when they turned down the sound on the projector and simply watched her gestures. They decided to teach a nonvocal language to a chimpanzee, and they chose a language that is used by a significant population of Americans—American Sign Language, or Ameslan. Ameslan is a gestural language that employs a syntax analogous to that of spoken English (Stokoe, Casterline, & Croneberg, 1965). A compelling reason for using Ameslan was that chimpanzees naturally communicate gesturally both in the wild (van Lawick-Goodall, 1968; Kortlandt, 1967) and in captivity (Yerkes, 1943; Schenkel, 1964; van Hooff, 1971). Furthermore, chimpanzee hands are subject to rather fine motor coordination (Witmer, 1909; Kohts, 1935; Hayes & Hayes, 1952; Riesen & Kinder, 1952).

The Gardners initiated "Project Washoe" in 1966, when they acquired a wild-caught female chimpanzee between the ages of 8 and 14 months whom they named Washoe (Gardner & Gardner, 1969, 1971). Washoe was reared at the Gardners' home in Reno, Nevada, where she had her own house trailer in their back yard. Her environment was enriched, as compared with that of the typical captive chimpanzee, by human companionship during all of her waking hours. Her companions communicated exclusively in Ameslan in her presence, and they continually conversed with her in this mode. The Gardners observed very little manual babbling by Washoe during the first months of the project, but after a few months babbling seemed to increase in frequency. After the second year of the project, manual babbling was rare. The Gardners felt that this decline was probably a function of Washoe's accelerating sign vocabulary; the signs began to replace the babbling.

Washoe acquired individual signs by imitating the human signs around her just as do human children. She was taught some signs by molding her hands into the correct form in the presence of the appropriate referent. Washoe also acquired several signs simply through observational learning. Immersed in an environment of sign language, Washoe occasionally acquired a sign after several months' exposure to it but without any concerted effort by the research team to teach it: These signs, then, were spontaneously acquired by Washoe. Washoe's vocabulary and sign usage were systematically recorded by the research team. When she was tested under double-blind conditions, her vocabulary errors fit into conceptually related categories; for example, if the referent was an animal, her errors usually took the form of other animal signs.

Vocabulary size, however, is not the most salient feature of language, in human or chimpanzee. Washoe's sign combinations were much more interesting and important and she began to produce signed sequences by the time she had a vocabulary of 8 or 10 signs. Her combinations proved to be used in contextually correct situations (e.g., *key open please blanket* to have locked blanket cupboard opened), and she evidenced a preference for sign order that can be interpreted as demonstrating a syntactical capacity on her part. Using a method similar to that proposed by Brown (1970) for children's utterances, the Gardners analyzed Washoe's two-sign sequences. They found that Washoe's earliest two-sign combinations were comparable to the earliest two-word combinations of human children in terms of semantic classes and expressed meanings.

Washoe's combinations were segmented in much the same fashion that human signers segment their combinations. She would keep her hands raised in the signing space until she had completed a sequence and would often terminate a sequence by contacting or handling an object or surface, comparable to a human signer's hands in repose.

Project Washoe was terminated in 1970, when Roger Fouts brought Washoe to the Institute of Primate Studies in Norman, Oklahoma. At this point, Washoe had a vocabulary of approximately 130 signs. The Gardners (1975) have since begun a project involving the rearing from birth of two chimpanzees by researchers who are deaf or whose parents are deaf.

The Institute for Primate Studies is directed by Dr. W. B. Lemmon and houses a large colony of chimpanzees. The institute's facilities have provided an excellent opportunity to expand Ameslan teaching to other chimpanzees. In addition to the chimpanzees at the institute, several chimpanzees are being raised in human homes in the Norman area, and some have been taught sign language.

One of the first studies completed here (Fouts, 1973) examined whether chimpanzees other than Washoe could acquire signs. All four chimpanzee subjects acquired all 10 of the signs attempted, and distinct individual differences in acquisition were apparent. Since this study, signs have been taught to several other chimpanzees, and studies of the linguistic and conceptual abilities of chimpanzees are ongoing. Some of the linguistic studies that are particularly appropriate to this volume are described in the following sections.

COMPLETED LINGUISTIC STUDIES

Although the linguistic research completed at the institute has involved several chimpanzees, one in particular has been involved in more signing or sign-related projects than any other chimpanzee to our knowledge. For that reason it is appropriate to mention a few things about his background. Ali (formerly spelled Ally in other publications) was born at the Institute for Primate Studies on October 15, 1969, and was taken from his natural mother on December 6, 1969. He was raised in a human home from then until he rejoined the chimpanzee colony at the institute in June 1974. Much of his early use as a subject involved the study of sign acquisition, but his value as a subject in many of the studies to be presented relies on his prerequisite signing ability. Ali has a sign language vocabulary of approximately 130 signs and a comprehension of English vocabulary at least equal to that.

Psycholinguistic Studies

Comprehension and Production

Fouts, Chown, Kimble, and Couch (1976) showed that a chimpanzee could respond correctly to signed commands (demonstrating comprehension) as well as respond correctly to spatial arrangements of objects by signing descriptive sequences of signs in Ameslan (demonstrating productivity [Hockett, 1958]). The subject, Ali, had a vocabulary of 88 reliable signs and was nearly 4 years of age at the beginning of this study.

Assessment of productive linguistic knowledge may be based on comprehension of constructions as well as on structure analysis of spontaneous communications. If a chimpanzee can comprehend the individual units of a linguistic system and the relationships among these constituents, it is probable that it successfully understands the linguistic system.

In the first experiment, Ali was instructed via a signed command either to put an object in a particular location or to give an object to a particular person. Ali was to select the objects from a box in order to ensure that the experimenter could not see the selection or influence Ali's choice. Training involved two groups. In Training Group 1, five common objects (flower, ball, doll, brush, and hat) were to be put in either of two locations (purse and box) or given to an experimenter (Larry). In Training Group 2, objects were kept selectively novel to specific places, so although Ali was to place common objects in both purse and box, he also had objects that were to be placed only at one specific location (e.g., leaf in box or toothbrush in purse). Objects to be given to Larry were those kept specific to box and purse (e.g., *Ali give Larry toothbrush*). Double-blind procedures were used during part of the training and all of the testing. This eliminated any cuing between experimenter and subject.

Results for both training groups showed that Ali scored well above chance (7%) for total commands correct (43% for mean in Training Group 1 and 55% for mean in Training Group 2). If the categories within the total commands are examined, Ali did much better with the object than with the location in both training groups (Training Group 1 mean correct: 84% for object, 52% for location; Training Group 2 mean correct: 87% for object, 55% for location).

Testing was conducted in two phases, Test 1 and Test 2. Fifty-eight commands were used during Test 1, 29 of which were identical to those used in training and 29 of which were new commands. In Group 1 of Test 1, an additional location (chair) was added to the commands used in Training Group 1. In Group 2 of Test 1, the objects used for specific locations in Training Group 2 were reversed (e.g., *put leaf in purse*). In addition, Ali was to put objects on the recessed seat of a chair. For Test 2, new commands included using additional experimenters (e.g., *give Roger toothbrush*), new objects with training locations (e.g., *put spoon in purse*), and totally novel combinations (e.g., *give Bill fruit*). Test commands were presented in a random order with the restriction that neither object nor location could be presented twice in succession.

Results show that for all commands in Test 1, Ali improved on object selection (98%) but decreased his performance for location (38%). This can be attributed to Ali's inability to respond to chair as a location. If chair was omitted, the location performance increased to 47% for all commands. In Test 2 Ali scored well with the object portion of the commands (92% correct; 20% is chance) and scored 67% correct (33% is chance) for location. Overall total commands correct was 61% (chance performance is 7%).

The second experiment was designed to demonstrate the active application or productive use of a syntactic system to express spatial relationships between objects in the environment. Such a system need not be complex, since the number of signs to express spatial relationships may be as few as three. The relationship is expressed by the order of the signs, or syntax, as well as by the functional meaning of the sign.

Ali, again the subject, was taught the relationships—*on, in,* and *under*—by first associating the specific preposition to the specific spatial relationship and later by asking him to describe the situation in Ameslan. The grammar of the requested response consisted of an ordered sequence: subject (which was an object such as ball), preposition (*in, on,* or *under*), and location (which was an object such as purse). Training consisted of teaching Ali to describe a variety of arranged objects. He would be shown the objects and then asked, "Where's X?" (X referring to the subject). If he did not respond or if his response was incorrect, he would be prompted or corrected by molding his hands in the proper fashion. Once Ali had described 8 out of 10 relationships correctly twice in a row for 3 days, he proceeded into testing. In testing he was required to describe spatial relationships utilizing novel as well as familiar objects as subjects and locations. Eighty trials were given per session and were arranged so that neither subject nor location occurred on consecutive trials.

Results of the experiment on productive use show that Ali learned to describe correctly the spatial relationships during training. During the first 9 days of training (Block 1), Ali on the average signed the preposition correctly on 49.1% of the trials (chance level is 33%). The percentage mean correct for the location was 29.3% (16.7% was chance). Totally correct responses for Block 1 had a mean of 18%. During Blocks 2 and 3, Ali's performance continued to improve. In Block 3, for example, Ali scored 84.3% mean correct responses for preposition and 61.6% mean correct for location. Overall mean correct response was 50.2%. In Block 4, Ali reached testing criterion with prepositions averaging 96% correct. In testing, Ali performed similarly to the last 10 days of training. There was a slight decrement in the percentage of prepositions correct (80% in testing; 87% in training); however, the locations and the total percentage of correct relationships stated were slightly higher in testing than in training (location: 68% in testing, 66% in training; total: 55.8% in testing, 55.6% in training). Responses to novel relationships were slightly lower than all relationships tested, but they were still far superior to chance response (preposition: 77% mean correct; location: 64% mean correct; and overall: 50% mean correct).

Frame (a)

Frame (b)

Figure 6.1(a–c). Ali describes the appropriate relationship (baby on pillow) to researcher George Kimball at the Institute for Primate Studies.

Frame (c)

The results of both experiments indicate that the chimpanzee can (a) understand and produce signed commands in sequences he has never seen before; and (b) master a simple syntactic system. In both experiments, the responses during testing approximated the performance generated during training. With the exception of a few commands that involved the chair in Experiment 1, Ali clearly demonstrated an ability to carry out correctly the actions specified by new commands. In Experiment 2, Ali showed he could describe relationships of various degrees of novelty by using the syntactic system he had learned (see Figure 6.1).

Because there were no restrictions on the possible responses he could sign, he had to construct each description completely on his own. All errors he did make were errors of naming within the relational category (e.g., *on* may have been used for *in*). Ali always ordered his signed sequence: subject–preposition–location, or preposition–location—that is, he never made a grammatical error.

Transferred Response from Vocal English to Ameslan

Chimpanzees raised in human homes generally comprehend a certain amount of the language spoken by their "parents." We conducted studies with two chimpanzees while they were in their human homes to investigate the relationship between their Ameslan vocabularies and their vocal English vocabularies.

Lucy has been raised in a home in the Norman, Oklahoma, area since she was 2 days old. Her Ameslan training did not begin until she was 5 years old; thus, vocal English was her first language even though she could not herself produce it. In a preliminary study, Lucy was taught the sign for "car," using only the vocal word *car* as a referent. On the following day, a second experimenter (who did not know the status of the sign) showed Lucy a toy car and asked her in Ameslan what it was. Lucy correctly signed *car* to the toy. This accomplishment corresponds to second-language acquisition in humans, who are able to pick up foreign words without benefit of their direct association with the physical referent.

Prior to Ali's arrival at the institute, a similar but more extensive study was conducted to determine his ability to transfer a signed response from vocal English stimuli to the actual physical stimuli (Fouts, Chown, & Goodin, 1976). First, Ali's comprehension of 10 English words was tested by giving him commands to follow. For instance, he was vocally instructed to "pick up the spoon" out of an array of items scattered around the room. If he correctly selected the spoon five consecutive times, he met the criterion for comprehension of the vocal word *spoon*. In training, the 10 signs corresponding to the words were randomly divided into two lists of 5 signs. Experimenter 1 taught a sign to a vocal word in list 1 without referring to the actual referent of the word. Experimenter 2 did the same thing with signs on List 2 during another session. During the latter part of each session, each experimenter tested for the acquisition and transfer of signs from the other experimenter's list to the actual referents without referring to the vocal words. This was done by asking Ali, *What that?* in Ameslan, indicating the physical referent. Experimenter 1 would arrive in the morning and attempt to teach a sign from List 1 using only the vocal word as referent. Later, Experimenter 2 would test Ali on all 5 of the objects in List 1; he did not know which signs had been taught or acquired. He would question Ali on all 5 objects in Ameslan without vocally producing the English word. Thus, the experimenter doing the testing was blind with regard to Ali's acquisition of signs to the English referents. Ali successfully transferred the signs he acquired for vocal English referents for all 10 of the objects attempted. Note that this study has cross-modal implications. In pretraining, the visual (objects) and auditory (vocal words) stimuli were associated. In training, Ali was taught to produce a gestural response (a sign) to an auditory stimulus (a vocal word), and then in testing he successfully transferred the gestural response to the visual stimulus (the object).

Sociolinguistic Studies

Whether or not a linguistic chimpanzee initiates and terminates conversations and interactions is one of many questions asked by linguists. The question is important, since it continues in the tradition of language scrutiny. Mounin (1976) believes that chimpanzees do not initiate conversations, particularly in natural social settings. Furthermore, he contends that the artificiality of the experimental situations used in chimpanzee linguistic research is a poor setting in which to test language competence.

In a study (Mandel & Fouts, 1976) attempting to answer this question, a linguistic chimpanzee was observed as it participated in conversation and other interactions with two humans. The subject, Lucy, who was 10 years old at the time, had a vocabulary of approximately 98 signs in Ameslan. The human participants had different roles. One was passive, that is, not initiating conversation nor moving about. This permitted recording of all the dialogue during the sessions. The other participant had an active role, following Lucy about the house and interacting in conversations. Both human participants let the situation be as spontaneous as possible.

The sessions were analyzed in terms of their general features and in terms of the quantifiable units of (*a*) solitary actions (e.g., walking around or other self-engaged behaviors); (*b*) nonsigning interactions (i.e., some action between Lucy and at least one human, such as grooming); and (*c*) Ameslan conversations. The initiator, the maintainer, and the terminator of each interaction were recorded during the session. The sessions took place in the subject's house and lasted from 1 to 2 hours each.

In the 15 sessions that were analyzed, solitary actions comprised 22.8% of the total activities recorded. Interactions other than signing comprised 20.9% of the total activities recorded. Conversations, which occurred between Lucy and at least one human or involved Lucy signing to herself, comprised 56.3% of all actions.

Also of interest was the analysis of initiator and terminator components of the action. Of the 99 total acts of interaction other than signing, 96.9% were initiated by Lucy, while 39.4% were terminated by her. Lucy both initiated and terminated 36.4% of the interactions. Conversations were also largely initiated by Lucy (77.9% of the 267 separate conversations were initiated by her). Lucy terminated 54.7% of all the conversations, and she both initiated and terminated 42.7% of the conversations.

In conclusion, there seems every indication that Lucy not only participated in two-way interactions and conversations with her human companions but was also an *active* participant in these sessions in terms of initiating and terminating conversation with them.

Sociolinguistic variables, such as variations or differences in signing, are important in the functional analysis of Ameslan when it is examined in social situations. Variations may be due to differences in dialects (e.g., state, regional, racial, social, sexual, and even school-related differences in signs), individual differences (i.e., where and how signs are formed by the individual), or code switching (Berko-Gleason, 1973); that is, the kinds of signs and how they are used depend on the interactant and the situations.

Another study (Gorcyca, Garner, & Fouts, 1975) was conducted to determine whether or not such sociolinguistic variables could be applied to a group of chimpanzees and a group of deaf children. Three male chimpanzees and three deaf children (two females, one male) were examined in separate signing situations: with a teacher, with a stranger, and with a peer (chimp to chimp, or child to child). The sessions were videotaped for 5 minutes for each situation. Topics of discussion during the sessions dealt primarily with food sharing for the chimpanzees and with ball playing for the children.

The following questions were investigated: What are the species-specific signing and nonsigning communication variations across situations for chimpanzees and deaf children; and what are the similarities across species?

Other categories that were analyzed in this study are

1. Touching. This behavior is determined by social relationships and denotes a level of intimacy that may be absent from formal situations. It was assumed in both species that the amounts of touching would increase as social relationships became less formal.
2. Eye contact. This is an important variable in suggesting dominance hierarchies, which play a major role in social behavior. The amount of eye contact with an interactant and the dominance of the individual would be expected to vary between species. For deaf children, more formal and dominant settings would promote more eye contact, but the reverse of this was expected in chimpanzees.
3. Initiations. This variable may reflect social relationships. It was assumed that as social relationships became less formal, there should be an increase in the less formal, nonsigned initiations (e.g., tapping a person or clapping hands) for both species.
4. Average number of signs per segment. It was felt that in less formal situations, the number of signs per segment for both species would increase.
5. Variations. This variable has been mentioned briefly, and it was assumed that with both species there would be increased variation in signing as the social situations became less formal.

It was found that social setting and resultant dominance dictated touching behavior in both the chimpanzee and the child groups. When an individual higher in the dominance hierarchy was present, the situation was more formal, as evidenced by the fact that touching behavior was less likely to occur than when both individuals were equal in dominance.

With the chimpanzees, an inverse relationship existed between the amount of dominance one possessed and the amount of eye contact with others. The amount of eye contact for the deaf, however, varied directly with dominance. For chimpanzees, high dominance and respect dictate a lack of eye contact, but the reverse is true in our society.

When interacting with the teacher or a stranger, the majority of the children's initiations were accomplished through the use of signs. Initiations between children were mainly nonsigned. In contrast, the chimpanzees had more signed initiations. In fact, the expectation of increased nonsigned initiation in less formal settings or across situations was not realized. Only with one chimpanzee, Bruno, was a trend of this sort suggested. Signing by chimpanzees generally involved discussion of food items, and while all chimpanzees would sign, there was a difference in the number of signs initiated by each chimpanzee. This difference can best be explained by dominance. Ali, the smallest and least dominant chimpanzee, was quite hesitant to sign to Booee, the most dominant chimpanzee. When Ali was hesitant in signing for food, Booee would poke Ali to get his attention and then sign *you give me food*. Booee continued this spontaneous signing until Ali signed his necessary sentence. When Ali made the appropriate request for food, Booee would cease his prompting and deliver the requested item.

For both chimpanzees and deaf children, the signing variation increased as the formality of the situation decreased. In the formal situation (teacher or stranger), the chimpanzees mainly used the signs the teacher had taught them. As the situations became less formal, they increased the number of different signs.

Cultural Linguistic Studies

One of the most exciting aspects of language is its cultural evolution. We have thus far demonstrated language acquisition by a chimpanzee, signed communication between chimpanzees and humans, and signed communication between two chimpanzees. But what can we say about chimpanzee language potential from a cultural perspective?

We have realized for some time now that the demonstration of the transmission of signs by chimpanzees across generations would have profound implications for language theory, but numerous difficulties surround research appropriate to such a demonstration. First of all, the population of chimpanzees fluent with signs is severely limited. Second, the only reliable bond between chimpanzee generations is the mother–infant bond (van Lawick-Goodall, 1968); therefore, we must start with a signing female subject capable of bearing offspring. But female chimpanzees do not reach reproductive maturity until about 11 years of age, and then they produce infants at most once in 4 years. Our most desirable prospective subject for such a project is Washoe, who is presently 11 years old and who has a vocabulary of about 200 signs.

Washoe is presently of child-bearing age. She gave birth to her first infant on August 18, 1976; unfortunately, the baby lived only 4 hours. During this time, Washoe demonstrated that she would be an excellent mother. She was observed sucking the mucus from the infant's nose and mouth, carrying the infant in the proper fashion, and carefully grooming the infant. After 3 hours, the infant showed few signs of life, and Washoe's grooming became more intense. Occasionally the infant would move, and when this happened, Washoe would hold the infant close to her chest. Twice, when the infant was inactive, Washoe laid the infant beneath her, signed *baby* to it, and cried. After several lengthy attempts by Washoe to revive the infant, she repeatedly started to offer the infant to her human companions watching outside her cage; but she changed her mind on each occasion. Finally, it was decided to anesthetize Washoe and remove the baby, who was taken to a hospital. En route it was given cardiopulmonary resuscitation, but this proved futile. A postmortem showed that the baby had a serious congenital heart defect and a concussion to the back of the head. It was assumed that Washoe birthed the infant over the edge of a bed 8 feet from the floor. This was indicated by the fact that the umbilical cord was severed (resulting in a premature loss of blood) and by the distribution of the blood on the floor. Often, human mothers report that the pressure during birth resembles the feeling associated with a bowel movement, which might explain why Washoe possibly birthed over the edge. Also, the birth was discovered less than ½ hour after it occurred. She was observed at 7:30 A.M. and showed no signs of labor; however, by 8:00 A.M. she had delivered the baby.

Washoe revealed the general appearance of depression during the following 2 weeks. However, at the present time, she is doing well and is being housed with several males so that she can become pregnant again.

This incident, although very unfortunate, has shown us that Washoe is capable of becoming pregnant and that she will be an excellent mother—which is unusual in primiparous females. It also demonstrates that she would sign to the infant, which is very encouraging for the future of this type of research.

When Washoe gives birth to her second infant, humans will cease to sign in the presence of the infant, to ensure that any signs produced by the infant can be ascribed to the tutelage of the mother. The possibility that an infant chimpanzee will acquire signs from his or her mother is not farfetched, as a great deal of chimpanzee behavior appears to be culturally transmitted from mother to offspring at an early age. Feral chimpanzee skills, such as insect fishing, are probably learned through observation of the mother (van Lawick-Goodall, 1968, 1975; McGrew, 1974). The transmission of language from Washoe to her offspring would answer an important linguistic and anthropological concern.

ADDITIONAL LINGUISTIC RESEARCH
WITH CHIMPANZEES

Other Approaches

It is appropriate to briefly mention the works of Premack (1972), Premack and Premack (1971a,b, and Rumbaugh, Gill, von Glasersfeld (1973), all of which concern the linguistic ability of the chimpanzee. Their methodology, however, relies heavily on instrumental mediation and artificial languages. The Premacks showed that the chimpanzee could demonstrate the ability to use language constituents called exemplars (e.g., word, sentence, copula, metalinguistics, etc.), provided the overall instruction of the exemplar was broken down into lessons that could be comprehended by the subject. The language medium consisted of plastic pieces of various colors and shapes that represented words or phrases. The subject, Sarah, by placing the pieces on a magnetized board, produced a linguistic response. The Premacks (1972) summarize their results with the following statement: "We have been teaching Sarah to read and write with variously shaped and colored pieces of plastic, each representing a word. Sarah has a vocabulary of about 130 items that she uses with a reliability of between 75 and 80% [p. 92]."

Using an even more elaborate instrumental methodology, Rumbaugh et al. (1973, 1974) have shown that a chimpanzee can communicate to humans or a computer using a devised language of geometric figures or lexigrams. The subject, Lana, lives in a plastic room surrounded by electronic equipment. To communicate, she must press a series of keys, each of which has a lexigram etched onto it. The lexigrams represented holographic phrases at first, but later they represented words. The sequence of her responses is based on a predetermined grammar. Whenever Lana presses a key, not only is she informed of her choice, but so are the experimenter and the computer, the latter of which records the selections and decides whether to accept or reject the input. This highly instrumental technique puts the chimpanzee in a position that allows for rapid learning of the desired language skills as well as continued use of the skills. Since the chimpanzee has continuous access to the computer, she may communicate whenever she feels hungry or wants entertainment (she may ask for movies, etc.).

Current Research at the Institute

In a study currently underway, one of us (Shapiro) is attempting to determine whether or not a chimpanzee can comprehend useful signed information provided by another chimpanzee. Although chimpanzee-to-chimpanzee signing has been observed (Fouts, 1975b), it is difficult to decide if a chimpanzee receiver has comprehended the signs of a chimpanzee sender. Most signed conversations between chimpanzees are one-way, with the signer actively requesting some food item or game and the receiver usually reacting either neutrally or negatively (by ignoring or leaving the dyad).

In this project, the sender and the receiver will be one and the same. Ali, the subject, has been filmed signing three-sign combinations specifying subject–preposition–location (e.g., *berry in box*). These will be shown to him in training and testing phases of the experiment, after which he will attempt to find the hidden object specified in the film. This method is being used, rather than another chimpanzee, in order to circumvent the problems inherent in managing two apes in a controlled situation. Results thus far in training indicate that Ali can obtain information from the film. His mistakes are similar to those made when information is signed manually to him. Use of the film method will also make testing other chimpanzees relatively easier.

Another study underway at the institute (O'Neil) utilizes the communicative abilities of signing chimpanzees to examine their conceptual world. The acquisitional sequence of such relational concepts as *big* and *little* is the topic of this study. We have adapted a format already used with human children as subjects (Klatzky, Clark, & Mackin, 1973) to accommodate our primates. The Klatzky *et al.* study attributed the distinct developmental sequence of polar adjective acquisition in humans (Clark, 1973) to conceptual rather than linguistic variables. We are looking at acquisition of both the comprehension and the production of relational adjective pairs in our chimpanzees.

In a third study, two groups of chimpanzees are being tested in a color study involving perceptual and recognition tasks. Prior to performing these tasks, one group was taught the sign names for four focal hues: red, green, blue, and yellow. The other group did not learn these signs. The purpose of this study is to determine whether the ability to name the colors will affect performance and accuracy in color matching and color recognition.

RELATED RESEARCH WITH OTHER PRIMATES

Although chimpanzees have been used as subjects in the studies presented thus far, the ability to use sign language or any contrived language does not seem to be limited to the species *Pan troglodytes*. In several studies (Fouts, 1973; Shapiro, 1975; Patterson, 1974), apes other than chimpanzees learned to use the language system as instructed by the experimenter.

Pongo pygmaeus (Orangutan)

The use of an orangutan as a subject in a linguistic study is by no means novel. Furness (1916) showed that an orangutan could learn to speak two words, *papa* and *cup*, though the words were sounded in a hoarse whisper. Although this was not an impressive demonstration of language ability, it was not any less productive than other attempts to induce speech in chimpanzees. Could an orangutan, like the chimpanzee, learn to use a language system successfully if the discourse was via the visual mode?

In a short exploratory study (Fouts, 1973), it was found that an infant orangutan could acquire signs, although the rate of sign acquisition appeared to be slower than that of a chimpanzee of equal age receiving similar training. The male subject, Foots, did acquire signs (e.g., *drink, food, tickle,* etc.), and he also combined them into two-sign combinations. Because of the lack of time on the experimenter's part, the study has not been continued. Although the study was not a definitive one, it can be stated that at least one infant orangutan is capable of acquiring signs.

In a 21-month study (Shapiro, 1975), a 4-year-old female orangutan was taught a language system similar to Premack and Premack's (1972). However, plastic children's letters were used as the word–symbols representing the referents. A developing grammar was taught over a period of 5 months to the subject, Aazk, by the addition of functional word categories to the existing categories. The grammar went from *object* to *action–object*, to *donor agent–action–object*, and finally to *donor agent–action–object–recipient agent.* In order to use the system properly, Aazk had to choose the appropriate word–symbols from an array and place them in the proper sequence according to the situation and the grammar at the time. Not only could she produce sentences (e.g., *Gary give apple* [to] *Aazk*), but she could read them as well (e.g., *Aazk take cup* [from] *Dick*). Near the termination of the production and comprehension part of the study, Aazk was producing correct responses 78% of the time and was comprehending sentences 80% of the time (chance correct was 1.2% and 8.33%, respectively).

Aazk was also allowed to produce sentences whenever she wanted. This gave her the opportunity to tell the experimenter what she wanted. There was a 4:1 ratio of requests for objects (mostly edible objects) over requests for activities (e.g., swinging, hugging, etc.). She also used the grammar taught during the earlier production portion of the study. The mean word–symbol length of all correct sentences produced was 4.25.

Aazk also demonstrated productivity (i.e., the generation of new words or phrases not specifically taught to the subject) when she took two plastic symbols that represented different referents and combined them to describe an item that seemingly shared properties of both the former items yet was unique in itself. Orange juice had been brought in as a reward for requests involving inedible items; but after tasting the juice, Aazk quickly wrote *Gary water orange*—a grammatically incorrect sentence but one that aptly described the orange juice. She later used the hybrid word correctly when asking for orange juice.

Gorilla gorilla (Gorilla)

In an ongoing study, F. Patterson (1974) has been teaching a 6-year-old female gorilla named Koko to use Ameslan. Koko began learning Ameslan when she was 1 year old, and she has acquired nearly 300 signs. Koko uses the signs in combinations much like the chimpanzee and human. In fact, Koko's two-sign combinations fall under the same functional categories as proposed by Brown (1970) when he compared Washoe's early linguistic ability to that of human children.

Homo sapiens (Man)

We have always considered our research to have direct implications in the realm of comparative psychology. The chimpanzee is considered the closest relative to man on a number of behavioral and biomedical measures (van Lawick-Goodall, 1975; King & Wilson, 1975). We now have access to another organism with language abilities that we can compare with human language abilities. When we have a chimpanzee as the subject for linguistic research, we can exercise relatively strict control over its exposure to and experience with language—something that is not ethically feasible with human subjects. Comparisons between sign language acquisition in chimpanzees and in deaf children are particularly interesting.

But the deaf are not the only users of sign language. We have been able to apply lessons learned from our signing chimpanzees to the sign language training of noncommunicating children who have no discernible vocal or auditory impairments (e.g., autistic children or children with cerebral palsy). Our chimpanzees provide a valuable proving ground for gestural language instruction techniques.

Speech training of autistic children has proved discouragingly time-consuming and unproductive (Hingtgen and Churchill, 1969). Recent evidence (Gillies, 1965; Lovaas, 1966; Bryson, 1970 and 1972) indicates that the vocal–auditory mode may be inappropriate for language in these subjects because cross-modal visual–auditory associations may be impaired. Autistic children also seem to be more adept at tasks requiring primarily visual integration than at tasks requiring primarily auditory integration (Davis, 1970). These children, however, do seem to use nonverbal gestures in a meaningful way (Jakab, 1972). Other researchers (Provonost, Wakstein, & Wakstein, 1966; Rutenberg & Gordon, 1967) note that autistic children respond to the gestures and facial expressions of others and that communication is impossible without such nonverbal signals. Lovaas (1966) and Senn and Solnit (1968) reported that autistic children are particularly responsive to tactile stimulation. In response to the above considerations, Fulwiler and Fouts (1976) elected to teach sign language to a noncommunicating autistic child. A manual language seemed singularly appropriate for such children for several reasons:

1. It capitalizes on the senses (visual and tactile) to which the autistic child is most responsive.
2. It avoids problems with cross-modal (visual–auditory) associations.
3. It utilizes the autistic child's naturally communicative gestures and expressions.

After 20 hours of sign language training, the 5-year-old male subject used approximately 25 signs appropriately and combined them into two- and three-word phrases. The most exciting outcome of the project, however, was the spontaneous generation of vocal words and phrases by the subject. Although the "total comnunication" technique (simultaneous vocal and nonvocal communication) was used, the experimenters had not intentionally tried to elicit vocal responses. Another by-product of the training sessions was a general improvement in behavior. Attentiveness and initiations of social contacts increased, as did manageability in general. Several other researchers (Miller & Miller, 1973; Webster, McPherson, Sloman, Evans, & Kucher, 1973) have noted both an increase in meaningful vocalizations and behavior improvement as a result of sign language training of autistic children.

We had similar success with a nonspeaking 8-year-old child with cerebral palsy who had control over gross motor movements of his arms and hands. After 13 30-minute training sessions, the child had acquired about 73 signs and had produced approximately 150 different sign combinations, including sequences up to 6 signs in length. Toward the end of the training sessions, the child showed an increase in vocalizations, although no comprehensible spoken words were recorded.

Premack's (1974) work with chimpanzees has also been applied to language therapy for children. Carrier (1973) adapted Premack's language system for children, resulting in "Non-SLIP" (Non-Speech Language Initiation Program), which incorporates a set of plastic symbols, a simple set of grammatical rules, and a limited vocabulary of concrete words. This program produced communicative behavior in 178 of 180 retarded mute children, many of whom also began to vocalize.

CONCLUSION

Our work at the institute has proceeded through several phases thus far. We concentrated initially on basic research into language capabilities of chimpanzees. We proceeded to comparative studies of linguistic and conceptual abilities in humans and chimpanzees. Now we have reached the point of applying our research to human therapies. The linguistic and conceptual sophistication of chimpanzees is still under scrutiny, and the more we discover about chimpanzee intellect, the more we will discover about our own. Language intervention in noncommunicating children is but the first and most direct of the possible applications of the language research with chimpanzees.

REFERENCES

Berko-Gleason, J., Code switching in children's language, In T. E. Moore (Ed.), *Cognitive development and the acquisition of language.* New York: Academic Press, 1973. Pp. 159–169.

Brown, R. W. The First Words of Child and Chimpanzee. In R. Brown (Ed.), *Psycholinguistics: Selected Papers,* Free Press: New York, 1970, 208–231.

Bryson, Q. Systematic identification of perceptual disabilities in autistic children. *Perceptual and Motor Skills,* 1970, *31,* 239–246.

Bryson, Q. Short-term memory and cross-modal information processing in autistic children. *Journal of Learning Disabilities,* 1972, 5, 81–91.

Carrier, J. K. Application of functional analysis and nonspeech response mode to teach language. *American Speech and Hearing Association,* Monograph 18, 1973. Pp. 47–95.

Clark, E. What is a word? On the child's acquisition of semantics in his first language. In T. E. Moore (Ed.), *Cognitive development and the acquisition of language.* New York: Academic Press, 1973.

Davis, B. J. A clinical approach to the development of communication in young schizophrenic children. *Journal of Communication Disorders,* 1970, 3, 211–222.

Fouts, R. S. Acquisition and testing of gestural signs in four young chimpanzees, *Science,* 1973, *180,* 978–980.

Fouts, R. S. Capacities for language in great apes. In R. H. Tuttle (Ed.), Socioecology and psychology of primates. The Hauge/Pans: Mouton, 1975. Pp. 371–390. (a)

Fouts, R. S. Communication with chimpanzees. In E. Eibl-Eibesfeldt & G. North (Eds.), *Hominisation and Verhalten.* Stuttgart: Gustav Fischer Verlag, 1975. Pp. 137–158. (b)

Fouts, R., Chown, W., & Goodin, L. Transfer of signed responses in American Sign Language from vocal English stimuli to physical object by a chimpanzee *(Pan). Learning and Motivation,* 1976, 7, 458–475.

Fouts, R., Chown, W., Kimball, G., & Couch, J. Comprehension and production of American Sign Language by a chimpanzee *(Pan).* Paper presented at the XXI International Congress of Psychology in Paris, France, 1976.

Fouts, R. S. & Rigby, R. L. Man–chimpanzee communication. In *How animals communicate.* T. A. Sebeok (Ed.). Bloomington: Indiana Univ. Press, 1975.

Fulwiler, R. & Fouts, R., 1976. Acquisition of American Sign Language by a noncommunicating autistic child. *Journal of Autistic and Childhood Schizophrenia,* 1976, 6, 43–51.

Furness, W. H. *Proceedings of the American Philosophical Society,* 1916, 55, 281.

Gardner, B. T., & Gardner, R. A. Two-way communication with an infant chimpanzee. In A. Schrier & F. Stollnitz (Eds.), *Behavior of Non-Human Primates,* New York: Academic Press, 1971. Pp. 117–184.

Gardner, R. A., & Gardner, B. T. Teaching sign language to a chimpanzee. *Science,* 1969, *165,* 644–672.

Gardner, R. A., & Gardner, B. T. Early signs of language in child and chimpanzee. *Science,* 1975, *181,* 752–753.

Gillies, S. Some abilities of psychotic children and subnormal controls. *Journal of Mental Deficiency Research,* 1965, 9, 89–101.

Gorcyca, D., Garner, P., & Fouts, R. Deaf children and chimpanzees: A comparative sociolinguistic investigation. Paper presented at the Speech Communication Association Convention, Houston, Texas, December, 1975.

Hayes, C. *The ape in our house*. New York: Harper, 1951.

Hayes, K., & Hayes, C. The intellectual development of a home-raised chimpanzee. *Proceedings of the American Philosophical Society,* 1951, 95, 105–109.

Hayes, K., & Hayes, C. Imitation in a home-raised chimpanzee. *Journal of Comparative and Physiological Psychology,* 1952, 45, 450–459.

Hayes, K., & Nissen, C. Higher mental functions of a home-raised chimpanzee. In *Behavior of nonhuman primates*. A. Schrier & F. Stollnitz (Eds.). Academic Press: New York, 1971. Pp. 39–115.

Hingtgen, J., & Churchill, D. Identification of perceptual limitations in mute autistic children: Identification by the use of behavior modification. *Archives of General Psychiatry,* 1965, 21, 68–71.

Hockett, C. *A course in modern linguistics,* New York: Macmillan, 1958.

van Hooff, J. A. R. A. M. *Aspects of the social Behavior and Communication in Human and Higher Non-Human Primates*. Rotterdam: Bronder-Offset H.V., 1971.

Jakab, I. The patient, the mother, and the therapist: an interactional triangle in the treatment of the autistic child. *Journal of Communication Disorders,* 1972, 5, 154–182.

Kellogg, W. N., & Kellogg, L. A. *The ape and the child: A study of environmental influences on early behavior*. New York: Hafner, 1967.

King, M. C., & Wilson, A. C. Evolution at two levels in humans and chimpanzees. *Science,* 1975, 188, 107–116.

Klatzky, R., Clark, E., & Mackin, M. Asymmetries in the acquisition of polar adjectives: Linguistic or conceptual? *Journal of Experimental Child Psychology,* 1973, 16, 32–46.

Kohts, N. *Infant ape and human child (Instincts, emotions, play, and habits)*. Moscow: Scientific Memoirs of the Museum Darwinian, 1935.

Kortlandt, A. Experimentation with chimpanzees in the wild. In Starck, Schneider, & Kahn (Eds.), *Progress in Primatology,* Stuttgart: Gustav Fischer Verlag, 1967. Pp. 208–224.

van Lawick-Goodall, J. The behavior of free-living chimpanzees in the Gombe Stream Reserve. *Animal Behavior Monographs,* 1968, 1, 165–311.

van Lawick-Goodall, J. The chimpanzee. In v. Goodall (Ed.). *The quest for man*. London: Phaidon Press, 1975.

Lieberman, P. Primate vocalizations and human linguistic ability. *Journal of the Acoustical Society of America,* 1968, 44, 1574–1584.

Lieberman, P., Crelin, E., & Klatt, D. Phonetic ability and related anatomy of the newborn and adult human, Neanderthal man, and the chimpanzee. *American Anthropologist,* 1972, 74, 287–307.

Lovaas, O. A program for the establishment of speech in psychotic children. In T. K. Wing (Ed.), *Early childhood autism: Clinical, educational and social aspects*. London: Pergamon Press, 1966.

Mandel, B., & Fouts, R. Human-chimpanzee conversations in a social-setting: Initiations/terminations. Paper presented at the 70th Annual Meeting of the American Sociological Association, August 25–29, 1976.

McGrew, W. Evolutionary implications of sex differences in chimpanzee predation and tool use. Paper presented at the Burg Wartenstein Symposium, No. 62, July, 1974.

Miller, A. & Miller, E. Cognitive developmental training with elevated boards and sign language. *Journal of Autism and Childhood Schizophrenia,* 1973, 3, 65–85.

Mounin, G. Language, communication, chimpanzees. *Current Anthropology*, 1976, *17*, 1–21.

Patterson, F. Sign language acquisition by an infant gorilla: Some preliminary data. Unpublished manuscript, Stanford University, 1974.

Premack, D. Language in chimpanzee? *Science*, 1971, *172*, 808–822.

Premack, D. On the assessment of language competence in the chimpanzee. In A. Schrier & F. Stollnitz (Eds.), *Behavior of nonhuman primates* (Vol. 4). New York: Academic Press, 1971. Pp. 185–228. (b)

Premack, D. Teaching visual language to apes and language-deficient persons. In R. L. Schiefelbusch & L. L. Lloyd (Eds.), *Language perspectives–acquisition retardation, and intervention*, Baltimore: Univ. Park Press, 1974.

Premack, A. J., & Premack, D. Teaching language to an ape. *Scientific American*, 1972, *227*, 92–99.

Provonost, W., Wakstein, P., & Wakstein, P. A longitudinal study of the speech behavior of fourteen children diagnosed as atypical or autistic. *Exceptional Children*, 1966, *33*, 19–26.

Riesen, A. H., & Kinder, E. F. *Postural development in infant chimpanzees*. New Haven: Yale Univ. Press, 1952.

Rumbaugh, D., Gill, T., & von Glasersfeld, E. Reading and sentence completion by a chimpanzee (Pan). *Science*, 1973, *182*, 731–733.

Rumbaugh, D., von Glasersfeld, E., Warner, H., Pisani, P., & Gill, T. Lana (chimpanzee) learning language: A progress report. *Brain and Language*, 1974, *1*, 205–212.

Rutenberg, B. A., & Gordon, E. G. Evaluating the communication of the autistic child. *Journal of Speech and Hearing Disorders*, 1967, *32*, 314–324.

Schenkel, R. Zur Ontogersis des verhalten bei gorilla and mensch. *Zeitschrift fur morphologie and anthropologie*, 1964, *54*, 233–259.

Senn, M., & Solnit, A. *Problems in child behavior and development*. Philadelphia: Lea and Febiger, 1968.

Shapiro, G. Teaching language to a juvenile orangutan (abstract only). *American Journal of Physical Anthropology, 42:* 329. Paper presented at the Forty-fourth annual meeting of the American Association of Physical Anthropologists, Denver, Colorado, April, 1975.

Stokoe, W. C., Casterline, D. C., & Croneberg, C. G. *A dictionary of American sign language on linguistic principles*. Washington, D.C.: Gallaudet College Press, 1965.

Webster, C. D., McPherson, H., Sloman, L., Evans, M. A., & Kuchar, E. Communicating with an autistic boy by gestures. *Journal of Autism and Childhood Schizophrenia*, 1973, *3*, 337–346.

Witmer, L. A monkey with a mind. *The Psychological Clinic*, 3 (7), 1909, 189–205.

Yerkes, R. M. *Almost human*, New York: Century, 1927.

Yerkes, R. M. *Chimpanzees: A laboratory colony*, New Haven: Yale Univ. Press, 1943

7

Development of Sign Language in Autistic Children and Other Language-Handicapped Individuals

JOHN D. BONVILLIAN

Vassar College

KEITH E. NELSON

New School for Social Research
The Pennsylvania State University

INTRODUCTION

The apparent ease and rapidity with which most young children master their native language often succeeds in masking the complexity and enormity of this intellectual accomplishment. Over the past two decades, a number of longitudinal investigations have added much to our knowledge of how the young child actively re-creates his own language. The investigations of sign language acquisition and usage among the deaf have added to our understanding of the process of language acquisition. These studies have often highlighted the many cognitive processes common to sign and speech by revealing the many structural similarities in the acquisition process between young deaf children learning to sign and young hearing children learning to speak. However, it is the sharply contrasting failures of language development, as seen in mute, echolalic, or other speech-disordered youngsters, that underline for us the importance of this feat of language acquisition and that emphasize how little we still understand of how the process actually occurs. Here we will examine some past and current efforts in assisting language-limited children to learn language, giving special emphasis to directions for future educational and theoretical efforts.

Most therapeutic intervention programs with mute or speech-limited or speech-disturbed children have focused on stimulating speech. Perhaps the best known program for fostering speech in previously-mute children has been the behavior therapy programs carried out by Lovaas and his associates (Lovaas, 1967; Lovaas, Koegel, Simmons, & Long, 1973). By rewarding mute autistic children for normal behavior and punishing them for psychotic behavior, Lovaas *et al.* have reported success in decreasing inappropriate social behavior (e.g., tantrums and self-destructive behavior) and in increasing social interaction, I.Q., and facility with spoken words or phrases. Similar behavior modification programs have been used with retarded and aphasic children, with much success in eliciting some speech and in increasing social skills. However, one of the difficulties in these treatment programs is that they do not appear to be effective in promoting the acquisition of spontaneous speech: The children involved often learn the elements of language they are taught, but they fail to generate new sentences spontaneously and to use their "language" outside the treatment situation. In fact, many of the children to be discussed later in this chapter received extended behavior modification training on speech, failed to develop spontaneous speech, and then entered treatment regimens involving sign language.

In the subsequent sections of this chapter, we wish to examine and make comparisons among the small number of programs that have recently experimented with using sign language as an avenue of communication for autistic, retarded, and aphasic children. First, we will raise some lines of discussion that will apply throughout the paper. Next, we will focus on the case history of an autistic boy, Ted, learning to communicate through sign language. His progress over several years illustrates some of the different techniques often used in the sign language programs, the variety of social and communicative changes that may occur, and the major obstacles that often remain after years of training. Then we review the results of other reported programs of sign language for the language-handicapped children. Finally, we will pull all the studies together in a comparative discussion that points toward needed refinements of method and theory.

In the set of studies reported to date, there have been some remarkable instances of children's transition from nearly total lack of language to high levels of communication in sign or in speech and sign. As we review these studies, however, we will look not only at what has been achieved but at the many questions and goals that have not yet been answered or met. In addition, we will try to specify the kinds of steps that must be taken and the kind of information that must be gained if further educational and theoretical advances are to be forthcoming.

Our discussion and conclusions will focus on four major themes, themes that will also be resonant in our review of our own case study with Ted and of each of the other research efforts.

1. A first theme is one of *diversity*. Different children in the same program show strikingly different outcomes. Different programs share common elements of sign language training but vary in the way the total educational effort is put together. And so far no one can predict very well which child will benefit from what program.

2. A second theme is the *relatively low exposure to fluent sign language communication* that most children have received in their educational programs to date. If we are going to discover how autistic and retarded children can most efficiently make strides toward language mastery, it may be necessary to bring the child directly and regularly into interaction with signers who are highly fluent and who use signing at a high level of complexity. Also we need to discuss what the child can learn from observing other communication partners fluently conversing in sign and to set up research programs allowing evaluation of this factor's potency in relation to direct teaching efforts with the child.

3. Our third point of emphasis is that we need to know much more about these children's *receptive language abilities in each mode:* in sign alone, in speech alone, and in speech and sign together. As the data below will make evident, the educational procedure and assessment efforts have so far permitted only the sketchiest of conclusions on this topic. Additionally, current theoretical discussions on language acquisition in autistic children give heavy emphasis to intermodal factors in language reception; such discussion will be shown to be weak not only on internal consistency but also on empirical support.

4. The final theme concerns the need for the *reporting of similar background and evaluation measures* by different investigators. We

believe this plea is more than the usual complaint from reviewers of scientific literature about the frustration of making sense of numerous studies where no two studies give comparable information on subjects or employ the same procedures. In this area of research on the role of sign or sign-related communication in aiding language mastery by language-limited children, there are a few kinds of data that will have to be reported for each study before the study's theoretical and practical implications can be assessed. Until more common background and evaluation information begins to appear in literature accounts, we will see no meaningful replications, no systematic assessments of the effects of program modifications, and little progress toward determining why programs work at all or which children need what sorts of instructional programs.

ACQUISITION OF SIGN LANGUAGE
IN A MUTE AUTISTIC CHILD

Before we examine studies of sign language acquisition in autistic children, it should be noted that the impairments in language functioning of autistic children typically include delayed onset of speech, echolalia, and mutism. Some comparisons of autistic children's language skills with those of children diagnosed as aphasic show autistic children's language development to be more deviant and their comprehension deficit more severe (Bartak, Rutter, & Cox, 1975; Cohen, Caparula, & Shaywitz, 1976). In addition to their serious language handicap, and perhaps in part because of this handicap, autistic children typically show ritualized movements, impaired social relations, and other profound disturbances in behavior.

The case history (Bonvillian & Nelson, 1976) that will be examined in some detail concerns a 12-year-old boy, Ted, who has been learning sign language since shortly after his ninth birthday. At the time of his introduction to sign language, Ted had never spoken, and he had experienced a long history of failure not only in language but in social development as well. His parents recalled that as an infant he did not cuddle when he was held, and he often appeared insensitive to pain. After failing to make even any approximations to speech by the time he was nearly 3 years old, Ted entered a "computer interaction language program," in which he participated for 18 months. Although this program of utilizing computer-accessed games to assist language-handicapped children combine English sounds and letters into words and expressions clearly helped most nonspeaking children, Ted remained unimproved (Colby, 1968). Supplementary individual language training and group play therapy were also ineffective in stimulating his speech or social development. At age 6½ years he was diagnosed as infantile autistic. In addition to an absence of speech, Ted still exhibited at that time the bizarre, stereotyped gestures and tantrums that had characterized his early development. After a year in a residential facility, Ted entered the day treatment center he now attends. After over a year of operant training, in which both food and tokens were used as rewards for verbalization, Ted still failed to use words or even to imitate sounds; however, his attention to his teacher–therapist appeared to have improved as a result of the reinforcement program. In spite of this small improvement, he remained an uncommunicative and severely disturbed child at the time we initiated the sign language program.

The first step in teaching Ted sign language was to teach him to use individual signs correctly. New signs were introduced in a daily half-hour language session by showing him pictures or examples of the signs and by saying the appropriate English equivalent. Ted's production of the signs was promoted by having his teacher–therapist model the sign and then mold Ted's fingers into the correct arrangement before guiding his hands through the proper motion. Initially, successful performance was rewarded by both praise and a token reward system. Eventually, as Ted's vocabulary became quite extensive and his ability to learn new signs improved, we phased out the token reward system. Ted's daily language period was supplemented with informal training at home by his mother, who learned sign language by attending a weekly sign class. Later, after expansion of the sign-teaching program to include other autistic children and new staff members, Ted began interacting in sign language with other children and teachers at the center.

Records of Ted's performance in the language sessions over the first 6 months of the study showed that he made gradual, consistent progress toward a sign lexicon. During this period, Ted's rate of acquisition increased slightly from a rate of less than two new signs a week to an average of three new signs each week. Such slow but steady progress after hours of practice is not unusual in studies of sign acquisition by autistic children; the task is difficult for the child, and considerable patience is demanded of the teacher. Nor did Ted succeed in mastering during this 6-month period all the signs to which he was introduced—he failed to learn nearly 30% of the signs presented.

However, the majority of the signs that he did not master during this initial period were those that had been most recently introduced. In the ensuing months, Ted would eventually gain facility in using the majority of these signs. Still, certain individual signs appeared to be more difficult for Ted to master. Those signs that involved more complex finger configurations (especially the extension of his little finger) and those two-hand signs that required a different hand configuration or motion with each hand (e.g., the sign AIRPLANE) proved more difficult to learn. At the same time, those signs he used correctly once (without preceding imitation or molding) were likely to be retained permanently (96% of cases). Records of Ted's vocabulary over the following 2½ years have shown that he has continued to learn new signs and retain mastery of old signs. Current estimates of his total vocabulary indicate about 400 individual signs. A lexicon this size enables him to converse on a variety of topics, although in comparison with normal children, his conversations are still limited in their range of subject matters. Yet he has not undergone the rapid burst of language learning observed in normal hearing and deaf children, who, after a slow beginning, greatly increase their vocabularies with each succeeding month during their second through fourth years. Although neurological factors might be responsible for his slow rate of acquisition in comparison with normal children, part of the explanation may reside in the fact that he is not constantly exposed to fluent signers, nor does he continually feel a need to match the particular signs he encounters with his motivation to learn those particular signs. With regard to this last point, a specific example demonstrating the speed with which he can acquire signs when he obviously wants to learn is pertinent. Not long ago, he appeared quite confused by the names of the months on a calendar and pointed to them with a quizzical look on his face. He was then shown the signs for the different months and acquired many of them within minutes. In contrast, all previous attempts to teach him any of the names had resulted in failure. In addition, the fact that Ted's vocabulary continues to grow indicates that he does not have a small, finite language capacity, as has sometimes been reported of autistic children learning speech.

Ted first spontaneously combined signs after 3 months of training in production of individual signs. Within the next several months, Ted produced hundreds of sign combinations, and analyses of these combinations indicated a wide range of semantic relations. Comparison of the semantic relationships observed in Ted's early sign combinations with those reported for young children in the two- to three-word sentence stage (Brown, 1973) revealed a number of similarities. As would be expected of a young normal child, Ted showed knowledge of such basic semantic components as agent, location, experiencer, possession, object, and instrument. Examples of Ted's two-sign combinations and their structural interpretations included: DADDY EAT (agent and verb), GO SCHOOL (verb and location), MOTHER CAR (possession and object), FATHER HAIRCUT (experiencer and verb), EAT COOKIE (verb and object), and TOMORROW RAIN (time and verb). Other similarities with normal young children's early speech included Ted's use of the sign MORE to request or signal recurrence (e.g., MORE COOKIE) and his use of the sign for negation before another sign to signal nonexistence or refusal (e.g., NO FOOD, NO GO).

Although Ted's first combinations closely resembled those of a normal young child's in terms of structure, Ted's subsequent combinations over the following 2½ years have not kept pace in terms of their average length with those reported for normal children. Most of Ted's sign sentences remain 2 or 3 signs in length. At the same time, his relatively short sign combinations do not appear to be the result of a memory or production deficit, as he will on rare occasions produce a combination of up to 12 to 15 signs in length. An additional point of interest is Ted's limited success in picking up many of the aspects of the SEE (Signing Exact English) signs, to which he was introduced in his second year of sign training. Rather than incorporating the inflections, auxiliary verbs, and other grammatical markers that make SEE largely isomorphic with English, Ted's signing continues to consist predominantly of ASL (American Sign Language) signs roughly equivalent to nouns, verbs, and adjectives.

Both at home and at school, Ted often engages others, and on some days spends much of his time in sign conversations. Indeed, his persistent inquiries and running commentaries have even become tedious at times, as was witnessed recently when his mother, finally overtaxed by his sign volubility, told him to SHUT-UP. Later, she reflected that she had never believed that she would ever have the chance, or cause, to tell him to keep still. Examination of Ted's sign conversations indicate that although most are only one or two interchanges long, and some involve perseveration, at other times he will pursue and discuss topics for many minutes. For example, one night he spent about 15 minutes inquiring of guests where they lived, what they did for a living, and so forth. Most of the time in these conversations Ted produces only short sign utterances, one, two, or three signs in length, although it is quite possible that his sign utterances would become longer and more complex if the other signers in his environment increased their still-limited facility in sign. Regardless, these conversations reveal a level of functioning not previously discerned. Ted's more recent conversations also suggest a developing sense of humor. On one occasion his mother returned from the beauty parlor with a tightly curled natural, and Ted laughingly inquired if the hairdo was "for Halloween."

Another approach to enhancing Ted's communication and educational skills has been an attempt to teach him to read English words via sign language. In this recent phase of the project, Ted was taught to respond with the sign equivalent to an English word printed on a small white card. The signs utilized in this aspect of the project were ones he had previously mastered in earlier language sessions. Although learning was difficult at first, Ted's ability to sight-read has gradually improved, and he currently responds with the correct sign to 42 printed words. After Ted mastered a small vocabulary of printed English words, his teacher began arranging the printed cards so that they formed short English sentences. Ted was then required to sign each sentence at sight. Eventually the sentences were combined to form several brief stories, with Ted evidencing the ability to read and sign the stories and to answer questions on their content. In addition, Ted also learned to form sentences by placing the printed cards in order to make acceptable English sentences (predominantly with subject–verb–object order).

Over the past year, work has also continued on the development of Ted's speech skills. His speech therapist, recognizing Ted's many difficulties in controlling his oral movements, has focused the training on improving Ted's tongue mobility and control through a series of exercises designed to improve his purposeful tongue placement. For example, ice cream is systematically placed at different positions around his mouth, and he is encouraged to lick the spoon clean without moving his head. Progress in Ted's acquisition of spoken language, however, remains exceedingly slow. He has now learned a spoken vocabulary of 19 words (e.g., *mama*) that are intelligible when said in conjunction with signs, but most of his attempts at spoken utterances are largely unintelligible. Another interesting aspect of these speech sessions is their occasional stressfulness for Ted. Whereas today Ted rarely exhibits the stereotypic movements and gestures that he produced in great quantity 3 years ago, he sometimes makes these bizarre repetitive gestures under the apparent stress of his speech instruction.

GENERAL REVIEW OF SIGN PROGRAMS
WITH AUTISTIC CHILDREN

During the past 5 years, in addition to the study just reported, a number of other investigators (Barnes, 1973; Baron & Isensee, 1976; Creedon, 1973; Fulwiler & Fouts, 1976; Leibovitz, 1976; Miller & Miller, 1973; Schaeffer, Kollinzas, Musil & McDowell, 1976; Webster, Konstantareas, & Oxman, 1976; Webster, McPherson, Sloman, Evans, & Kuchar, 1973) have also reported success in teaching previously-mute autistic children to communicate in sign language. At the time most of these projects were initiated, it appears that the different investigators were working independently—with clear exceptions in the recent work by Leibovitz, by Baron and Isensee, and by Schaeffer and his colleagues. (An early indicator of the potential effectiveness of sign language for autistic children is reported very briefly in one case history by Churchill [1972].) For some time news of procedures and successes remained unshared among the programs. The immediate goal of these projects appeared to be to see if sign language could be learned and used at all by these children, rather than systematic investigations of the best way to teach sign language. We begin by reviewing the results of these studies; later we will suggest new procedures or methods that we feel should be examined.

Webster and colleagues, in an early study (Webster et al., 1973), reported on the relative effectiveness of manual and speech messages with one autistic boy. After they had unsuccessfully attempted to teach this child to follow very simple spoken commands, they began a sign-training program. During 24 1-hour language sessions over 3 months, the boy quickly learned to respond accurately when a limited repertoire of commands were given in sign and gesture (80% correct), whereas his performance remained low (44% correct) when the information was given verbally. The Millers (Miller & Miller, 1973) worked with 19 mute autistic children ranging in age from 5 to 23 years (median age = 11 years). The teachers paired signs with spoken words as the children walked along elevated boards several feet off the ground. The use of the elevated boards was an attempt to enhance the children's awareness of their bodies and to focus their attention on functional activity. There is no evidence to indicate that superior performance on the elevated boards was related to any change in language use, in either sign or speech. However, a number of the subjects in the program made substantial improvements in sign—after training in sign use for periods of 4 to 36 months. The median number of receptive signs learned was 27, while the median number of expressive signs mastered was 8. In contrast, although two children made the transition to some spontaneous speech, most of the children mastered few spoken words (median = 0). A larger proportion (four of six) of the nonverbal children who participated in a study by Barnes (1973) showed at least some increase in verbalization after sign language training began. All six nonspeaking boys initially learned a sign lexicon (ranging in size from 12 to 50 signs), produced these signs spontaneously, and in one case learned to combine the signs into more complex phrases. In addition, all but one of the six improved in personal and social behavior over the 6-month duration of the study.

The relative ease with which some autistic children may acquire a productive sign vocabulary although showing little or no speech is emphasized also by Fulwiler and Fouts (1976). Whereas hundreds of hours are often needed to teach only a few spoken words or "sounds" in speech-oriented programs, Fulwiler and Fouts reported a rapid growth in sign vocabulary and usage (to more than 25 signs) in only 20 hours of sign-with-speech training with their "nonverbal" autistic subject. However, the boy's initial levels in language production and comprehension were reported in detail, so it is not possible to determine the full extent of communicative advance in this study.

Similarly, fairly rapid learning within 20 hours of training was observed by Leibovitz (1976). She taught an autistic boy to imitate a small set of words (eight in all); the child learned in 3½ weeks to imitate both signs and spoken words. In ongoing research by Webster et al. (1976), four children with a mixture of autistic and retarded characteristics have received over 34 weeks of training from teachers using simultaneous communication in sign and speech. Each child has so far produced at least 50 different signs in spontaneous fashion. Additional evidence on the rapid acquisition of sign language in a program of simultaneous communication has been reported by Baron and Isensee (1976). The results of a series of tests with a 12-year-old nonverbal autistic girl showed that signs were rapidly learned and that they were easily transferred from items in one representational context to another (e.g., from objects to pictures). Baron and Isensee later made systematic tests of language comprehension in sign language alone and speech alone, finding that sign language produced higher response accuracy. Interestingly, when instructions to this subject were given in spoken English, she frequently signed spontaneously before making the appropriate behavioral response, suggesting that she might be using signs to mediate spoken input.

Schaeffer et al. combined sign language instruction with a behavior modification program for teaching oral language. Their three subjects, who ranged in age from 4½ to 5½ years, began learning sign language in two 45-minute daily language sessions. They were taught to imitate words in two daily speech sessions also 45 minutes in duration. The two means of communication were initially taught independently for the most part, and the children signed before they used signs and speech simultaneously. The children progressed from spontaneous sign language to combined signing and speech after about 4 to 5 months of spontaneous signing, and then, after the use of signs was systematically faded, to spontaneous speech alone. Although the children made a dramatic improvement over the 18 months of the study, it should be noted that they were still quite limited in their speech skills: One of the two originally mute children in the study produced only an average of 14 spontaneous spoken utterances per day; the other child, 24. Nevertheless, despite the apparent low frequencies of their spontaneous utterances in either sign or speech, each of the children learned to produce spontaneous two- or three-word utterances in sign or in speech or in simultaneous speech and sign.

Finally, Creedon (see Offir, 1976), using a program of simultaneous sign and speech in her classrooms, has reported success in the acquisition of sign language skills in all of her 30 original subjects. Of these, 7 eventually acquired facility in spoken English, and about another 40% developed some speech. Beyond this, the levels of language production and comprehension achieved are not specified except in general terms. However, it is clear that quite different outcomes held for different children. For example, even though most advanced to one-element and two-element productions both in sign and in speech, one child failed to acquire speech but learned to produce spontaneous phrases in sign.

Although none of the nearly 70 subjects in these studies failed to acquire at least one sign, the final outcome, in terms of each individual subject's linguistic performance, appeared to vary widely. For example, some of the children, after acquiring facility in sign language, learned to use spoken English and eventually made the transition to public school classrooms. At the other extreme, a small number of children never learned to use more than a handful of signs, although in several of these cases the children reportedly comprehended a much larger number of signs but experienced difficulty in the gestural production. Most of the children, however, succeeded in acquiring a working vocabulary (from a dozen up to several hundred signs) over a period of several years, and they learned to combine the signs spontaneously into phrases or sentences conveying a wide range of ideas.

In comparison with the very limited progress toward effective communication previously exhibited by the children, their progress in sign acquisition was remarkable. Furthermore, nearly all the children showed concomitant improvement in social behavior: Tantrums, soilings, and stereotyped repetitive movements markedly decreased in frequency or disappeared in the children.

Analysis of the techniques used to teach sign in the different studies reveals a number of common procedures, several of which merit further discussion. Each of the studies employed simultaneous speech and sign in an apparent attempt to provide the child with an oral environment to which he might transfer his sign language skills. However, the emphasis on bimodal input, both auditory and visual, might provide difficulties for autistic children, who reportedly perform poorly on cross-modal tasks (Bryson, 1970). If an autistic child does have difficulty when both auditory and visual information are combined, it is possible that simultaneous presentation of sign and speech might hinder, rather than help, the child (e.g., see Leibovitz, 1976). An alternative approach might be to introduce children to a program where sign language alone would initially be the sole method of communication. In such a program, if the therapists wished to try teaching speech, they would wait until the children had evidenced mastery of sign language skills. If, on the other hand, the use of both spoken and signed input proved to be more advantageous for some children than sign alone, then other forms of redundancy could also be helpful to such children. As one example, perhaps the pairing of the printed word with the signed and spoken word in the learning of the sign would provide a useful memory cue as well as facilitating these children's development of reading.

A second point that should be made with regard to the experimental procedures is that most of the experimenters' and staffs' sign input to the children was that of English syntax (signing in English), not the grammar of the sign language most widely used by the deaf (ASL). Although English signing has the possible advantage that word order similar to English might make a transfer to spoken or printed English easier for the autistic child, such use of signs in English word order could prove to be more difficult to the autistic child initially learning to combine signs. One reason for thinking this is true is that many signers fluent in both ASL and English signing find that they can more effectively and efficiently transmit information in ASL. Related to this discussion of the most effective form of sign input is the fact that although the staffs in most of the projects acquired at least a limited vocabulary of signs, it appears that with one exception (Creedon,

1973) the experimenters and their staffs did not communicate among themselves very extensively in sign language in the child's presence and that the child was not immersed in an environment in which sign language was widely used as the means of communication. Such use by the staff, and by the child's parents, might lead to increased use by the child and help generalize the child's signing beyond the therapeutic setting.

In spite of the limited pretraining data on the subjects in the existing studies, a review of these studies suggests several tentative generalizations about an autistic child's prognosis for later language achievement. First, with few exceptions (Miller & Miller, 1973), the younger children in the programs appeared to show greater success, both in sign and in speech, than those who had already reached adolescence. This finding might be related, of course, to the older children's previous experiences of failure in therapeutic settings or to such biological factors as the lateralization of function in the cerebral hemispheres. Second, duration in the programs was positively correlated with the number of signs learned and the production of sign phrases. Finally, several measures of degree of disability (e.g., high Creak scores, low scores on scales of language age) appeared to be directly related to difficulty in mastering sign language. In contrast, measures of intelligence were not clearly predictive of success in language training.

What reasons might account for the relative success of sign language in fostering communicative skills in these children, when other techniques emphasizing speech had often repeatedly failed? One possibility is the relative ease of teaching the child an individual sign: The therapist can easily mold the child's hands into the appropriate configuration, guiding the hand movements while visual feedback is available to the child. Another probable advantage of sign language as it has been used in programs to date is that some of the signs that the children initially learned were highly iconic or closely resembled their referent, as opposed to the largely arbitrary relation between a word and its referent in speech and between most signs and their referents in ASL. Further reasons for using a visual–motor means of communication stem from previous research (O'Connor, 1971; Tubbs, 1966) that reported that autistic children's visual and motor responses appeared to be quite similar to those of normal children, whereas the autistic children's auditory–vocal skills were much more deviant. Thus a visual–motor language, like sign, might take advantage of underlying skills that were relatively unimpaired in contrast to speech handicaps. This last point has taken on increased significance in the light of a recent investigation (Hauser, DeLong, & Rosman, 1975) using pneumoencephalography that found pathological enlargement in the left temporal horn in 15 of the 18 autistic children examined. If such pathology or dysfunction were to prevent normal speech development, any system of communication that could be processed in a different area in the brain might facilitate acquisition of communicative skills. Neville's (1977) study of hemisphere differences in language processing, which suggested that sign language may be processed in the right hemisphere in the deaf, and the findings of differential impairment of speech and sign after left-hemisphere strokes in the deaf (Battison & Markowicz, 1974) would support an interpretation that autistic children may be processing sign in a different location in their brains. These speculations, of course, require validation, and they must be reconciled at some future point with the findings that some of these autistic children move beyond sign communication to verbal communication.

PROJECTS USING SIGN WITH
RETARDED AND APHASIC CHILDREN

Some mentally retarded persons never acquire speech. These individuals frequently must live in institutions, and they often experience difficulty in communicating their basic needs and desires. Although it is unclear why some subnormal persons acquire speech and others do not, those who fail to acquire even the rudiments of oral language tend to be those with the lowest tested I.Q.s (Sheehan, Martyn, & Kilburn, 1968). With this population of nonspeaking, severely retarded individuals, several investigators have recently set up programs for teaching sign language communication skills.

The results of three studies (Briggs, 1974; Grecco, 1974; Richardson, 1974, 1975; see also Wilson, 1974) show that many nonspeaking subnormals can develop limited facility in sign language. Of the more than 60 subjects in these studies, only 1 failed to acquire some expressive or receptive sign skills, and many of the participants succeeded in acquiring an expressive vocabulary of more than 200 signs. The length of participation in the sign-training programs was moderately, but positively related to the number of signs mastered. For example, in the Briggs study, in which total training ranged from 25 to 75 hours, only one subject acquired more than 100 signs, whereas in the multiyear, 12½ hours-per-week training that characterized the other two studies, Grecco reported an average lexicon of over 200 signs and Richardson a median of over 100 signs (with some students mastering nearly 600). Whereas duration of participation appeared to be related to the size of a sign vocabulary, an individual's performance on a standardized I.Q. test did not ($r = -.11$, Grecco, 1974). Considering that most of the subjects had I.Q.s well below 50, the I.Q. tests may not have accurately differentiated the performance capabilities needed to master sign among this limited range of very low scores.

The ability to combine signs spontaneously was more difficult for the subjects than was the mastery of individual vocabulary items. Less than half (35%) of the participants in the Grecco study were observed spontaneously combining signs, and these combinations rarely exceeded two or three signs in length. In terms of grammatical structure, most of the sign combinations could be described as a simple combination of a noun plus a descriptive word, although evidence of use of verbs, pronouns, negatives, and conjunctions in sign combinations was also occasionally reported (Grecco, 1974). In addition, Richardson noted that after 3 years of training, only a very small fraction of his subjects' sign combinations reached five signs in length.

Aside from providing the participants with an effective means to communicate many of their daily needs for the first time, the programs also reportedly led to both improved classroom concentration and enhanced overall social behavior among the subjects. Yet at the same time that these studies underlined the need for further and continuing programs, they introduced intriguing questions that need to be investigated. What, for example, would happen if the participants were placed in classroom and living environments where sign was used as the primary or sole means of communication all the time, rather than the current maximum involvement of about 12½ hours per week? On a limited basis this kind of full-time sign language environment has recently been tried with the Pennhurst Communication Center (Kopchick, Rombach, & Smilovitz, 1975). Despite the fact that the staff involved possessed only limited sign facility, an all-day, every-day program in which the staff used simultaneous speech and sign as the exclusive mode of language led each of 11 nonverbal, mentally retarded men to acquire several dozen or more signs over a period of 6 months. Also, what if younger, nonspeaking retarded individuals participated? At present, most of the participants were already well past the age of normal language acquisition (many in their late teens to early 30s), and changes in the plasticity of the subjects' nervous systems associated with increased chronological age might have adversely affected their progress.

Sign language may also facilitate the acquisition of receptive English language skills in retarded children and adults with severe oral language handicaps. In the acquisition of English word meanings, sign has definitely proved valuable. When taught the sign corresponding to an object and its English equivalent, nonverbal retarded children showed improved performance in pairing objects to appropriate verbal stimuli (Bricker, 1972).

Sign language has also been used with aphasic children. Although progress in sign acquisition has been briefly noted for several such children by Hughes (1974/75) and Cohen et al. (1976), few reports explain program details or the outcome measures. However, Cohen et al. provide a case history of one child who lost, at about age 4, both receptive and productive facility in speech. By age 10, receptive abilities in speech were good, but still no speech was produced. At this point, ASL was introduced and the child mastered its production, still demonstrating no productive speech skill. Given this report and the other sketchily documented cases of sign language progress by aphasic children and adults, and given the many similarities in aspects of productive language disability in aphasic and autistic children, it may not be too optimistic to expect increasingly successful use of sign language in communication programs for aphasic children and adults.

In the remainder of this chapter we will discuss material from the studies on the retarded and aphasic together with the sign studies on autistic children.

ON DIVERSITY OF SUBJECTS, PROCEDURES, AND OUTCOMES

Considerable differences in language, social, and cognitive skills characterized the subjects in the studies reviewed above prior to any treatment with sign language programs. Within as well as between studies, it is impossible to speak accurately of any homogeneous group of children, whether labeled "autistic" or "aphasic" or whatever. For anyone interested only in children with one clearly identifiable set of deficiencies, this is a disadvantage; predicting what sort of child will benefit most from a sign language program is not yet possible. But the diversity in subjects is encouraging in one sense. That is, the studies show there is at least some positive impact on communication of sign language training for a wide range of language-handicapped individuals; those with and without general cognitive impairment, with and without severe emotional or behavioral disorders, and those completely mute as well as those with some speech.

The wide variation in programs and outcomes should make us pause before deciding that there is one best way of using sign language or before expecting signs or sign language to be a panacea, to be dramatically effective with every speech-limited child. Any serious comparative program evaluation is for the future, when highly similar groups of subjects can be tested before training and then evaluated as they move through contrasting educational curricula. In the following discussion we will make some recommendations on what data need to be specified on all subjects in such evaluation efforts. Here we offer a few reminders of just how many different factors did vary among the set of studies examined. Only three of the studies directly involved any of the parents in sign training (Bonvillian & Nelson, 1976; Schaeffer *et al.*, 1976; Creedon, 1973). Only two of the studies (the latter two just cited) worked toward a systematic transition from sign-and-speech reliance to attempted reliance on speech alone. Miller and Miller (1973) focused on a sensory–motor task (walking along a board) with the children as a major part of training. Token or food or praise were made contingent on sign production in our early work with Ted. No other studies on autistic children detail such contingent reinforcement, but the presence of some such system is strongly implied in several other studies with autistic children. Contingent reinforcement systems were also used in the projects with retarded children and adults. Work on reading was reported only rarely.

Despite the remarkable diversity there are three fundamental observations that applied to all the studies. One is that each program relied on sign or sign language as one central element of the language-training program. The second is that all but one of the children acquired some elements of productive and/or receptive sign language, ranging from a few individual signs to considerable ability in spontaneous sentences. The third is that for children who progressed in speech as well as sign, the progress in sign language appeared crucial as a foundation for the changes in speech skills: The sign progress predated and appeared to guide or support the spoken language advances. Taken together, this set of studies very powerfully suggests that sign language itself, rather than other elements of the treatment programs, was essential in opening up communicative exchanges with many of the children and to advances in speech production, speech comprehension, and social behavior as well as sign production and comprehension.

COMMUNICATION MODES: SIGN, SPEECH,
SIGN AND SPEECH

Discussions by many investigators of why sign language is proving effective in opening up communication in autistic children and of why speech had been blocked or disturbed in these children show recurrent reference to possible deficits in combining or integrating auditory and visual information. In a review, Dalgleish (1975) argues that integration of cross-modal information is an essential deficit of autism. Fulwiler and Fouts (1976), Lovaas, Schreibman, Koegel, and Rehm (1971), Rimland (1964), Creedon (1973), and Schaeffer et al. (1976) all refer to the difficulties of autistic children in attending to or remembering or processing the auditory information of speech in conjunction with related information in other modes. In the projects just reviewed there are no tests or measures on the children learning sign language that empirically confirm or deny these theoretical speculations. And the literature more generally provides only limited and somewhat inconsistent support for the idea that autistic children generally have trouble combining auditory information with nonauditory information. In future intervention or educational efforts with autistic children, tests of the children separately on auditory–verbal processing, visual processing, and processing of information in both modes prior to the onset of training in sign language would serve practical and theory-building ends. Across many studies it should be possible to determine the typical patterns of information-processing deficits by mode that characterize autism and aphasia. Further, it should prove feasible to determine how different kinds of sign language and speech programs fare in dealing with children showing typical deficit patterns and with children whose pattern of processing by mode is exceptional.

The theoretical conceptions of cross-modal or selective processing difficulties in autism have been used as arguments that speech and sign should be presented together in language programs for the autistic. In fact, such combined presentation has been central in all the projects reviewed in the preceding discussion. However, the reasoning about the need for such combined presentation shows inconsistencies and contradictions. In particular, it has been argued that speech and sign together provide redundant information for the child, allowing the child to make up in one mode what may have been poorly processed or remembered in the other. But such "redundancy" could only be helpful to the child who indeed was successfully processing considerable information in each of the modes; two channels of unprocessed information may constitute noise for the child rather than redundancy. With at least equal force one can argue that language training in *one mode only* should be the most effective initial language program with any language-handicapped children who have severe difficulty in processing multiple modes or channels of information. This idea, to our knowledge, has not yet been put to the test with sign language as the *exclusive* mode of training and communication. If the child can give his undivided attention to the sign of the teacher and if the teacher can apply undivided attention to providing clear, fluent production in sign rather than in sign and speech, then for some children who have failed in speech-only programs some remarkable language learning might well occur. After substantial progress in sign, use of speech or writing in the program might be introduced with greater effectiveness than if it had been used from the beginning.

Three related points on this issue deserve mention. One is that because so little information was provided on the pretraining receptive language abilities of most of the autistic children in the sign-plus-speech projects reviewed earlier in the chapter, it is distinctly possible that the programs' success for some children was based on supplementing already-established skills in comprehension of speech with a productive capacity in sign. If so, once two-way communication involving sign was established, then the further steps to some productive speech and to increases in receptive speech levels also became more likely. The second point is that a pattern of relatively good receptive abilities in speech and production difficulties is more common with aphasic than with autistic children. Especially for such children, the prospects may be favorable for establishing productive skills in sign language to complement receptive skills in speech. This, of course, is precisely what Cohen *et al.* (1976) reported for the child who mastered ASL after age 10. The third and final point on this issue is that written language may prove a useful additional mode for reception, production, or both reception and production of language. The visual features as well as the timing and sequencing involved are sufficiently different from those involved in sign that some children who have difficulty processing sign may experience few problems in processing pointing and writing (or vice versa). The combination of receptive language skill in speech and writing but productive skill only in orthographic language is also illustrated by the boy whom Lenneberg (1962) reported to have receptive language mastery only and who then went on to master reading, writing, and typewriting (Fourcin, 1975).

Fluent Sign Communication

We made clear in the preceding discussion that none of the sign-training programs to date have tested the efficacy of sign language when used for a period as the only language available to the child. The further step of trying only sign language in settings where the parents and all the teachers are highly fluent in sign language may deserve serious consideration, too. After all, this would place the mute child in a situation comparable to that of the hearing child learning to talk—an environment where all (or virtually all) the adults communicate with psychological ease and linguistic fluency in just one language mode. In comparison with the speech-plus-sign settings that have prevailed thus far in research on sign learning by language-handicapped children, such a setting may not only make better use of the child's processing skills (as just argued) but may have beneficial effects on the child's motivation for learning language and for interacting socially. We certainly do not recommend any crash program to institute sign-only settings for most children with severe disorders of speech acquisition; but for some children the parents and teachers may be well advised to try out this approach. Perhaps the most logical candidates for a sign-only, total setting approach would be children who have no useful speech and who react with frustration and anger to repetitive and unsuccessful attempts at teaching beginning skills in speech.

Within programs that rely, as past studies have, on some combinations of speech and sign language modes by teachers, the limits of effectiveness have probably not been approached. This is true for many reasons, including the accumulation of experience that teachers are gaining. One of the most important reasons for thinking effectiveness can be improved is that by necessity most projects have been training teachers in sign concurrently with training the children; future studies are therefore likely to be able to employ much more fluent signers. In thinking about the sequence of steps a child moves through in future language-training programs, some care needs to be taken to avoid locking in sequences for the teacher's language use—such as, one-sign, then two-sign, and only much later many-sign productions by the teacher—which once were unavoidable until the teacher's own skills advanced. To put it another way, the children at early points in a training program may be able to profit from much more complex sentences in sign language than the current "generation" of students ever saw.

The child's opportunities for observing sign communication between other children, between adults, and between adults and other children may also prove much more important in future projects than they could be in the first generation of efforts in sign instruction. There have been some opportunities of this sort, most notably in work by Creedon (1973) and her colleagues, but frequent opportunities to observe fluent signers in interaction have been lacking. As soon as the child is able to use and understand the rudiments of sign language communication, films and videotapes could prove to be a valuable supplement in the sense that examples of fluent sign communication could be provided while teachers in the programs are themselves mastering sign. Also when a program is just starting, there will be no children who are fluent signers, and the films and videotapes could provide important models of fluent child signers.

NEEDED INFORMATION ON SUBJECTS' BACKGROUNDS AND ON LANGUAGE PROGRESS

One shortcoming of most of these studies has been a relative dearth of background information with regard to the subject populations. Such absence of thorough background data makes it very difficult to predict which children will most benefit in future sign language programs. Aside from the results of thorough physical and neurological examination (including, if possible, electroencephalogram, pneumoencephalogram, brain scan, audiometric evaluation, urinalysis, and urine tests for genetic screening) and reports on the severity of autistic or behavioral symptoms, future studies should probably provide results on intelligence tests (including nonverbal or performance items) and on scales of language and motor development. Scales of receptive language and articulatory skills might prove especially important in predicting whether a specific mute child might master sign and might later acquire speech after learning sign. As many autistic children are "untestable" because their outbursts and lack of communication prevent formal testing, any failures to respond and any behavioral difficulties should probably also be carefully documented. These measures need to be obtained before treatment and at regular intervals (annually at least) during the treatment period.

We recommend with particular emphasis that comprehension of and memory for pantomime and gesture be used as predictive measures for language-training programs with language-disordered children. Three lines of thought lend credence to the possibility that such measures might predict well for sign and sign–speech programs alike.

One is that the manually produced and visually observed elements of sign, gesture, and pantomime obviously have much in common. Another is that there are arguments and some data suggesting that prior to representation through speech there is symbolic representation through nonverbal actions both in the development of the individual (Piaget, 1951) and in the development of our species (Hewes, 1976). Yet another line of thought comes from observations that pantomime and gesture and other nonverbal aspects of representation may often be spared in speech aphasics (Zangwill, 1975) and other language disorders.

Finally, for direct measures of language skill it is clear that consistent reporting is needed on a few measures that are easily obtained, even though no single study reviewed in this chapter reported on all (or even half) of them. First, in each report some *systematic* (if not exhaustive) account of the range of semantic and syntactic structures in the children's productive and comprehension repertoires is needed rather than the mere provision of a few exemplary productions. Second, separate information is needed on spontaneous and nonspontaneous production along with some data on its relation to context. Third, testing on imitation and comprehension needs to be done in three ways—sign alone, speech alone, and simultaneous sign and speech—even if the instructional program focuses on sign and speech combined (for beginnings along these lines, see Webster *et al.*, 1976; Baron & Isensee, 1976; and Leibovitz, 1976). This will provide much useful feedback to the program teachers about the kinds of progress being made, and it will allow an assessment of such theoretical questions as whether (and if so, how) comprehension advances in one mode may provide the foundation for productive advances in the other mode. Once this kind of information is routinely reported, attempts to describe the processes of language acquisition in language-disordered children may at last take on some theoretical substance and order. Moreover, it should become possible to use the ongoing assessments of a child's progress, along with some theoretical structure, to make ongoing revisions that are sensibly tailored to each child's particular pattern of progress.

CONCLUSION

Recent work by many investigators with widely varying backgrounds has shown that language programs involving simultaneous speech and sign are effective in teaching rudiments of sign language to autistic, retarded, and aphasic children and adults who have severe deficits in oral language skills. Beyond this, for the first time in their lives many of these individuals learned to communicate complex messages through spontaneously produced phrases or sentences in sign language. A small minority of subjects also began to use spontaneous speech after developing facility in sign language. Social skills in most cases advanced along with advances in language.

Despite such successes, few if any of the exploratory studies reported here should be repeated in closely similar forms. What is needed instead is a new set of studies that will support much more refined conclusions than that "sign works." In this chapter we have offered many suggestions to this end. Among the necessary improvements in future designs will be the employment of sign teachers who are highly skilled (rather than students themselves in elementary sign language) and whom the autistic, or retarded, or aphasic children will observe signing to other sign teachers as well as to themselves. Another crucial element of more informative research will be the testing of production and comprehension skills initially and periodically during treatment for both sign language and speech. Finally, and of particular importance for understanding the processes of language acquisition and for devising effective language-teaching programs, some of the investigations should provide clear-cut comparisons among programs that offer all communication with the children and in the presence of the children in just one of four ways: in ASL only, in English signing (syntax based on English) only, in speech alone, or in speech simultaneously combined with English signing.

ACKNOWLEDGMENTS

The authors gratefully acknowledge the assistance and support of the Peninsula Children's Center in Palo Alto, California, at which their case study of sign language acquisition in a mute autistic boy was conducted. Special thanks are due Rachel Vasiliev, Kelly Flanagan, Deborah Bresler, Gloria Leiderman, and the child's parents for their many hours of help and for the numerous suggestions and improvements they contributed to the study.

REFERENCES

Barnes, S. *The use of sign language as a technique for language acquisition in autistic children: An applied model bridging verbal and nonverbal theoretical systems.* Unpublished doctoral dissertation, California School of Professional Psychology, 1973.

210   John D. Bonvillian and Keith E. Nelson

Baron, N. S., & Isensee, L. M. *Effectiveness of manual versus spoken language with an autistic child.* Unpublished paper, Brown Univ., Providence, Rhode Island, 1976.

Bartak, L., Rutter, M., & Cox, A. A comparative study of the infantile autism and specific development receptive language disorders: I. The children. *British Journal of Psychiatry,* 1975, *126,* 127–145.

Battison, R., & Makowicz, H. *Sign aphasia and neurolinguistic theory.* Unpublished paper, Gallaudet College, 1974.

Bonvillian, J. D., & Nelson, K. E. Sign language acquisition in a mute autistic boy. *Journal of Speech and Hearing Disorders,* 1976, *41,* 339–347.

Bricker, D. D. Imitative sign training as a facilitator of word-object association with low-functioning children. *American Journal of Mental Deficiency,* 1972, *76,* 509–516.

Briggs, T. *Sign language in alingual retardates.* Paper presented at the American Association of Mental Deficiency Conference, Toronto, Canada, 1974.

Brown, R. *A first language.* Cambridge, Massachusetts: Harvard Univ. Press, 1973.

Bryson, C. Q. Systematic identification of perceptual disabilities in autistic children. *Perceptual and Motor Skills,* 1970, *31,* 239–246.

Churchill, D. W. The relation of infantile autism and early childhood schizophrenia to developmental language disorders of childhood. *Journal of Autism and Childhood Schizophrenia,* 1972, *2,* 182–197.

Cohen, D. J., Caparula, B., & Shaywitz, B. Primary childhood aphasia and childhood autism: Clinical, biological, and conceptual observations. *Journal of the American Academy of Child Psychiatry,* 1976, *15,* 604–645.

Colby, K. M. Computer-aided language development in nonspeaking children. *Archives of General Psychiatry,* 1968, *19,* 641–651.

Creedon, M. P. *Language development in nonverbal autistic children using a simultaneous communication system.* Paper presented at the biennial meeting of the Society for Research in Child Development, Philadelphia, Pennsylvania, 1973.

Dalgleish, B. Cognitive processing and linguistic reference in autistic children. *Journal of Autism and Childhood Schizophrenia,* 1975, *5,* 353–361.

Fourcin, A. J. Language development in the absence of expressive speech. In E. H. & E. Lenneberg (Eds.), *Foundations of language development: A multidisciplinary approach* (Vol. 2.). New York: Academic Press, 1975, 263–268.

Fulwiler, R. L., & Fouts, R. S. Acquisition of American Sign Language by a noncommunicating autistic child. *Journal of Autism and Childhood Schizophrenia,* 1976, *6,* 43–51.

Grecco, R. V. *Results of a manual language program for nonverbal hearing and hearing impaired retarded.* Paper presented at the Connecticut Speech and Hearing Convention, 1974.

Hauser, S. L., DeLong, G. R., & Rosman, N. P. Pneumographic findings in the infantile autism syndrome. *Brain,* 1975, *98,* 667–688.

Hewes, G. W. The current status of the gestural theory of language origin. In S. R. Harnad, H. D. Steklis, & J. Lancaster (Eds.), *Origins and evolution of language and speech.* (*Annals of the New York Academy of Sciences,* 1976, *280,* 482–504.) New York: New York Academy of Sciences, 1976.

Hughes, J. Acquisition of a non-vocal "language" by aphasic children. *Cognition,* 1974/75, *3,* 41–56.

Kopchick, G. A., Jr., Rombach, D. W., & Smilovitz, R. A total communication environment in an institution. *Mental Retardation,* 1975, *13,* 22–23.

Leibovitz, S. *Sign versus speech in the imitation learning of a mute autistic child.* Unpublished master's thesis, School of Human Communication Disorders, McGill Univ., 1976.

Lenneberg, E. H. Understanding language without ability to speak: A case report. *Journal of Abnormal and Social Psychology*, 1962, 65, 419–425.

Lovaas, O. I. A behavior therapy approach to the treatment of childhood schizophrenia. In J. P. Hill (Ed.), *Minnesota Symposia on Child Psychology* (Vol. 1). Minneapolis: Univ. of Minnesota, 1967, 108–159.

Lovaas, O I., Koegel, R., Simmons, J. Q., & Long, J. S. Some generalization and follow-up measures on autistic children in behavior therapy. *Journal of Applied Behavior Analysis*, 1973, 6, 131–166.

Lovaas, O I., Schreibman, L., Koegel, R., & Rehm, R. Selective responding by autistic children to multiple sensory input. *Journal of Abnormal Psychology*, 1971, 77, 211–222.

Miller, A., & Miller, E. E. Cognitive-developmental training with elevated boards and sign language. *Journal of Autism and Childhood Schizophrenia*, 1973, 3, 65–85.

Neville, H. Electroencephalographic and behavioral specialization in normal and congenitally deaf children: A preliminary report. In S. Segalowitz (Ed.), *Language development and neurological theory.* New York: Academic Press, 1977. Pp. 121–131.

O'Connor, N. Visual perception in autistic children. In M. Rutter (Ed.), *Infantile autism: Concepts, characteristics and treatment.* Edinburgh: Churchill, Livingstone, 1971.

Offir, C. W. Visual speech: Their fingers do the talking. *Psychology Today*, 1976, 10, 72–78.

Piaget, J. *Play, dreams and imitation in childhood.* New York: W. W. Norton, 1951.

Richardson, T. *Sign language as a means of communication for the institutionalized mentally retarded.* Unpublished paper, Southbury Training School, Southbury, Connecticut, 1974.

Richardson, T. *The third year of the gestural language program at Southbury Training School 1974–1975.* Unpublished paper, Southbury Training School, Southbury, Connecticut, 1975.

Rimland, B. *Infantile autism.* New York: Appleton, 1964.

Schaeffer, B., Kollinzas, G., Musil, A., & McDowell, P. *Spontaneous verbal language for autistic children through signed speech.* Unpublished paper, Univ. of Oregon, 1976.

Sheehan, J., Martyn, M. M., & Kilburn, K. L. Speech disorders in retardation. *American Journal of Mental Deficiency*, 1968, 73, 251–256.

Tubbs, V. K. Types of linguistic disability in psychotic children. *Journal of Mental Deficiency Research*, 1966, 10, 230–240.

Webster, C. D., Konstantareas, M. M., & Oxman, J. *Simultaneous communication with severely dysfunctional nonverbal children: An alternative to speech training.* Unpublished Working Paper in Child Development and Care, Univ. of Victoria, 1976.

Webster, C. D., McPherson, H., Sloman, K., Evans, M. A., & Kuchar, E. Communicating with an autistic boy by gestures. *Journal of Autism and Childhood Schizophrenia*, 1973, 3, 337–346.

Wilson, P. S. *Sign language as a means of communication for the mentally retarded.*

Paper presented at the Annual Meeting of the Eastern Psychological Association, Philadelphia, Pennsylvania, 1974.

Zangwill, O. L. The relation of nonverbal cognitive functions to aphasia. In E. H. Lenneberg & E. Lenneberg (Eds.), *Foundations of language development: A multidisciplinary approach* (Vol. 2). New York: Academic Press, 1975. Pp. 95–106.

8

Iconicity: Effects on the Acquisition of Sign Language by Autistic and Other Severely Dysfunctional Children

M. M. KONSTANTAREAS
J. OXMAN
Clarke Institute of Psychiatry

C. D. WEBSTER
University of Victoria

As is true of most facets of human functioning, knowledge of linguistic dysfunction appears to provide valuable insights into normal functioning. The work of Lenneberg (1967), Whittaker (1971), and Krashen (1972) furnish good examples of the fruitfulness of this approach. Much has been gained in our understanding of language development and a possible critical period hypothesis for language through such work.

This work was supported (in part) under National Health Research and Development Project No. 606–1240–44 to Dr. M. M. Konstantareas and (in part) by the Ruth Schwartz Foundation Grant No. 821–32.

UNDERSTANDING LANGUAGE THROUGH SIGN LANGUAGE RESEARCH

213

Studying communication disorders is, of course, invaluable in its own right, since a child's ability to communicate with others is intricately interwoven with almost every other aspect of his development and behavior. That this may be true can best be appreciated in the case of a very severe developmental disorder, early infantile autism, first described by Kanner (1943). The original conceptualization of the disorder hinged on psychogenic factors. Because of this emphasis on an environmental contribution, and more specifically on a parental one, most early treatment programs tended to focus on improving the affect–isolation component from which autism takes its name. Communication difficulties had been recognized for some time but were never thought to be central to the autistic child's handicap. With the upsurge of radical behaviorism and its application to language, which was renamed verbal behavior (Skinner, 1957), however, a systematic effort to improve communication in autistic and autistic-like children began, first by Hewitt (1965) and shortly thereafter by Lovaas, Berberich, Perloff, and Schaeffer (1966). Crucial to this approach was an emphasis on speech training. The rationale behind speech training was that improvement in the verbal ability of the autistic child would provide him with naturally occurring social reinforcement opportunities and thereby reduce his social isolation (see Lovaas, Koegel, Simmons, & Long, 1973). For the first time, the traditional focus on the autistic child's alleged "affect isolation," the feature that dynamic theorists had considered to be the sine qua non of the disorder, ceased to guide treatment.

A decade after the first report on the use of the speech-training program, we can attempt, with some justification, to evaluate, first, the rationale behind an emphasis on *language,* and second, the general effectiveness of *speech training.* With respect to the rationale, recent evidence provides ample support for the radical behaviorists' concentration on language. A series of studies of diverse methodological and theoretical orientation concur with clinical observation on the validity of the premise that lack of language, and more particularly of inner language, is central to autism (e.g., Ricks & Wing, 1975; Rutter, 1968, 1974).

Emphasizing language and communication deficiencies as central to the syndrome is also independently supported by theoretical and empirical work on normal child development. The significance of language as a functional system mediating a wide variety of social–interactional and personality processes has been well documented (e.g., Bruner, Olver, & Greenfield, 1967; Nelson, 1973, 1974; de Ajuriaguerra, 1966). The "experiential deficiencies" of deaf children due to limited language availability are also well documented (cf. Liben, 1975). Since autistic children appear to have central information-processing deficiencies of a severe nature (Churchill, 1972; Ricks & Wing, 1975; Rutter, 1974), it may be understandable that their affective and social development appears even more distorted than that of deaf children.

Language is not only linked to social and affective development, of course, it is also intimately related to cognitive functioning. A number of studies (e.g., Reese, 1962; Spiker, 1963) have pointed to the facilitative use of linguistic mediation in discrimination learning, memory, and problem solving in normal children. The exact prerequisites for language acquisition are not agreed upon. Responding to the position of the nativists (e.g., Chomsky, 1972) on the innateness of linguistic structure and organization, a number of developmental psychologists (e.g., Piaget & Inhelder, 1969) and psycholinguists (Cromer, 1974; Huttenlocher & Strauss, 1968; Nelson, 1974) argue that cognition antedates language acquisition and makes it possible. Despite the fact that the debate is far from reaching a satisfactory closure, however, there is virtual agreement among psychologists and psycholinguists that language and thought tend to act in a mutually facilitative fashion.

A number of workers in the area (Rutter, 1974; Shopler, 1974) have come to the conclusion that most autistic children are also severely mentally retarded, with an I.Q. below 50. Indeed for Shopler (1974) this figure may be as high as 90%. Although it is futile at this point to debate whether these children's low cognitive ability is responsible for their linguistic impairment or the reverse, we may nonetheless say that their cognitive and linguistic skills are both severely impaired and that any attempt at improving the one will probably have some influence on the other. To the extent that cognition and affectivity are postulated to be rather closely linked (Piaget, 1970), improvement in either language or cognition may have positive influences on these children's affective and social functioning as well. There is, then, little doubt that the behaviorists' emphasis on improving the *language* of autistic children was quite insightful and well justified.

What remains, of course, is the second issue we raised a little earlier, the exclusive focus on building vocal language. A few years ago this would have been a rather meaningless consideration. As recently as 1968, most linguists considered *vocal sign* to be the defining characteristic of language (Bloomfield, 1933; Lyons, 1968; Sapir, 1966). But the outcome of the speech-training approach, in conjunction with a number of other developments in research on autism, constitutes one more demonstration of the now well-recognized fallacy of equating speech with language. Although some success was evidenced with a number of children in the Lovaas *et al.* (1973) follow-up, not all 19 children in the sample benefited from speech training. Speech training was apparently particularly ineffective with the mute children. An earlier study by Hingtgen and Churchill (1969) had, in fact, also reported on the relative unproductiveness and extensive time involvement needed for even minimal progress. Churchill (1972) also reported the case of an autistic child who was unable to form visual–vocal and auditory–visual associations, despite massive training. Work carried out at our institute with 54 autistic children over approximately 6 years, employing a comparable procedure, yielded similar findings. Although many children did show some progress in speech, not all of them benefited from training (Mack & Webster, 1974).

Our aim in this chapter is twofold: (*a*) to summarize some of the main findings on the peculiarities of information processing in autistic and autistic-like children as they relate to the communication modality suitable to their needs; and (*b*) to present evidence from our research on some of the variables that influence sign language acquisition in these children.[1]

PECULIARITIES IN INFORMATION PROCESSING

A steadily accumulating body of evidence on the overall functioning of autistic and autistic-like children leaves little doubt as to their obvious and severe problems in negotiating the developmental tasks every normal child has to achieve. Indeed, despite its very low incidence, the syndrome has been accorded a great deal of attention and research probing in recent years. As early as 1966, for example, using the Illinois Test of Psycholinguistic Abilities, Tubbs demonstrated that, compared with normal and subnormal children, "psychotic" children of the same mental age were inferior in their decoding and encoding of auditory information. It was of interest that the groups did not significantly differ from each other in their processing of visual

---

[1] The children we worked with have all been diagnosed as "autistic" or "autistic-like." Along with Bonvillian and Nelson (Chapter 7, this volume) however, we would like to stress the heterogeneity of our treatment population specifically, and the clinical entity of "autism" more generally. We have therefore employed the term *severely dysfunctional* in the title of this chapter to refer to the broader class of children who are operationally (i.e., in terms of their presenting strengths and weaknesses) indistinguishable from the autistic.

input. This work, although interesting, did not fit with any existing evidence on the disorder at that time. A few years later, however, Hermelin and O'Connor (1970) summarized their own findings on the autistic child's information-processing deficiencies. Relying on a number of behavioral and neurophysiological techniques, these investigators were able to demonstrate that there was abnormal responsiveness to stimuli within the auditory, tactile, kinesthetic, and visual modalities in these children.

In general, the children were less attentive to or able to employ auditory as opposed to visual, tactile, and kinesthetic inputs in problem-solving situations. This evidence therefore supports the conclusion Tubbs (1966) presented, that these children have a relatively greater deficit in auditory processing, and it may explain the failure of many of them to acquire speech.

Related to this evidence is a series of findings on the autistic child's tendency to "overselect," that is, to favor one of a number of modalities in discriminating a complex stimulus. Lovaas and Schreibman (1971) and Reynolds, Newsom, and Lovaas (1974), among others, were able to demonstrate this phenomenon by presenting a multimodal stimulus complex, typically including auditory, visual, and tactile components appearing simultaneously, to autistic, retarded, and normal children. After they learned to respond reliably to the complex, autistic children were subsequently unable to respond to each one of the component modalities when presented alone. The children could apparently only respond to one of the contributing modalities to the exclusion of the rest. Normal children, on the other hand, could respond to each component in turn, demonstrating thereby their ability to process and respond to all of them. More recently, it has been shown that the overselectivity of autistic children appears to hold not only across but within modalities as well (Koegel & Wilhelm, 1973; Kovattana & Kraemer, 1974). As to the preferred modality, different autistic children responded to different modalities, complicating the picture painted thus far, since some tended to favor the auditory, whereas others favored the visual. Clearly more research is needed before any implications for treatment can be drawn. This need is well highlighted by other work by Lovaas and his co-workers.

Following their own speech-training approach, Lovaas et al. (1971), for example, reported that after a great many trials, 1 of the 19 children undergoing training could not acquire the vocalization "ah." Eventually, after 1760 trials, the child could imitate the therapist's "ah." However, when the therapist covered his mouth, the previously acquired vocal response was immediately lost. According to the authors, the child had apparently been attending to the visual components of the task (i.e., the therapist's mouth and facial movements) to the exclusion of the simultaneous auditory input.

As indicated by Bonvillian and Nelson in the previous chapter, Webster, McPherson, Sloman, Evans, and Kuchar (1973) reported similar observations in their work with an autistic boy who was discovered to rely upon visual cues (i.e., facial expression, direction of gaze, and body movement) for understanding the therapist's spoken messages. In both instances, overselectivity to the visual modality was clearly evident.

Recently, Condon (1975) provided additional evidence on the autistic child's auditory dysfunction. Employing linguistic and microkinesic techniques of sound–film analysis (see Condon, 1970), he reported that the autistic children he studied responded in a peculiar fashion to auditory (speech and nonspeech) stimuli. Generally, these children responded to discrete stimuli (e.g., the sound of a wooden block hitting the floor, the phonemes of a spoken utterance, etc.) more than once. A first response apparently occurred within the normal latency, whereas a second response, greater in amplitude, appeared up to a full second (or 24 frames of regular film speed) after the first. In some instances, even a third response to the same stimulus was identified. Examples of a microkinesic response would be a slight and barely perceptible raise of the brow or right shoulder, a fine movement of the torso, a slight opening of the eyelid or mouth, etc.

These findings alert one to the possibility that autistic children may experience severe difficulties in speech acquisition because of their repetitive pattern of responsiveness to speech sounds, and because of the distinct possibility that they hear the same sound more than once. These children are described by Condon as being "dyssynchronous," compared with normal children and adults, who move in a rhythmic and finely modulated fashion (imperceptible by ordinary means of observation) to the speech sounds of others. What is interesting for our purposes here is that such "synchronous" movements are integrally related to the articulatory patterns of speech and, to a lesser extent, to the patterns of visual information presented to the hearer. Furthermore, autistic children not only fail in "interactional synchrony," that is, in their movement to the speech of others, they also lack self-synchrony, that is, they do not synchronize their movements to their own vocalizations.

No doubt considerable work is still needed to clarify fully the phenomena Condon (1975) described, including early screening and precise longitudinal monitoring of children at risk. Nonetheless, these striking findings would argue against a speech-oriented approach in communication training with these children.

ALTERNATIVES TO SPEECH TRAINING

This brief review serves to place in perspective the considerable problems autistic children encounter in decoding and encoding information, particularly aural information. The most obvious implication of this research for therapy is that speech training alone may be inadvisable in our effort to help many of these children to acquire a functional language. How many "autistic" children require an alternative to speech is not certain. As reported earlier, Lovaas et al. (1973) found that mute autistics were particularly inaccessible through vocal language training. Although it may be premature to draw implications for therapy from the limited findings of Lovaas and his co-workers and from some of our own observations in assessing these children, it may not be too early when it comes to research in this area. From some preliminary findings of our own, we would like to suggest that, in future research, dividing the autistic group into "mute" and "vocalizing" may provide us with some valuable insights in understanding the possible differential information-processing deficits these two groups display. It is conceivable that whereas the verbal autistic children are good candidates for speech training, the mute ones are not.

Our immediate concern, of course, is how to help noncommunicating children acquire the rudiments of language. Fortunately, an alternative to speech-only training became available, largely through the work of Gardner and Gardner (1971), who demonstrated that a gestural system, when employed with primates, can result in effective communication acquisition, whereas speech cannot (Hayes, 1951; Kellogg, 1968). The extensive pioneering work of Stokoe (1972); Klima and Bellugi (1975); and Bellugi, Klima, and Siple (1975), among many others, provided further support for this alternative, since it demonstrated that a manual communication system, such as American Sign Language (ASL), is indeed a language obeying a well organized and integrated set of principles.

Two years ago we put this notion to the test in a brief but intensive 5-week program, utilizing sign and speech in a simultaneous fashion. Our results (Konstantareas, Oxman, & Webster, 1977) and those of others working in the same paradigm (e.g., Creedon, 1973; Miller & Miller, 1973) have been promising. Many of the 18 children we treated for various lengths of time had, in fact, been previously exposed to systematic speech training with little or no success. With the introduction of speech and sign in a simultaneous manner, their responsiveness to training was rather dramatic. Most were able to acquire a number of signs and could communicate either when prompted or spontaneously. Indeed, for many, this was the first time they could use a sign to represent a referent, even though they were 10 years old at the time. A number of other investigators have since reported comparable findings using either single subjects or groups (cf. Bonvillian & Nelson, 1976; Miller & Miller, 1973).

In the process of monitoring the acquisition of sign language in our subsequent, more intensive work, we became intrigued with the question of whether sign language possessed special features of its own that rendered it more suitable to the information-processing capacities of these children.[2] In our earlier work, we had observed that the children seemed to acquire first, and most easily, those signs that to us appeared to provide clues to meaning. Vocal languages very rarely have this interesting feature, which in sign language is identified by the term *iconicity*. In his treatment of some of the main aspects of sign language, Schlesinger (in press) considers iconicity to be its single most striking feature. He defines as iconic those signs whose physical appearance has some resemblance to what is denoted by them. Iconicity is apparently expressed in various ways, such as (*a*) by performing an abbreviated imitation of a characteristic part of the referent (e.g., EAT or WRITE); (*b*) by outlining in the air the object referred to (e.g., HOUSE); (*c*) by evoking a property or state (e.g., FAT); and (*d*) by mimicking a property or state in a fragmentary manner (e.g., SLEEP).

A number of other writers have also defined iconicity in terms of a relationship between a sign and its meaning. Iconicity could be traced to the early origins of signs in pantomime, although many writers in the area are quick to point out that only a few signs are so clearly transparent in their iconicity that a nonsigner can guess their meaning without some additional cues. Most do concede, nonetheless, that "from the point of view of the outside observer, many of the signs of a visual language like American Sign Language appear not to be totally arbitrary [Bellugi, Klima & Siple, 1975, p. 97]." Our use of the term *iconicity* is comparable to that of others, such as Klima and Bellugi (1975), and incorporates three of the six relationships Stokoe, Casterline, and Cronberg (1965) considered in their treatment of the observ-

[2] Our concentration on sign language rather than speech acquisition has been necessitated by the inability of most of our children to produce speech, although they all seem to have some receptive speech capabilities.

able relationship between a sign and its referent. Their pantonymic, imitative, and metonymic signs, we believe, are roughly equivalent to what we call iconic signs.[3]

Although we believed clues to meaning may have rendered iconic signs easier to acquire than noniconic signs for the children with whom we worked, careful investigation of this hypothesis seemed warranted. For deaf adults of normal intelligence, for instance, Bellugi *et al.* (1975) found distinctive morphological features, rather than iconic attributes, of signs to be the basis for encoding and decoding processes. For the autistic child who suffers from information-processing impairments and concomitant cognitive deficits, however, there seemed reason to believe that iconicity might assume a unique significance.

Extensive documentation attests to these children's concreteness of thought and their limited symbolic representational capabilities (Churchill, 1972; Ricks & Wing, 1975). Iconic signs may therefore compensate to some extent for these limitations by making the task of symbolic representation easier (i.e., more concrete) for these children. In general, sign language requires visual representation rather than auditory skills. It is interesting to note that Hewes (1973) and Kimura (1974) hypothesize that existing communication through speech might have evolved from an original early foundation on gesture. That is, the phylogenetic development of language may have proceeded from pantomime and gesture to speech. Premack's (1972) contention that the autistic child's inability to acquire speech is due to his as yet limited auditory representation strategies is also relevant. Considered together, these two hypotheses would suggest that, in both evolutionary and developmental terms, manual language and visual representation may constitute the basic elements as well as the crucial antecedents to speech development (see also Bruner, 1974). If there is any validity to these speculations, the next step would be to argue that any clues to meaning in the early communication acquisition will render the task of communication training easier for the autistic child.[4]

[3] Schlesinger (in press) describes iconicity as involving the relationship between the sign and its base, that is, the concept directly described by the sign, whereas the related term *transparency* refers to the relationship between a sign and its referent. In signing COFFEE, for example, iconicity refers to the relationship between the sign (grinding movement of fists) and the base (grinding of coffee beans), whereas transparency encompasses both iconicity and the kind of transfer of meaning that occurs (the base–referent relationship).

[4] No doubt iconic signs may be easier to acquire by everyone but this may not be *as crucial* for sign language acquisition as with severely impaired children acquiring language for the first time.

Our first hypothesis therefore was that, other things being equal, iconic signs would be easier to acquire than noniconic signs.

Although our knowledge of language acquisition in normal children has considerably increased in recent years (Bloom, 1970; Brown, 1973), there is a paucity of evidence on language acquisition in autistic children, perhaps because it is only recently that language deficits have been viewed as central to their problem. We were therefore interested in possible parallels between normal and autistic language acquisition, being aware all the while that (a) we were dealing with sign language; (b) we were superimposing words over signs; and (c) we were studying children who were not able to extract spontaneously the linguistic rules of their native tongue but were exposed to systematic language training by active and intrusive therapists. We were particularly interested in a possible differential acquisition of three grammatical categories—verbs, nouns, and adjectives. This conventional grammatical distinction, it should be noted, provided a general way of categorizing the referents of the signs used in the experiment. The verb–noun–adjective distinction is not always easily made, either in sign language or in spoken English. In the present case, nouns clearly referred to concrete objects, adjectives to attributes of objects, and verbs to actions performed or descriptions of states of being. We postulated that verbs and nouns would be easier to acquire than adjectives, as others have shown to be true of normal language acquisition (cf. Bloom, 1970).

A third question we asked related to the issue of the relative stimulus control, that is, stimulus effectiveness, of the two modalities involved in the simultaneous communication training we employed. In view of the previous review, we were interested in determining if these children's receptive ability for visual information was superior to their auditory, or if the combination of the two tended to act in a synergistic fashion, thereby facilitating communication acquistion. This question is of particular relevance to applied concerns since, as has also been pointed out by Bonvillian and Nelson (Chapter 7), there is very little systematic evidence on the relative merit of employing a simultaneous versus a sign-only approach with these children.

METHOD

Subjects

Three boys and two girls, ranging in age from 7 years, 7 months, to 11 years, 5 months (mean age 9 years, 1 month), participated in the study. Table 8.1 lists the chronological age, developmental levels, and diagnosis for each child.

All five children had been diagnosed as "autistic" or "autistic-like." As is reflected in their developmental age scores in Table 8.1, all were particularly impaired in the areas of communication and social interaction skills.

TABLE 8.1

Chronological and Developmental Ages[a] and Diagnoses for the Sample

Subject	C.A.	Alpern and Boll developmental age scores					Diagnosis
		Phys-ical	Self-Help	Social	Aca-demic	Communi-cation	
Mary	9–6	3–2	3–6	3–2	2–6	2–2	Severe mental retardation with autistic features
Larry	9–3	4–6	3–6	2–2	1–10	1–10	Autism with severe mental retardation
Lee	7–7	7–6	5–8	1–10	3–4	1–0	Neurosensory deafness, bilateral; behavior disorder with autistic features
Brian	11–5	2–10	4–2	2–6	2–8	2–0	Mental retardation with autistic features
Maureen	7–10	5–6	3–6	2–4	3–2	1–8	Autism with mental retardation

[a] Developmental ages determined from the Alpern and Boll Developmental Profile (1972) at time of pretesting.

Procedure

Determining the "Iconicity" of Signs for Presentation

While the literature offers documentation of the iconic nature of sign language systems (e.g., Klima & Bellugi, 1975; Schlesinger, in press), it was necessary in the present context to determine which particular signs in the Ontario dialect of American Sign Language for the Deaf, were to be considered "iconic" and which "noniconic." To this end, we adopted as an operational definition of iconicity "the degree of physical similarity between a sign and its referent, in conjunction with the extent to which a sign offers the perceiver a clue to meaning." With the aid of fluent signers and through access to a number of catalogues of signs of the Ontario Sign Language system, we arrived at an initial list of 126 signs. These signs appeared to have, in most cases, possible functional utility for, and at levels of abstraction in accord with, our autistic sample's cognitive ability. Ratings as to the degree of iconicity for each of these signs were obtained from a group of 41 undergraduate students in psychology and from 25 first-grade children, none of whom had any prior knowledge of sign language. These ratings were employed to determine, by consensus, which of the signs were to be considered as iconic and which noniconic for normal children and young adults.

The group of 126 signs presented for rating included an approximately equal number of nouns, verbs, and adjectives and comprised what appeared to the investigators to be an equal number of iconic and noniconic signs within each of the three grammatical categories. Signs were chosen in an attempt to keep the motor coordination required for their production at a low or moderate level, all signs being generally equivalent in this regard.

Signs were presented with their spoken counterparts to the adult and child raters. The adults rated each sign on a four-point scale, from "highly iconic" to "not at all iconic," by means of a written checklist. For the child raters this task was simplified to a two-choice situation, where a raise of the hand indicated a judgment of a sign appearing iconic.

To compare their judgments with those of the children, the adults' original four-point scale was collapsed into a two-point one, iconic and noniconic. The proportions of children and adults rating each sign as iconic or noniconic were then determined. Overall, the children's and adults' ratings of iconicity were highly similar ($r = .567$, $df = 124$; $p < .005$). Although the considerable agreement that was obtained across raters was encouraging, there were still some cases where a discrepancy in judgment for particular signs did occur between the two groups. In these cases we relied upon the children's ratings, making the assumption that there would be a greater similarity between the normal and the severely dysfunctional children's perception of signs.

The 10 signs within each grammatical category (noun, verb, adjective) judged by the largest proportion of raters as iconic and those 10 judged by the largest proportion as noniconic were selected for presentation in the experiment proper. These 60 signs are listed in Table 8.2.

TABLE 8.2

Signs Chosen for Iconicity Training on the Basis of Ratings by Adult and Children Groups

	Iconic			Noniconic	
Nouns	Verbs	Adjectives	Nouns	Verbs	Adjectives
CARDS	BREATH	HOT	MOUSE	START	DARK
UMBRELLA	RACE	HIGH	REFRIGERATOR	FILL	SHARP
GATE	REST	CHOPPED	SHEEP	SHARE	SOFT
DEODORANT	TASTE	COLD	MIRROR	KNIT	HEAVY
IRON	SCRATCH	FAT	COFFEE	JOIN	DEEP
PIPE	KNOCK	BALD	FOOT	LOCK	CLOSE
HEEL	PUNISH	WIDE	CANDLE	MOW	SWEET
HOUSE	EXCHANGE	WHOLE	BASKET	SCATTER	THICK
COLLAR	SEPARATE	FULL	GRASS	AWAKEN	EMPTY
SUN	COVER	LONG	STAR	SKI	OLD

Stimulus Materials and Training Procedures

The referent for each of the 60 signs was drawn on a separate 15 × 22-centimeter piece of white cardboard. In several cases (e.g., for the adjective *long*) it was necessary to illustrate the referent by means of a comparison. Therefore, two cards for each of those particular signs were used (e.g., one card showing a long and the other a short stick). Figure 8.1 shows six of the stimulus cards employed in training.

Prior to the study, is was ascertained that none of the five children either understood or could produce, through speech or sign, any of the 60 signs to be presented for training. Experimental sessions consisted of teaching sign–words (i.e., signs and their vocal counterparts) through simultaneous communication procedures, where speech and sign are used together. Following previously designed training procedures (cf. Konstantareas *et al.*, 1977), experimental sessions focused upon the child's performance in three categories of communication skill: reproductive, receptive, and elicited signing.

For each sign–word, training proceeded in the same order. Four training trials were given for each sign–word within each of the three communication categories. Training procedures were as follows:

Figure 8.1. Examples of the stimulus materials used for training. HOUSE, EX-CHANGE, and COLD represent iconic signs and MOUSE, SKI, and EMPTY represent noniconic signs.

1. *Reproductive signing.* The appropriate stimulus card was presented. *E* (the experimenter) directed the child's attention to the card, and then to his (*E*'s) modeled sign for the referent depicted while vocalizing the corresponding word. The child was prompted to imitate *E*'s sign. If the child incorrectly reproduced the sign, his hands were "molded" into the proper configuration and movement.

2. *Receptive signing.* Those three cards relevant to a given training session were presented. *E* asked the child to pick up a particular card by signing and speaking the name of the referent shown on it (prior to the experimental sessions, all children were trained to respond to this, and other, task relevant instructions). Appropriate feedback was offered by *E* as to the correctness of the child's response upon its emission.

3. *Elicited signing.* A stimulus card was presented and the child was prompted to respond with its appropriate sign label. Feedback was offered as to the correctness of the response. In the event of no signing response, or an incorrect or poorly articulated one, the child was shown the appropriate sign for the stimulus card, which remained in front of him.

Three sign–words were presented to each child during each training session, iconic and noniconic signs being presented alternately. Nine different orders of sign–word presentations were determined for the three grammatical categories used, and these orders were randomly employed for each child until all sign–words were exhausted. Throughout training, positive reinforcement in the form of praise was offered for the child's effort and correct responding, and appropriate feedback and correction were given for incorrect responding or failure to respond.

All experimental sessions were carried out in a room familiar to the children and were conducted by the same experimenter. A maximum intersession interval of 4 days was observed, each session lasting for approximately 25 minutes. The experimenter conducting training rated each child's vocal and signing performance through the course of each session. Reliability ratings from an independent judge were obtained for 50% of the trials. Scoring proceeded according to the following criteria: score "1" for an incorrect response or a failure to respond; score "2" for an approximation to a correct response (e.g., correct sign or vocalization offered but poorly articulated); score "3" for a correct response.

Testing for Stimulus Control in the Receptive Category

Because all items were presented for training through a simultaneous communication approach—that is, speech and sign were used together—testing was conducted at the completion of each training session to determine what modality or modalities were operative in the child's understanding of the training items. For each of the three sign–words presented during a training session, a stimulus control assessment was administered at the end of that session. In a procedure similar to that employed for training the receptive category (see p. 227), two trials were given within each of the three modes of presentation involved—sign only, speech only, and sign and speech combined. Scoring criteria were the same as during training, but no reinforcement or feedback was offered to the children during this assessment.

RESULTS

Reliability

Although reliabilities were obtained by an independent observer for 50% of all trials for both signing and vocalization, we will report only data pertaining to the children's signing performance and their understanding of signed, spoken, and simultaneous cues. This choice is due to the fact that only two of the five children in the sample could produce even approximately correct renditions of the vocal counterparts of signs, rendering data on vocal output in this context extremely limited. Percentage agreement between raters across 50% of the trials for all children was 94.48%, with a range of 89.90% to 96.35% for individual children.

Assessment of Iconicity, Grammatical Category, and Linguistic Competence

A $2 \times 3 \times 3$ analysis of variance for iconicity, grammatical category of sign, and level of linguistic competence revealed significant main effects for iconicity [$F(1,3578) = 18.41, p < .0001$], grammatical category [$F(2,3578) = 6.52, p < .002$], and linguistic competence level [$F(2,3578) = 176.06, p < .0001$]. Significant interactions were obtained for iconicity and grammatical category [$F(2,3578) = 3.63, p < .026$] and for grammatical category and level of linguistic competence [$F(4,3578) = 2.76, p < .026$]. These results are shown in Table 8.3.

TABLE 8.3

Analysis of Variance Summary Table for Sign Acquisition as a Function of Iconicity, Grammatical Class, and Level of Linguistic Competence

Source	Sum of squares	df	F	Prob.
Iconicity (I)	7.654	1	18.414	.0001
Part of speech (P)	5.417	2	6.516	.0019
Linguistic competence (L)	146.374	2	176.060	.0001
I × P	3.014	2	3.625	.0260
I × L	.124	2	.149	.8620
P × L	4.584	4	2.757	.0260
I × P × L	.498	4	.299	.8785
Error	1487.346	3578		

Regarding the main effect for iconicity, the children's performance, defined in terms of mean score across trials for each sign, was better for iconic than for noniconic signs. A Duncan multiple range test applied on the significant effect for grammatical category revealed that verbs and adjectives were acquired more easily than were nouns ($p <$ .05). Verbs and adjectives were comparable to each other. The interaction between iconicity and grammatical category appears in Figure 8.2. Examination of these six means through the Duncan test revealed

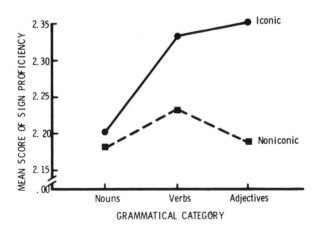

Figure 8.2. The interaction between iconicity and part of speech.

that iconic signs for verbs and adjectives were equivalent, and significantly superior ($p < .05$) to the other four means, none of which
differed significantly from one another.

A Duncan test applied to the significant main effect for level of
linguistic competence showed all three levels to differ significantly
from one another. Receptive performance was significantly superior to
reproductive performance, which in turn was superior to elicited
performance. Examination of the significant grammatical category by
level of linguistic competence interaction revealed a complex picture,
which is best appreciated by considering Figure 8.3. A Duncan test
applied to the nine means involved in this interaction yielded results
generally consistent with the two main effects considered separately,
with receptive verbs reflecting the best performance and elicited
nouns the poorest ($p < .05$). Performance for receptive verbs was not
significantly different from that for receptive nouns or receptive and
reproductive adjectives. Performance on the latter two categories as
well as on reproductive verbs was superior to that on reproductive
nouns, however, while elicited verbs and adjectives resulted in poorer
performance ($p < .05$ in all cases).

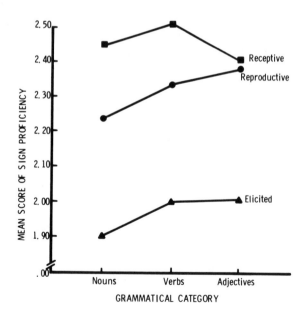

Figure 8.3. The interaction between level of linguistic competence and part of
speech.

Assessment of Stimulus Control

A 3 × 3 × 2 analysis of variance for sensory modality (auditory, visual, or auditory and visual), grammatical category, and iconicity was computed for performance on the stimulus control test within the receptive category of linguistic competence. Significant effects were obtained only for sensory modality [$F(2,1778) = 44.74$, $p < .0001$]. These results are shown in Table 8.4.

TABLE 8.4

Analysis of Variance Summary Table for Stimulus Control as a Function of Iconicity, Grammatical Class, and Sensory Modality

Source	Sum of squares	df	F	Prob.
Iconicity (*I*)	2.722	1	2.930	.0871
Part of speech (*P*)	.324	2	.175	.8410
Modality (*M*)	83.114	2	44.737	.0001
I × *P*	.751	2	.404	.6734
I × *M*	1.008	2	.524	.5871
P × *M*	2.502	4	.673	.6135
I × *P* × *M*	3.529	4	.950	.5644
Error	1651.643	1778		

A Duncan test applied on the data showed that the visual modality (sign only) was as effective as the visual-and-auditory modality (sign and speech combined), whereas both were superior ($p < .05$) to the auditory modality (speech only).

DISCUSSION

The results of this study offer some insights about the manner in which signs are acquired by autistic or autistic-like children. Although our sample size was small, our findings, collected over an extensive period of training, would seem to have some important implications for simultaneous communication-training procedures with autistic children and for further inquiry into the formal characteristics of sign language.

That iconic signs were learned better than noniconic signs across both the receptive and the two productive levels of linguistic competence seems to fit well with the notion that iconicity facilitates the decoding and encoding of sign language. Although we may only guess at this point, perhaps the iconic nature of some signs makes them accessible to the concrete representational capacities of autistic children (cf. Churchill, 1972; Wing, 1966). While Bellugi, Klima, and Siple (1975) found that deaf adults process signs on the basis of their distinctive configurational features (as opposed to semantic or iconic origin codes), the children we have studied appear to have been relying upon the iconic and transparent nature of signs for their learning when such clues to meaning were available.

Though the children studied would appear to be operating differently from fluent adult signers, we do not know as yet whether or not they are similar in this respect to deaf children learning sign language for the first time. If the latter is indeed the case, it would perhaps provide an optimistic similarity between the autistic and the normal deaf child's use of sign. An extension of Bellugi, Klima, and Siple's (1975) research paradigm or of the present one may help answer this question.

It was of interest that we consistently obtained superior performance for iconic verbs and adjectives. We cannot offer any definitive explanation for this finding, although we can think of two possibilities. First, in our initial assessment of the iconicity of 126 signs, both the child and adult raters tended, in general, to perceive verbs and adjectives as more iconic than nouns. Thus the signs we chose to consider in the original rating task may have included adjectives and verbs that were actually more iconic than nouns. A more appealing possibility comes from theoretical work in the area of developmental psycholinguistics. In her "functional core" theory of concept formation and language acquisition, Nelson (1974) suggests that verbs are semantically and conceptually the least complex words for the child to acquire. With the young child operating within an action-oriented, sensorimotor framework, verbs, especially verbs of action, which largely comprised the sample in this study, offer the best cognitive and perceptual fit with the child's learning and cognitive–organizational strategies. That iconic verbs were among the easiest for the children in the present sample to acquire may, therefore, be consistent with this notion. It is also of interest to note that in Fillmore's (1968) "case grammar" model, adjectives are seen as a subclass of verbs, both arising from the same generic semantic class. Applied to the present case, Fillmore's model would suggest that, semantically, verbs and adjectives are more similar to each other than either of them is to nouns. Although there is much dispute regarding Fillmore's model (cf. Brown, 1973), the notion that verbs and adjectives are generically and semantically related, and thus also related in terms of early language acquisition, is supported by the present findings.

The significant effect for performance at the three levels of linguistic competence employed—receptive, reproductive, and elicited—is in accord with acquisition data from our previous research (Konstantareas *et al.*, 1977) and parallels evidence that in speech development, comprehension tends to antedate production (e.g., Fraser, Bellugi & Brown, 1963; Bloom, 1970; Brown, 1973; Clark, 1971; Huttenlocher, 1974).

The interaction obtained between level of linguistic competence and grammatical category is difficult to explain. However, the means involved do tend to parallel the main effects for grammatical category and linguistic competence. That these two variables interact in a rather complex manner, however, should alert us to the need for more extensive research in this area, both with dysfunctional and with normal populations.

In the testing of stimulus control for receptive communication, the finding that sign used alone and speech used simultaneously are superior to speech use alone is confirmed by our own clinical observation as well as by the previously reported findings pertaining to the autistic child's difficulties in dealing with auditory information. In the case of the combined speech and sign presentation, speech did not result in improved receptive communication. At the same time, it is important to note that it did not adversely affect the children's receptive performance, as a deficit in auditory–visual association might lead one to expect. This outcome is also not consistent with the autistic child's double responding to sound reported by Condon (1975), since superimposition of sound on sign should be expected to interfere with performance. It is possible, of course, that the children in the present sample elected to respond to sign alone, disregarding the second component of the simultaneous message. This would be consistent with the previously cited evidence of selective responding by autistic children (cf. Lovaas *et al.*, 1971). What is clearly needed at this point is to determine if comparable findings can be obtained not only for receptive but also for productive performance.

It has been anecdotally reported that exposure to a simultaneous communication approach has a facilitative effect on speech and vocalization by these children (e.g., Creedon, 1973). Elsewhere we have reported preliminary data suggestive of such a facilitative effect for five children in our own simultaneous communication program (Oxman, Konstantareas, & Webster, 1976). We have also found that the minimal receptive speech abilities of some of our dysfunctional children aid them in their sign acquisition. Especially in the early stages of training, the child's understanding of at least some words seems to augment his subsequent understanding through signs of the fact that specific symbols can be employed to stand for specific referents. That the vocal component in the present study did not interfere with receptive sign acquisition implies that the use of speech along with signs may be defensible at this point.

This issue requires further investigation, however, for two main reasons: First, these findings have relevance for *receptive* communication acquisition *only*, and, second, since the use of sign language with children younger than those so far reported in the literature is becoming more and more prevalent, we must consider the long-term effects of the presence or absence of the speech component. With the apparent success of simultaneous communication, it is now easier to argue persuasively for the use of signs with 3- and 4-year-olds, or even with younger mute autistic and autistic-like children. The need to determine whether sign alone or a simultaneous use of sign and speech in terms of both receptive and productive training is more appropriate for these younger children ought to be an immediate priority.

In conclusion, the fact that the children in the present study found iconic signs easier to learn than noniconic ones and that the superimposition of speech neither facilitated nor interfered with their receptive communication acquisition, have important implications for treatment relying on simultaneous communication-training procedures. Capitalizing upon these findings in training may facilitate sign language acquisition by the nonverbal autistic or autistic-like child. With continued research of this kind, especially within a longitudinal framework and with chronologically younger groups, we might hope to further clarify both the information-processing peculiarities of these children and the intricate process of language acquisition.

ACKNOWLEDGMENTS

The authors would like to express their appreciation to Mrs. Donna Taylor and Miss Thora Richards, child care workers, for their multifaceted contribution to the project, and to Dr. Leon Sloman for his psychiatric consultation and support. Thanks are also extended to Dr. Peter Reich for his invaluable comments and criticisms.

REFERENCES

de Ajuriaguerra, J. Speech disorders in childhood. In E. C. Carterette (Ed.), *Brain function: Volume III—speech, language, and communication,* Los Angeles: Univ. of California Press, 1966.

Alpern, G. D., & Boll, T. J. *Developmental profile.* New York: Psychological Development Publications, 1972.

Bellugi, U., Klima, E. S., & Siple, P. Remembering in Signs. *Cognition,* 1975, *3,* 93–125.

Bloom, L. *Language development: Form and function in emerging grammars.* Cambridge, Massachusets: The M.I.T. Press, 1970.

Bloomfield, L. *Language.* New York: Holt, Rinehart and Winston, 1933.

Bonvillian, J. D., & Nelson, K. E. Sign language acquisition in a mute autistic boy. *Journal of Speech and Hearing Disorders,* 1976, *41,* 339–347.

Brown, R., Cazden, C., & Bellugi, U. The child's grammar from I to III. In C. A. Ferguson & D. I. Slobin (Eds.), *Studies of child language development.* Toronto: Holt, Rinehart and Winston, 1973.

Brown, R. *A first language: The early stages.* Harvard Univ. Press, Cambridge, Massachusetts, 1973.

Bruner, J. S., Olver, R. R., Greenfield, P. M., *et al. Studies in cognitive growth: A collaboration at the center for cognitive studies.* London: John Wiley & Sons, 1967.

Chomsky, N. *Language and mind.* New York: Harcourt, Brace and World, 1972.

Churchill, D. N. The relationship of infantile autism and early childhood schizophrenia to developmental language disorders of childhood. *Journal of Autism and Childhood Schizophrenia,* 1972, *2,* 182–197.

Clark, E. V. Some aspects of the conceptual basis for first language acquisition. In R. L. Schiefelbusch & L. L. Lloyd (Eds.), *Language perspectives—acquisition, retardation, and intervention.* London: Univ. Park Press, 1974.

Clark, E. V. On the acquisition of the meaning of before and after. *Journal of Verbal Learning and Verbal Behavior,* 1971, *10,* 266–275.

Condon, W. S. Method of micro-analysis of sound films of behavior. *Behavior Research Methods & Instrumentation,* 1970, *2*(2), 51–54.

Condon, W. S. Multiple response to sound in dysfunctional children. *Journal of Autism and Childhood Schizophrenia,* 1975, *5,* 37–56.

Creedon, M. *Language development in nonverbal autistic children using a simultaneous communication system.* Paper presented at the Society for Research in Child Development Meeting, 1973.

Cromer, R. F. The development of language and cognition:The cognition hypothesis. In B. Foss (Ed.), *New perspectives in child development.* Harmondsworth: Penguin Books, 1974.

Fillmore, C. J. The case for case. In E. Bach & R. T. Harms (Eds.), *Universals in linguistic theory.* New York: Holt, Rinehart and Winston, 1968.

Fraser, C., Bellugi, U.,& Brown, R. Control of grammar in imitation, comprehension, and production. *Journal of Verbal Learning and Verbal Behavior,* 1963, *2,* 121–135.

Gardner, B. T., & Gardner, R. A. Two way communication with an infant chimpanzee. In A. Schrier and F. Stollnitz (Eds.), *Behavior of nonhuman primates, Vol. IV.* New York: Academic Press, 1971. Pp. 117–184.

Hayes, C. *The ape in our house.* New York: Harper, 1951.

Hermelin, B., & O'Connor, N. *Psychological experiments with autistic children.* Toronto: Pergamon Press, 1970.

Hewes, G. H. Primate communication and the gestural origin of language. *Current Anthropology*, 1973, *14*, 5–24.

Hewitt, F. M. Teaching speech to autistic children through operant conditioning. *American Journal of Orthopsychiatry*, 1965, *35*, 927–936.

Hingtgen, J. N., & Churchill, D. N. Identification of perceptual limitations in mute autistic children. *Archives of General Psychiatry*, 1969, *21*, 68–71.

Huttenlocher, J. The origins of language comprehension. In R. L. Solso (Ed.), *Theories in cognitive psychology*. The Loyola Symposium. Potomac, Maryland: Lawrence Erlbaum Assoc., 1974.

Huttenlocher, J., & Strauss, S. Comprehension and a statement's relation to the situation it describes. *Journal of Verbal Learning and Verbal Behavior*, 1968, 7, 300–304.

Kanner, L. Autistic disturbances of affective contact. *Nervous Child*, 1943, *2*, 217–250.

Kellogg, W. N. Communication in language in the home-raised chimpanzee. *Science*, 1968, *162*, 423–427.

Kimura, D. The neural basis of language qua gesture. In H. Avakian-Whitaker & H. A. Whitaker (Eds.), *Current trends in Neurolinguistics*. Mouton, 1974.

Klima, E. S., & Bellugi, U. *Proceedings for neuroscienc research programs*. Boston, Massachusetts: in press.

Koegel, R., & Wilhelm, H. Selective responding to the components of multiple visual cues. *Journal of Experimental Child Psychology*, 1973, *15*, 442–453.

Konstantareas, M. M., Oxman, J., & Webster, C. D. Simultaneous communication with nonverbal children: An alternative to speech with autistic and other severely dysfunctional non-verbal children. *Journal of Communication Disorders*, 1977, *10*, 267–282.

Kovattana, P. M., & Kraemer, H. C. Response to multiple visual cues of color, size, and form by autistic children. *Journal of Autism and Childhood Schizophrenia*, 1974, *4*, 251–261.

Krashen, S. D. The development of cerebral dominance and language learning: More new evidence. In *Psycholinguistic development: Theory and applications*, 1976.

Lenneberg, E. H. *Biological foundations of language*. New York: Wiley, 1967.

Liben, L. S. *A developmental approach to the experiential deficiencies of deaf children*. Paper presented at the Society for Research in Child Development Meeting, 1975.

Lovaas, O. I., Berberich, J. P., Perloff, B. F., & Schaeffer, B. Acquisition of imitative speech by schizophrenic children. *Science*, 1966, *151*, 705–707.

Lovaas, O. I., Koegel, R., Schreibman, L., & Rehm, R. Selective responding by autistic children to multiple sensory input. *Journal of Abnormal Child Psychology*, 1971, *77*, 211–222.

Lovaas, O. I., Koegel, R., Simmons, J. Q., & Long, J. S. Some generalization and follow-up measures on autistic children in behavior therapy. *Journal of Applied Behavior Analysis*, 1973, *6*, 131–166.

Lovaas, O. I., & Schreibman, L. Stimulus overselectivity of autistic children in a two-stimulus situation. *Behavior Research and Therapy*, 1971, *9*, 305–310.

Lyons, J. *Introduction to theoretical linguistics*. Cambridge, Massachusetts: Harvard University Press, 1968.

Mack, J., & Webster, C. D. Where are they now and how are they faring? Substudy 74–19. Unpublished manuscript, Clarke Institute of Psychiatry, 1974.

Miller, A., & Miller, E. E. Cognitive-developmental training with elevated boards and sign language. *Journal of Autism and Childhood Schizophrenia*, 1973, *3*, 65–85.

Nelson, K. Structure and strategy in learning to talk. Monograph SRCD, *149*, 1973.

Nelson, K. Concept, word, and sentence: Interrelations in acquisition and development. *Psychological Review*, 1974, 8, 267–285.

Oxman, J., Konstantareas, M. M., & Webster, C. D. *The possible function of sign language in facilitating verbal communication in severely dysfunctional children.* Paper presented at the Univ. of Louisville Interdisciplinary Linguistics Conference, Louisville, Kentucky, 1976.

Piaget, J. The developmental psychology of Jean Piaget. In *Carmichael's manual of child psychology.* P. Mussen (Ed.), New York: J. Wiley, 1970.

Piaget, J., & Inhelder, B. *The psychology of the child.* New York: Basic Books, 1969.

Premack, D. Two problems in cognition: Symbolization, and from icon to phoneme. In T. Alloway, L. Krames, & P. Pliner (Eds.), *Communication and affect: A comparative approach.* New York: Academic Press, 1972.

Reese, H. W. Verbal mediation as a function of age level. *Psychological Bulletin*, 1962, 59, 502–509.

Reynolds, B., Newsom, C. D., & Lovaas, O. I. Auditory overselectivity in autistic children. *Journal of Abnormal Child Psychology*, 1974, 2, 253–264.

Rutter, M. Concepts of autism: A review of research. *Journal of Child Psychiatry and Psychology*, 1968, 9, 1–25.

Rutter, M. The development of infantile autism. *Psychological Medicine*, 1974, 4, 147–163.

Ricks, D. M., & Wing, L. Language, communication, and the use of symbols in normal and autistic children. *Journal of Autism and Childhood Schizophrenia*, 1975, 5, 191–221.

Sapir, E. In *Culture, language and personality.* Mandelbaum (Ed.), Berkeley: Univ. of California Press, 1966.

Schlesinger, I. M. Some aspects of sign language. In E. Cohen, L. Namir, & I. M. Schlesinger (Eds.), *A new dictionary of sign language: Part 1.* Mouton: The Hague, in press.

Shopler, E. The stress of autism in ethology. *Journal of Autism and Childhood Schizophrenia*, 1974, 4, 193–195.

Skinner, B. F. *Verbal behavior.* New York: Appleton-Century-Crofts, 1957.

Spiker, C. C. Verbal factors in the discrimination learning of children. In J. C. Wright & Y. Kagan (Eds.), *Basic cognitive processes in children.* Monograph of SRCD, 1963, 28, 53–69.

Stokoe, W. C. *Semiotics and human sign languages.* Mouton, The Hague, 1972.

Stokoe, W. C., Jr., Casterline, D. C., & Croneberg, C. G. A dictionary of American Sign Language on linguistic principles. Washington: Gaulladet College Press, 1965.

Tubbs, V. K. Types of linguistic disability in psychotic children. *Journal of Mental Deficiency Research*, 1966, 10, 230–240.

Webster, C. D., McPherson, H., Sloman, L., Evans, M. A., & Kuchar, E. Communication with an autistic boy with gestures. *Journal of Autism and Childhood Schizophrenia*, 1973, 3, 337–346.

Whitaker, H. A. Neurolinguistics. In W. O. Dingwall (Ed.), *A Survey of linguistic science.* Linguistics Program, Univ. of Maryland, 1971, 137–244.

Wing, J. K. Diagnosis, epidemiology, aetiology. In J. K. Wing (Ed.), *Early childhood autism: Clinical, educational and social aspects.* London: Pergamon Press, 1966.

9

Patterns of Cerebral Specialization in Congenitally Deaf Adults: A Preliminary Report

HELEN J. NEVILLE

University of California, San Diego,
and The Salk Institute for Biological Studies

URSULA BELLUGI

The Salk Institute for Biological Studies

INTRODUCTION

One of the most distinguishing characteristics of the organization of the human brain is the differential functional specialization of the left and right hemispheres. In most adults, the left cerebral hemisphere is more important in speech and language functioning, and the right hemisphere is more important in the performance of certain nonlanguage perceptual tasks.

Evidence for this specialization of function comes from studies of behavioral deficits in neurological disease, and also from behavioral and evoked potential studies of normal people. The evidence from neuropathology shows that speech and/or language functioning is very likely to be disrupted following damage to left hemisphere but is only

This work was supported, in part, by National Institutes of Health Grant No. NS-09811 and by National Science Foundation Grant No. BNS-76-12866 to The Salk Institute for Biological Studies.

UNDERSTANDING LANGUAGE
THROUGH
SIGN LANGUAGE RESEARCH

rarely affected following right-hemisphere lesions (Luria & Karasseva, 1968; Milner, 1964; Weinstein, 1962). On the other hand, certain perceptual skills, such as the recognition of faces and the ability to orient oneself in space, are more likely to be disrupted after right- than after left-hemisphere lesions (Milner, 1971; Newcombe & Russell, 1969).

Behavioral studies of healthy adults show that verbal material is more accurately reported when presented to the right ear or right visual field, presumbly because these have stronger or more direct connections with the left hemisphere than do the left ear and left visual field (Kimura, 1961, 1967; McKeever & Huling, 1971). Similarly, certain nonlanguage materials, like environmental sounds and unfamiliar faces, are more accurately perceived when presented to the left ear or left visual field, which have stronger or more direct access to the right hemisphere (Berlucchi, 1974; Curry, 1967; Klein, Moscovitch & Vigna, 1976; Knox & Kimura, 1968; Spreen, Spellacy, & Reid, 1970).

Evoked potential studies of normal adults report that certain components of the evoked potential are of higher amplitude and occur at shorter latencies from the left than from the right hemisphere during tasks engaging language processes (Neville, 1974; Neville, Schulman, & Galambos, 1977; Wood, 1975; Wood, Goff, & Day, 1971). Other studies report greater amplitude of evoked potential components recorded from the right hemisphere with the presentation of nonlanguage stimuli (Dustman & Beck, 1974; Neville et al., 1977; Vella, Butler, & Glass, 1972).

The results from these different approaches to the study of cerebral specialization are all interpreted as supporting the notion that the left hemisphere is specialized for speech and language functions and the right hemisphere is specialized for nonlanguage perceptual skills in the normal human adult.

We have been particularly interested in the relationship between cerebral functional specialization and the acquisition of speech and language. However, rather little is known about the phylogeny and ontogeny of cerebral specialization of function.

The human species appears to be the only mammal that shows clear evidence for hemispheric specialization of function. There are some studies in both cats and monkeys showing preferential retention and acquisition by one hemisphere of tasks learned initially by that hemisphere (Gazzaniga, 1963; Webster, 1972), and these results have been interpreted as suggestive of the specialization seen in the human brain.

However, more recent studies have questioned the existence of a homologue of cerebral specialization in infrahuman primates. Hamilton (1977), studying rhesus monkeys, looked for asymmetries in the retention of visual tasks designed, on the basis of experiments with human subjects, to reveal hemispheric specialization. His tasks included the discrimination of orientation of lines and the discrimination of monkeys' faces. No evidence was found to suggest that the two hemispheres were differentially specialized for processing these types of information. Doty and Overman (1977) studied the acquisition of a maze learning task in macaque monkeys and also failed to find evidence for hemispheric specialization of function.

There is clear evidence of lateral functional specialization for bird song in at least four species of birds. The lateralization of control is both peripheral and central. If the tracheosyringealis branch of the left hypoglossal nerve is cut in an adult male, only a fragment of the bird's song remains intact. When a similar lesion is made on the right only a fragment of the song is lost (Nottebohm, 1970; 1974). Similarly, left-sided brain lesions of the hyperstriatum ventrale, pars caudale, and of the robust nucleus of the archistriatum result in severe disruption of song, but similar, right-sided lesions do not (Nottebohm, 1977).

The lack of strong evidence for hemispheric specialization in mammals other than man and the absence of speech and language in any animal but ourselves has led many people to propose that the development of cerebral specialization and the development of language occurred together in phylogeny (Gazzaniga, 1970; Levy, 1969). The studies demonstrating lateralized control of bird song suggested to some investigators the hypothesis that cerebral specialization has developed specifically for the unilateral motoric control of vocalization (speech or bird song) which may be more easily disrupted were the two hemispheres to share control of the midline structures (larynx or syrinx) (Liberman, 1974; Marler, 1970). In support of this proposition is the fact that many studies find speech production to be more strongly lateralized than language comprehension or the performance of nonlanguage skills (Levy, 1974; Sperry, 1968; White, 1969).

Most of what we know about the ontogeny of cerebral specialization comes from studies of the effects on behavior of left- and right-hemisphere lesions at different ages. These show, by and large, that the functional specialization of the two hemispheres is not immutably determined in the human brain until around puberty. In children of 3 years or less, damage to the right hemisphere interferes with language to the same extent as damage to the left hemisphere, suggesting that both hemispheres are involved in language acquisition at that time

(Lenneberg, 1967). Between 3 years of age and puberty, recovery from language deficits following left-hemisphere insults is much more likely to occur than in an adult (Kinsbourne, 1974; Lenneberg, 1967; 1974). Moreover, whereas left hemispherectomy in a right-handed adult usually eliminates both speech production and language comprehension, the same operation performed in infancy or childhood does not preclude the attainment of perfectly normal or even superior speech and language skills (Smith & Sugar, 1975), although in some cases language acquisiton has been reported to be slightly delayed after early left hemispherectomy (Dennis & Whitaker, 1976). Thus, although there may be an early predisposition for the left and right hemispheres to govern different cognitive skills, the remarkable regulatory capacity or plasticity of the immature brain permits modification of functional specialization until around the end of childhood. The data from clinical neuropathology indicate the increasing determination or specialization of cortical tissue with age; in order to describe the functional interrelationships between the two hemispheres in the normal child we can employ behavioral and electrophysiological tests of hemispheric specialization.

There are only a few behavioral studies of the ontogeny of cerebral specialization, and the results from these are equivocal. Some studies find that the right-ear advantage for verbal material is found to the same extent in children and adults (Berlin, Hughes, Lowe-Bell, & Berlin, 1973; Kimura, 1963; Schulman-Galambos, 1977). Others, however, find that the right-ear advantage, and presumably left-hemispheric specialization for language, increases from 5 to 13 years of age (Bryden, 1970; Bryden & Allard, 1973; Satz, Bakker, Teunissen, Goebel, & Van der Vlugt, 1975).

Other studies report behavioral asymmetries in young infants that may be related to the functional asymmetries seen in older children and adults. Turkewitz (1977) and Kinsbourne (1972) report early asymmetrical turning tendencies; Entus (1975) reports better right-ear discrimination for verbal material and a left-ear advantage for nonverbal stimuli in infants only a few weeks of age. Consistent with these behavioral studies is the report of material specific evoked potential asymmetries in infants from 1 week to 10 months of age, (Molfese, Freeman, & Palermo, 1975), although these are not precisely parallel to the evoked potential asymmetries seen in adults (Molfese, 1977). Also, there are studies showing anatomical asymmetries between the left and right hemispheres in newborns which are similar to those found in adults (Wada, 1973; Wada et al., 1975; Witelson & Pallie, 1973). Thus, these early signs may be indicative of eventual developmental preferences, given normal neurological development and a normal language and cognitive environment.

Neville (1975; 1977) investigated cerebral specialization for non-language material in 16 children aged 9–13 years. The subjects were asked to identify line drawings of common objects and evoked potentials (EPs) were recorded from left and right temporal sites (T5 and T6 in the International 10–20 System). The EPs from the right hemisphere were significantly larger and the amplitude of certain components peaked earlier, than did EPs from the left hemisphere. Moreover, this EP asymmetry was larger in older children, suggesting some increase in cerebral specialization with age.

In the same study, Neville also looked for EP evidence of cerebral specialization in congenitally deaf children to try to determine the relationship between the acquisition of speech and the development of cerebral specialization. The 15 deaf children ranged in age from 9–13 years and had normal nonverbal I.Q.s. They had profound (i.e., > 100 dB loss binaurally) sensori-neural deafness diagnosed to be of hereditary etiology. All deaf children had a family history of sensori-neural deafness; 8 of the 15 had at least one deaf parent. All of the children were free from other neurological disorder. These deaf children were chosen to be subjects because, while they were of normal nonverbal intelligence, they were functionally without speech according to (a) evaluations made by their teachers; and (b) the results of a series of simple language tests given by Professor Eric Lenneberg. The deaf children showed no asymmetry of amplitude or latency of EP components. Their performances on the task and their EPs were very similar to those of the hearing children, but there was no evidence of lateral asymmetry. Further analysis of the data revealed that the 8 deaf children of deaf parents had learned American Sign Language (ASL), from their parents and these subjects did have asymmetrical EPs: The amplitude of certain components of the EP from the left hemisphere were significantly larger than from the right hemisphere (i.e., an asymmetry opposite in direction to that of the hearing children).

The remaining seven deaf children who could not speak and did not know sign language did not show evidence of cerebral specialization; the EPs from the left and right hemispheres were symmetrical. These children did communicate with other people, largely by way of gesture and pantomime, but they did not show evidence of using a formalized system of rules like those inherent in oral languages and in American Sign Language. American Sign Language has developed quite separate from English in any form. As it is used by deaf people of deaf parents, who learned sign language as their first language, ASL shows structural properties which mark it as a distinct language. See Klima and Bellugi (in press); Battison (1977); Frishberg, 1976, Supalla and Newport (Chapter 4, this volume); and Stokoe, Casterline and Croneberg (1965) for further details.

Thus, these results suggest that the acquisition of aural–oral speech and language is not the relevant variable in the development of cerebral specialization, since even children whose only language is manual–visual (ASL) showed asymmetrical EPs. Perhaps the acquisition of some formal language is a critical variable in the development of hemispheric specialization for both language and nonlanguage skills.

These results raise a number of questions. Perhaps most intriguing is the result suggesting that the left hemisphere of deaf signers shows specialization in a nonlanguage task in which hearing children show right hemisphere specialization. This may be accounted for by one of the following propositions: (a) Deaf signers acquire sign language in a manner similar to the way in which hearing children acquire speech, that is with left-hemisphere specialization playing a role. Because their language has strong visuo-spatial components, however, nonlanguage visual–spatial tasks are also preferentially performed by the left hemisphere; or (b) Owing to its strong visual–spatial structure, sign language is acquired with right-hemisphere specialization, thereby leaving the left hemisphere to specialize for nonlanguage skills.

There is very little evidence that bears on the question of hemispheric specialization for sign language. The evidence from neuropathology consists of published case reports of language testing of deaf adults following left-hemisphere damage. Two of these reports do not bring evidence to bear on the question of aphasia for sign language. The patient reported by Grasset (1896) appears only to have suffered motor disability of the right hand; he could express himself by fingerspelling with the left hand. Critchley's report (1938) concerns a man who only became deaf in his teens, well after speech acquisition had occurred. It is conceivable that hemispheric specialization for a second language (whether spoken or sign) is determined by which hemisphere is dominant for the language first acquired. Thus, for example, if the left hemisphere is in some fundamental way well suited to be the neural substrate for speech, any other languages learned after primary speech acquisition may also be preferentially processed by the left hemisphere, for reasons of parsimony. Three other case reports (Douglass & Richardson, 1959; Sarno, Swisher, & Sarno, 1969; Tureen, Smolik, & Tritt, 1951) do concern congenitally deaf patients who knew sign language. These studies suggest that the production and reception of sign language were impaired in these subjects following left-hemisphere lesions. However, it is not clear how early in life these patients acquired sign language, nor is it clear whether sign language was the first language acquired. All three of the patients had some ability to speak, and they also showed deficits in their speech following the left-hemisphere lesions.

In order to describe hemispheric specialization for sign language and for other nonlanguage visual tasks, one would like to see measures of lateral asymmetry in otherwise normal congenitally deaf adults whose first language was sign language. Two recent studies address this question. McKeever, Hoemann, Florian, and VanDeventer (1976), employed the visual half-field technique, mentioned earlier, to investigate lateral asymmetries for the perception of written English and for the perception of line drawings of the manual alphabet and signs of ASL. The subjects in this study were right-handed congenitally deaf females who communicated in ASL, and hearing control subjects whose familiarity with ASL ranged from 1 to 20 years experience.

The hearing subjects showed a significant right-field advantage in (verbally) reporting written words, whether presented unilaterally or bilaterally. The deaf subjects showed a significant right-visual-field advantage for unilaterally, but not bilaterally presented written English words. Unfortunately, manual alphabet and sign language stimuli were only presented bilaterally. The data for these two different groups of stimuli when analyzed together showed a significant left-visual-field superiority for hearing subjects, and no significant field advantage for deaf subjects.

The data for the hearing subjects may be interpreted as showing left-hemisphere specialization for the perception of written English and a right-hemisphere advantage in the perception of line drawings of manual alphabet and sign language stimuli.

The interpretation of the data for the deaf subjects is made difficult by a number of factors. First, the significant right-visual-field advantage on the unilateral words task suggests left-hemisphere specialization for the perception of English even in subjects for whom this is not primarily an oral–aural language. The failure to find a significant field advantage in the bilateral word condition might be attributable to numerous task and strategy variables that differ in unilateral and bilateral presentation situations. For example, in the bilateral situation where a word appears in both visual fields on each trial, a subject can maximize his score by selectively focusing his attention, (not

necessarily his gaze) on one field preferentially. Subjects may selectively attend to and report one field for a few trials, and then shift
attention to the other and so forth, and end up with equal scores for the
two fields. In our own work we have noticed this pattern of performance; and, in fact, deaf subjects have reported using just this
strategy. The question remains, of course, why hearing subjects do not
demonstrate this strategy. It may be that deaf users of sign language
are particularly adept at selectively picking up peripherally located
visual information because of the nature of sign language: In sign
discourse, the eyes look forward at the eyes of the addressor(ee) and
the signed information is perceived with peripheral vision. In any
event, given this pattern of results for written words, the lack of field
effects for bilaterally presented manual alphabet and sign stimuli is
difficult to interpret. Perhaps lateral asymmetries would have
emerged if these stimuli had been presented unilaterally as well.

Manning, Goble, Markman, and La Breche (1977) also employed
the visual half-field technique to study lateral asymmetries in the deaf.
They also presented stimuli bilaterally only. Their congenitally deaf
subjects did not show significant lateral asymmetries for either English words or sign language stimuli. Hearing subjects were not tested
on the sign stimuli but did show the usual right-visual-field advantage
in the word task. Neither hearing nor deaf subjects showed significant
field effects on a task requiring perception of random shapes.

A few methodological points concerning this type of study should
be mentioned. First, the line drawings of sign and manual alphabet
are often asymmetrical; they present different information foveally
when in the left- and right-visual fields. Since visual acuity is greater
closer to the fovea, experimenters should present a sign stimulus to
one field and its mirror image to the other visual field to control for
lateral asymmetries based simply on differences in visual acuity for
information presented to the left- and right-visual fields. While this
factor is unlikely to produce large and consistent field effects, it may
well introduce random fluctuations in accuracy that may obscure any
field effects due to functional asymmetry. An important part of the
visual half-field technique is the presentation of a central fixation
digit, to be reported before the lateral stimuli, to ensure that the
subject was focusing centrally at the time of stimulus presentation.
This digit is typically arabic in studies of this type. Perhaps a line
drawing of a signed digit would help to ensure that subjects maintain
an ASL mode in sign language tasks. Klein *et al.* (1976) report data
which suggest that the nature (e.g., verbal–nonverbal) of recently
performed tasks significantly affects the magnitude of functional
asymmetries obtained in hemifield recognition tasks. A related matter

concerns the response requirements in tasks like these. Lateral asymmetries for written English, for example, may be obscured by requiring the subject to translate into sign before responding. A written response may keep the subject in an English language *mode*. Similarly, responding in ASL only, without accompanying vocalization, may help to ensure that only the processing of sign language is determining the results.

We incorporated these methodological points in an experiment designed to determine cerebral specialization for sign language and for nonlanguage visual–spatial performance in congenitally deaf adults.

METHODS

Subjects

Our subjects were 14 congenitally deaf adults who were profoundly deaf and whose major form of communication was American Sign Language. They ranged in age from 15 to 35 years and all were right-handed. No subject had a history of any other neurological disorder. All subjects participated in the sign language testing but only 8 of these took part in the nonlanguage task. We also ran 8 hearing subjects on the nonlanguage task. They were all right-handed and were of the same age range as the deaf subjects.

Stimuli and Apparatus

Sign Language

These were line drawings of a person making various signs of ASL. The signs were chosen in such a way that they were distinctive and easily recognizable from the line drawings.[1] We chose 22 signs which are made with the two hands symmetrically placed in front of the torso.[2] Because they are symmetrical, these signs present the same information to the same point on the retina whether in the left- or right-visual-field. An example is shown in Figure 9.1a. We also pre-

[1] Certain conventions were used to enable distinctive recognition of signs: choice of signs with differentiated handshapes and with movements that could be represented either by flicker lines or by indicating onset and offset. We pretested the drawings for ease of recognition, changing either the drawings or revising our choice of signs until we obtained a set for which rapid recognition was possible.

[2] The English glosses for these signs are TOWN, CHAIR, SENTENCE, WITH, MEET, OPPOSITE, PROBLEM, MORE, EGG, CLEAR, SWEETHEART, BODY, JAIL, BUT, WEDDING, LOVE, NAME, BUTTERFLY, INTERPRET, MEASURE, QUIET, and SHOES.

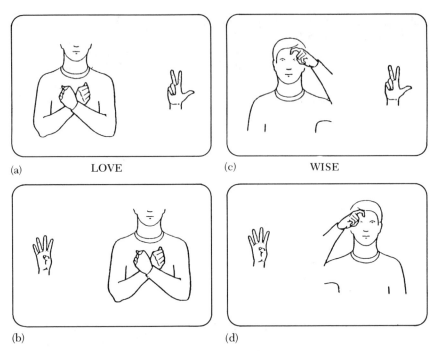

Figure 9.1. Examples of stimulus cards for unilateral presentation of symmetrical signs (LOVE) made on torso (a) and (b), and asymmetrical signs (WISE) made on the face (c) and (d). The digits shown are THREE and FOUR.

sented 20 signs which are made on the face, and which are asymmetrical, being made with one hand only.[3] In order to be sure that the same information was presented the same distance from the fovea for both left- and right-visual-field presentations, these signs were presented with the right hand in the right visual field and the left hand in the left visual field.[4] An example is seen in Figure 9.1b. A digit (from 1–9) was placed in the center of each stimulus configuration and it was also signed (see Figure 9.1).

[3]The English glosses for the signs are GUM, WRONG, EAT, SUGAR, SECRET, TELEPHONE, HEAD, YESTERDAY, WISE, CHINESE, CANDY, HOME, BLACK, APPLE, MOTHER, CAT, GIRL, BOY, COW, and ONION.

[4]We also pretested for ease of recognition if signs when presented with left hand active versus right hand active. Signs were equally recognizable either way. Some signers are right hand dominant, some are left hand dominant with respect to signing. A signer who is left hand dominant will in fact make one-handed signs consistently in citation form with his left hand active. Thus there are no minimal pairs in ASL distinguished by the use of one hand rather than another; nor is handedness significant in case of recognizing signs. In fact, we have noted that deaf people may not even notice that a signer is left-handed.

All signs were presented so that the nearest point of the drawn figure began 2 degrees 30 minutes of visual angle laterally from fixation. All signs were 3 degrees 15 minutes wide and 3 degrees 30 minutes high.

Nonlanguage Stimuli

We chose a dot localization task similar to that used by Levy and Reid (1976),[5] since they reported strong left-visual-field advantages in normal hearing subjects on this task. These stimuli were single dots located in 1 of 20 possible positions in a rectangle. The nearest edge of the rectangle began 2 degrees of visual angle out from fixation and was 3 degrees 30 minutes wide and 4 degrees high (see Figure 9.2a and b). An arabic digit (from 1–9) was placed in the center of each stimulus configuration.

All stimuli were presented on 4 × 5 inch cards in one channel of a two-channel Scientific Prototype Tachistoscope. A fixation field was presented in the second channel.

Procedure

Sign Language Task

All instructions were given in ASL. These were prerecorded on videotape. Just prior to stimulus presentation a fixation field, consisting of a black cross, was presented. Subjects were told to fixate the center of the cross and that a digit would appear there and a sign would appear either to the left or right of center (unilateral task). Each subject also participated in a bilateral sign language task, and he was told that two different signs would appear, one to the left and one to the right of center. Subjects were asked first to report the digit and then to report the sign(s). In bilateral conditions, signs could be reported in any order. All responses were signed. Trials on which the digit was reported incorrectly were discarded.

Unilateral and bilateral tasks were performed in separate blocks, and order of presentation was counterbalanced across subjects. Each sign occurred once in the left and once in the right visual field. Stimulus duration was 100 milliseconds.

Dot Localization

This task was performed approximately 2 weeks after the sign language task. Instructions were given in written English. Subjects first

[5] We are very grateful to Dr. Jerre Levy for providing us with full details of this task.

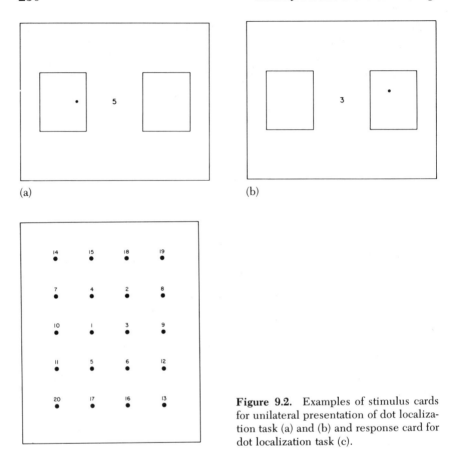

Figure 9.2. Examples of stimulus cards for unilateral presentation of dot localization task (a) and (b) and response card for dot localization task (c).

reported the digit and then pointed to the location of the dot(s) they had just seen from a 4 × 5 matrix of dots. This response matrix is shown in Figure 9.2c. A dot appeared in each possible dot location once in the left and once in the right visual field. Stimulus duration was 100 milliseconds. Only the deaf subjects were run in a bilateral version of this task, since the hearing subjects found it too difficult.

DATA ANALYSIS

We employed nonparametric procedures to test for the significance of the differences between visual fields within subject groups (Wil-

TABLE 9.1

Mean Percentage Correct Left Visual Field and Right Visual Field Scores and Difference Scores for All Tasks

	Unilateral presentation			Bilateral presentation		
	Left visual field	Right visual field		Left visual field	Right visual field	
Deaf						
Signs	41.2	50.1	8.9	34.5	34.7	.2
Dots	38.1	61.3	23.1	41.4	41.4	0
Hearing						
Dots	57.5	45.6	−11.9			

coxen sign test of differences, all two-tailed) and across subject groups (Mann-Whitney U test) (Hays, 1963).

RESULTS

The mean left- and right-visual-field scores and hemi-field difference scores for both tasks are shown in Table 9.1. The results for signs made on the torso and signs made on the face were not different and so the data for these two sets of stimuli were combined. The deaf subjects showed a significant right-visual-field advantage for the unilateral presentation of signs ($T = 11.0, N = 14, z = 2.61, p < .01$) but no differences between hemi-fields for bilateral presentations.

The deaf subjects also showed a significant right-visual-field advantage for the unilateral presentation of the dot localization task ($T = 2.0, N = 8, z = 2.24, p < .03$) but no difference between hemi-fields for bilateral presentations. The percentage correct for left and right visual fields for the sign task and the dot localization task are plotted in Figure 9.3.

The hearing subjects showed a significant left-visual-field advantage on the unilateral dot localization task ($T = 4.0, N = 8, z = 1.96, p < .05$). The results showing opposite laterality effects for hearing and deaf subjects on this task were significant ($U = 7.5, z = 2.58, p < .01$) and this interaction is plotted in Figure 9.4.

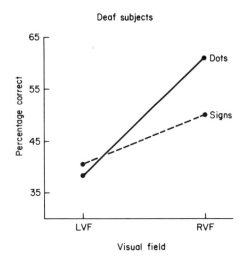

Figure 9.3. Percentage correct recognition of deaf subjects for unilateral left- and right-visual-field presentation of sign task and dot localization task.

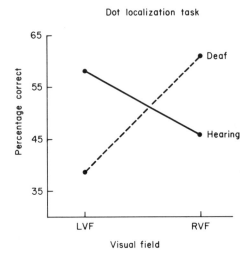

Figure 9.4. Percentage correct recognition of hearing and deaf subjects for unilateral presentation of dot localization task.

DISCUSSION

The results showing lateral asymmetries in deaf subjects for language and nonlanguage tasks with unilateral but not bilateral stimulus presentation suggests that these subjects may indeed be switching attention to one visual field preferentially in the bilateral situation, as was suggested in the Introduction. While this proposition remains to be explicitly tested, many of our subjects did volunteer the information that they employed this field switching strategy in bilateral conditions. The significant lateral asymmetry obtained here but not in the studies mentioned above may, therefore, be attributable to unilateral presentation, but also be in part due to other methodological differences including the use of a signed fixation digit, symmetrical stimuli for left- and right-visual fields and a nonlanguage task which produces strong lateral asymmetries in hearing subjects.

The significant lateral asymmetries in the performance of both sign language and nonlanguage tasks in these congenitally deaf adults suggests that the development of cerebral specialization is not necessarily dependent on either the acquisition of speech (Gazzaniga, 1970) or on auditory stimulation (McKeever et al., 1976).

The fact that the asymmetry favored the right visual field suggests that sign language, like spoken language, is acquired with left hemisphere specialization even though it is acquired in the visual–haptic modalities.

The results showing a right visual field advantage on the dot localization task is consistent with the earlier report (Neville, 1975, 1977) of left hemisphere specialization in the perception of line drawings in congenitally deaf children who knew sign language. This result suggests that since spatial localization is an important aspect of the grammar of sign language,[6] it may be adaptive to bring together

---

[6] Spatial location is a significant aspect of American Sign Language in many different ways. First, lexical signs themselves are made in different places of articulation with respect to the head and torso (SUMMER on the forehead; AUTUMN on the lower arm; WINTER in front of the torso). Second, some signs are distinguished only by differences in spatial location, all other parameters being identical. (The same hand configuration and movement at the forehead is SUMMER, at the nose is UGLY, at the chin is DRY). Thus location is a distinguishing feature of a sign which differentiates it from all other signs. Third, temporal notions are often realized spatially in ASL signs. Signs for future move forward from the ear; signs for past move backward.

Spatial location is not only important in the ASL lexicon, it also figures in highly significant ways in the grammar of the language. ASL signs are made by the hands moving in space; it is dimensions of space and movement which the language uses for its grammatical processes. Planes in signing space figure as distinct locations for different inflectional processes. Within the planes, specific target points and patterns of lines, arcs, and circles are called into play. Both the spatial pattern and its planar locus are distinguishing dimensions. Target loci in signing space identify points for pronominal reference: the equivalent of I, you, he. Specific target loci signal a reciprocal inflection (we gave to each other); movement along an arc or circle signals inflections for number and for distributional aspect (give something to each of them, to all of them). Thus at all levels, spatial location is crucial to the signs and grammar of this language of the hands in space.

these two functions within the same hemisphere. This result is perhaps analogous to the evidence which suggests that in hearing people nonlanguage judgments of temporal order are preferentially performed by the left hemisphere (Carmon & Nachshon, 1971; Efron, 1963a,b; Halperin, Nachshon & Carmon, 1973), possibly because the perception of small differences in temporal patterning is an intricate part of speech perception. In hearing people, visual–spatial skills are not brought into play in speech perception, and are typically the province of the right hemisphere. Perhaps judgments of small differences in temporal order, which do not play a particularly important role in the perception of sign language, are predominantly made by the right hemisphere in congenitally deaf adults whose first language is sign language. We are currently investigating this and other questions related to cerebral specialization in the deaf.

The results presented here must be taken as preliminary because of the small number of subjects involved and because of their unexpected nature. Nonetheless, the evidence to date suggests that the two cerebral hemispheres are not irreversibly preprogrammed or hardwired to specialize for particular functions. The data from the deaf subjects suggest that both biological and experiential factors, such as language acquisition and the *mode* of language acquisition, interact in determining the functional organization of the brain.

ACKNOWLEDGMENTS

We are grateful to Frank A. Paul for providing illustrations specifically designed for this study.

REFERENCES

Battison, R. *Lexical borrowing in American Sign Language: Phonological and morphological restructuring.* Unpublished doctoral dissertation, Univ. of California, San Diego, 1977.

Berlin, C. I., Hughes, L. F., Lowe-Bell, S., & Berlin, H. L. Dichotic right ear advantages in children aged five to thirteen. *Cortex,* 1973, 9, 393–401.

Berlucchi, G. Cerebral dominance and interhemispheric communication in normal man. In F. O. Schmitt & F. G. Worden (Eds.), *The Neurosciences Third Study Program.* Cambridge, Massachusetts: MIT Press, 1974.

Bryden, M. P. Laterality effects in dichotic listening: Relations with handedness and reading ability in children. *Neuropsychologia,* 1970, 8, 443–445.

Bryden, M. P., & Allard, F. *Dichotic listening and the development of linquistic pro-

cesses. Paper read to International Neuropsychological Society, New Orleans, 1973.

Carmon, A. & Nachshon, I. Effect of unilateral brain damage on perception of temporal order. *Cortex,* 1971, *7,* 410–418.

Critchley, M. Aphasia in a partial deaf-mute. *Brain,* 1938, *61,* 163–169.

Curry, F. A comparison of left handed and right handed subjects on verbal and non-verbal dichotic listening task. *Cortex,* 1967, *3,* 343–352.

Dennis, M., & Whitaker, H. A. Language acquisition following hemidecortication: linguistic superiority of the left over the right hemisphere. *Brain and Language,* 1976, *3,* 404–433.

Doty, R. W., Sr. & Overman, W. H., Jr. Mnemonic role of forebrain commissurs in macaques. In S. Harnad, R. W. Doty, L. Goldstein, J. Jaynes, & G. Krauthamer (Eds.), *Lateralization in the Nervous System.* New York: Academic Press, 1977.

Douglass, E., & Richardson, J. C. Aphasia in a deaf-mute. *Brain,* 1959, *82,* 68–80.

Dustman, R. E., & Beck, E. C. The evoked response: Its use in evaluating brain function of children and young adults. Preprint, 1974.

Efron, R. Temporal perception, aphasia, and déjà vu. *Brain,* 1963a, *86,* 403–424.

Efron, R. The effect of handedness on the perception of simultaneity and temporal order. *Brain,* 1963b, *86,* 261–284.

Entus, A. R. *Hemispheric asymmetry in processing of dichotically presented speech and nonspeech stimuli by infants.* Paper presented at biennial meeting of the Society for Research in Child Development, Denver, Colorado, April, 1975.

Frishberg, N. *Some aspects of historical change in American Sign Language.* Unpublished doctoral dissertation, San Diego: Univ. of California, 1976.

Gazzaniga, M. S. Effects of commissurotomy on a preoperatively learned visual discrimination. *Experimental Neurology,* 1963, *8,* 14–19.

Gazzaniga, M. S. *The bisected brain.* New York: Appleton-Century-Crofts, 1970.

Grasset, J. Aphasie de la main droite chez un soud muet. *Le Prog. Med.,* 1896, *4,* 281.

Halperin, Y., Nachshon, I. & Carmon, A. Shift of ear superiority in dichotic listening to temporally patterned nonverbal stimuli. *Journal of the Acoustical Society of America,* 1973, *53,* 46–50.

Hamilton, C. R. Investigations of perceptual and mnemonic lateralization in monkeys. In S. Harnad, R. W. Doty, L. Goldstein, J. Jaynes, & G. Krauthamer (Eds.), *Lateralization in the nervous system.* New York: Academic Press, 1977.

Hays, W. L. *Statistics.* New York: Holt, Rinehart and Winston, 1963.

Kimura, D. Some effects of temporal lobe damage on auditory perception. *Canadian Journal of Psychology,* 1961, *15,* 156–165.

Kimura, D. Speech lateralization in young children as determined by an auditory test. *Journal of Comparative and Physiological Psychology,* 1963, *56,* 899–902.

Kimura, D. Functional asymmetry of the brain in dichotic listening. *Cortex,* 1967, *3,* 163–178.

Kinsbourne, M. Eye and head turning indicate cerebral lateralization. *Science,* 1972, *176,* 539–541.

Kinsbourne, M. Mechanisms of hemispheric interaction in man. In M. Kinsbourne & W. L. Smith (Eds.), *Hemispheric disconnection and cerebral function.* Springfield, Illinois: L. L. Thomas, 1974.

Klein, D., Moscovitch, M., & Vigna, R. Attentional mechanisms and asymmetries in tachistoscopic recognition of words and faces. *Neuropsychologia,* 1976, *14,* 55–66.

Klima, E. S., & Bellugi, U. *The signs of language.* Cambridge, Massachusetts: Harvard Univ. Press, in press.

Knox, C., & Kimura, D. Cerebral processing of nonverbal sounds in boys and girls. *Neuropsychologia*, 1968, 6, 1–11.

Lenneberg, E. *Biological foundations of language*. New York: John Wiley & Sons, 1967.

Lenneberg, E. (Ed.), *Language and brain: Developmental aspects. Neurosciences Research Program Bulletin*, 1974, 12(4).

Levy, J. Possible basis for the evolution of lateral specialization in the human brain. *Nature*, 1969, 224, 614–615.

Levy, J. Psychobiological implications of bilateral asymmetry. In S. J. Dimond & J. G. Beaumont (Eds.), *Hemisphere function in the brain*. New York: John Wiley & Sons, 1974.

Levy, J., & Reid, M. Variations in writing, posture and cerebral organization. *Science*, 1976, 194, 339–339.

Liberman, A. M. The specialization of the language hemisphere. In F. O. Schmitt & F. G. Worden (Eds.), *The Neurosciences Third Study Program*. Cambridge, Massachusetts: MIT Press, 1974.

Luria, A. R., & Karasseva, T. A. Disturbances of auditory–speech memory in focal lesions of the deep regions of the left temporal lobe. *Neuropsychologia*, 1968, 6, 97–104.

Manning, A. A., Goble, W., Markman, R., & La Breche, T. Lateral cerebral differences in the deaf in response to linguistic and nonlinguistic stimuli. *Brain and Language*, 1977, 4, 309–321.

Marler, P. Birdsong and speech development: Could there be parallels? *American Scientist*, 1970, 58, 669–673.

McKeever, W. F., & Huling, M. P. Lateral dominance and tachistoscopic word recognition performance obtained with simultaneous bilateral input. *Neuropsychologia*, 1971, 9, 15–20.

McKeever, W. F., Hoemann, H. W., Florian, V. A., & VanDeventer, A. D. Evidence of minimal cerebral asymmetries for the processing of English words and American Sign Language in the congenitally deaf. *Neuropsychologia*, 1976, 14, 413–423.

Milner, B. Some effects of frontal lobectomy in man. In J. M. Warren & K. Akert (Eds.), *The frontal granular cortex and behavior*. New York: McGraw-Hill, 1964.

Milner, B. Interhemispheric differences in the localization of psychological processes in man. *British Medical Bulletin*, 1971, 27, 272–277.

Molfese, D. L., Freeman, R. B., Jr., & Palermo, D. S. The ontogeny of brain lateralization for speech and nonspeech stimuli. *Brain and Language*, 1975, 2, 356–368.

Molfese, D. Infant cerebral asymmetry. In S. Segalowitz & F. Gruber (Eds.), *Language development and neurological theory*. New York: Academic Press, 1977.

Neville, H. F. Electrographic correlates of lateral asymmetry in the processing of verbal and nonverbal auditory stimuli. *Journal of Psycholinguistic Research*, 1974, 3 (2), 151–163.

Neville, H. J. *Cerebral specialization in normal and cogenitally deaf children*: An evoked potential and behavioral study. Unpublished doctoral dissertation, Cornell Univ., Ithaca, New York, 1975.

Neville, H. J., Schulman, C., & Galambos, R. *Evoked potential and behavioral correlates of functional hemispheric specialization*. Paper presented at Fifth Annual Meeting of International Neuropsychology Society, Santa Fe, 1977.

Neville, H. J. Electrographic and behavioral cerebral specialization in normal and congenitally deaf children: A preliminary report. In S. Segalowitz (Ed.), *Language and development and neurological theory*. New York: Academic Press, 1977.

Newcombe, F., & Russell, W. Dissociated visual perceptual and spatial deficits in focal lesions of the right hemisphere. *Journals of Neurology, Neurosurgery, and Psychiatry*, 1969, 32, 73–81.

Nottebohm, F. Ontogeny of bird song. *Science*, 1970, 167, 950–956.

Nottebohm, F. Cerebral lateralization in birds. In E. Lenneberg (Ed.), *Language and brain: Developmental aspects. Neurosciences Research Bulletin*, 1974, 12(4).

Nottebohm, F. Asymmetries in neural control of vocalization in the canary. In S. Harnad, R. W. Doty, L. Goldstein, J. Jaynes, & G. Krauthamer (Eds.), *Lateralization in the nervous system*. New York: Academic Press, 1977.

Sarno, J. E., Swisher, L. P., & Sarno, M. T. Aphasia in a congenitally deaf man. *Cortex*, 1969, 5, 398–414.

Satz, P., Bakker, D. J., Teunissen, J., Goebel, R., & Van der Vlugt, H. Developmental parameters of the ear asymmetry: A multivariate approach. *Brain and Language*, 1975, 2, 171–185.

Schulman-Galambos, C. Dichotic listening performance in elementary and college students. *Neuropsychologia*, 1977, 15, 577–584.

Smith, A., & Sugar, O. Development of above normal language and intelligence 21 years after left hemispherectomy. *Neurology*, 1975, 25(9), 813–818.

Sperry, R. *Mental unity following surgical disconnection of the cerebral hemispheres.* The Harvey Lectures, Series 62, New York: Academic Press, 1968.

Spreen, O., Spellacy, F. J., & Reid, J. R. The effect of interstimulus interval and intensity on ear asymmetry for nonverbal stimuli in dichotic listening. *Neuropsychologia*, 1970, 8, 245–250.

Stokoe, W. C., Casterline, D., & Croneberg, C. *A dictionary of American Sign Language on linguistic principles*. Washington, D.C.: Gallaudet College Press, 1965.

Teuber, Hans-Lukas. Why two brains? In F. O. Schmitt & F. G. Worden (Eds.), *The neurosciences third study*. Cambridge, Massachusetts: MIT Press, 1974.

Tureen, L. L., Smolik, E. A., & Tritt, J. H., Aphasia in a deaf-mute. *Neurology*, 1951, 1, 237–244.

Turkewitz, G. The development of lateral differences in the human infant. In S. Harnad et al. (Eds.), *Lateralization in the Nervous System*. New York: Academic Press, 1977. Pp. 251–259.

Vella, E. J., Butler, S. R., & Glass, A. Electrical correlates of right hemisphere function. *Nature*, 1972, 236, 125–126.

Wada, J. Sharing and shift of cerebral speech dominance and morphological hemispheric asymmetry. *Excerpta Medica International Congress Series*, 1973, 296, 252.

Wada, J. A., Clarke, R., & Hamm, A. Cerebral hemispheric asymmetry in humans:Cortical speech zones in 100 adult and 100 infant brains. *Archives of Neurology*, 1975, 32, 239–246.

Webster, W. G. Functional asymmetry between the cerebral hemispheres of the cat. *Neuropsychologia*, 1972, 10, 75–87.

Weinstein, S. Differences in effects of brain wounds implicating right or left hemispheres. In V. B. Mountcastle (Ed.), *Interhemispheric relations and cerebral dominance*. Baltimore: Johns Hopkins Press, 1962.

White, M. J. Laterality differences in perception: A review. *Psychological Bulletin*, 1969, 72, 387–405.

Witelson, S. F., & Pallie, W. Left-hemisphere specialization for language in the human newborn: Neuroanatomical evidence of asymmetry. *Brain*, 1973, 96, 641–646.

Wood, C. C. Auditory and phonetic levels of processing in speech perception: Neurophysiological and information processing analyses. *Journal of Experimental Psychology: Human Perception and Performance*, 1975, 10, 3–20.

Wood, C. C., Goff, W. R., & Day, R. S. Auditory evoked potentials during speech perception. *Science*, 1971, 173, 1248–1251.

IV

PSYCHOLINGUISTIC RESEARCH

10

A Child's Representation of Action in American Sign Language

RUTH ELLENBERGER
MARCIA STEYAERT

University of Minnesota

INTRODUCTION

Use of the visual modality presents the signer with a large variety of means of representing actions, ranging from pantomimic reenactment to the highly systematized forms available in a sign language. The existence of such a wide range of communicative possibilities raises an interesting question about the order in which they will be learned by a child exposed to them. This study traces the development of means of representing action in the communication of a deaf child learning American Sign Language (ASL) as a first language.

Data were obtained from a series of videotapes of a deaf child of deaf parents who learned ASL as a first language and relied on it as his primary means of communication.[1] The language development of this

The research reported herein was performed pursuant to a grant from the Bureau of Education for the Handicapped, U.S. Office of Education, Department of Health, Education and Welfare to the Center of Research, Development and Demonstration in Education of Handicapped Children, Department of Psychoeducational Studies, University of Minnesota. (Grant No. OE–09–332189–4533(032) and 300–76–0036).

[1] Both the subject and his parents have profound hearing losses and use sign as the primary means of communication in the home.

child was followed between the ages of 43 and 71 months, as part of a longitudinal study of deaf children of deaf parents. Several earlier tapes, made as part of a different study, were also analyzed but were found to contain little pertinent information. The films recorded spontaneous conversation between the child and his mother (or, occasionally, an investigator) in the child's home. All interpretations of signed sequences cited in this chapter were verified by adult deaf signers who were quite familiar with children's signing styles.

BACKGROUND INFORMATION

In ASL, signs representing physical actions are often stylized reproductions of the actions themselves. For example, in one commonly used sign for WALK, two "B" hands reproduce the alternating motion of the feet in walking.[2] Such stylized reproductions of actions are unlike pantomime, however, in that they respect the phonological constraints of ASL[3] and require less context to make their meaning "transparent." Thus, although there are some cases in which it is difficult to distinguish sign from pantomime, Bellugi and Klima (1975) note that "from the point of view of signers . . . there appears to be a perceived difference between the extremes of what is clearly signing and what is clearly pantomiming [p. 179]."

In signed representation of an action, it is sometimes possible to incorporate into the sign itself reference to participants and places involved in the action. For example, if a signer wants to indicate that Harry gave George something and they are both present, he can direct the sign GIVE from Harry toward George. If they are not physically present, he can point to a location,[4] signing or spelling George's name to indicate that this refers to him, and similarly specify another loca-

[2] In this chapter, capitalized English glosses are used to represent signs. Although somewhat standardized, these English glosses often only approximate the meaning of a given sign. Many of the handshapes used in signs are the same as signs for numbers or symbols of the manual alphabet, so handshapes in signs will be described in terms of the letter or number symbols they resemble, although this resemblance is often coincidental. Letters and numbers used to refer to handshapes will be enclosed in quotation marks, and letters will be capitalized. The letters of the manual alphabet are shown in Figure 1.1 (Chapter 1).

[3] For discussion of some of these phonological constraints, see Battison, Markowicz, and Woodward (1975). Some discussion of distinctions between sign and pantomime is given in Newkirk (1975).

[4] Pointing is not the only means for establishing reference locations. Other commonly used conventions for this purpose include direction of gaze and body shifts. See Friedman (1975, 1976) and Baker (1976).

tion as referring to Harry. (These reference locations are commonly placed in space at various angles to the signer's body.) The fact that Harry gave George something can then be represented by moving the sign GIVE from Harry's location to George's location, thus incorporating the reference locations into the action sign.

Semantically, signs such as GIVE involve source and goal; the sign normally moves from the reference location of the source to that of the goal. Certain other signs, such as BREAK, are normally performed at a single location representing the person, object, or body part acted upon. For example, the sign BREAK done on the leg indicates a broken leg. In this chapter, spatially modifiable signs like GIVE will be referred to as source–goal signs; spatially modifiable signs like BREAK will be called locational signs. When possible, both types of signs tend to be spatially modified; in fact, source–goal signs rarely occur in citation form.[5]

In some action signs, each hand visually symbolizes a participant in the action. In such signs, the handshapes used may indicate something about the nature of the participants in the action. For example, in the sign CRASH, in which two "A" hands meet abruptly, each "A" hand represents one of the colliding objects. The "A" handshape is used in the citation forms of many such signs and gives little information about the participants other than that they are solid objects. If the signer wants to impart more specific information about the participants, he can replace the "A" by another handshape, such as the "3," which represents a vehicle, usually an automobile. Use of two "3" handshapes in the sign CRASH, then, would indicate that there were two cars that crashed. These symbolic handshapes, which are meaningless unless incorporated into action representations, have been called classifiers (Kegl & Wilbur, 1976). In addition to their use in well-established signs, as just discussed, classifiers may be used in representing motions for which there are no standardized action signs, for example, a car moving along a winding road or going over a steep hill.

The signer can also alter the motion of a sign, such as CRASH, to incorporate more specific information about the motions of the participants. For instance, if there had been a collision between a moving and a stationary object, the signer could represent this collision by crashing a moving "A" into a motionless "A."

From the preceding discussion, it is clear that depictions of actions

[5] The citation form of a sign is its "dictionary" form, the form used when it is made out of context.

in ASL are in some sense more concrete and pictorial and less arbitrary than their counterparts in spoken language, though certainly not so iconic as to be comprehensible to someone unfamiliar with the conventions used. One might expect that such a representational system, because of its somewhat pictorial nature, could be easily grasped by a child, and would thus be acquired at an early age by a child learning ASL as a first language. However, the present study of a deaf child indicates that some aspects of this representational system seem to have been acquired by this child only at the end of the period studied.

DISCUSSION

First Stage

The subject's representation of action in the earliest films, beginning at age 43 months, was characterized by use of pantomime and citation form signs. The pantomime used at this time frequently involved role playing, in which the child acted like another person or animal. For example, when he pretended to be a dog, he pawed the air with his hands and walked around on his hands and knees. It was not always clear whether such pantomime was intended as communication or was simply play. Pantomimes representing single actions, such as chewing, were also used. This latter type of pantomime resembles that used by adults.

Almost all of the action signs used at this time, which include PLAY, EAT, and BRUSH-TEETH, are among those which are not usually subject to spatial modification. Source–goal signs, such as TELL, GIVE, and SHOW, which seldom occur in citation form, were not found in these films. Locational signs, such as BITE, BREAK, and SEW, occurred only rarely in the early films. It may be that souce–goal and locational signs are not used at this time because spatial modification can result in great variation in the appearance of a sign. Because of this variation, the child may not yet have succeeded in abstracting out the recurring features of such signs or mastered their complex reference system well enough to feel confident in using them.[6]

---

[6] It is possible that the use of small toys as stimuli in these films may have encouraged physical manipulation at the expense of linguistic output. The unfamiliarity of the filming situation may also have adversely influenced the language on these early films.

Second Stage

The next group of films, covering the period beginning at age 54 months and separated from the earlier ones by a period of several months, was characterized by less use of pantomime, especially where the child assumed the identity of an animal, for instance, and imitated its general behavior. The pantomime that did occur more closely resembled that of the adult in that it could be segmented into series of discrete actions.

Source–goal signs such as GIVE, which did not occur in the earlier films, and locational signs such as BREAK, which then occurred only rarely, occurred frequently in these later films. While these signs did not yet incorporate arbitrarily established reference locations used to represent people or things not physically present, they were moved between or performed on people and objects in the signer's immediate surroundings. For example, the subject indicated that he wanted to give something to someone across the room by moving the sign GIVE from himself toward that person.

Another tendency evident at this time was for the child to provide some sort of concrete backup or context for his action signs. One way in which this was done was the use, within a single utterance, of both a pantomime or gesture and a sign representing the same action. For example, the child performed the sign BITE on his mother's knee and then leaned over and pretended to bite it.

Another type of concrete backup noted was the frequent performance of action signs on appropriate places in pictures or on concrete objects. For example, in a story in which a dog was jumping through a series of hoops, a series of JUMPs was done between the hoops on the page. When talking about an automobile collision, the child made the sign CRASH with one hand hitting a toy car instead of his other hand.

In several instances, the sign itself was concretized in some way. The sign EAT, in which a flat "O" hand is brought up to the mouth, was actually inserted into a wide open mouth. The sign BITE, in which a closing hand represents the action of the mouth, was performed in front of the mouth instead of in its usual location on the arm in neutral space.

The appearance of these various types of concretization suggests that the subject was becoming aware of the relationship between an action and the formalized way it is represented in a sign and was playing with that relationship.

The most interesting phenomenon seen in this group of films was the development of the subject's ability to provide additional information about the participants in an action by modification of the handshapes and/or motion of a sign, as described earlier. In the following examples, it is clear that the child was using each hand to represent one participant.

In one example, the subject represented one skier following another down a hill by placing his hands side by side in "B" shapes so that the palms faced each other, and then moving them on a wavy path down and away from himself. One hand was placed slightly behind the other. He periodically interrupted this skiing action to indicate the identity of the lead skier. This was done by placing a fingerspelled "K," the first initial of the other skier's name, on top of the leading "B" hand. After each such interruption, the "K" hand again assumed the "B" shape, and the skiing action was resumed. By designating the leading hand as the other skier, the child made it clear that he followed his companion down the hill.

Another example involved modification of the sign SKI, normally made with the hands held parallel in the "X" configuration and moving forward. The episode involved the subject snowplowing to keep from colliding with a tree. His efforts failed, and he broke his skis against the tree. At one point in this story, the two "X"s of the sign converged on each other from the sides, indicating the snowplowing position of his skis. He had analyzed the sign SKI into its two components, one representing each foot, and had used this knowledge in modifying the sign. The two "X"s collided. The sign BREAK was then made with the hands still in the "X" configuration to indicate that the skis broke.

The other examples of this phenomenon also involved either skiing or skating collisions. In one case, the subject waved a "K," indicating the name of the same skiing companion, and then signed TREE with the other hand while converting the "K" into the more neutral "A" handshape of the sign CRASH. This "A" hand was then crashed into the "tree." By substituting the sign TREE for the other "A" handshape of CRASH, he indicated that the object his friend hit was a tree. He thus identified both participants in the action.

In a final example, he identified the participants in an action by using two different, significant hand configurations throughout the execution of the sign. One hand was held in the "X" configuration of the sign SKI to indicate a skier, while the other formed the sign TREE. The "X" collided with the "tree" and hooked on the thumb, indicating that the skier had become entangled in the tree's branches.

In the earlier films, the subject generally either used pantomime to depict action sequences or used single or unmodified signs. In these later films, he was able to use the signs more flexibly and sometimes simultaneously to depict complex action sequences. He seems to have realized that in many action signs, the hands symbolize two separate objects, and he was able to use this knowledge to produce meaningful modifications of his signs.

Third Stage

The ability to structure the space in which action signs move, as described at the beginning of this chapter, was the most important new development evident in the subject's narratives in the next and final group of films, covering the age range of 61 to 71 months. In some instances, the subject used what we will call shape descriptors to set up a spatial framework for his action signs. Shape descriptors are commonly used following nouns to indicate the shape and/or size of an object; for example, two "F"s starting together and moved outward to the sides represent a long, slender, solid object. The general forms of these shape descriptors are standardized, although some modifications are possible in order to indicate details of size and shape. Shape descriptors can also be placed in space to designate reference locations for the objects they describe.

In one case, the child was describing a barrier over which his horse jumped. He first signed ROCK (an "X" hand under the chin) followed by a shape descriptor in the form of two "C" hands placed off to one side, thereby establishing a location for the rock. He repeated the sign ROCK and placed a similar descriptor off to the other side to indicate a second rock. Then he signed WOOD, followed by a shape descriptor in the form of two "C" hands starting together and moving off to the sides where the rocks were located. This represented a thick log placed across the rocks. He then signed HORSE, placed one arm in roughly the position established for the log, and moved the sign JUMP over the log. The child thus clearly indicated through his structuring of space that the horse jumped over a barrier formed by a log laid over two rocks.

At this stage, such spatial structuring alternated with the use of English-like word order as a means of organizing narratives. The use of the latter probably resulted from the child's school program, in which signs were used in English word order.

Another characteristic of this final set of tapes was the frequent and creative use of classifiers. As mentioned on page 263, classifiers are standardized handshapes that may be used in some action signs to represent various entities such as cars, planes, and people. In contrast to the substitutions used in the previous stage (e.g., TREE, SKI), they are usually meaningless unless they occur in action representations.

For example, the subject often used the standard "3" handshape to represent a car in such actions as one car running over another, a car getting stuck, and cars being piled in a junkyard. In one instance, he described a car getting stuck and the driver continuing his journey on foot by moving his hand along a single path while changing the handshape from that of the car classifier to that of the person classifier (a "V" handshape). By such use of these two classifiers, one beginning at the point where the other left off, the child was able to indicate the continuity of the action. Such classifiers provide one way for the child to represent simultaneously the nature of both the moving entity and the action itself.

CONCLUSION

Several clear trends were observed in the child's developing system of action representations. The earliest action signs used seemed to be the citation forms of signs that are not normally spatially modifiable. Spatially modifiable signs (source–goal or locational signs) first occurred in the second group of films, in which action signs were often accompanied by some type of concretization. These concretizations suggest that the child had realized that there can be a relationship between a real action and the formalized way it is represented in a sign, and he was playing with this relationship. He had evidently also recognized that in some action signs, each hand symbolizes one participant in the action and was able to modify his signs accordingly, altering the shape or motion of a hand to provide additional information about the participant it represents. It was only later that the child acquired the ability to modify action signs significantly by the structuring of space and the use of classifiers.

Thus, the child's acquisition of action representations seemed to manifest a clear developmental progression from early use of citation forms of signs not usually subject to spatial modification to acquisition of adult-like spatial structuring.

While one might expect spatial modifications to appear earlier because of their pictorial nature, they are, in fact, relatively late acquisitions, perhaps because such representations may require a fairly advanced mastery of cognitive skills involving spatial relationships.

Also, setting up a spatial framework as a background for the subsequent representation of an action requires a type of advance planning that may be beyond the capabilities of a younger child.

One promising area for future research growing out of this study would be inquiry into the relationship between the cognitive skills discussed earlier and linguistic expressions representing actions in ASL. Another possible area for future research would be the influence on child sign language of modifications made by parents in their signing to children; for example, the previously noted tendency to use concrete backups for action signs may simply result from imitations of similar parent-to-child signing. Because language development can differ considerably between children, it would also be interesting to compare this child's development with that of other children learning ASL as a first language, to determine whether trends similar to those found for this child characterize their language acquisition as well.

ACKNOWLEDGMENTS

We wish to thank Vicki Anderson, Shirley Egbert, and Carol Finke for their assistance as translators and informants in this study.

REFERENCES

Baker, C. What's not on the other hand in American Sign Language. In *Papers from the Twelfth Regional Meeting of the Chicago Linguistic Society*, 1976.

Battison, R., Markowicz, H., & Woodward, J. A good rule of thumb: Variable phonology in American Sign Language. In *Analyzing Variation in Language*, R. Shuy & R. Fasold (Eds.). Washington, D.C.. Georgetown Univ. Press, 1975.

Bellugi, U., & Klima, E. Aspects of sign language and its structure. In J. Kavanagh & J. Cutting (Eds.). *The Role of Speech in Language*. Cambridge, Massachusetts: MIT Press, 1975.

Friedman, L. Space, time and person reference in American Sign Language, *Language*, 1975, *51*(4), 940–961.

Friedman, L. The manifestation of subject, object, and topic in the American Sign Language. In C. Li (Ed.), *Subject and Topic*. New York: Academic Press, 1976.

Kegl, J., & Wilbur, R. Where does structure stop and style begin? Syntax, morphology, and phonology vs. stylistic variation in American Sign Language. In *Papers from the Twelfth Regional Meeting of the Chicago Linguistic Society*, 1976.

Newkirk, D. Some phonological distinctions between citation-form signing and free pantomime. Salk Institute for Biological Studies, working paper, 1975.

11

Discrimination of Location in American Sign Language

HOWARD POIZNER[1]
HARLAN LANE

Northeastern University

A sign in American Sign Language (ASL) seems to be composed of at least four distinct parameters: shape of the hands, orientation of the palm, location of the hand, and movement of the hand (Bellugi, Klima, & Siple, 1975). The four parameters represent large inventories of alternate choices. According to Stokoe, Casterline, and Croneberg (1965, 1976), the handshape parameter contains 19 values, or primes; location of the hand, 12 primes; and movement, 24 primes. (They include changes in palm orientation among the movement and location primes.) Representatives of these parameters are combined simultaneously, but they function separately to contrast minimally different signs. Bellugi and Siple (1974) and Bellugi *et al.* (1975) have shown in short-term memory tests for signs that a significant number of multiply occurring errors were of a formational rather than a semantic nature. These formational errors in recall maintained many of the parameter values of the original stimulus, often changing only one

This research was supported, in part, by National Institute of Mental Health National Research Service Award 1 F31 MH 05640–01 to H. Poizner, by a grant from the NIMH Small Grants Section, Division of Extramural Research Programs (F. Grosjean and H. Lane, principal investigators), and by a grant from the National Science Foundation.

[1] Now at The Salk Institute for Biological Studies.

UNDERSTANDING LANGUAGE THROUGH SIGN LANGUAGE RESEARCH

271

prime of one parameter. Klima and Bellugi (1975) further report the interchange of individual formational parameters of signs in spontaneous errors occurring in sign production. Rarely did signers interchange entire signs, but they transposed representatives of formational parameters, with the resulting gestures often being nonsigns. Studies of historical change in ASL have also shown changes along these four parameters (Frishberg, 1975). These results lend support to the position that deaf signers code ASL in terms of independent linguistic parameters.

One way to learn about submorphemic structure in sign language is to study how subjects perceive the parameters of signs. Lane, Boyes-Braem, and Bellugi (1976) have obtained a set of distinctive features for the handshape parameter, much as Miller and Nicely (1955) had done for consonants. The present study is likewise concerned with the internal structure of one parameter of ASL signs—namely, the locations in which the signs are made. The 14 location primes we used are shown schematically in Figure 11.1: They comprise the 12 listed in the Stokoe *et al.* (1976) dictionary of ASL, plus 2 additional primes for some handshapes used as locations. Two locations lie off of the body. First, the area directly in front of the head (cf. ASL PRETTY) is represented by the face profile, although the location is in front of the face. Second, the area in front (and to the side) of the trunk of the body, the "neutral space," (cf. ASL PREACH) is drawn as a rectangle. Next, the supine and prone wrist and hand provide a base in various signs.

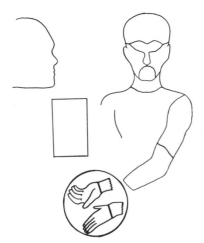

Figure 11.1. A response sheet containing a schematic representation of 14 locations in ASL.

These four locations are portrayed in the enlarged circle. The supine wrist (palm up) appears, for example, in DOCTOR, and the prone wrist in DUTY (a minimal pair). Similarly, SCHOOL and WARNING are contrasted primarily by the supine (prone) base hand. Finally, signs utilizing the other eight locations generally contact the body in the areas roughly outlined.

This study asks fundamentally two questions about the perception of location in ASL. First, is each of the dozen or so locations in ASL distinct from every other, or do the locations form classes based on shared features? Second, does the class structure obtained from native ASL users differ from that obtained from naïve observers, and if so, in what ways? The answers to these questions can throw light on language processing in general, as well as on ASL in particular. First, if there is evidence for the psychological reality of a level of description in this manual–visual language below the level of the prime (phoneme), as there is in spoken language, then it is tempting to infer that featural analysis, in view of its modality invariance, is a more general cognitive strategy. Second, if the classes of combining elements (primes) based on these shared features prove to be the same for native signers as for naïve observers, at least in part, then it is tempting to infer that the phonological feature system is tuned in part to the sensory constraints of the observer.

Alternatively, native signers might confuse locations as naïve observers do because the identification task does not engage their linguistic knowledge or because they have no relevant knowledge at that level. Related experiments in the literature on speech perception make it clear that a speaker's perception of phonemes is heavily determined not only by his phonological knowledge but also by more universal sensory processes. As an example of the former, the phonemes /r/ and /l/, which contrast in English but not Japanese phonology, are more accurately discriminated by American than by Japanese listeners (Miyawaki, Strange, Verbrugge, Liberman, Jenkins, & Fujimura, 1975). Similarly, Thai partitions the voicing continuum differently from English, and the discrimination functions of Thai and English speakers are correspondingly different (Abramson & Lisker, 1970). Moreover, Thai and American listeners are differently affected in their consonant perceptions by one and the same adapting stimulus, depending upon how their respective languages categorize that stimulus along the voicing continuum (Donald, 1976).

Contrasting with this phonological determination of language perception, there are certain regularities that seem to transcend language boundaries and provide evidence for psychophysical determination of language perception. For example, speakers of several languages proved more accurate in discriminating consonant nasality than they did consonant friction—not only in their respective native languages but in each others' languages as well. Singh and Black (1966) found the same rank order of seven features applied to the intelligibility of consonants for Hindi, English, Arabic, and Japanese listeners. Likewise, Stevens, Liberman, Studdert-Kennedy, and Ohman (1969) found that Swedish and American listeners discriminated series of steady-state vowels in nearly the same way, including a set that was phonemic only in Swedish.

Comparing the patterns of discrimination of location by deaf and hearing subjects can cast some light on the phonological and psychophysical determination of the perception of language stimuli. In the cross-language studies just cited, all stimuli were linguistic for all subjects. The subjects' experiences with the stimuli differed, but they all spoke some language, and their particular native language unavoidably played a role in their perceptions of the sounds of the other languages. The study of ASL with native and naïve users, however, is less confounded. Because the formational structures of manual and spoken languages differ so greatly, naïve subjects do not have some linguistic visual code other than ASL; rather they have no code whatsoever. The native language of these naïve subjects presumably does not play a role in their perception of ASL phonology.

While the patterns of discrimination of the native signers and naïve subjects may prove fundamentally different, giving weight to phonological determinism, it would be surprising indeed if the linguistic code took little or no account of the most salient psychophysical properties of the stimulus array. Consequently, we should rather expect some overlap between the similarity structure of locations based purely on their psychophysics and that based, in part at least, on their roles within a formational system.

METHOD

Subjects

Two groups of five subjects were used, each with three male and two female adults, ranging in age from 17 to 24, with normal eyesight. The first group consisted of congenitally deaf signers of deaf parents. All had learned ASL as a first language and used it as their normal means of communication. The second group comprised hearing English speakers who had no knowledge of ASL at all.

Stimuli and Apparatus

The 14 location primes have been described earlier. Three values of each of the other three sign parameters were selected for their high discriminability. For handshape, the primes were (a) flat hand; (b) compact hand; and (c) the index and second finger, side by side, extended—B, A, and U, in Stokoe notation. For the orientation parameter, the primes were palm facing (a) away from the signer; (b) toward the signer; and (c) down toward the floor. For movement, the primes were (a) medial twists of the wrist; (b) counterclockwise circular movements of the arm; and (c) a short repeated horizontal movement. When each of the 14 location primes were used with each of the 27 combinations of handshapes, orientations and movements, 378 gestures, mostly permissible but nonoccurring as signs in ASL, were the result.

A deaf native signer recorded each of these "signs" in random order, one every 8 seconds, on videotape; she presented the sign for 1 second, and the experimenter covered the camera lens for 7 seconds. An additional blank of several seconds was inserted after every tenth sign to help subjects maintain proper ordering of responses. Three test tapes were then generated by mixing (Sony SEG) differing amounts of visual noise with the sign videotape (AV 3650) while copying it (AV 3600). The noise appeared as "snow" on the video monitor only during the 1-second sign presentation and during the blank ½-second immediately preceding and following this presentation. The noise was recorded (AV 3600) from an idling video recorder (AV 3650). The signal-to-noise (S/N) ratios of the three test tapes were −4.5 decibels, −7.9 decibels, and −13.0 decibels. Pilot tests indicated that these ratios produced an appropriate range of test difficulty.

Three practice tapes were also prepared by sampling approximately 100 items from each of the test tapes. Each practice tape started out with unsnowed signs and then presented signs with higher and higher noise levels until the S/N level of the appropriate test tape was reached.

Procedure

The observer was seated 2 feet from an 8-inch video monitor (Sony CVM 950) whose brightness and contrast controls were set on maximum. The subject received written instructions explaining the nature of the test materials and the response requirements, augmented by spoken explanation for the hearing group or signed explanation (by a native sigñer) for the deaf subjects. Their task was to identify the location of each sign presented on one of the test tapes by placing a check on a schematic representation of the 14 possible locations. Figure 11.1 is a sample response sheet. The practice tape corresponding to the test tape to be shown that session was then presented, and feedback regarding correct responding was given. By the end of the practice tape, all subjects understood the task requirements and were adjusted to the S/N level they would receive that session. Each test tape lasted approximately 1 hour, with subjects given a short break after 30 minutes. Subjects were tested individually, each one viewing one test tape on each of 3 days. The order of presentation of the three test tapes was independently randomized for each subject in one group, with the same order of presentation for the subjects of the other group.

Data Reduction

The Shepard–Kruskal method of nonmetric multidimensional scaling (Shepard, 1962; Kruskal, 1964a, b) provides a spatial representation of the stimuli such that the distance between any two stimuli corresponds to the obtained confusion frequency of that pair. Thus, the closer together two locations are in the spatial solution, the more similar they appeared to the observer. However, any uniform expansion, contraction, or rotation of the points does not affect the solution. Nonmetric multidimensional scaling uses only ordinal information in the data to construct their spatial representation. The scaling proceeds by iteratively adjusting the points, in a specified number of dimensions, from some initial configuration (chosen randomly here) in the direction of the sharpest decrease in stress until a configuration of the stimuli is achieved in which stress is (locally) minimum. Stress is thus a measure of poorness of fit of the spatial solution to the similarity scores; more exactly, it is a measure of how well the data are predicted by the best fitting monotonic function relating the similarity scores to interpoint distances. Shepard (1974) suggests using as many as 20 random starting configurations to be quite sure a global minimum value for stress has been achieved. All stress values reported here are minima obtained from scalings with 20 random starting configurations. Stress Formula 1 and the primary approach to ties are used throughout.

A complementary method of representing structure in confusion matrices is the use of hierarchical clustering. Johnson's (1967) clustering procedures were used to represent such structure in the form of a binary tree. Stimuli are grouped together in discrete clusters whose organization is strictly hierarchical (and nondimensional). Location groupings represent location similarity. Johnson's clustering program provides for two different clustering methods, the "connectedness" and "diameter" procedures. Only the diameter method is used here, since it has been found the most satisfactory for representing speech (Johnson, 1967; Shepard, 1972) and nonspeech confusions (Shepard, Kilpatric, & Cunningham, 1975).

RESULTS AND DISCUSSION

Subjects were 76% correct in identifying locations at the highest S/N level, 67% at the intermediate, and 44% at the lowest. A three-way analysis of variance using group (deaf or hearing), location, and S/N level as factors was performed on the accuracy of identifying the locations.[2] Significant F values were obtained for the following effects: (a) for the various locations [$F(13, 104) = 39.8$, $p < .001$], indicating that some locations were more accurately identified than were others; (b) for the S/N levels [$F(2, 16) = 44.4$, $p < .001$], with higher accuracy for the higher S/N ratios; (c) for the location by S/N level interaction [$F(26, 208) = 3.1$, $p < .001$], indicating that some locations were more accurately identified at some S/N levels than at others; and (d) for the group by location interaction [$F(13, 104) = 2.4$, $p < .01$], indicating that the deaf subjects identified certain locations more accurately than the hearing subjects, and conversely, the hearing subjects identified other locations more accurately than the deaf. (There was no difference between the two groups in overall accuracy.) Table 11.1 presents mean percentage of correct identifications of location by each group.

The final column of Table 11.1 shows the difference in these means between groups. Positive difference scores indicate that deaf subjects were more accurate in identifying the location, whereas negative difference scores reflect greater accuracy by hearing subjects. Differences in accuracy ranged from +15% at the chin location, to little difference at the upper arm and neutral space locations, to −15% at

---

[2]It is common practice to transform proportions (p) by $\theta = \arcsin \sqrt{p}$ to improve homogeneity of variance and normality of distribution. This transformation was applied to the percentage correct data in the present experiment and the data reanalyzed by analysis of variance, with virtually the same results. Every source of variance that was significant in one analysis was also significant in the other, while all nonsignificant terms remained so.

TABLE 11.1

Mean Percentage Correct Identification of Location[a]

Location	Deaf	Hearing	Deaf − hearing
Full face	67	72	− 5
Forehead	77	68	9
Midface	62	68	− 6
Cheek	59	53	6
Chin	64	49	15
Neck	71	86	−15
Trunk	85	82	3
Neutral space	67	65	2
Upper arm	87	89	− 2
Forearm	69	78	− 9
Wrist up	38	41	− 3
Palm up	64	51	13
Wrist down	36	47	−11
Palm down	18	25	− 7
Mean	62	62	0

[a] Each entry is based on 405 identifications, 27 at each of three signal-to-noise levels, by each of five subjects.

the neck location. Strikingly, this pattern of differences in accuracy between groups was significantly correlated (Rho = .62, p < .05, two-tailed) with the frequencies of occurrence of the individual locations in the Stokoe *et al.* (1965, 1976) dictionary of American Sign Language (see Table 11.2 for a list of these frequencies). Deaf subjects were more accurate in perceiving the locations listed most frequently in the dictionary, and hearing subjects were more accurate in perceiving the less frequently listed ones.

The possibility exists that patterns of response bias may have produced the observed differences in accuracy for identifying the locations. A tendency to respond by marking a given location irrespective of the location presented would increase the accuracy of identifying that location at the expense of some other locations. To check on this possibility, the total number of times subjects used a given location as a response was taken as an approximate measure of response bias.[3] (Klatt [1968] has also used this statistic as a measure of response bias in confusion matrices.) If responses were equally distributed over the 14 locations, each location would have been used 7.1% of the time. Table 11.2 shows that the actual distribution of responses ranged from

[3] No stimulus bias exists in the present data, since each location was presented an equal number of times and subjects made a response to each presentation.

TABLE 11.2

Percentage Response Biases and Bias Differences of Deaf and Hearing Groups, for Each Location,[a] and the Percentage of Occurrence of Each Location in the Stokoe *et al.* (1965, 1976) Dictionary of American Sign Language

Location	Deaf	Hearing	Deaf − hearing	Occurrence in dictionary
Full face	7.7	7.5	.2	5.4
Forehead	7.3	5.4	1.9	7.5
Midface	6.7	8.2	−1.5	3.6
Cheek	7.0	6.6	.4	3.3
Chin	8.3	5.5	2.8	11.5
Neck	6.8	9.1	−2.3	0.9
Trunk	7.9	9.0	−1.1	8.2
Neutral space	8.4	7.2	1.2	43.0
Upper arm	6.5	7.0	− .5	0.4
Forearm	7.2	7.4	− .2	1.2
Wrist up	6.1	5.5	.6	0.2
Palm up	11.3	9.5	1.8	8.3
Wrist down	5.4	6.6	−1.2	2.3
Palm down	3.4	5.5	−2.1	4.2
N	5670	5670		2025

[a] Responses were pooled over all signal-to-noise levels.

3.4% at the palm-down location to 11.3% at the palm-up. The last column of the table lists the frequency of each location in the Stokoe *et al.* (1965, 1976) dictionary as a percentage of total lexical entries. The difference between groups at each location in response bias correlated with the lexical frequency of the location, Rho = .50 (.05 < p < .10, one-tailed).

Confusion matrices, with columns listing the location presented and rows listing the location responded, provide a means of testing and correcting for bias. If response biases exist in the data, the confusion matrices will not be symmetric; that is, for pairs of locations A and B, response A will not be given to stimulus B as often as response B is given to stimulus A. The Pearson correlation coefficients between the lower and upper halves of confusion matrices for data pooled over all S/N levels were r = .68 and r = .70 for deaf and hearing subjects, respectively. Correlations revealing similar asymmetry were obtained from the confusion matrices of each group at each S/N level (where they ranged from .56 to .70). The confusion matrices were then corrected for response bias by multiplying each cell in the matrix by the ratio of the largest row total (response bias) to its own row total. The increase in the symmetry of the matrices was substantial: $r = .90$ and $r = .86$ for the deaf and hearing groups, respectively.

After the correction for bias, the accuracies of the deaf and hearing subjects at each location were recalculated, subtracted from one another, and correlated anew with the frequencies of the locations in the Stokoe *et al.* (1965, 1976) dictionary. The correlation was significant, though slightly reduced in magnitude from that obtained with uncorrected scores (Rho = .55, $p < .05$, one-tailed). We have some evidence, then, that the deaf brought their linguistic knowledge to bear on this perceptual task and that it affected perceptual accuracy as well as response probability.

An assumption of the scaling and clustering procedures is that the confusion matrices are symmetric (Shepard, 1962; Johnson, 1967). After the correction for bias yielding matrix symmetry, the lower and upper half matrices were pooled and normalized following Shepard's formula (1962, 1972): $S_{ij} = (f_{ij} + f_{ji})/(f_{ii} + f_{jj})$, where f_{ij} is the confusion frequency of response j to stimulus i, f_{ji} the confusion frequency of response i to stimulus j, and f_{ii} and f_{jj} the frequencies of correct responding to stimuli i and j, respectively. The result is a half matrix of similarity scores, diagonal absent, one score for every pair of stimuli. Individual subjects resembled each other, within groups, in the sorts of confusions they made at the various S/N levels. Coefficients of concordance (based on corrected similarity scores) are presented in Table 11.3.

TABLE 11.3

Kendall W Coefficients of Concordance for the Deaf and Hearing Groups, at Three Signal-to-Noise Levels[a]

	Pooled over all levels	Signal-to-noise level		
		−4.5 dB	−7.9 dB	−13.0 dB
Five deaf subjects	.76	.77	.76	.62
Five hearing subjects	.81	.76	.74	.74

[a] All similarity scores were corrected for response bias.

Kendall's W ranged from .62 to .81, (all $\chi^2 > 278$, $p < .001$), reflecting relatively stable confusion patterns among subjects in each group. Next, the data were pooled over the three S/N levels. This not only increases the sample size on which to base the analysis of confusions but, as Table 11.3 shows, slightly enhances the agreement among hearing subjects on the relative similarities of the locations.

Multidimensional scaling solutions were obtained in up to four dimensions for each group and for a set of actual physical distances (the similarity scores were the reciprocals of the Euclidean distances separating the pairs of locations on the signer who had produced the stimuli). Figure 11.2 presents the clustering solution superimposed on the two-dimensional scaling solution for the actual physical distances. Stress values were .258, .100, .058, and .040 in one through four dimensions, respectively. The stress value decreased sharply from one to two dimensions, decreasing more slowly thereafter.

The spatial positions of the locations are those obtained from the scaling solution. The boundaries are drawn in by hand and represent the hierarchical clusterings obtained from the clustering program. If the fit between the scaling and clustering solutions were perfect, all clusters would be surrounded by simple, concave curves that do not intersect.

A nearly perfect spatial representation of the topography of the ASL locations appears in the figure, as we would expect. The vertical

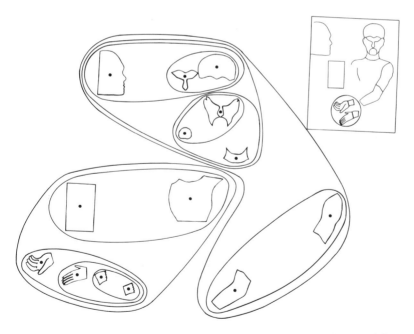

Figure 11.2. Clustering solution superimposed on the scaling solution of the actual physical distances separating all pairs of locations.

dimension of the scaling arranges the locations roughly according to their actual vertical positions relative to the signer: The hand locations are close to the space in front of the chest, while the forearm region merges with the upper arm and eventually with the neck and lower and upper facial regions. The horizontal dimension basically distinguishes those locations that lie off the body (neutral space and the palm and wrist locations) from those that contact the body. These two dimensions, vertical distance along the body and horizontal distance from the body, mirror important physical dimensions necessary to specify the position of each location.

To provide a baseline, Figure 11.3 presents the two-dimensional scaling and the clustering solution for a set of random numbers input as similarity scores for the various pairs of locations. The scaling and clustering solutions have indeed randomly positioned and grouped the locations. The two-dimensional stress is rather high, .25, and the match between the scaling and clustering solutions is very poor, as indicated by the clustering of nonadjacent items. All in all, the two-dimensional scaling solution does not, of course, provide a good fit to the random data.

Turning to the scaling solution for the location confusions of deaf and hearing observers, stress values in one through four dimensions

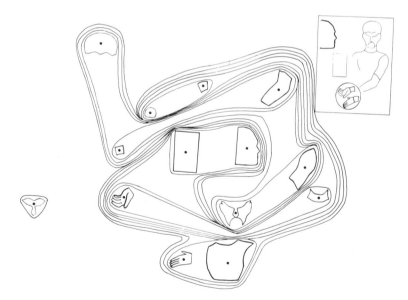

Figure 11.3. Clustering solution superimposed on the scaling solution for a set of random numbers defining the similarity among locations.

were .308, .151, .083, and .042 for the deaf subjects; and .206, .084, .050, and .023 for the hearing subjects. Again, the most rapid decrease in stress is from one to two dimensions; both two-dimensional stress values were acceptable, with the three-dimensional solution offering no greater interpretability. Further evidence for the fact that the two-dimensional scaling solution captures the important relationships in the data is provided by the excellent match between the clustering and two-dimensional scaling within each group. Figures 11.4 and 11.5 present the clustering solution superimposed on the two-dimensional scaling solution for the deaf and hearing subjects, respectively.

Figures 11.4 and 11.5 clearly show a similarity structure for ASL locations and point to controlling properties of the visual stimuli. The first major division in the clustering solution for the deaf group (Figure 11.4) is between the upper facial region (forehead, midface, and full face) and all other locations. Next, the central body region (trunk, neutral space, and upper arm) is separate from the remaining large grouping of the palm, wrist, forearm locations, in one subgroup, and the neck and lower facial region (chin and cheek), in another sub-

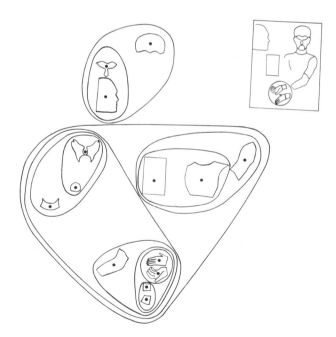

Figure 11.4. Clustering solution superimposed on the scaling solution for the group of deaf subjects, with confusions pooled over all signal-to-noise levels.

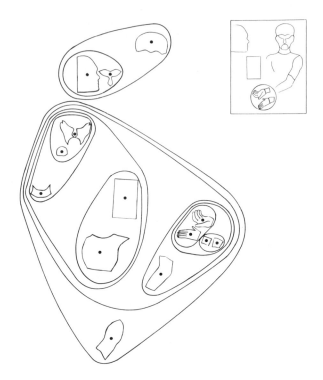

Figure 11.5. Clustering solution superimposed on the scaling solution for the group of hearing subjects, with confusions pooled over all signal-to-noise levels.

group. These locations all have small surface area, contrasting in this respect with trunk, neutral space, and upper arm. Possibly this feature served as an organizing principle for the perceptual judgments of the deaf observers. The three clusters are, however, roughly equidistant in the scaling solution.

The solution for the hearing subjects in Figure 11.5 also shows a major initial grouping of the upper facial region (forehead, midface, and full face) versus all remaining locations. However, the next break (excluding the isolated cluster of the upper arm location alone) separates the palm, wrist, and forearm locations from the physically proximate neutral space, trunk, neck, and lower facial cluster. The central body locations then separate from the neck and lower facial region.

The solutions for the deaf, hearing, and physical distance data share certain properties. In each solution, lower facial locations group together as do the upper facial ones; the wrist and palm locations consistently cluster together, and the trunk and neutral space areas form a cluster located roughly equidistant from other clusters.

The scaling and clustering solutions obtained from the actual physical distance data, however, quite reasonably group the lower and upper facial regions together, whereas both the deaf and hearing solutions isolate the upper facial region from everything else. This discrepancy may be attributable to the salience of the nose, which demarcates the upper from the lower facial regions, a topographical cue that is available to an observer but that had little effect on our measurement of the distance separating the upper facial locations from the rest.

Overall, the deaf and hearing scaling solutions are fairly congruent: The distances separating all pairs of points in the two solutions correlate $r = .82$. Further, the deaf and hearing clustering solutions shared 83% common clusters.[4] The scaling solution for the hearing subjects matches that obtained from the actual distances slightly better ($r = .75$) than does the solution for the deaf subjects, $r = .69$ ($Z = .79$, n.s.). The clustering solutions from both the deaf and hearing subjects shared 50% common clusters with the solution based on the actual physical distances.

This experiment provides some evidence for the phonological determination of perceptual judgments of a visual language. Native signers proved more accurate than naïve observers in identifying locations that are frequent in ASL and less accurate in identifying infrequent locations. In addition, native signers responded more often with the more frequent locations and less often with the infrequent ones. Scaling and clustering analyses of the similarity structure of these locations for native speakers and naïve observers, however, yielded substantially the same results for the two groups, providing evidence for psychophysical determination of the perception of ASL location.

ACKNOWLEDGMENT

We are indebted to Dr. Phipps Arabie of the University of Minnesota for assistance in implementing the scaling and clustering computer programs.

[4]The average percentage agreement between pairs of clustering solutions of three random sets of similarity scores for 14 objects was 8.4% shared clusters. Thus, agreement in the range of 80% is considerably above chance level.

REFERENCES

Abramson, A. S., & Lisker, L. Discriminability along the voicing continuum: Cross-language tests. In *Proceedings of the Sixth International Congress of Phonetic Science*. Prague: Academia, 1970. Pp. 569–573.

Bellugi, U., Klima, E. S., & Siple, P. Remembering in signs. *Cognition: International Journal of Cognitive Psychology*, 1975, 3, 93–125.

Bellugi, U., & Siple, P. Remembering with and without words. In F. Bresson (Ed.), *Current problems in psycholinguistics*. Paris: Centre Nationale de la Recherche Scientifique, 1974. 216–236.

Donald, S. L. The effects of selective adaptation on voicing in Thai and English. In Haskins Laboratories: Status report on speech research SR-47, 1976, 129–135.

Frishberg, N. Arbitrariness and iconicity: Historical change in American Sign Language. *Language*, 1975, *51*, 696–719.

Johnson, S. C. Hierarchical clustering schemes. *Psychometrika*, 1967, *32*, 241–254.

Klatt, D. H. Structure of confusions in short-term memory between English consonants. *Journal of the Acoustical Society of America*, 1968, *44*, 401–407.

Klima, E. S., & Bellugi, U. Perception and production in a visually based language. In D. Aaronson & R. W. Rieber (Eds.), *Developmental psycholinguistics and communication disorders*. New York: The New York Academy of Sciences, 1975. Pp. 225–235.

Kruskal, J. B. Multidimensional scaling by optimizing goodness of fit to a nonmetric hypothesis. *Psychometrika*, 1964, *29*, 1–27. (a)

Kruskal, J. B. Nonmetric multidimensional scaling: A numerical method. *Psychometrika*, 1964, *29*, 115–129. (b)

Lane, H., Boyes-Braem, P., & Bellugi, U. Preliminaries to a distinctive feature analysis of handshapes in American Sign Language. *Cognitive Psychology*, 8, 1976, 263–289.

Miller, G. A., & Nicely, P. E. An analysis of perceptual confusions among some English consonants. *Journal of the Acoustical Society of America*, 1955, *27*, 339–352.

Miyawaki, K., Strange, W., Verbrugge, R. R., Liberman, A. M., Jenkins, J. J., & Fujimura, O. An effect of linguistic experience: The discrimination of /r/ and /l/ by native speakers of Japanese and English. *Perception and Psychophysics*, 1975, *18*, 331–340.

Shepard, R. N. The analysis of proximities: Multidimensional scaling with an unknown distance function, I & II. *Psychometrika*, 1962, *27*, 125–140, 219–246.

Shepard, R. N. Psychological representation of speech sounds. In E. E. David & P. B. Denes (Eds.), *Human communication: A unified view*. New York: McGraw-Hill, 1972, 67–113.

Shepard, R. N. Representation of structure in similarity data: Problems and prospects. *Psychometrika*, 1974, *39*, 373–421.

Shepard, R. N., Kilpatric, D. W., & Cunningham, J. P. The internal representation of numbers. *Cognitive Psychology*, 1975, 7, 82–138.

Singh, S., & Black, J. W. Study of twenty-six intervocalic consonants as spoken and recognized by four language groups. *Journal of the Acoustical Society of America*, 1966, *39*, 372–387.

Stevens, K. N., Liberman, A. M., Studdert-Kennedy, M., & Ohman, S. Cross-language study of vowel perception. *Language and Speech*, 1969, *12*, 1–23.

Stokoe, W. C., Casterline, D. C., & Croneberg, C. G. *A dictionary of American Sign Language*. Washington, D.C.: Gallaudet College Press, 1965.

Stokoe, W. C., Casterline, D. C., & Croneberg, C. G. *A dictionary of American Sign Language* (Rev. ed.). Silver Spring, Maryland: Linstok Press, 1976.

12

Categorical Coding of Sign and English in Short-Term Memory by Deaf and Hearing Subjects

HARRY W. HOEMANN

Bowling Green State University

Proactive interference has played an important role in the development and testing of theories of memory. Additionally, it has provided a number of investigators with a reliable dependent variable for their research. As a phenomenon it is less well understood by the intelligent layman than its counterpart, *retroactive interference*. Retroactive interference is relatively easy to think about, since we can all draw upon our subjective experiences for examples. We have all looked up a telephone number in a directory, had our attention momentarily distracted, and then found that we could no longer remember the number. The distraction interfered with our recall. Since the interference occurred *after* the information had been coded and stored, it is called retroactive interference.

Proactive interference is more difficult to conceptualize, because we are typically not aware of it when it occurs. When we are unable to recall something at will, we are more likely to blame our "poor mem-

The preparation of this report was supported in part by National Institutes of Health Research Grant NS–09590–04A1 from the National Institute of Neurological and Communicative Diseases and Stroke and in part by the psychology department of Bowling Green State University.

ory." But it is a fact that material already stored in memory may interfere with the storage or retrieval of additional information. When the interference stems from an event that occurred *before* the additional information is processed, it is called proactive interference (PI).

STUDIES OF PROACTIVE INTERFERENCE

Peterson and Peterson (1959) first reported that forgetting progresses at different rates depending on the amount of controlled rehearsal of the stimuli, and they concluded that short-term retention is an important aspect of the acquisition process. Keppel and Underwood (1962) showed that both long- and short-term memory are subject to the effects of PI. Besides contributing to the theoretical discussion concerning similarities and differences observed in long- and short-term memory, Keppel and Underwood documented the generality of PI as a reliable phenomenon.

Paradigmatic research on the effects of PI in short-term memory has been carried on since the early 1960s by Wickens and his associates at Ohio State University. After demonstrating that PI is a function of stimulus similarity (Wickens, Born, & Allen, 1963), Wickens directed a series of studies exploring the circumstances in which PI might occur and the conditions required for its release (Wickens, 1970, 1972). He concluded that information is coded categorically in short-term memory on the basis of attributes that various classes of stimuli share in common. Wickens and his associates evaluated the saliency of particular encoding dimensions by noting the magnitude of the releases from PI that occurred when the subjects were switched to different classes of materials on a subsequent trial.

A typical trial in a study demonstrating PI and its release involves auditory or visual presentation of groups of three or four stimulus items for about 3 seconds followed by an interpolated task that prevents rehearsal. Subjects may see pictures of a cow, horse, and pig for 3 seconds and then be given the number 86, from which they are to count backward by threes (86, 83, 80, 77, 74, etc.) until told to stop. The length of the interpolated task may be varied, but 15 to 20 seconds seems to be sufficient to permit satisfactory recall on the first trial and to allow the effects of PI to be observed on subsequent trials. Subjects are given about 3 seconds to recall the previously presented items, and they are then shown the stimulus items associated with the next trial. Control subjects receive four trials drawn from the same conceptual category. Experimental subjects are switched to a different category, for example, from animals to furniture, on the fourth trial. Half the experimental subjects are typically switched in the opposite direc-

tion (furniture to animals). Since there are 24 combinations of sequences for four trials, complete counterbalancing in the Wickens
paradigm requires at least 48 experimental subjects, 24 switched from
category A to category B and 24 switched from category B to category
A. An additional 48 subjects are assigned to control (no-switch) conditions, 24 to category A for four trials and 24 to category B for four trials.
Random assignment of the subjects to one of the four conditions
protects the results from any bias stemming from that source. The
counterbalancing of trial sequences ensures that performance differences due to stimulus variables will be averaged out across trials and
that any significant trend or trends observed will be a function of the
trials rather than of the nature of the stimuli.

The results of a PI release study are typically plotted as mean
percentage correct as a function of trials. Attention is focused on the
performance of the experimental groups on the third and fourth trials.
A significant improvement on Trial 4 compared with Trial 3 is taken as
evidence for categorical encoding of the stimuli, inasmuch as the
category shift produced a release of the PI that had built up on the
previous trials. Since the amount of release may depend on which
aspect of the stimuli was altered, the Wickens paradigm can serve as a
sensitive indicator of cognitive organization.

CATEGORICAL CODING OF LINGUISTIC STIMULI BY
BILINGUAL SUBJECTS

Kolers (1963) has suggested that different languages may have separate memory stores. This hypothesis is testable by means of the Wickens paradigm. If stimuli from language A are stored separately from
language B, any interference built up in the one language domain
should have no effect on the other. Thus, vocabulary items drawn from
the same conceptual category and presented in language A should
result in a build-up of PI across two or more trials. But bilingual
subjects switched to language B on the last trial should experience a
release of PI and a corresponding improvement in their recall. If the
two languages share the same memory store, there should be only a
very small improvement on the last trial or none at all.

Goggin and Wickens (1971) conducted a language-switch study
using English and Spanish as the target languages. They observed a
release of PI with switches from English to Spanish and vice versa,
even when the category remained unchanged, confirming Kolers's
hypothesis. They commented that the effect seemed to be more pro-
nounced in persons who were equally fluent in both languages. Indi-

viduals lacking genuine competence in one of the languages might engage in covert translating. In that case a switch into their first language would not be likely to result in a release of PI, since they would have been translating the stimuli into that language all along.

CATEGORICAL CODING OF ENGLISH AND MANUAL ALPHABET CHARACTERS

The studies described in the balance of this chapter were conducted to determine whether the linguistic stimuli from a manual and a spoken language are coded categorically. This is the result that would be predicted by the Goggin and Wickens (1971) data, but when one of the languages is a manual language, there are some unique considerations. Since the two languages are transmitted through different sensory systems, they can be executed simultaneously. One can speak and sign at the same time. Moreover, the manual alphabet appears to derive its status at least in part from its one-to-one correspondence with the English alphabet. Deaf persons may use the manual alphabet as a device for nominal referencing simply by spelling out English words.

The coding of manual and English alphabet characters was selected as the primary focus of the reported studies rather than sign and English vocabularies, since the presentation of sign vocabulary items out of context and without facial expression presents special problems for sign language study. The citation forms of signs are often markedly different from the executions seen in a linguistic context. In contrast, the citation forms of the manual alphabet are a close match for the hand configurations actually seen in fingerspelled words.

The first study was conducted at Gallaudet College, where 48 undergraduate students were recruited as volunteer subjects. The subjects understood that they were expected to have a fluent knowledge of American Sign Language (ASL). A questionnaire administered during the course of the experiment elicited information regarding the subjects' hearing levels, age of onset of their hearing loss, etiology (if known), and years of experience with ASL usage. It was determined that 40 of the 48 subjects were prelingually deaf. Twenty-eight subjects had losses averaging 80 decibels or more in the better ear, 11 had losses averaging 60 to 80 decibels in the better ear, 6 had moderate losses, and the losses for 3 were unknown. Etiologies were reported for 31 subjects. Ten were hereditary. The remainder were spread across a wide variety of categories. Birth trauma, childhood diseases, head injury or other accident, blood factor, spinal meningitis, rubella, "infection," and "weak nerves" were all mentioned at least once. All of the subjects had at least 4 years of experience with ASL usage. Twelve had deaf parents and had acquired ASL as their first language.

The 48 subjects were randomly assigned to one of four conditions: (*a*) manual-to-English experimental switch; (*b*) English-to-manual experimental switch; (*c*) manual alphabet control (no switch); and (*d*) English alphabet control (no switch). The English alphabet characters were presented one at a time at the rate of 1 second each in a 1 × 1¾-inch window of a cardboard sleeve. The manual alphabet characters were presented at the rate of 1 second each by the examiner with his right hand. The interpolated task was to count backward by threes for 15 seconds. Subjects were encouraged to respond in spoken English or in a manual mode or both, as they wished. Trial sequences were counterbalanced in order to ensure that each group of stimuli was used as the switch condition for an equal number of trials.

The results are presented in Figure 12.1 with the manual-to-English switch and the manual control groups in the left panel and the English-to-manual switch and English control groups in the right panel. The decline in performance across the first three trials on the part of all of the subjects reflects the buildup of PI for letters of one or the other alphabet. The control groups showed no recovery on the last trial. The improvement in performance between Trials 3 and 4 on the

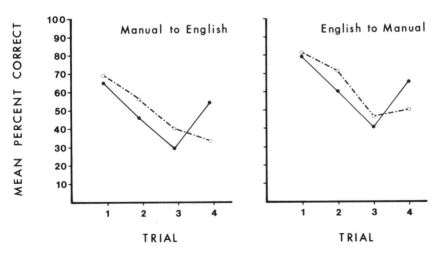

Figure 12.1. Gallaudet College students' performances on the alphabet test (— = Experimental; o—··—··o = Control).

part of the experimental groups reflected the release from PI occasioned by the switch from the one set of alphabet symbols to the
other.

The statistical significance of PI effects can be evaluated by means
of a 2 × 2 × 4 (category × condition × trials) analysis of variance.
The category variable reflects the initial assignment to a manual alphabet trial series or an English alphabet trial series. The term
condition refers to "switch" or "no switch" and reflects the experimental manipulation of switching half the subjects to the other alphabet on the fourth trial. The trials variable reflects the buildup of PI,
and a significant trials effect indicates that the decline in performance
across Trials 1 to 4 of the control group and Trials 1 to 3 of the
experimental group is not likely to have occurred by chance.

The release from PI on the part of the experimental groups will
show up statistically as a significant interaction effect between condition and trials. To verify that the interaction is due entirely to the
experimental groups' improvement on the last trial, a second analysis
of variance can be carried out on the first three trials only, and the
interaction effect should no longer appear.

The data depicted in Figure 12.1 satisfy all of these requirements.
The trials effect was significant ($F = 15.2$, $df = 3, 132$, $p < .01$), and the
trials-by-condition interaction effect was significant when all four
trials were included in the analysis ($F = 3.03$, $df = 3, 132$, $p < .05$).
When the last trial was excluded, the interaction effect was not significant ($F = .32$, $df = 2, 88$, $p > .05$). Although the scores in the right
panel of Figure 12.1 appear to be slightly elevated compared with
those in the left panel, the difference was not statistically significant.
It appears that the two conditions yielded initially similar performance scores, a similar buildup of PI across the subsequent trials, and
a symmetrical release from PI by the experimental groups on the
fourth trial. The results support the conclusion that manual and English alphabet characters are coded categorically by deaf persons.

It might be objected that the presentation of English letters in a
window of a cardboard shield and the presentation of manual letters
on the hand constitutes enough of a stimulus change to yield a release
all by itself. Consequently, another study was conducted with 48
subjects drawn from the high school division of Saint Rita School for
the Deaf, Cincinnati, Ohio. In this study both the English and the
manual alphabet characters were drawn in ink on cardboard strips and
presented in a window of a cardboard shield. The results are presented in Figure 12.2 with the manual-to-English switch and the

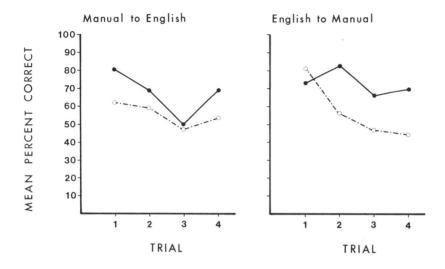

Figure 12.2. Saint Rita School for the Deaf pupils' performances on the alphabet test (———— = Experimental; ··—··— = Control).

manual control groups in the left panel and the English-to-manual switch and English control groups in the right panel.

It appears that the presentation of a line drawing of a hand is not perceptually equivalent to the presentation of the citation form of a manual alphabet character on the hand. There was no release of PI observed in the English-to-manual switch condition in the right panel. This outcome, however, does not controvert the conclusion drawn earlier that English and manual alphabet characters are coded categorically. The manual-to-English switch group manifested a significant improvement from Trials 3 to 4 ($t = 2.71$, $df = 15$, $p < .01$, one-tailed), and such an improvement is unlikely to have occurred if the two alphabets had been coded similarly. Given the significant improvement in the experimental group in the left panel of Figure 12.2, it is plausible to suppose that the unusual manner of presenting the manual alphabet characters to the Saint Rita subjects obscured the release that might otherwise have been observed in the performances depicted in the right panel. Deaf pupils at Saint Rita would be unlikely to have seen such representations of the manual alphabet except on novelty items such as T-shirts or posters. If the line drawing presentations of the manual alphabet characters encouraged covert translating into English, this could also account for a nonsymmetrical release of

PI. A switch from English to the manual alphabet is not a switch for those who are translating the manual alphabet into English.

CONTROL TASK

As an extra precaution, to ensure that the release of PI would not be attributable to any obvious change in the physical appearance of the stimuli, a control task was presented to the Gallaudet student subjects in which the switch condition involved a switch from upper-case to lower-case letters of the English alphabet (lower to upper for half the subjects). The subjects assigned to the experimental group in the alphabet task were assigned to the control group (no switch) in the control task. The results are presented in Figure 12.3. Inspection of the slopes of the four lines depicted in Figure 12.3 reveals that the switch from upper to lower case or vice versa resulted in no release of PI. Although the trials effect was significant ($F = 24.2$, $df = 3,132$, $p <$ .01), there were no significant interaction effects or significant improvements from Trials 3 to 4. Thus, the control task replicated the findings of the alphabet task with respect to the buildup of PI, verifying that letters of a language's alphabet are coded categorically. But a change in physical appearance has no effect as long as it leaves the category itself unchanged.

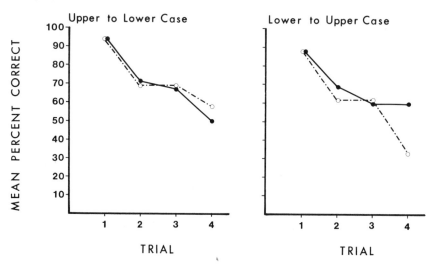

Figure 12.3. Performances on a control task in which the switch was between upper-case and lower-case letters of the English alphabet (— = Experimental; ·—·—· = Control).

This conclusion would be strengthened by data from spoken languages whose alphabets are written differently, such as English and Greek. If the alphabets of each language are assimilated to the language system to which it belongs, then a switch between any two dissimilar alphabets should yield a release of PI among bilingual subjects. Whether languages that come from the same family, such as Hebrew and Arabic, will yield releases of the same magnitude remains to be determined. Data are lacking, but the procedures just described could be used to conduct studies such as these, and it seems likely that the Wickens paradigm will one day be applied to the alphabets of more or less dissimilar languages.

SWITCHES BETWEEN MANUAL AND ENGLISH VOCABULARIES

Classroom experience in teaching ASL and in conducting ASL vocabulary tests for examination purposes has revealed that the citation forms of signs presented out of context are often ambiguous, even to persons who have had considerable experience with the social use of ASL (Hoemann, 1977). Signs sharing two aspects, such as movement and hand configuration, are easily confused with one another, and the loss of the redundancy or predictability occasioned by the absence of a context seems to add considerably to the task demands of a vocabulary test comprised of citation forms of signs.

Since the procedures of the memory task used in the present research are tantamount to a vocabulary test (the subjects must be able to recognize the signs if they are to remember them), there are grounds for concern over the feasibility of using the Wickens paradigm to evaluate switches from sign to English or vice versa. The problem is made even more serious when the signs are executed by an examiner whose dialect of ASL differs from the dialect used by the linguistic community from which the subjects were drawn.

Of the two subject populations from which subjects were recruited for the present studies, Gallaudet College and Saint Rita School for the Deaf, the former was more likely to yield participants who were able to recognize the examiner's signs, since the examiner had been a member of the Gallaudet professional community for 9 years (1960 to 1969). The Gallaudet data are, therefore, presented first (see Figure 12.4). The same subjects participated as had participated in the alphabet test. A sign–word association test was administered between

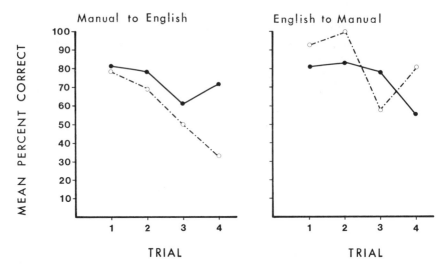

Figure 12.4. Gallaudet College students' performances on the vocabulary test (— = Experimental; ·—··— = Control).

the two memory tasks in order to allow time for any PI to dissipate before beginning the vocabulary task.

The switch from signs to English, presented in the left panel of Figure 12.4, appears to have resulted in the expected release of PI, but the switch from English to signs, presented in the right panel, yielded no release at all. The downward trend across trials was significant (F = 11.31, df = 3,132, p < .01), and the nonsymmetrical release from PI resulted in a triple interaction effect, category × condition × trials (F = 4.96, df = 3,132, p < .05), which disappeared when the analysis was carried out on Trials 1 to 3, excluding Trial 4.

The apparent "recovery" from Trial 3 to Trial 4 on the part of the control group in the right panel of Figure 12.4 was not statistically reliable. A conservative approach to the data would attribute it to chance.

Taken by themselves, these data are too tenuous to merit much comment. However, the Saint Rita data, presented in Figure 12.5, provide a replication that is remarkably faithful in detail. First of all, there was a significant trials effect, reflecting the buildup of PI (F = 10.47, df = 3,132, p < .01). Second, the manual-to-English switch condition again yielded a significant improvement (t = 2.71, df = 15, p < .01), and the English-to-manual switch condition did not. The expected significant interaction effect disappeared when the analysis was limited to three trials. This replication of the Gallaudet trends is more convincing than a statistical test to determine whether the re-

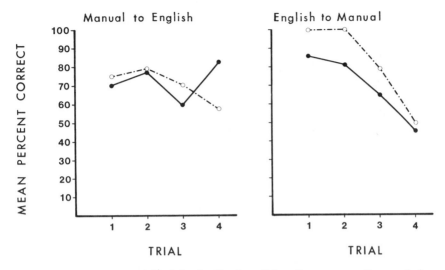

Figure 12.5. Saint Rita School for the Deaf pupils' performances on the vocabulary test (—— = Experimental;   ·–··– = Control).

sults in both cases are reliable. It appears safe to conclude that English vocabulary and sign vocabulary items are coded categorically in short-term memory by deaf subjects.

The absence of a symmetrical release could be a result of covert translating. The signs used in the task (MOTHER, UNCLE, COUSIN, etc.) were signs for which there are clear English equivalents, and they were executed without facial expression. Since the release of PI may be less likely to occur when the switch is out of the first language and into the second, it is noteworthy that among the Saint Rita students the switch from signs to English yielded a release. If covert translating accounts for the lack of symmetry in the Saint Rita and in the Gallaudet data, it must be assumed that the presentation of vocabulary in sign for three successive trials created a set or expectancy that was altered when English words were shown on the fourth trial. On the other hand, presenting English words for three trials followed by signs having ready English equivalents required no basic change in the subjects' encoding strategies.

HEARING DATA

The question remains as to what kinds of performances on these tasks one might obtain with hearing subjects who are bilingual in

English and sign. Sufficient data are lacking for drawing clear conclusions. Expecially needed are data from hearing children of deaf parents who have used sign from birth. In the absence of data from hearing subjects with such native sign competence, conclusions must be considered very tentative.

The data that exist were gathered from 16 hearing staff members of Saint Rita School for the Deaf. The results are presented in Figure 12.6, with the alphabet task in the left panel and the vocabulary task on the right. Years of exposure to ASL usage ranged from 2 to 20, with a mean of 9. Performances on the vocabulary task indicated that the subjects were able to deal better with the English stimuli than with the sign stimuli. Half the subjects ($N = 8$) received English vocabulary items for three trials and were switched to sign vocabulary on the fourth trial. The other half of the subjects received sign vocabulary for three trials and were switched to English vocabulary on the fourth trial. On Trial 1, which reflected performances prior to any buildup of PI, all 8 subjects receiving English stimuli obtained perfect scores of 3 out of 3; only 3 of the 8 subjects receiving sign stimuli on Trial 1 obtained perfect scores.

Depressed performances on Trial 1 jeopardize the results of the test, since a release of PI can only be observed as an improvement in performance relative to previous trials. As a matter of fact, the data on the vocabulary task reveal very little more than that the hearing subjects' ability to recognize and recall sign vocabulary items was inferior

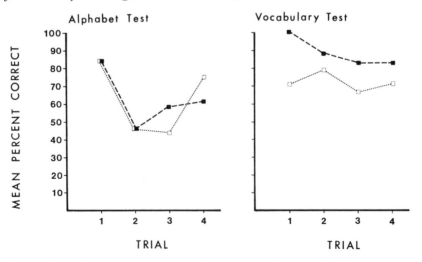

Figure 12.6. Hearing data on the vocabulary test and on the alphabet test (■----■ = English to Manual; □ . . . . □ = Manual to English).

to their ability to recognize and recall English vocabulary items. Lack of familiarity with the signs used in the task seems to have interfered with recall, depressing performances on the first three trials of the manual-to-English switch condition and possibly obscuring any release of PI that may have occurred on Trial 4 of the English-to-manual switch condition.

It should be added that the subjects' lack of competence with the sign vocabulary presented in this task cannot be taken as an accurate measure of their manual communicative competence with their pupils. Citation forms were executed that may have differed considerably from the ordinary way the children executed the same signs. Some of the signs (UNCLE, AUNT, HUSBAND, WIFE, NEPHEW, COUSIN) may have been used very infrequently by the child population with whom the staff members were in daily contact. Moreover, all the signs were executed out of context and without facial expression.

Performances across the first three trials by the group exposed to English vocabulary revealed the expected decline, but it was not statistically significant.

The data from the alphabet task obtained from the hearing subjects were more gratifying. Performances on Trial 1 were identical for both groups, regardless which alphabet was used for the first trial. The trials effect, which reflected the buildup of PI, was statistically significant ($F = 8.38$, $df = 3,42$, $p < .01$). There was no clear release from PI for the English-to-manual switch condition, but the switch from manual to English letters yielded a release that approached significance ($t = 1.97$, $df = 5$, $p < .10$). These data are consistent with the data from the deaf subjects. The data do not support a "covert translating" explanation for the absence of a symmetrical release, since the hearing subjects seemed to have experienced a release into rather than out of their first language; however, it would be appropriate to withhold judgment until hearing persons can be tested who learned ASL from deaf parents. Meanwhile, the data indicate that hearing persons also code manual and English alphabet characters categorically. This result was observed even in subjects who appeared to be somewhat less fluent in ASL than in English.

IMPLICATIONS AND CONCLUSIONS

There is a great deal of consistency in the present data, especially when it is considered that they were gathered from a diverse subject pool including hearing staff and deaf pupils from Saint Rita School for the Deaf and deaf students from Gallaudet College. The switch from manual to English stimuli, whether alphabet characters or vocabulary items, consistently yielded a release from PI. Moreover, when the manual alphabet characters were presented live on the hand, the release was symmetrical, occurring also with the English-to-manual switch. Since this is the normal mode of presentation of the manual alphabet, it is tempting to accept the symmetrical release as the outcome from which to draw conclusions and to attribute the lack of symmetry in the other situations to covert translating effects induced by the nature of the stimuli or their mode of presentation, for example, as line drawings rather than live on the hand. Fortunately, the main conclusion of the study, that deaf persons code manual and English language stimuli categorically, is not jeopardized by a nonsymmetrical release.

The data are compatible with the results reported by Goggin and Wickens (1971) and with Kolers's (1963) hypothesis that different languages have separate memory stores. Even the manual alphabet, which appears to derive its status from its ability to represent English letters by means of a manual symbol, appears to be not merely a code for English, even though it may be used as one, but part and parcel of the manual system of communicating used by large numbers of deaf persons in the United States and Canada. This may be true even for hearing persons who use the manual alphabet primarily as a way to spell English words. It is certainly true for deaf children of deaf parents, since their fluency in fingerspelling develops along with their fluency to communicate in a manual system.

A close relation between the manual alphabet and ASL can be seen in other phenomena. Battison (1976) has gathered a generous body of data that show that fingerspelled loan words constitute a significant aspect of ASL lexical usage. Loan words are executed with a gestalt that is constrained by usage, and they take on features such as movement and orientation, which serve as distinctive features of sign (Stokoe, 1972). Second, initialized signs are widely used by deaf persons. These are complex symbols whose movement and location reference a field of meaning associated with a conventional sign from ASL and whose hand configuration references, at the same time, an associated English word (Hoemann, 1976). There is no counterpart to such bilanguage referencing in any spoken language. Its presence in ASL indicates that the symbols of the manual alphabet perform functions within ASL that go far beyond representing corresponding letters of the English alphabet.

Even for hearing persons there are grounds for suspecting that manual alphabet letters are not perceived merely as English letters in another guise. Tachistascopic presentations of conflicting linguistic stimuli in the left and right visual fields reveal that English language stimuli—words and letters—tend to be processed by the left hemisphere by right-handed persons, while manual language stimuli—signs and letters—tend to be processed by the right hemisphere by the same hearing persons (McKeever, Hoemann, Florian, & VanDeventer, 1976).

The view that the manual alphabet is an integral feature of ASL rather than a method for spelling English is also compatible with some unpublished data from our laboratories in which we found a different error pattern in deaf children's live fingerspelling than in their written English spelling performances for the same word list. Omission errors, for example, accounted for only about 42% of the errors in a written spelling test (Hoemann, Andrews, Florian, Hoemann, & Jensems, 1976), but they accounted for 78% of the errors when the responses were made in fingerspelling. This dissimilar performance suggests that fingerspelling is acquired primarily as a means of communicating rather than as a way to spell English words. A communication channel must be relatively tolerant of noise due to interference or missing information if it is to function effectively. Insistence on 100% spelling accuracy in order for fingerspelling to serve as a means of communicating would be an excessive demand that would render fingerspelling ineffectual for ordinary conversational use.

Besides clarifying the status of the manual alphabet by relating it to its users and its uses, the research described in this chapter also sheds some light on an issue that has recurred from time to time in the memory literature dealing with deafness. It has long been assumed that audition plays an important role in the coding process. Observed deficiencies in deaf subjects' performances have sometimes been attributed to the absence of auditory coding strategies (Pintner & Paterson, 1917) or to the absence of acoustic mediators (Koh, Vernon, & Bailey, 1971). An alternative position holds that deaf people's memory can function effectively without auditory involvement (Carey & Blake, 1974; Hoemann, Andrews, & DeRosa, 1974; Ross, 1969). The present data are compatible with the latter view. Regardless how central a role audition may sometimes seem to play in the mental processes of people who can hear, auditory experiences are apparently not essential for the processes to function at all. There is no clear evidence that the coding strategies used by deaf persons are inevitably inferior to those used by hearing persons. Our data argue for the assumption that the memory function of deaf persons lies within the normal range of human adaptations and that it is responsive to their intellectual and social needs.

Finally, the results of the present investigation illustrate the utility and the diverse applicability of the Wickens paradigm as a research tool. Its applicability to some basic questions regarding the status of certain components of deaf people's communicative devices is borne out by the present research. An extension of the findings to other aspects of ASL, to other manual languages, and to other language systems is within the scope of currently available research methods.

ACKNOWLEDGMENTS

The cooperation of the students and administrators of Gallaudet College and of Saint Rita School for the Deaf is gratefully acknowledged. Suzanne Farquharson, a senior psychology major at Bowling Green State University during the 1975–1976 academic year, participated in the planning of the research and in the gathering of the Gallaudet data. A preliminary report coauthored by Farquharson was presented at the Conference on Sign Language and Neurolinguistics, September 24–26, 1976, Rochester, New York.

REFERENCES

Battison, R. Fingerspelled loan words in American Sign Language: Evidence for restructuring. Conference on Sign Language and Neurolinguistics, Rochester, New York, September 24–26, 1976.

Carey, P., & Blake, J. Visual short-term memory in the hearing and the deaf. *Canadian Journal of Psychology*, 1974, 28, 1–14.

Goggin, J., & Wickens, D. D. Proactive interference and language change in short-term memory. *Journal of Verbal Learning and Verbal Behavior*, 1971, 10, 453–458.

Hoemann, H. W. *American Sign Language: Lexical and grammatical notes with translation exercises*. Silver Spring, Maryland: National Association of the Deaf, 1976.

Hoemann, H. W. *Teaching American Sign Language: A rationale*. Paper presented at the National Symposium on Sign Language Research and Teaching. Chicago, Illinois, May 30–June 3, 1977.

Hoemann, H. W., Andrews, C. E., & DeRosa, D. V. Categorical coding in short-term memory by deaf and hearing children. *Journal of Speech and Hearing Research*, 1974, 17, 426–431.

Hoemann, H. W., Andrews, C. E., Florian, V. A., Hoemann, S. A., & Jensema, C. J. The spelling proficiency of deaf children. *American Annals of the Deaf*, 1976, 121, 489–493.

Keppel, G., & Underwood, B. J. Proactive inhibition in short-term retention of single items. *Journal of Verbal Learning and Verbal Behavior*, 1962, 1, 153–161.

Koh, S. D., Vernon, M., & Bailey, W. Free-recall learning of word lists by prelingual deaf subjects. *Journal of Verbal Learning and Verbal Behavior*, 1971, 10, 542–547.

Kolers, P. A. Interlingual word associations. *Journal of Verbal Learning and Verbal Behavior*, 1963, 2, 291–300.

McKeever, W. F., Hoemann, H. W., Florian, V. A., & VanDeventer, A. D. Evidence of minimal cerebral assymetries for the processing of English words and American Sign Language in the congenitally deaf. *Neuropsychologia*, 1976, *14*, 413–423.

Peterson, L. R., & Peterson, M. J. Short-term retention of individual verbal items. *Journal of Experimental Psychology*, 1959, *58*, 193–198.

Pintner, R., & Paterson, D. A comparison of deaf and hearing in visual memory for digits. *Journal of Experimental Psychology*, 1917, *16*, 76–88.

Ross, B. M. Sequential visual memory and the limited magic of the number seven. *Journal of Experimental Psychology*, 1969, *80*, 339–347.

Stokoe, W. C., Jr. *Semiotics and Human Sign Languages*. The Hague: Mouton, 1972.

Wickens, D. D. Characteristics of word encoding. In A. W. Melton & E. Martin (Eds.), *Coding processes in human memory*. Washington, D.C.: Winston & Sons, 1972, 191–215.

Wickens, D. D. Encoding categories of words: An empirical approach to meaning. *Psychological Review*, 1970, *77*, 1–15.

Wickens, D. D., Born, D. G., & Allen, C. K. Proactive inhibition and item similarity in short-term memory. *Journal of Verbal Learning and Verbal Behavior*, 1963, *2*, 440–445.

V

HISTORICAL AND COMPARATIVE STUDIES

13

Sign Language and Creoles

SUSAN D. FISCHER

San Diego State University

INTRODUCTION

As I write this, it has been about 6 years since I started working on
American Sign Language (ASL). At that time, those of us working on
ASL had a special sort of psycholinguistic or sociolinguistic ax to
grind. This ax very easily evolved into a political one as well. We were
all interested in showing that ASL really was (and is) a real, live,
natural language—that just because it is produced in space and perceived by the eyes makes it no less a language. As neophytes in the
business, we were concerned, quite naturally I think, with having the
stamp of legitimacy placed on our research, and on our conclusions.
Thus, there was a lot of work that—although allowing, of course, for
differences in modality—concentrated largely on the parallels between sign language and oral language. See, for example, Bellugi and
Fischer (1972), Stokoe (1972), Fischer (1972, 1974), and Woodward
(1973a). I, for one, was particularly eager for ASL to receive appropriate recognition in the area of generative syntax.

It became apparent all too soon, however, that it was difficult to
maintain that ASL was totally parallel to oral languages, and the
pendulum began to swing in the direction of concentrating on the
differences between the two modalities rather than on the similarities.
A number of persons (e.g., Friedman, 1976) began remarking on the

noticeably freer-seeming grammar of ASL as compared with oral languages. Even the specter of "sign language has no grammar," which we thought we had demythologized out of existence, began rearing its head again.

I would like to nudge the pendulum back in the other direction. The impetus for this nudge comes from consideration of a class of languages that has long had the same status vis-à-vis "establishment" languages as ASL. That class of languages is creoles. If we compare sign languages with creoles rather than with "establishment" languages, the parallels become much closer; one can once again talk about the similarities rather than the differences between signed and oral languages. It is simply necessary to choose *which* class of oral languages one makes the comparison with. Further, the considerations that permit us to make this sort of close comparison provide us with evidence about the process of creolization, the process of language learning in children, and, ultimately, the process of creation of language. In this chapter, I shall give a sociolinguistic sketch of sign language and creoles, some short grammatical (i.e., syntactic) descriptions, and then speculations on a possible explanation for the striking parallels between the two systems.

SOCIOLINGUISTIC DESCRIPTION

The first thing I would like to do is to provide a sociolinguistic sketch of a particular language; it could be one of many. By sociolinguistic sketch, I mean a brief description of the social context in which it exists. This language, which we will call ZZZ for convenience, has long been on the fringes of respectability. In a society whose most powerful members use standard English (SE), users, especially monolingual users, of ZZZ are low on the power totem pole; hence, they are also low on the prestige totem pole as well, and too often low on the financial one, too. It would be out of the question, for example, for a monolingual user of ZZZ to get a job in a bank, though it might be possible to get a job selling used cars.

ZZZ is viewed with opprobrium particularly by educators. Many educators would be relieved if ZZZ disappeared from the face of the earth. They feel that there is something "primitive" about it. One will often hear teachers say things about it like, "ZZZ has no grammar," or "It's just broken English," or "ZZZ can express only concrete notions; you could never have a discussion of abstract concepts or philosophy in it." In most schools its use is frowned upon, if not prohibited entirely, with the justification that if students are permitted to use it, they will grow to depend on it as a crutch and will never be able to learn the prestige variety of English. This prohibition does not, however, prevent children from using ZZZ on the playground or when they are out of sight of adults who do not share their subculture. Forty years ago, it was standard to have two sets of schools, one for those who had "good English" and the other, with much lower prestige, naturally, for those who had "bad English," that is, the ZZZ-using rejects from the first set of schools.

ZZZ is often labeled "inferior," and one of the reasons this is all too easy to do is the difficulty one faces in trying to write it down. Much of the flavor, and even certain aspects of the grammar, as we shall be discussing later on, are in the intonation rather than at the segmental level; because intonation is notoriously difficult to capture on paper, the end result of trying to write the language down may indeed appear at first glance like "broken" or impoverished English, since so much is missing from the transcript. For this and other reasons, there is very little literature in ZZZ that is written, a fact that lends even more ammunition for those who wish to put it down as inferior; such persons have much less respect for oral literature, it would seem, than for the written word.

Based mostly on the (mis)apprehension that ZZZ is "primitive," most persons who are not native in ZZZ think that it is quite easy to learn, a notion that itself seems to enable nonnatives to consider ZZZ inferior to English. An interesting corollary of this view is that even native users of ZZZ share the same feeling; perhaps they have been told for so long that ZZZ is inferior that they themselves have come to believe it. As a result, many persons native in ZZZ, especially those with some command of SE, will even refuse to admit that they know the language. A user of ZZZ, when conversing with a nonnative, will often make his or her language approach SE as much as his or her competence permits. I once met a young woman who said of ZZZ, "Oh, I used it as a kid, but I've forgotten it all now." I suspected from the way she used SE that she had not forgotten ZZZ, but it was not until she was able to realize that it was acceptable to use ZZZ in an academic setting that it came out that she really knew ZZZ and still used it. It is perhaps this adjustment of level of grammar on the part of native users of ZZZ that gives outsiders the impression that it is so easy for them to learn. However, the outsider who manages to observe two natives using ZZZ entirely between themselves without their being aware of his or her presence will quickly be disabused of this opinion. Indeed, using the most un-English form of the language is a

device by which persons skilled in ZZZ can effectively exclude outsiders from participation in the conversation. However, even among
themselves, users of ZZZ may use more "Englishy" forms, especially
when they are trying to impress their interlocutor with how educated
they are, or when they are talking about academic or intellectual
topics.

Thus, whereas native users themselves may view their own
language as inferior in some ways, they paradoxically use it as a marker
of in-group solidarity. Outsiders who know ZZZ very well are ac-
cepted into the community, while those who do not know it well are
not. Even among users of ZZZ, there are different degrees of facility
with it that seem to be more than simply rhetorical. Facility is prized
within the in-group and is often the mark of leadership in the community.

Fortunately, the picture has changed somewhat in recent years. The
students who attended the "bad English" high school 30 years ago
have now achieved a great deal of political power. ZZZ is gaining
more acceptance in at least some schools, and some literature has
begun to appear. Users of ZZZ have gained a new pride in their
language, and for the first time in a very long while, they are starting to
stand up for their right to use their native language. One can even see
the language used in the mass media.

It often occurs that the parents of users of this language are not
themselves speakers of the language, although this picture is in constant flux. Perhaps for that reason, ZZZ has changed extraordinarily
fast, not so much in the area of syntax, but particularly in the area of
vocabulary, though even some syntactic change has occurred. If one
were doing glottochronology, one's hypotheses as to how old ZZZ is
would probably be off by at least several centuries.

The final point I would like to make in this description is that, due
perhaps to the fact that ZZZ has been an underground language for so
long, there is a lack of standardization. Any discussion of grammaticality
within ZZZ by two users always ends in an argument.

For someone who is familiar with ASL and the deaf community in
the United States, most of this description will come as no surprise.
However, this is *not*, in fact, a description of ASL in the deaf and
hearing worlds; rather, it is a description of Hawaiian Creole English
(HCE) and the community of speakers of HCE in Hawaii.

That there should be such a striking similarity between attitudes
toward ASL and attitudes toward HCE is interesting. Even more interesting, however, are the grammatical similarities between ASL and
HCE or other creoles. Before I discuss specific parallels, however, I

would like, for the benefit of those readers who are unfamiliar with creole languages, to give a brief introduction to pidgins and creoles and to some of the analogies between these and signing systems.

PIDGINS AND CREOLES

What happens when an adult tries to speak a second language without any formal training? At the beginning, utterances may come out sounding like the "me Tarzan, you Jane" variety. Similar utterances will even be made by a native speaker trying to communicate with a nonnative speaker. Ferguson (1971) suggests that this "foreigner talk" is the source for pidgin languages. A pidgin develops as a contact vernacular among speakers of several languages. Often, though not always, it develops in a colonial situation. For example, a plantation in the Indian Ocean or in Hawaii may import workers from a number of different language families. In Hawaii, workers have been brought in from Portugal, China, Japan, the Philippines, and Samoa, in addition to native Hawaiians, who were essentially colonized by Britons and Americans; such a mix may lead to a number of different "pidgin" languages.

According to Hall's (1966) definition, a pidgin is nobody's first language and has no history of ever having had native speakers. Although pidgin speakers of different language backgrounds will often have different-sounding pidgins even if they are in the same geographical area—that is, the phonology may be different, and the syntax approaches, though is not identical to, that of the speaker's first language—there will be one language that largely serves as a lexical base for the pidgin(s), usually the lexicon of the language of power. In Hawaii, that language is largely English, though there are quite a few Hawaiian and Japanese words as well as a few Chinese words commonly used by pidgin speakers. That the vocabulary would be borrowed though the syntax and phonology of the pidgin speaker's first language remain fairly constant should not be surprising. One is constantly learning vocabulary throughout one's lifetime, even in one's native language, but syntactic and phonological learning usually stops sometime during childhood.[1] Thus, it would be logical that if

---

[1] See Lenneberg (1967). Zaidel (in press) has brought out that in the split-brain patients he has examined, the minor hemisphere seems to learn vocabulary about 3, but only 3, years behind the major; whereas in the case of syntax, the development of the minor hemisphere seems to stop at age 5.

anything is to adapt to a new linguistic environment, the vocabulary is going to be in the lead. This process is often termed "relexification."

A pidgin language, not being anyone's first language, is used only in situations of contact among speakers of different languages. Partially because of this limited usage, and probably partially because of most adults' limited language-learning capabilities, the language itself is often rather severely limited. Pidgin languages (though not creoles, as we shall see in the following discussion) thus are seen as fulfilling many of the commonly held stereotypes of languages like ASL. Their vocabularies are small, their syntaxes really do look primitive, and the kinds of expressive devices, whether grammatical or rhetorical, are far fewer in number than those in "establishment" languages. They do, however, serve the purposes of limited interactions such as trade quite adequately.

The vast majority of pidgin languages are transitory—they last only the lifetimes of the first participants in a colonial situation. The children of pidgin speakers will speak a creole rather than a pidgin (see the following discussion). There are, however, a few exceptions. The original lingua franca, with a lexical base of Italian, has existed in Asia Minor since the times of the Crusades; it was originally a trade jargon.

Syntactically and morphologically, pidgins are characterized by simplification vis-à-vis the languages they are related to. This simplification is in specific directions. Thus, a pidgin will have virtually no inflectional or even derivational morphology; grammatical relations are indicated by word order, and there is a minimum of redundancy.

There are examples of pidgin sign systems as well. Woodward (1973b, Woodward & Markowicz, 1975) characterizes what he calls Pidgin Signed English as that variety of sign language used, among other things, as an interface between deaf signers and hearing speakers. Pidgin Signed English is thus used as a second language by both groups. Generally, it follows English word order using signs from ASL, but it may lack the redundancy of either English or ASL.

There are examples of pidgin sign languages other than the one Woodward describes. So-called "homemade" signs have most of the characteristics of pidgin languages (see the ones described by Frishberg, 1975). Some signing systems used in schools that prohibit signing may be pidgins also, which would contribute to the low regard in which they are held. Another familiar example is the phenomenon of one's being able to understand, and to make oneself understood in, an unfamiliar sign system more quickly than an unfamiliar spoken language. If I may cite a personal example, in 1972, I went to Japan and in a few days was able to pick up quite a few (perhaps 150 to 200) Japanese signs. In comparison, the number of spoken Japanese words I picked up in 3 weeks totaled perhaps 40. Even though some of the grammatical mechanisms in JSL (Japanese Sign Language) are similar to those in ASL, I am certain that the variety of JSL I was able to use after a few days was a pidgin, and not at all "good" JSL. (It was, however, good enough to enable me to interpret fairly accurately for my companion.) The sign language used by the Plains Indians for trade among tribes that do not otherwise have a common language is a good example of the exception just discussed, that of a pidgin that continues for more than a couple of generations.

A creole is conventionally defined as the language that the children of pidgin speakers learn, or—to put it more accurately—create. Where a pidgin is a second language, a creole is a first language. Where a pidgin is generally limited in usage and structure, a creole is varied and rich. It has been said (D. Bickerton, personal communication), "All pidgins are different, and all creoles are alike," and indeed there are certain structural characteristics that seem to be common to all creoles (see pp. 318–325). Some examples of creoles include the French-based creoles in Haiti, Louisiana, and the Indian Ocean islands of Mauritius and Réunion. One English-based creole is Gullah, spoken off the coast of South Carolina. Dillard (1972) argues that so-called Black English is also a creole, though if it is indeed a creole, it must have evolved a great deal since its initial creolization. There are also creoles spoken in Guyana and the West Indies. One can even view Modern English as a former creole; 1066 certainly changed the English language a great deal. There are obvious differences between, say, Middle English and other creoles, but these may be due to the fact that only two, rather than several, languages were involved.

Many creoles have a Portuguese lexical base, and there are theories that assert that all creoles are relexified versions of one Portuguese protocreole; such a "monogenesis" theory would account for the fact that creoles all over the world are so similar grammatically. If, as I shall try to show, ASL behaves like a creole, even though it has had no contact with spoken Portuguese, that theory will thereby be weakened. Perhaps one reason why ASL looks so much like a creole is expressed in the speculation voiced by Woodward (Chapter 14, this volume) that present-day ASL resulted from a creolization process between indigenous American Sign Language and the French Sign Language that was brought over by Gallaudet in the early 1800s. However, that was 150 years ago, and we will, in a later section, still want to explain why ASL *still* looks like a creole.

If, through continued contact, speakers of a creole continue to be exposed to a "standard" language, that is, the language that provided the lexical base for the creole, then there may develop what has been variously called a postcreole continuum, or a decreolizing gradatum (Bailey, 1974). One end of this continuous scale may be so drastically different from the other end that it may be unintelligible to a person who knows only the other end. This postcreolized continuum bears an intimate relation to Ferguson's (1959) notion of diglossia. If we extend the theory to look at two ends of a diglossic *continuum*, the "High" variant of the language is used on formal occasions and may be considered the "prestige" dialect. The "Low" variant is used on less formal occasions and is generally considered the "low-prestige" dialect. In his pioneering work, Stokoe (1970) has discussed the notion of a diglossic continuum with respect to ASL. Stokoe sees the continuum as running between something like Manual English on one end and "super-deaf" sign on the other (these are not his terms). Lou Fant (1972) has proposed a similar scale, though he seems to view it as much less of a continuum, with the opposite poles of Siglish (Signed English) and Ameslan (American Sign Language).

The distinction I wish to draw is along somewhat different axes. I do not doubt that there are High and Low forms of ASL; clearly, there are both lexical and grammatical differences between the various sorts of signing a deaf person will use in a platform speech as opposed to what she or he will use in a bar with friends. One example would be the two different sentence negators DON'T[2] (two B hands, palms down, are crossed in front of the body, then separated) and NOT (thumb of a fist hand brushes under the chin). DON'T is used in more formal situations, whereas NOT is used in ordinary conversation. DON'T is no more standard English than NOT; a more formal style of language need not be closer to a standard. Differently expressed, a diglossic continuum is responding to pressure from within the language's different social situations, whereas a postcreole continuum is responding to pressure from outside the language itself.

Creolists distinguish among roughly three levels of a postcreole continuum: the *acrolect*, the *mesolect*, and the *basilect*. The acrolect

[2] I follow the now established practice of using capital letters to gloss signs. Fingerspelled words will be shown with hyphens between the letters (e.g., O-F), and single signs that must be glossed with more than one English word will show hyphens between the words of the English gloss (e.g., REMOVE-WITH-SPOON). A plus (+) will be used to show two signs joined into a compound or cliticized form; with no immediately following word, it will signal repetition, usually fast reduplication. Crosshatches (# #) show slow reduplication. See Fischer (1972) for detailed discussions of these phenomena.

is closest to the standard form, though it may not quite reach it. The basilect bears the *least* resemblance to the standard. In a postcreole continuum, however, many speakers, often as a result of education and continued exposure to both the basilect and the acrolect, will commonly use the mesolect, which shares features of both and also contains features unique to that level. I will argue that there is an exact parallel between these three lects and the sociolinguistic structure of ASL, and probably other sign language systems as well.

It is no accident that even in its most "deaf" version, ASL *roughly* follows English word order (Fischer, 1974, 1975), or that JSL roughly follows Japanese word order, at least insofar as major constituents are concerned. Having been surrounded by hearing speakers of a standard language, especially hearing educators, has taken its toll, as has continued exposure to media. The acrolect of ASL is very close to SE, even though it is represented in a different modality. Several varieties of acrolect can be found, from pure fingerspelling (Rochester method) to visual English systems such as SEE (Signing Exact English) to Manual English. This is what Fant calls Siglish. It may not, however, be totally identical to SE. I recall a sentence uttered in ASL acrolect that was intended to mean that someone learned easily. The deaf person very carefully signed

(1) NANCY TRUE EASY TO LEARN.
     "Nancy is easy to learn."

The presence of the copula TRUE and the empty infinitive marker TO shows that the signer was doing her best to use SE, but did not quite make it.[3] In basilectal ASL, TRUE is not a copula but is used as an emphatic marker meaning "really." Moreover, TO is used only as a directional preposition, never as the marker for an infinitive.

The basilect of ASL is what Fant refers to as Ameslan; it has been variously called real deaf sign, old-time sign language, or even low verbal (meaning low English) signing. This is the variety of signing that hearing people cannot understand if they just know individual signs; it makes very little use of fingerspelling, a great deal of use of space, and a good deal of use of various parts of the body to signal grammatical form.

In between the acrolect and the basilect of ASL we find the mesolect. This corresponds to what Bernard Bragg (personal com-

---

[3] To be fair, even native speakers of SE sometimes don't quite make it either. I recall a dentist's receptionist from Ohio who said to me, "Your husband is difficult to understand what the doctor says," which is parallel to sentence (1).

munication) has called Ameslish. It does indeed share many properties of the extreme ends of the scale. An example of the difference
between the three levels is given in Table 13.1. Five versions of the
sentence "Have you been to Europe?" are given.

TABLE 13.1

Three Lects of American Sign Language, Including Respective Translations of "Have
You Been to Europe?"

Lect	Term	Sentence
Acrolect	Siglish, Manual English Rochester	HAVE YOU BE+EN TO EUROPE FINISH YOU B-E-E-N TO EUROPE? H-A-V-E Y-O-U B-E-E-N T-O E-U-R-O-P-E
Mesolect	Ameslish	YOU FINISH TOUCH EUROPE QUESTION?
Basilect	Ameslan	TOUCH+FINISH EUROPE, YOU? (question-eyes————————→)

A great deal of sound and fury has been generated over where one
draws the line between what is considered "pure" ASL and what
should be excluded from consideration as part of the language. I
personally feel that since deaf people themselves use all three varieties, they should all count. However, since I think that it would be a
waste of time to get involved in this dispute, I am going to limit
arbitrarily my discussion largely to the basilect of ASL, which
everyone will agree belongs in the category of American Sign Language. In any case, the distinction that has been made among lects in a
postcreole contiuum seems to be applicable to the various systems of
signing current in the United States.

SYNTACTIC AND LEXICAL CHARACTERISTICS OF
CREOLE LANGUAGES AND THE ANALOGY
TO AMERICAN SIGN LANGUAGE

In this section I shall summarize some facts about creole languages
and about ASL. Unless otherwise specified, I shall, when talking
about creoles, be referring to HCE, which is the creole language I
have had the most exposure to and which, since I am in Hawaii, I can
most easily find native informants for. Some of my discussion is based
on deCamp's (1971) excellent summary. The data from ASL come
largely from my own field notes and observations and has been
confirmed by a number of native signers.

Because intonation plays a fairly important role in this discussion, I shall attempt to capture it where necessary without going into great detail. I shall use punctuation marks such as [?] and [,] to signal question and comma intonation; at other times, more detail may be necessary. For ASL, I shall use two lines—one for segmental, and one for nonsegmental aspects of the signal—along lines similar to those employed by Liddell (Chapter 3, this volume) and Baker and Padden (Chapter 2, this volume). Since I am not interested in the phonological level, HCE will be written in SE orthography. It should be borne in mind, however, that all varieties of Hawaiian English—including Hawaiian Pidgin, HCE, and acrolectal forms approaching United States mainland English—have a phonology that is somewhat different from SE. For example, Sentence (4) in the following discussion would be represented phonetically as [gɛt plɛni tuːris big ailansai].

One of the first, and more superficial, factors that strikes one in looking at creoles and sign language is the remarkably similar content words used for grammatical purposes. It is a general characteristic of creole languages that some content words come to be used to express grammatical forms, and ASL and HCE are no exceptions. For example, in ASL there are two ways of forming existential sentences, one using TRUE, the other using HAVE. My impression is that HAVE is more basilectal and TRUE more mesolectal, but this may just be a regional variation. For example:

(2) HAVE SOMEONE HOME?
"Is there anyone home?"

(3) HAVE HERD SIGHT-SEE+ER YONDER (ARC) BIG IS-
LAND.
"There are lots and lots of tourists over on the Big Island (Hawaii)."

It is possible that the use of HAVE is a carryover from the French *y avoir* (*il y a*) construction. It is interesting, however, that in HCE one uses either *have* or *get* for existential constructions as well (*have* seems to be restricted to urban creole speakers according to one informant). Note the striking parallels between sentences (3) and (4), not only in the use of *get* or *have* but also in the suffix *-side*, which is used in apparently exactly the same way as YONDER in ASL:

(4) $\left\{ \begin{array}{l} Get \\ Have \end{array} \right\}$ *plenty tourist Big Island-side.*
"There are lots of tourists on the Big Island."

(5) *Makapuu get plenty shark(s).*
"There are lots of sharks around Makapuu."

Another lexical similarity is the use of some form of the verb FINISH as a perfective marker. HCE does not happen to use it (although the HCE word *pau,* from the Hawaiian for "finish," is used to mean "cut it out," just as the stressed form of FINISH is used in ASL). But there are many other creole languages which do, such as Guyanese and Mauritian creoles. We shall return to aspectual markers later in this section?

A third lexical similarity is the use of the word for "better" as an auxiliary for the polite imperative, or exhortative. In ASL, this would occur in a sentence like (6). In HCE, the phrase *more better* would occur in a sentence like (7); the usage is quite parallel.

(6) BETTER YOU HOME NOW+!
"You should go home right now."

(7) *More better you drink 'um fast.*
"You should drink it quickly."

A fourth lexical similarity, which approaches being a syntactic one, is the use of a form of *yes* plus a question intonation to form tag questions. In HCE this involves the word *yeah,* and in ASL it involves simultaneous signing, head nodding (or shaking in the case of a negative tag), and eye widening–eyebrow raising. We shall see in the following discussion the interesting way in which this interacts with rules of topicalization.

(8) *Good, yeah?*
"It's good, isn't it?"

(9) GOOD
YES? (head nod+question look)
"It's good, isn't it?"

Moving on to a comparison of the syntax of the two kinds of language systems, we again find striking similarities. There is a tendency for creoles to have very little in the way of tense marking (though they have more than pidgins do), but there is a very rich aspectual system. For example, in HCE time can be expressed, but in the case of the past, the concentration seems to be more on completion than time frame. The same holds true in ASL, where there are a few verbs, such as TOUCH or SEE, that can directly inflect for "tense" by incorporating the auxiliary FINISH. Most time reference is done, however, by time adverbs like IN-FUTURE ("later") (cf. HCE *bambai*), PAST (cf. *before*), or NOW. However, there are more ways for indicating aspect in either ASL or creoles than in a language like English. In both ASL and various creoles, there are two kinds of grammatical mechanisms used to express aspect: periphrastic "auxiliaries" and reduplication. ASL uses auxiliaries to express positive and negative perfective aspect (FINISH, NOT-YET [LATE]); continuation to or from a point (SINCE, HENCEFORTH); and two kinds of factive (SUCCESS, HAPPEN). It uses reduplication for signifying continuation, iteration, or habitual aspect (see Fischer, 1972). Reduplication is also used in the pluralization of nouns and some adjectives, in both ASL (e.g., SHOE+ for "shoes") and in creoles such as those in the West Indies (Craig, 1971).

In both ASL and creoles, there tends to be reliance on word order rather than bound morphemes to indicate case relations. The only exceptions seem to be the use of cliticized pronouns in both kinds of languages. Bickerton and Givon (1976) have shown that the cliticization of pronouns is one of the things that takes place in the transition between a pidgin and a creole, it can even have an effect on typological change in the creolization process. I have shown elsewhere (Fischer, 1975) that if one views the so-called directional verbs in ASL— that is, those verbs that change their motion and/or orientation to incorporate the location of the referents of various arguments in the sentence—as incorporating clitic pronouns, the same argument can hold for ASL as for HCE. An example of clitic pronouns substituting for word order is given in (10):

(10) BOY   GIRL   SHE-KICK-HIM.
      (point left) (point right) (right "kicks" left)
      "The girl kicks the boy."

One reason word order, sometimes in combination with cliticization, is particularly crucial is that ASL has no passive as such. This seems also to be the case with many creoles, including Jamaican (Craig, 1971). Instead of a passive, there is what one might call a middle voice, where the underlying object is made into the subject and the underlying agent is unspecified:

(11) RAIN, WELL?, WE POSTPONE PICNIC.
      "It rained, so we postponed the picnic."

(12) PICNIC POSTPONE BECAUSE RAIN.
      "The picnic was postponed on account of rain."

Cliticization can produce the same effect in ASL:

(13) ME NOT ME-INVITE-YOU MY PARTY.
"I'm not inviting you to my party."

(14) ME NOT SOMEONE-INVITE-ME HER PARTY.
"I'm not invited to her party."

Just because there are almost no inflections in ASL or in creoles does not mean that word order is completely fixed. Changing the word order, leaving behind intonational cues, is how topicalization or focalization is accomplished in both systems. Topicalization is one of many examples in which nonsegmental grammatical devices—which one can loosely term intonation—are crucial in making distinctions that in establishment languages would be conveyed syntactically or morphologically.

One example of topicalization is that the subject noun phrase being topicalized can move to the end of the sentence. For example:

(15) *She went Japan, my mother.*
"My mother went to Japan."

(16) GO-THERE JAPAN, MOTHER.
"My mother went to Japan."

In both ASL and HCE, topicalization is ordered after question formation. This can lead to some very interesting intonational convolutions:

(17) *Your brother, where he stay?*
"Talking about your brother, where is he?"

(18) YOUR BROTHER, WHERE LIVE NOW?
"Talking about your brother, where is he living?"

(19) *Good, yeah? the bus.*
"The bus (mentioned before) is good, isn't it?"

(20) GOOD, B-U-S.
YES?
"The bus is good, isn't it?"

Notice that in all four of the above sentences, there is a marked shift in intonation at the onset of the topicalized noun phrase (NP). In particular, in both (19) and (20), the question intonation stops *before* the topicalized NP—another striking parallel.

Relative clauses and conditionals are another two kinds of complex constructions that may be signaled by other than segmental means. The ASL equivalents of these constructions are discussed in detail in this volume (Chapters 2 and 3), so I shall only mention them roughly. In ASL, conditional sentences are not marked off with a conjunction

(IF is used in the mesolect), but rather with a special intonation contour, somewhat resembling a question:

(21) YOU WANT BECOME DOCTOR? (WELL), BETTER STUDY## HARD.
"If you want to become a doctor, you should study really hard."

Relative clauses are sometimes marked by the demonstrative THAT. Subject relatives are often marked by the emphatic marker SELF, as in (22):

(22) LONG-TIME-AGO HAVE BOY SMALL HIMSELF LIVE YONDER SMALL TOWN.
"Once upon a time, there was a little boy who lived in a village."

Quite often, however, relative clauses will be shown by means of pauses, hand switches, and/or changes in the angle of the body or head, as discussed by Liddell (Chapter 3).

Very similar processes operate in various creoles as well. The demonstrative *ia* (from English *here*), for example, is used as a relative marker in Melanesian Pidgin (where the term *pidgin* may be a misnomer) (Slobin, 1975). Consider also the following sentences in HCE, both conditionals and relatives.

(23) *You like come one doctor? you gotta study hard.*
"If you want to become a doctor, you have to study hard."

(24) *We gon sue the guy wen beat up my son.*
"We're going to sue the guy who beat up my son."

(25) *You know the policeman wen beat up the hippie? he gon court tomorrow.*
"The policeman who beat up the hippie is going to court tomorrow."

In (24) and (25) *wen* is a past marker, not a relative pronoun. Sentence (25) is particularly interesting, since it almost exactly parallels one of the sentences cited by Liddell (Chapter 3, page 73), with the use of *you know* as an introducer for the clause.[4]

In addition to the features of creoles and sign language already discussed, I would like to mention a number of references where creolists have listed various characteristics of pidgins and creoles and

[4]In fact, I think the use of *you know* or KNOW or REMEMBER is not so much a signal for the relative clause as an indicator of definiteness. In any case, however, once again similar mechanisms are being used in sign and creole.

compare these characteristics with those found in ASL. Both Bickerton (1974) and Tsuzaki (1971) give examples of the invariant order
they find in the aspectual system of HCE. For instance, Tsuzaki lists
the following order of elements: negative, modal, past, future, progressive, habitual, and, finally, the verb stem (pp. 332–333). (These
are my terms.) Bickerton's inventory covers a somewhat different
range and is thus not directly comparable. Some of these aspectual
markers in ASL, however, are *simultaneous* with the verb, as in the
case of habitual or continuous (progressive). It is interesting that these
are the closest to the verb in Tsuzaki's listing. Given that oral languages do not usually have simultaneously occurring morphemes, the
parallel can be said to hold.

Taylor (1971) lists 12 features shared in greater or lesser part by the
creole systems in the Caribbean. Of these 12, the creole languages
discussed have between 4 and 10. ASL has 6. These include such
things as the existence of a general locative marker, the use of the
third-person plural pronoun as a noun pluralizer, and the postposition
of various demonstratives.

Craig (1971) lists nine characteristics of English-based creole syntaxes. *Every one* is true of the syntax of ASL. This parallel holds not
only for those features that are notable for their absence, such as the
lack of case or sex markings in pronouns, but also the more positive
aspects of the syntax as well. Thus, Craig points out the use of what he
calls associative plurals. An example he cites is the use of /mieri-dem/
to mean Mary and her friends. ASL has more particular ways of
indicating associative plurals, but the principle is the same. Thus, in
ASL we have such phrases as HUSBAND TWO-OF-US, meaning "my
husband and me," and the use of the third-person plural pronoun as a
plural marker for the notion of a collective. Craig also points out the
use of reduplication for pluralization and habitual (p. 383), and he also
notes the use of what he terms the "inverted" sentence, a phenomenon which is quite prevalent in ASL, but which we used to call
copying. He cites the example /a ded im ded/, meaning "he's really
dead." In ASL, one finds analogs like that in (26).

(26) ME CAN'T A-F-F-O-R-D, CAN'T.
     "I absolutely can't afford it."

To summarize the findings on a comparison of grammars of creole
languages and ASL, there are characteristic ways in which semantic
content is expressed by grammatical form. This seems not to depend
on the particular "parent" languages involved but will require a
deeper explanation.

There are two more aspects of sign languages and creoles that have caused a number of methodological problems for investigators of these languages. The first is that because of the wide amount of variation and the tolerance of both linguistic and nonlinguistic context to provide redundancy, it is very difficult to define an obligatory context for the occurrence of a linguistic element. In order to do so, it is necessary to make the context so precise and lacking in clues that it may become artificial. Related to this is a second problem. The level of the sentence seems to be an inappropriate level of analysis. This is more obvious in the case of creoles and sign languages, but we are beginning to realize it more slowly in the case of establishment languages as well. In particular, conditions for deletion, pronominalization, topicalization, and focusing often operate across sentence boundaries.

Perhaps because of the latitude in lack of redundancy, there is a tendency to repeat sentences verbatim, as though to give the listener or viewer a second pass at the sentence:

(27) WHAT YOU WANT EAT, WHAT YOU WANT EAT?
    "What do you want to eat?"

(28) *What you like eat, what you like eat?*
    "What do you want to eat?"

Sometimes the second repetition will be a version that has slid in one direction or the other along the decreolizing continuum, and thus may have a sociolinguistic rather than a processing basis, but a tremendous amount of identical repetition goes on in both HCE and ASL.

There are, of course, places in which drawing parallels does not work for every comparison between every sign language and every creole, but many differences may be due largely to differences in modality. I believe that I have at least proved my point that there are more than an accidental number of parallels between sign languages and creoles at the syntactic as well as the sociolinguistic level. The next step is to try to account for the parallels in a nontrivial way.

SOME POSSIBLE EXPLANATIONS

We said earlier that a creole is the language the children of pidgin speakers speak. But where does a creole come from? It does not come totally out of thin air. It is somewhat based on pidgin(s). But things shift around a great deal. For example, content words often become function words with related meanings; some aspect markers become tense markers. In general, semantic markers become grammatical markers (Sankoff & Laberge, 1974). We really need to account for three phenomena:

1. Why does the process of creolization take place at all?
2. Why are creoles so alike whereas pidgins are so different?
3. Why does ASL still look like a creole?

A number of researchers within and outside of the field of pidgins and creoles have addressed the question of why the process of creolization occurs. One of the more important reasons seems to be that the scope of the language is so much wider than that of a pidgin. Recall that a pidgin is no one's native language. In a subcommunity within, say, a plantation, adults may be able to use their native language among themselves and will only have to resort to the pidgin in their contact with nonnative speakers. Thus, the situations in which it is used will be somewhat limited. A child, on the other hand, who is going to rely on the language almost exclusively, has a much wider range in which to use the language and will thus need the kind of richness to be found in a creole rather than in a pidgin. If a language is to become the main language of a community rather than an auxiliary one, it must especially become more efficient and more expressive. Thus, there will be pressure from the needs of communication for the language to grow richer.

There is a second factor that is important in accounting for the process of creolization. It has been emphasized by Bickerton (1974) that it is *children* who create a creole. Bickerton is arguing a rather strong nativist position, the details of which it is not necessary to agree with; however, his point is well taken. If we imagine a child being exposed to a pidgin language P, and we view the child of pidgin-speaking parents as making an attempt to learn P, what can be inferred as to the child's assumptions about his or her input? It is logical for any child to presuppose that the language to which he or she is being exposed is indeed a full-fledged language. Since children are supposedly used to being exposed to "degenerate" input, the child exposed to P may well assume that there must be more to the language than he or she is hearing, will try to "guess" the "real" grammar, and in doing so will literally create a language whose grammar is far richer and more complex than that of the pidgin. I once read a science-fiction story in which a group of scientists are shown a black box and told that it is an antigravity generator and that they must duplicate its effects.

Only when they succeed are they told that the black box is a clever hoax. The children who, exposed to pidgin, end up creating a creole are in a situation analogous to that of the scientists in the story.

If creolization occurs because a pidgin is being used as a first language and children expect it to be adequate, and hence jump to "wrong" conclusions about the structure of the language to which they are being exposed, we must still account for why creoles are so similar, especially syntactically. One can accept the monogenesis theory, but it is hard to see how such a theory will work in the case of ASL or other languages that historically have no record of contact with Portuguese creole. One can accept Bickerton's suggestion that the syntactic devices one finds in creoles are more "natural" than those found in more established languages. I am inclined to believe the outline of Bickerton's theory. However, the question then arises, "Natural" for whom? For indeed, the most complex and convoluted grammatical form will feel natural to one who has mastered it. The answer to this question must be "natural for the child." In order for this notion to be more than a truism, we need to have a more precise way of defining it, and there does seem to be a way of doing so. Slobin (1973) and Ervin-Tripp (1973) have both proposed various cognitive prerequisites and strategies for linguistic development. It is children, after all, who are creating their language, and very young children have characteristic ways of processing their language. Some grammatical forms will be difficult for a young child to process simply because he or she is not yet cognitively ready for them. Others will be relatively easy because they fall within the range of "do-able" processes. Implicit in the work of Bickerton and also Slobin is the notion that those structures that the child is cognitively prepared for will be those that occur most often in creole languages, since other kinds of structures require that there be adults around to provide models.

Slobin (1975) has explicitly tried to connect the disparate fields of child language, pidgin and creole studies, and diachronic linguistics by appealing to an interaction among these cognitive prerequisites and strategies and certain constraints on language, language development in children, and language change over time, which he calls charges. These charges are

(1) *Be clear.* Concretely, relations are expressed unambiguously. This may lead to such things as periphrastic constructions, where everything is spelled out in separate morphemes. This also leads to redundancy.
(2) *Be humanly processible in ongoing time.* "Language must con-

form to strategies of speech perception and production." (Slobin, 1975, p. 2)
(3) *Be quick and easy.* This charge counterbalances (1) and (2) to a
certain extent and allows for laziness and sloppiness in production.
(4) *Be expressive,* both semantically and rhetorically. Language
must be able to express the basic conceptual notions, and it must
have alternate ways of expressing the same thing, for the sake of
variety and the possibility of nuances.

There is a state of dynamic flux among these four constraints. The
speaker and the hearer are each trying to make things easier, but what
is easier to produce may not be easier to perceive, due to lack of
redundancy or the absence of cues to underlying relations. In addition, the need to communicate fully could lead to complex constructions that would be more difficult to process.

Slobin argues that children are more concerned with conditions (1),
(2), and (3) than they are with (4); these conditions by themselves
would lead to grammars remarkably similar to those of creoles or ASL.
If children are the primary agents in the process of creolization, then
they will create the kind of grammatical devices for which they are
cognitively ready. For example, Slobin (1973) suggests that children's
first tendency in the expression and interpretation of grammatical
relations is to rely on word order. A second example, not directly
discussed by Slobin but widespread in the literature, is young children's sensitivity to intonation. Over and over again in creole studies,
and in ASL as well, we find nonsegmental markers for grammatical
forms, such as the conditional and relative clauses discussed previously.

As a language develops over time, conditions (3) and (4) come more
and more into play; as certain forms become elided or contracted for
ease of production, the language may become superficially more complex. However, development into an "establishment" language may
take as long as a couple of centuries. It has been said that not until
Chaucer's time, for example, did English really assimilate its French
component.

If universals of children's cognitive and linguistic development can
account for the fact that all creoles are alike, why should ASL look like
a creole? Granted, Woodward (Chapter 14, this volume) has argued
that ASL was originally a creole, but that was 150 years ago, time
enough for ASL either to have completely decreolized or to have
turned into an unique but more "establishment" language. We need to
explain why neither alternative has in fact occurred.

I would like to speculate that there are two main reasons why neither process has been completed. First, as I have argued elsewhere (Fischer, 1975), countervailing pressures from educators (the acrolect) on the one hand and the modality in which ASL is communicated on the other prevents it from going all the way in one direction or the other.

The second, and I believe the more important, reason has to do with the social context in which ASL is learned. Woodward (1973b), among others, has pointed out that only 10% of deaf children have deaf parents. Even if we assume that a vast majority of that 10% are learning ASL as a first language, it still means that 90% of deaf children will learn sign language "in the streets," or more likely, in the dormitories of a residential school. If a deaf child of hearing parents is really fortunate, his or her parents (more often the mother, in my very limited observation) will attempt to learn ASL. However, as adult second-language learners, and as hearing persons who attach a strong positive value to English, the vast majority will use a form of pidgin signed English with their children, not ASL. This is also what most teachers of the deaf will use in a real classroom situation, if sign language is permitted in the school at all.

Thus, 150 years after the first creolization of ASL, most deaf children are forced to *re*creolize ASL in every generation. Continuity is provided by deaf adults and by peers with deaf parents, but many children are on their own. A case in point is the first hearing parent of a deaf child I ever met. She had taken the trouble to learn Visual English, which was also used by the teachers at her child's school. All the other children in the class had hearing parents. And yet this child's preferred language (she was able to use Visual English), though not totally congruent with ASL, looked a lot more like ASL than it did like Visual English. Again, this child clearly had degenerate data and was building up a different language from it, one that better suited her needs to express herself quickly, easily, and with rhetorical power; and that included grammatical devices she was cognitively ready to pay attention to.

CONCLUSIONS

ASL shares many of the social determinants of creoles; it also shares many similar means of grammatical expression. I have shown in this chapter that this is no accident; the process of creating a creole out of a pidgin is common to both situations. The very fact that the burden of creolization is on children who have characteristic learning strategies can largely provide explanation for this phenomenon on one level. Ultimately, however, we shall want to seek an explanation, not at the level of developmental sociolinguistics, or even at the level of developmental psycholinguistics, but at the level of developmental neurolinguistics. For this reason, it is particularly valuable that scholars from the disciplines of sign language and neurolinguistics are now talking and listening to each other and are addressing these very issues.

ACKNOWLEDGMENTS

I would like to thank Bob Papen and Derek Bickerton, who stimulated my interest in creole languages. Carol Akamatsu and Charlene Sato provided many of the native speaker judgments on Hawaiian Creole English, and Bonnie Gough taught me the ins and outs of ASL; I thank them all for their patience. Derek Bickerton, Richard Day, and Ann Peters read an earlier version of this chapter; I am grateful for their comments and criticisms. None of the above persons is responsible for any errors or conclusions on my part.

REFERENCES

Bailey, C.-J. Some suggestions for greater consensus in creole terminology. In D. DeCamp & I. Hancock (Eds.), *Pidgins and creoles: Current trends and prospects.* Washington: Georgetown Univ. Press, 1974.

Bellugi, U., & S. Fischer. A comparison of sign language and spoken language. In *Cognition: International Journal of Cognitive Psychology*, 1972, *1*, 173–200.

Bickerton, D. *Creolization, linguistic universals, natural semantax, and the brain.* Paper presented at the International Conference on Pidgins and Creoles, Honolulu, Hawaii, 1974.

Bickerton, D. & Givon, T. Pidginization and syntactic change: From SXV and VSX to SVX. In S. Steever, C. Walker, & S. Mufwene, (Eds.), *Diachronic Syntax.* Chicago: Chicago Linguistic Society, 1976.

Craig, D. Education and creole English. In D. Hymes (Ed.), *Pidginization and creolization of languages.* London: Cambridge Univ. Press, 1971.

DeCamp, D. The study of pidgin and creole languages. In D. Hymes (Ed.), *Pidginization and creolization of languages.* London: Cambridge Univ. Press, 1971.

DeCamp, D. & Hancock, I. (Eds.), *Pidgins and Creoles: Current trends and prospects.* Washington: Georgetown Univ. Press, 1974.

Dillard, J. *Black English: Its history and usage in the United States.* New York: Random House, 1972.

Ervin-Tripp, S. Some strategies for the first two years. In T. Moore (Ed.), *Cognition and the development of language.* New York: Academic Press, 1973.

Fant, L. *Ameslan: An introduction to American Sign Language* (teachers' manual) Silver Spring, Maryland: National Association of the Deaf, 1972.

Ferguson, C. Diglossia. *Word*, 1959, *15*, 325–340.

Ferguson, C. Absence of copula and the notion of simplicity: a study of normal speech, baby talk, foreigner talk, and pidgins. In D. Hymes (Ed.), *Pidginization and creolization of languages*. London: Cambridge Univ. Press. 1971.

Fischer, S. Two processes of reduplication in the American Sign Language. *Foundations of Language*, 1972, *9*, 469–480.

Fischer, S. Sign language and linguistic universals. In C. Rohrer & N. Ruwet (Eds.), *Actes du colloque Franco-Allemand de grammaire transformationelle, band II: Etudes de sémantique et autres*. Tubingen: Max Niemeyer Verlag, 1974.

Fischer, S. Influences on word order change in American Sign Language. In C. Li (Ed.), *Word order and word order change*. Austin: Univ. of Texas Press, 1975.

Friedman, L. A. The expression of subject, object, and topic in American Sign Language. In C. Li (Ed.), *Subject and topic*. New York: Academic Press. Pp. 125–148, 1976.

Frishberg, N. Arbitrariness and inconicity in American Sign Language. *Language*, 1975, *51*, 696–719.

Hall, R. A. *Pidgin and Creole languages*. Ithaca: Cornell Univ. Press, 1966.

Hymes, D. (Ed.) *Pidginization and creolization of languages*. London: Cambridge Univ. Press, 1971.

Lenneberg, E. *Biological foundations of language*. New York: Wiley, 1967.

Sankoff, G., & LaBerge, S. On the acquisition of native speakers by a language. In D. DeCamp & I. Hancock (Eds.), *Pidgins and creoles: Current trends and prospects*. Washington: Georgetown Univ. Press, 1974.

Slobin, D. I. Cognitive prerequisites for linguistic development. In C. Ferguson & D. Slobin (Eds.), *Studies of child language development*. New York: Holt, Rinehart and Winston, 1973.

Slobin, D. I. Language change in childhood and in history. Working Paper No. 41, Language Behavior Research Laboratory, Univ. of California, Berkeley, 1975.

Stokoe, W. Sign Language Diglossia. *Studies in Linguistics*, 1970, *21*, 27–41.

Stokoe, W. *Semiotics and human sign languages*. Mouton: The Hague, 1972.

Taylor, D. Grammatical and lexical affinities of creoles. In D. Hymes (Ed.), *Pidginization and creolization of languages*. London: Cambridge Univ. Press, 1971.

Tsuzaki, S. Coexistent systems in language variation. In D. Hymes (Ed.), *Pidginization and creolization of languages*. London: Cambridge Univ. Press, 1971.

Woodward, J. *Implication lects in the deaf diglossic continuum*. Unpublished doctoral dissertation, Georgetown Univ., 1973. (a)

Woodward, J. Some Characteristics of Pidgin Sign English. *Sign Language Studies*, 1973, *3*, 39–46. (b)

Woodward, J. & Markowitz, H. *Pidgin sign languages*. Paper presented at the International Conference on Pidgins and Creoles, Honolulu, 1975.

Zaidel, E. Auditory vocabulary of the right hemisphere following brain bisection or hemidecortication. *Cortex*, in press.

14

Historical Bases of
American Sign Language

JAMES WOODWARD

Gallaudet College

INTRODUCTION

Studies of sign language and the education of the deaf in the United States often remark upon the fact that T. H. Gallaudet and L. Clerc brought French Sign Language (FSL) to the United States (e.g., Stokoe, 1960, Frishberg, 1975). This seems a very unsatisfactory explanation from what is known about language variation and change. Stokoe (1960, p. 13) has stated his own dissatisfaction with this orthodox history of American Sign Language (ASL): "One may guess that some notion of the French system had preceded Gallaudet's formal introduction of it to the United States. How else explain the rapid flourishing of the language and the schools using the method to the point where a national college for the deaf was deemed necessary and established by an Act of Congress in 1864 for the higher education of the graduates of these schools?"

How else indeed, unless perhaps, as Fischer (1975, p. 7) has

This chapter was originally a paper presented at the Rochester Conference on Sign Language and Neurolinguistics, September 1976. Research on which this chapter was based was supported, in part, by NEH Research Grant No. RO–21418–75–196 and National Science Foundation Research Grants Nos. GS–31349 and SOC74–14724.

UNDERSTANDING LANGUAGE
THROUGH
SIGN LANGUAGE RESEARCH

333

suggested, there were some native influences of FSL from signs already existing in the United States. This chapter makes three contentions:

1. The great differences between modern FSL and modern ASL are not primarily the result of internal language change (by two men or the whole American deaf population), since internal language change involves constant, dynamic, but relatively rarely disruptive processes that are not related to influence from other languages.
2. The differences are more than those that arise out of normal language contact.
3. The differences are probably due to earlier creolization of FSL with sign languages already existing in the United States prior to 1816.

Language change that occurs in normal language contact would normally involve borrowing. In normal language contact, the language doing the borrowing might be more disrupted than it would be while undergoing its normal dynamic changes. However, the language doing the borrowing would still be easily recognizable as the same language before and after the borrowing. On the other hand, in creolization there is so much disruption that a new language is created, which is not mutually intelligible with any of the languages in the contact situation. The arguments for this creolization are both sociological and linguistic.

SOCIOLOGICAL EVIDENCE

Creolization usually involves one dominant and more than two subordinate language varieties that come into a special contact situation, usually because of colonization.[1]

In order to demonstrate the possibility of earlier creolization in ASL, it is necessary to demonstrate that some sign language varieties existed in the United States before 1816, that these varieties were widely divergent and perhaps mutually unintelligible, and that the

[1] As Whinnom (1971) points out, if there are only two language varieties in the contact situation, the result will be linguistic hybridization instead of creolization, since one group will probably eventually learn the other's language perfectly. Alleyne (1971) gives the examples of Caribbean creoles as fitting this general description of creoles. In addition, Alleyne makes the claim that creolization can (and, in fact, did in the Caribbean) occur without prior pidginization. While creolization without prior pidginization seems a minority opinion in creole studies, it does seem to fit the ASL situation. Apparently ASL was nativized especially quickly, perhaps too quickly for prior pidginization to have occurred.

language contact situation of FSL and ASL was sufficiently "colonial" to rule out borrowing or language mixture as the primary cause of change.

Lacking proper documentary history of ASL, one can only appeal to documented parallel situations in the past and in the present. Below are two examples of indigenous sign languages.

Épée himself states that deaf people in Paris were using a sign language (or languages) in Paris before he began any standardization attempts. There are no real records of this language, so we know nothing of its structure.

There is also one modern example of an isolated community that may very well closely parallel the language situation in the United States before 1816: Providence Island Sign Language (PISL) (cf. Washabaugh, Woodward, & DeSantis, 1976). PISL is a sign language used on an isolated island in the Caribbean. There has been no direct outside influence on PISL. There have been and are now no educational facilities for deaf people. The individual villages are quite isolated, with very infrequent intervillage contact. Yet there is a group of sign language varieties whose syntax does not follow the oral language.

Because of the absence of urbanization and educational facilities for deaf people, the isolation of villages, and a good amount of integration of deaf people into daily activities of the island, there is no single unified deaf community, nor does there appear to be local communities as such. In addition, there is also a great deal of sign variation among the villages.

The situation on Providence Island seems to be very similar to the situation that probably existed in the United States prior to 1816. Towns were isolated, transportation was poor, there was little urbanization, and there were no educational facilities for deaf people. In short, there were no factors to create a deaf community; it was a perfect place for home and/or town signs to develop as they have done on Providence Island.

But power and money have a way of changing things, and the search for education for Alice Cogswell and others became the motivating force for the transportation of FSL to the United States by Gallaudet and Clerc.

In America, FSL became a "colonial" language in the following senses:

1. FSL was one foreign standard language introduced into a heterogeneous-language local population.
2. FSL was introduced by a small minority of outsiders to the

heterogeneous local population. (Gallaudet was a hearing man with apparently no previous in-depth associations with deaf people. Clerc was a foreign educated deaf man.)

3. FSL as a language of education was the language of money, power, possible upward social mobility, and dominance.

However, meaningful acculturation of FSL cultural and linguistic norms was impossible because both Gallaudet and Clerc were poor models. Gallaudet was a poor representative because he was hearing and had only recently acquired some competence in FSL, and Clerc could serve only as an individual and not a group model.[2] The near veneration of Gallaudet and Clerc would also have proved to be more of a hindrance than a help in acquiring FSL cultural and linguistic traditions, since such veneration would have erected a boundary that maintained a vast social distance between the models and the learners. The logical outcome of this "colonization" was a new creolized culture with a new creolized language to act as one of its chief binding and identifying factors.[3]

Clerc himself in the collection of his writings at the Gallaudet College Library offers additional support for the possible creolization of FSL with indigeneous sign languages with old FSL. Clerc writes in 1852, only 35 years after his arrival in the United States:

> I see, however, and I say it with regret, that any efforts that we have made or may still be making, to do better than the Abbe Sicard, we have inadvertently fallen somewhat back of Abbé de l'Épée. Some of us have learned and still learn signs from uneducated pupils, instead of learning them from well instructed and experienced teachers.

Also in a letter to Clerc's son written in 1895, we find the following information about an event that happened in 1867, 2 years before Clerc's death.

> Soon after dinner at our hotel, he [Clerc], your father, asked me to take a walk with him which I said I would do. When we had walked two or three blocks, he stopped me, telling me that he wished to tell me something. He said with some tears in his eyes that the graceful signs which he and Gallaudet had brought from France to Hartford were being degenerated or changed into

---

[2] Because Clerc was an individual man, he could not have served alone as model for appropriate FSL conversational models in such areas as turn taking (cf. Baker, 1977). In addition he could not have adequately demonstrated female signing or cultural behavior to women naïve of FSL women's behavior.

[3] Padden and Markowicz (1975) and Markowicz and Woodward (1975) both contain discussions of the importance of language in maintaining modern community boundaries in the United States deaf community.

other ugly signs [both of these quotes are found in the collected writings of L. Clerc, Gallaudet College Library].

Additional support for the hypothesis of early creolization in ASL is seen in the obvious linguistic differences between modern FSL and modern ASL.

LINGUISTIC EVIDENCE

As Southworth (1971) points out: "brusque restructuring of features ... at all levels of structure [p. 260]" occurs in both pidginization and creolization, since they involve "a sharp break in transmission and the creation of a new code [p. 255]."

The linguistic arguments that follow aim at demonstrating restructuring at the lexical, phonological, and grammatical levels. Even though our comparative knowledge of FSL and ASL is still extremely slight, there is sufficient evidence of restructuring to support a hypothesis of early creolization in ASL.

Lexical Differences

Lexical differences between modern FSL and modern ASL are quite large, and the gap has widened at an astounding rate. This section utilizes the techniques of glottochronological analysis to illustrate just how astounding these changes are.

Gudschinsky (1964) provides an in-depth discussion of glottochronological analysis. Basically glottochronology attempts hypothetically to date time depths or separation between related languages. This involves several steps: "collection of comparable word lists from relatively stable core vocabulary, determining the probable cognates, computing the time depth, computing the range of error [p. 613]." The time depth is computed by a formula that assumes a constant retention rate of 80.5% in basic core vocabulary over 1000 years, "the average change over thirteen languages in which there are historical records (of such a span) [p. 613]." The range of error is a way of estimating the accuracy of the time depth. "The higher the level of confidence (i.e., the more certainty the true answer lies within the range cited) the wider the range of years [p. 619]."

As Hymes (1971) points out, glottochronology has many problems but has been useful in arguing for possible earlier creolization of a language (cf. Hymes, 1971; Cassidy, 1971; Frake, 1971; Southworth, 1971):

> The glottochronological distinctiveness of pidgins and creoles was first discovered by Hall (1959), who showed that Neo-Melanesian had diverged from its base language, English, at a rate far exceeding that normally found. Whereas glottochronology nromally errs in the direction of underestimating the time depth of divergence between languages, here it greatly overestimates the time-depth [p. 198].

In the discussion of glottochronology that follows, the classic procedures described by Gudschinsky (1964) have been followed. Let us now look at a comparison of modern FSL with modern ASL and of modern ASL with older ASL.

The data from modern FSL comes primarily from Oléron's (1974) dictionary of modern FSL signs and from my own field experience in Paris during the summer of 1975. The signs were compared with their ASL counterparts.[4] Four analyses comparing modern FSL and modern ASL were performed.

The first analysis compares data chosen on the basis of the Swadesh 200-word list, the normal list used for glottochronological analysis. Signs from ASL signers in their 20s and 30s were compared with data from Oléron's dictionary. All indexic signs and numerals were eliminated from the 200-word list. The results showed a 61% rate of cognates for 77 pairs of signs. This would hypothetically date the arrival of FSL in the United States between 504 A.D. and 1172 A.D. with a 90% level of confidence. This is between a 645- to 1300-year discrepancy from 1817, the actual date of FSL's arrival in the United States.

The second analysis compared the same FSL signs with those of a deaf American man in his eighties who attended the Kendall School for the Deaf in Washington, D.C. who studied under Hotchkiss. Hotchkiss, a deaf man, grew up on the campus of the American School while Clerc was residing, interacting with students, and teaching sign language at the American School. Thus our informant might be considered a second (linguistic) generation informant for ASL. The comparison of his signs showed the same rate (61% out of 77 pairs) of cognates. This would also indicate a 645- to 1300-year discrepancy.

The third analysis compared all of the 872 available FSL signs with their counterparts from younger ASL signers. The results showed a 57.3% rate of cognates from 872 pairs. This would hypothetically date the arrival of FSL in the U.S. between A.D. 584 and A.D. 802 with a 90% level of confidence. This is still 1000 to 1200 years off.

The fourth analysis compared all of the 872 available FSL signs with their counterparts from our informant in his 80s. The results

---

[4]ASL signs were not limited to any one regional, social, or ethnic group.

showed only a .7% difference with younger ASL signers, bringing the total of cognates to 58% out of 872 pairs. This would hypothetically date the arrival of FSL in the United States between A.D. 591 to A.D. 835, still 1000 to 1200 years off.

While we are not claiming that the glottochronological procedures should be completely accurate, they are deviant enough to suggest the strong possibility of massive abrupt change due to creolization. One objection could be raised to this argument, that sign language change occurs at a much faster rate than that of oral languages.

However, the evidence we have on language change within Russian Sign Language (Gejl'man, 1957) and within ASL supplies very nice evidence that sign languages do not change appreciably faster than oral languages. Three comparisons of data should serve to illustrate this fact.

1. Gejl'man (1957) made a comparison of 70 pairs of old Russian signs (from 1835) and found a 97.5% rate of cognates with modern Russian signs. Glottochronological analysis would yield a hypothetical time depth of 14 to 130 years, and the actual time separation was 122 years. Thus, the estimated time depth is very close to the actual one.
2. A comparison of 423 signs from Long's (1918) dictionary of ASL with modern ASL shows a 99% rate of cognates. Glotto-chronological analysis would show a hypothetical time depth of 5 to 41 years, but the actual time depth is at least 58 years. In reality, the actual time depth may be considerably greater if we can believe Long (1913), who states: "I am also indebted to Rev. Dr. Philip J. Hasenstab, of Chicago, who carefully went over the manuscript, verifying the descriptions, pointing out errors, and offering many suggestions which have added to the value of the completed material. Dr. Hasenstab received his early education in the Indiana school under early masters of the Sign Language who learned it at Hartford. This gives the assurance, therefore, that the descriptions conform to the original manner of making the signs [p. 11]."
3. A comparison of the 1913 film of Hotchkiss signing *Memories of Old Hartford* with modern ASL indicates results similar to the comparison of Long's dictionary with modern ASL. Hotchkiss says in the film that when he was a student at Hartford, he and the other students often talked with Clerc. We thus have data from a signer who talked often with one of the two men who brought FSL to the United States, and yet the percentage of

cognates of modern ASL with Hotchkiss's ASL is 99.6% for 251 pairs of signs. This would indicate a hypothetical time separation of 9 years, whereas the actual time separation is at least 63 years, and perhaps much older if we consider Hotchkiss's background.

In summary, glottochronological analysis has revealed very interesting results. Comparisons of older Russian and modern Russian and of older ASL and modern ASL yield expected results. The hypothetical time depths are reasonably accurate and, in fact, slightly slower than expected for ASL. However, the comparisons of modern FSL with modern ASL show wildly discrepant time depths, indicating a much more rapid change than what is expected from natural internal language change. This cannot be construed as proof of early creolization, but it certainly is not a bad argument.

In addition, the ASL data of Long and Hotchkiss indicate that the greatest amount of change from FSL came before Hotchkiss's time. This is a stronger argument for creolization, since almost all of the changes occurred before the mid- to late-1800s. The period of greatest change must have occurred in the early to mid-1800s, the time in which the proposed creolization would have occurred.

Phonological Restructuring

Evidence for phonological restructuring of FSL signs in ASL comes from Woodward's (1976) comparison of 873 FSL signs with their American counterparts. The restructurings discovered involve metathesis of movement and of handshape and maximal differentiation of movement and handshape. Metathesis and maximal differentiation appear to be very closely related, as we shall see, and perhaps may be two variants of one underlying type of restructuring.

Movement Metathesis

In movement metathesis there is a change in the hand that moves. That is, if the dominant hand moves in one variant, the nondominant hand moves in another variant, or vice versa. Movement metathesis occurs in the two signs BUY and APPROACH. Both signs in FSL have inward movement of the *nondominant* hand but in ASL have outward movement of the *dominant* hand. This change can be seen as natural since the nondominant hand in ASL very rarely moves unless the dominant hand also moves. In older ASL signs, where the nondominant hand moved in EARTH, the dominant hand now moves. However, the direction of EARTH's movement did not change, as in ASL BUY and APPROACH. A discussion of this type of movement change follows, under maximal differentiation.

Maximal Differentiation of Movement

Maximal differentiation of movement involves a reversal in the direction of movement of a sign.

FSL HISTORY (ASL TRADITION), which moves inward in FSL, moves outward in ASL. FSL signs with downward movement, such as GLAD, DIFFERENT, and SHAME, change to upward movement in ASL. FIGHT, PREVENT, NIGHT (ASL DARK), which are made with uncrossed arms in FSL, become crossed in ASL. FSL DO, which has the left hand moving left and the right hand moving right, corresponds to an ASL form with both hands first moving left and then right. The FSL sign for FRENCH is done with no movement in the Oléron dictionary, but with outward twisting movement (palm faces outward) by younger French signers. ASL FRENCH is done with an inward twisting movement (palm faces body).

Handshape Metathesis

In the metathesis of handshape, the nondominant hand takes on the handshape of the dominant, and vice versa. This change has been found to occur rarely in ASL (Woodward & Erting, 1975). Metathesis is found in three signs in the data: START (GV → VG), SHOW (GB → BG), REPRESENTATIVE (GB → BG).

Maximal Differentiation of Handshape

Maximal differentiation of handshape, like maximal differentiation of movement, involves a reversal of perceptible features. Handshapes in sign languages can be distinguished by relative openness (extension of fingers) or closure (nonextension of fingers). For example, looking at "A," "S," "G," "C," "B," "5" handshapes, we see that, with the exception of "G," all of these handshapes maximally contrast in openness or closure. "A" and "S" are maximally closed, with no fingers extended. "B" and "5" are maximally open, with all fingers extended. "C" is medially open, all fingers are extended but all are also bent.

It should be pointed out that these handshapes appear to be the most unmarked in sign languages. There are several reasons for this:

1. They occur in most, if not all, the world's sign languages.
2. They are among those acquired earliest by children learning ASL (Boyes, 1973; McIntire, 1974).

3. They are least restricted in occurrence in ASL (Battison, 1974), since they are the only handshapes that can be used as passive (nonmoving) hands in signs which have two different handshapes.

Characteristics 2 and 3 may be true of other sign languages as well.

Some signs that have maximally closed handshapes in FSL are related to signs that are open or maximally open in ASL. Maximally closed FSL "A" becomes medially open ASL C in DRINK and COMB-ONESELF and maximally open "B" in PAY-ATTENTION and PRINT. Maximally closed FSL S changes to maximally open ASL "5" in ACCLAMATION and DRESS and to maximally open ASL "B" in FALL (verb) and KISS.

Some maximally open handshapes in FSL are medially open or maximally closed in ASL. Maximally open FSL "B" changes to medially open ASL "C" in CONGRATULATE and to medially closed ASL bent "B" or very closed ASL "Y" in NOW. Maximally open FSL "5" changes to medially open ASL "C" in TIRED and HOW and to maximally closed "S" in PROTECT and maximally closed "A" in UNDER.

Medially open FSL "C" can become maximally open or closed. FSL "C" becomes maximally open ASL "5" in SAD and maximally closed "A" in AVOID. Medially open FSL "C" has also closed in ASL "O" in TEACH.

These variations are schematically demonstrated in the following diagram. C may be an intermediate stage in the process of maximal differentiation.

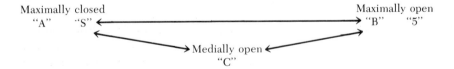

Maximal differentiation within ASL is only found in a few nonassimilated nondominant or passive handshapes, such as HARD (passive "B" or "S"). The number of signs that are definitely related by maximal differentiation across FSL and ASL is substantial in comparison.

Summary of Phonological Differences

Fifty-five percent of the signs with movement variations differed because of variations in metathesis and maximal differentiation.

Excluding initialized signs, 26.9% of the signs with handshape differences varied because of variations in metathesis and maximal differentiation. The fact that over one-half of the signs differing in movement and over one-fourth of the signs differing in handshape would differ in such radical ways suggests the possibility of some heavy earlier restructuring that would seem to be more related to creolization than to internal language change. This possibility becomes stronger when one looks at the paucity of metathesis and maximal differentiation within ASL (cf. Woodward & Erting, 1975).

Grammatical Restructuring

In addition to phonological differences, there are also grammatical differences between FSL and ASL. These differences appear in such area as word order in FSL and ASL grammar. However, word order change (cf. Fischer 1975) and a number of other differences apparently have happened over a fairly long period of time because of contact with English. Thus, a number of these changes do not appear to be sufficiently "brusque" to have occurred as a result of creolization.

However, there is one example of grammatical restructuring that is not due to contact with English and that apparently happened quite abruptly: negative incorporation. Negative incorporation in both FSL and ASL involves negating a small class of verb signs by a bound outward twisting movement of the hand(s) from the place where the sign is made. Woodward (1974) discusses the variability of the negative incorporation rule in ASL with five ASL verbs and has found an implicational pattern of the order HAVE implies LIKE implies WANT implies KNOW implies GOOD. Scalability was 97% for 108 northeastern deaf informants and 95% for 36 northwestern deaf informants. There was categorial negative incorporation with GOOD for American informants.

In the summer of 1975, Woodward and De Santis collected information from 60 French deaf informants from Paris, Toulouse, Albi, and Marseilles to determine if negative incorporation occurred in FSL. Woodward and De Santis (1976) found that variable negative incorporation did occur in FSL for the verbs HAVE, LIKE, WANT, and KNOW and that the ordering of the variability was identical to the American implication, with a 94.2% rate of scalability.

The surprising part of the data was that no French signer ever used negative incorporation with GOOD. In fact, the FSL sign BAD is not formationally related to FSL or ASL GOOD; it is a completely separate lexical item. FSL BAD is cognate with ASL WORSE, the only difference being that most French signers do not have assimilated handshapes for the sign, whereas American signers do.

Woodward and De Santis (1976) present evidence that negative incorporation began in FSL before 1816 as a process of phonological assimilation affecting in particular the signs KNOW, WANT, LIKE, and HAVE, in that order. When FSL was brought to America and creolized with existing varieties of sign language already there, negative incorporation was restructured as a grammatical process affecting the same four verbs and later GOOD in ASL.

Negative incorporation is a phonological process in FSL. Word order in old and modern FSL is Verb + NOT. FSL NOT is produced in neutral space in front of the body with a "G" handshape (index finger extended from the fist). The index finger points upward and the palm is outward from the body. The "G" hand moves repeatedly from side to side. In negative incorporation, FSL NOT assimilates location and handshape to that of the preceding verb sign and loses its movement. This results in an outward twisting movement (to obtain the outward orientation of FSL NOT) from the place where the verb sign is made. Thus these negated signs have the same phonological structure in FSL and ASL. However, assimilation adequately describes the process of negative incorporation in FSL but not in ASL.

This assimilation began affecting FSL verbs KNOW, WANT, LIKE, HAVE, in that order before 1816. Otherwise, there could be no negative incorporation in ASL, since ASL NOT has no formational relationship to FSL NOT. ASL NOT probably came from some sign variety in America, since old and modern FSL do not have cognates for ASL NOT. ASL NOT may have been in competition for a time with FSL NOT in America, however, ASL NOT appears to have won fairly quickly. The assimilated negative forms of KNOW, WANT, LIKE, and HAVE remained as single units in ASL.

These lexical units became generalized into a rule in ASL with the negative incorporation of ASL GOOD into ASL BAD during the creolization of FSL and existing varieties of signing in the United States. FSL and ASL GOOD are cognates. FSL BAD became ASL WORSE. Creolized ASL then had no single lexical unit for BAD, or this unit lost in competition with BAD as a negative incorporation of GOOD. GOOD then gradually moved to its appropriate place in the implicational pattern because of its phonological characteristics. Finally, negative incorporation of ASL GOOD has become categorical.

Further support for the salience of the negative incorporation grammatical rule in ASL comes from observations of children's signing in which it is overgeneralized. There have been reported over-generalizations by a child who already had the full implication. This child used the overgeneralized form *DON'T-LOVE. It is also interesting to note that hearing signers, once they realize that negative incorporation can apply to several verbs in ASL, begin making overgeneralizations—for example, *DON'T-THINK.

The restructuring of negative incorporation from phonological assimilation in FSL to a grammatical rule in ASL is extremely important. The restructuring of a grammatical variation to a phonological variation occurs in natural internal language change in oral languages—for example, is-deletion in Black English (Fasold, 1976). This situation is reasonable, and, in fact, expected, since phonology is more subject to change than is grammar. However, the restructuring of a phonological variation to a grammatical change is a very different situation. The restructuring in negative incorporation is much more likely to have been caused by the disruptive force of creolization than by natural internal language change.

SUMMARY AND IMPLICATIONS

This chapter has attempted to present sociological and linguistic arguments for possible earlier creolization in ASL. Evidence from the sociolinguistic situation in France before L'Épée and synchronic evidence from such isolated sign languages as PISL demonstrate the fact that sign languages have existed in extremely isolated situations where there have been no educational facilities.[5] Thus, there is the possibility that sign languages could have existed in the United States prior to 1816. Furthermore, sign languages in isolated signing communities such as Providence Island have shown great variations. Finally, the introduction of FSL in an educational situation in the United States could have offered the necessary "colonial" setting for the creolization of FSL and existing sign language varieties in the United States.

The linguistic evidence for possible earlier creolization in ASL is much stronger than the sociological evidence. There is evidence of restructuring at the lexical, phonological, and syntactic levels. Glottochronological analysis show expected time depths between older

---

[5] It is not unreasonable to assume that wherever there have been deaf people associating with each other, there has been sign language variety. These varieties developed through normal patterns of interaction, not through the invention of hearing people.

Russian Sign Language and modern Russian Sign Language and between older ASL and modern ASL. However the time depth for the
separation of FSL and ASL would indicate a far longer separation than
what actually occurred. This discrepancy may be due to the abrupt
changes in the process of creolization.

Such radical changes in sign language phonology as metathesis and
maximal differentiation account for a large percentage of the changes
in handshape and movement noted between modern FSL and modern
ASL signs. Finally, the restructuring of negative incorporation as a
phonological process of assimilation in FSL to a grammatical change
in ASL indicates an abrupt radical grammatical restructuring.

Although we are still far from knowing exactly the history of ASL
between 1816 and the mid-1800s, a hypothesis of creolization seems
quite feasible. Such a hypothesis has two important implications: one
theoretical and the other applied. The theoretical implication is that
sign languages are capable of undergoing not only sociolinguistic
processes of internal variation and change (e.g., Frishberg, 1975;
Woodward & De Santis, 1975) but also those massive but elusive
shifts that have been grouped under the heading of creolization.
Comparisons with oral language creolizations will be extremely valuable for sociolinguistic theory.

The applied implication may be somewhat deflating to those who
still like their heroes untarnished. T. H. Gallaudet and L. Clerc performed an admirable service by bringing FSL to the United States.
However, the fact is that FSL in the United States changed very
rapidly and dramatically (before the time of Hotchkiss) to meet the
needs of deaf individuals in the United States. On some introspection,
it seems more than a little ethnocentric of us hearies to maintain the
myth that two men—Gallaudet, a hearing man, and Clerc, a foreign
deaf man who apparently advocated assimilation into the hearing
community[6]—founded ASL as we know it. It seems time to give just a

---

[6]I would like to thank Harry Markowicz for pointing out the following quote. Clerc
(June 16, 1816) in his journal records a conversation with Mr. Wilder, another passenger
on the ship travelling to America.

> He asked me if I should like to marry a deaf and dumb lady handsome, young,
> virtuous, pious and amiable. I answered him that it would give me much
> pleasure but that a deaf and dumb gentleman and a lady suffering the same
> misfortune could not be companions for each other, and that consequently a
> lady endowed with the sense of hearing and the gift of speech was thought to
> be preferable and indispensable to a deaf and dumb person. Mr. Wilder
> replied nothing, but I am sure that he found my argument just.

Contrast the above statement with the findings by Fay (1898) that 85% of marriages little credit to the American deaf people, who drastically modified (if not creolized) FSL to satisfy their needs.

ACKNOWLEDGMENTS

I would like to thank Carol Padden for her help in the preliminary analysis of data in the comparison of FSL and ASL cognates and Susan De Santis for her assistance in analyzing the Hotchkiss film.

I would also like to thank Charlotte Baker, Susan De Santis, Harry Markowicz, William Stokoe, and William Washabaugh for their comments and criticisms on this chapter. Finally, I would like to dedicate this chapter to Wally Edington.

REFERENCES

Alleyne, M. Acculturation and the cultural matrix of creolization. In D. Hymes (Ed.), *Pidginization and creolization of languages*. New York: Cambridge Univ. Press, 1971. Pp. 169–186.

Baker, C. Regulators and turn-taking in American Sign Language discourse. In L. L. Friedman, (Ed.) *On the other hand: New perspectives on American Sign Language*. New York: Academic Press, 1977.

Battison, R. 1974. Phonological deletion in American Sign Language. *Sign Language Studies*, 1974, 5, 1–19.

Boyes, P. *A study of the acquisition of dez in American Sign Language*. Working paper, Salk Institute for Biological Studies, La Jolla, California, 1973.

Cassidy, H. Tracing the pidgin element in Jamaican Creole. In D. Hymes (Ed.), *Pidginization and credolization of languages*. New York: Cambridge Univ. Press, 1971. Pp. 203–222.

Clerc, L. Private Journal. *The Diary of Laurent Clerc's voyage from France to America in 1816*. West Hartford, Connecticut: American School for the Deaf, 1952. (Originally published, 1816).

Fasold, R. One hundred years: From syntax to phonology. In *Diachronic syntax*, Chicago: Chicago Linguistic Soceity, 1976.

Fay, E. A. *Marriages of the deaf in America*. Washington, D.C.: Volta Bureau, 1898.

Fischer, S. Influences on word-order change in American Sign Language. In C. Li (Ed.), *Word order and word order change*. Austin: Univ. of Texas Press, 1975.

Frake, C. Lexical origins and semantic structure in Philippine Creole Spanish. In D. Hymes (Ed.), *Pidginization and creolization of languages*. New York: Cambridge Univ. Press, 1971. Pp. 223–242.

Frishberg, N. Arbitrariness and iconicity: Historical change in American Sign Language. *Language*, 1975, 51, 696–719.

Gejl'man, I. F. *The manual alphabet and the signs of the deaf and dumb*. Moscow: Vsesojuznoe Kooperativnoe Izdatel'stvo, 1957.

among deaf people in the United States were endogamous and by Ranier and others (1963) that 95% of marriages of women born deaf in New York State and 91% of marriages of women who became deaf at an early age in New York were endogamous.

Gudinschinsky, S. The ABCs of lexicostatistics (glottochronology). In D. Hymes (Ed.), *Language in Culture and Society*. New York: Harper and Row, 1964. Pp. 612–623.

Hall, R. Neo-Melanesian and glottochronology. *International Journal of American Linguistics*, 1959, *25*, 265–267.

Hotchkiss, J. B. *Memories of Old Hartford*. National Association of the Deaf film. Gallaudet College Library, Washington, D.C., 1913.

Hymes, D. *Pidginization and creolization of languages*. New York: Cambridge Univ. Press, 1971.

Long, J. S. *The Sign Language*. Washington, D.C.: Gallaudet College, reprinted in 1962. (Originally published, 1918.)

Markowicz, H. & Woodward, J. *Language and the maintenance of ethnic boundaries in the deaf community*. Paper presented at the Conference on Culture and Communication, Philadelphia, March, 1975.

McIntire, M. *A modified model for the description of language acquisition in a deaf child*. Unpublished thesis, California State University, Northridge, California, 1974.

Oleron, P. *Elements de repertoire du language gestuel des sourds-muets*. Paris: Centre National de la Recherche Scientifique, 1974.

Padden, C. & Markowicz, H. *Crossing cultural boundaries into the deaf community*. Paper presented at the 1975 Conference on Culture and Communication, Philadelphia, March 1975.

Ranier, J. D., K. Z. Altshuler, & F. J. Kallman (Ed.), *Family and mental health problems in a deaf population*. New York: New York State Psychiatric Institute, Columbia, 1963.

Southworth, F. C. Detecting prior creolization: An analysis of the historical origins of Marathi. In D. Hymes (Ed.), *Pidginization and creolization of languages*. New York: Cambridge Univ. Press, 1971. Pp. 255–274.

Stokoe, William C., Jr. Sign language structure: An outline of the visual communication system of the American deaf. *Studies in Linguistics*, 1960, Occasional Paper 8, 1960.

Washabaugh, W. Woodward, J. & De Santis, S. *Providence Island Sign Language*. Paper presented at the Annual Meeting of the Linguistic Society of America, Philadelphia, December, 1976.

Whinnon, K. Linguistic hybridization and the 'special case' of pidgins and creoles. In D. Hymes (Ed.), *Pidginization and creolization of languages*. New York: Cambridge Univ. Press, 1971. Pp. 91–116.

Woodward, J. Implicational variation in American Sign Language: Negative incorporation. *Sign Language Studies*, 1974, *5*, 20–30.

Woodward, J. Signs of change: Historical variation in American Sign Language. *Sign Language Studies*, 1976, *10*, 81–94.

Woodward, J. & De Santis, S. *Two to one it happens*. Paper presented at the Annual Meeting of the Linguistic Society of America, San Francisco, December 1975.

Woodward, J. & De Santis, S. *Negative incorporation in French and American Sign Languages*. Paper presented at the Annual Meeting of the Linguistic Society of America, Philadelphia, December, 1976.

Woodward, J. & Erting, C. Synchronic variation and historical change in American Sign Language. *Language Sciences*, 1975, *37*, 9–12.

15

French Canadian Sign Language: A Study of Inter-Sign Language Comprehension

RACHEL I. MAYBERRY[1]

McGill University

In all North American cities there are groups of deaf individuals who use sign language as a major means of communication. The sign language common to these groups, dialectal and situational variations aside, is American Sign Language (ASL). However, in the province of Québec and in the city of Montréal there are two sign languages: One is ASL and the other is French-Canadian Sign Language (FCSL). If one asks Québecois deaf signers how similar the two sign languages are, or whether having fluency in one sign language allows for communication with individuals fluent in the other, the variety of responses seem characterized by contradiction. Some Québecois deaf signers note that the two sign languages are very similar and that inter-sign language comprehension is easy. Others note that the two sign languages are very different and that inter-sign language comprehension is next to impossible. In one sense these viewpoints seem diametrically opposed. But similar viewpoints are occasionally ex-

This study was supported by Grant No. 605–1326–44 from the Canadian Department of National Health and Welfare to Donald G. Doehring.

[1] Currently with the Department of Communication Disorders, Northwestern University, Evanston, Illinois.

pressed by speakers of English and French. If, for example, a native Québecois English speaker is asked about the similarities and differences between French and English, the response may depend upon his or her familiarity with French. Since the individual opinions and experiences of Québecois deaf signers are so varied, some systematic investigation of the relationship between FCSL and ASL was clearly in order.

A review of the literature in terms of sign language universality and inter-sign language comprehension will set the background for discussing the inconclusive results of a FCSL experiment that yielded more information about the complexity of inter-sign language comprehension, research designed to explore this question, and suggestions for such research than about the relationship of FCSL to ASL.

SIGN LANGUAGE UNIVERSALITY

Signers and nonsigners alike frequently ask whether having fluency in a sign language permits fluid communication with foreign individuals fluent in another sign language. At first glance it would seem that there are two mutually exclusive, possible answers: yes or no. However, this question is more complicated than a first glance suggests and is not so easily answered. The literature reflects this complexity in that several different answers occur. Generally speaking, the yes responses are typical of early writings about sign language, whereas the no responses are more typical of current sign language literature.

Early Writings

According to Battison and Jordan (1976), writers of the nineteenth and early twentieth centuries seemed to think that sign language was universally understood by individuals who knew sign language. Battison and Jordan note that it was common practice to refer to sign language as "*the* sign language." Interestingly, they also note that many of the early speculations concerning the universal nature of sign language came from individuals who were familiar with signing of one kind or another. For example, a deaf writer named Berthier suggested that " 'for centuries scholars from every country have sought after a universal language, and failed. Well, it exists all around, it is sign language'." Garrick Mallery made a similar suggestion in 1881 after he studied North American Indian signing. Mallery thought that both deaf and Indian signing " 'constitute together one language—the gesture speech of mankind—of which each system is a dialect' (Battison & Jordan, 1976: 54)." Not all early writers found this question adequately answered by a simple yes or no. Michaels, an American author of a sign language text, wrote in 1923 that " ' . . . though all nations do not use the same mode of signs, one having a knowledge of the signs herein delineated will experience little, if any difficulty in understanding other modes, and of being understood by those who use a different mode' (Battison & Jordan, 1976: 54)." Here the response is qualified: The differences in the world's sign languages are insufficient to impede inter-sign language comprehension.

Perhaps one of the more detailed responses to this question was proposed by a nineteenth-century psychologist. Wilhelm Wundt studied the sign language of German deaf children in an effort to discover universal properties underlying all languages. Wundt thought that sign language was, to a certain extent, universally understood; that universality was related to what might be labeled as concrete concepts. In the terminology of current sign language literature, Wundt's response suggests that sign language universality is found at the level of individual transparent, or iconic, signs:

> Systems of signs that have arisen in spatially separate environments and under doubtlessly independent circumstances are, for the most part, very similar or indeed closely related; this, then, enables communication without great difficulty between persons making use of gestures. Such is the much-lauded universality of gestural communication. Further, it is self-evident that this universality extends only to those concepts of a generally objective nature: for example, you and I, this and that, here and there, or earth, heaven, cloud, sun, house, tree, flower, walking, standing, lying, hitting, and many other such objects and actions perceived according to their basic features [Wundt].

The notions of *concreteness, iconicity,* and *universality* are often all closely tied or used interchangeably in popular lay beliefs about sign language. If sign language symbolizes only concrete concepts, then signs may be mainly iconic and hence universally understood, cultural differences aside. The reasoning also runs the other way around. If sign language is universally understood, then it is probably iconic and limited to concrete and picturable concepts. Given the common assumptions made about sign language at the time, it is easy to understand why early writers might have thought sign language to be universal. This would have been corroborated by the fact that unfamiliar sign languages can look much alike to naïve eyes, just as unfamiliar spoken languages can sound much alike to naïve ears.

Current Writings

Of course, there is greater opportunity today than ever before for individuals curious about sign language universality to observe different sign languages. This is especially true of international conferences and athletic events attended by deaf signers. If sign language were universal, then there would be no need for the numerous interpreters who can be observed interpreting from one sign language to another, as well as from spoken to sign language and vice versa. Lack of universality in sign language is also supported by attempts of the World Federation of the Deaf (1971) to create an "international sign language" (the sign language equivalent to Esperanto).

Fingerspelling would not be expected to be universal, since it is a manual symbol system for written alphabets which, in turn, are written symbol systems for spoken languages. In fact this is the case. Carmel (1975) has collected 28 different hand alphabet charts from around the world. Since many fingerspelling handshapes constitute part of the phonology of sign languages, this diversity in fingerspelling certainly suggests a lack of universality at the phonological level of sign languages. In terms of actual phonological comparisons, Bellugi and Klima (1975) have reported some striking phonological differences between ASL and Chinese Sign Language.

There is now ample published evidence that numerous sign languages exist in the world today. In a review of sign language dictionaries, Bornstein and Hamilton (1972) list works from 13 different countries in addition to the United States including Denmark, Sweden, Finland, Russia, Ukrania, Bulgaria, Germany, England, Spain, Brazil, Poland, Haiti, and Japan. Of course, the fact that these various sign language dictionaries are available does not, in and of itself, address the question of sign language universality or inter-sign language comprehension. For the most part these dictionaries are listings of individual lexical items with no references to differences or similarities in vocabulary with other sign languages. In addition to these dictionaries, linguistic descriptions of different sign languages are beginning to appear. For example, Hansen (1975) and Sørensen (1975) have both described portions of Danish Sign Language; Sallagoity (1975) has briefly described sign language in southern France; Peng (1974) has discussed kinship signs in Japanese Sign Language; and Kuschel (1973) has described some signs of the only deaf person on the Polynesian island of Rennell. Once again, these various linguistic descriptions do not address themselves to the question of sign language universality or inter-sign language comprehension. However, readers familiar with the linguistic structure of one sign language can make their own inter-sign language comparisons, which may or may not be predictive of inter-sign language communication in real life situations.

Many sign language papers do make reference to the notion of universality, although this is rarely the topic at hand. Early speculations regarding the universal nature of sign language are typically referred to as "misconceptions" or "myths" by recent sign language researchers. Today it is common practice to begin papers by setting the record straight, so to speak, sometimes with what strikes the reader as being an unusually strong position regarding inter-sign language comprehension given the current state of knowledge. The counterexample most often cited is the reported mutual unintelligibility of ASL and British Sign Language (for example: Battison & Jordan, 1976; Bellugi & Klima, 1975; Fischer, 1974; Lane, 1976; Mayberry, 1976, 1978; Stokoe, 1972, 1974; Stokoe, Casterline, & Croneberg, 1965; Wilbur, 1976). No doubt this example is cited frequently because it illustrates the suggestion that the linguistic boundaries of sign and spoken languages do not necessarily coincide.

Inter-Sign Language Comprehension

Despite the great interest in inter-sign language comprehension, there is only one investigative study. Jordan and Battison (1976) examined intra- versus inter-sign language comprehension using the following sign languages: American, Danish, French, Chinese (Hong Kong), Italian, and Portuguese. Their experiment consisted of asking pairs of signers fluent in these sign languages to describe to one another pictures from six 36-picture displays. Jordan and Battison videotaped these descriptions and then selected those descriptions that resulted in the highest communication accuracy, that is, senders' descriptions that enabled receivers to select correctly the target pictures. They then showed these selected videotaped descriptions to signers who were fluent in the sign languages of the videotapes and to those who were not. Again these receivers' task was to select the target picture being described. Unfortunately Jordan and Battison do not report the accuracy scores for pairs of different sign languages. Nor is it clear which sign languages were represented in the inter-sign language group, since Jordan and Battison report only the percentage

correct for "shared language" and "foreign language" by target picture. However, they do conclude from their data that "deaf signers can
understand their own sign language better than they can understand
sign languages foreign to them [p. 78]." If sign languages were universally understood, this clearly would not be the case.

The fact that sign language is not universally understood does not
automatically mean that all sign languages possess a high and equivalent degree of mutual *un*intelligibility. Many of Jordan and Battison's
subjects were able to comprehend some utterances from sign languages foreign to them. In fact, there are probably varying degrees of
mutual intelligibility among sign languages that may be a function of
group membership and/or shared historic–linguistic influences.

Spoken languages form genetically related groups whereby there
are greater linguistic similarities within than among groups. Stokoe
(1974) has suggested that sign languages also form genetically related
groups and that the linguistic similarities of sign languages are a
function of their group membership. For spoken languages, interlan-
guage comprehension is often used as a tool to determine whether two
groups of people speak two different languages or dialects of one
language. As Bender and Cooper (1971: 32) point out, this tool is
based "on the common-sense assumption that people who 'speak the
same language' can understand one another and conversely if they
cannot understand each other they must be speaking 'different languages' [Hockett, 1958]." Bender and Cooper also note that there are
degrees of inter-spoken language comprehension. The degree of
comprehension may serve as a means of determining language group
or subgroup membership. This hypothesis should also apply to sign
languages. Stokoe (1974) used this reasoning when he classified
British Sign Language as being outside the group of sign languages
that were influenced by or developed from French Sign Language. As
someone familiar with ASL, Stokoe felt he experienced far more
difficulty communicating with individuals using British Sign Language than with individuals using French Sign Language. He attributed this to ASL as having been influenced heavily by French Sign
Language, and British Sign Language as having developed without
such influence.

Thus inter-sign language comprehension, in conjunction with his-
torical data, should serve the dual purposes of determining whether
FCSL and ASL are two separate languages, and whether FCSL, like
ASL, is a member of the sign language group headed by old French
Sign Language.

FRENCH CANADIAN SIGN LANGUAGE

FCSL is the sign language used by deaf Québecois French individuals who use sign language as a major means of communication. It is learned as a first language by both the deaf and normally hearing children of these individuals. Unlike many sign languages, FCSL is embedded in a linguistic milieu consisting of another sign language—ASL—and two spoken languages—French and English. Like many sign languages, educational policies in the schools for the deaf seem to have heavily influenced FCSL's origin and development.

Historical Background

Until 6 years ago, the Québecois French schools for the deaf prohibited classroom use of sign language. However, students at the Institut des Sourds Muets (the boys' school) and the Institute des Sourdes Muetes (the girls' school) clandestinely created sign systems. The boys' sign system may have been marginally influenced by French Sign Language. Faculty monks made sporadic attempts to obtain French Sign Language texts for the boys. Such texts were scarce because sign language had been prohibited in French schools for the deaf since the beginning of the nineteenth century. The girls' sign system may have been influenced by ASL. Deaf nuns from the United States occasionally joined their faculty. Today FCSL is a composite of these two sign systems, although it is impossible to determine at what point the two systems joined and filtered through the schools and signing community.

Thus the relation of FCSL to ASL appears to be a close and complicated one. Historically, French is the spoken language within which eighteenth-century French Sign Language emerged. French Sign Language exerted some undetermined influence on the development of ASL; ASL developed within spoken English. Presently FCSL and ASL exist side by side in Québec, with FCSL signers also being fluent in French to varying degrees, and ASL signers also being fluent in English to varying degrees.

If FCSL's development was indeed influenced by both ASL and French Sign Language, then ASL signers should be able to understand some, but not all, FCSL utterances. However, if FCSL evolved without such influence, then ASL signers should be able to understand very few, if any, FCSL utterances. Since transparency in some

signs is conceivably an influencing factor in inter-sign language comprehension, naïve subjects' comprehension of FCSL utterances
should provide a control against which ASL signers' comprehension
of FCSL can be measured.

Method

Stimuli Utterances

Since picture-generated utterances have proven useful as an objective technique to assess sign language communicative efficiency and
comprehension (Bode, 1974; Jordan, 1975; Jordan & Battison, 1976;
Schlesinger, 1971), this technique was used both to generate FCSL
utterances and to assess the subjects' comprehension of these utterances. The pictures were 21-picture sets, 4 to a page, of the Northwestern Syntax Screening Test (Lee, 1969). The pictures were simple
line drawings of people, objects, and their relationships. These particular pictures were chosen because they were designed to test a
variety of English syntactic structures. It was hoped that by using
these pictures a variety of FCSL syntactic structures would be elicited
for later analysis. Figure 15.1 shows one example of these pictures.

A FCSL–English interpreter instructed four FCSL senders to generate an utterance or utterances that described each of the 21 target
pictures so that future FCSL receivers would be able to select the
target picture from among the four alternatives. The four FCSL senders were all deaf adults living in Montréal. They were considered by
their peers to be fluent in FCSL. The utterances were videotaped and
then edited so that the four senders and their 21 descriptions appeared
in a mixed order. Since the senders spontaneously generated their
picture descriptions, each utterance differed from every other utterance, so that there were $4 \times 21 = 84$ different utterances.

Subjects

The subjects consisted of three receiver groups. The first group
consisted of eight FCSL subjects. These subjects were deaf students
at the Lucien Page High School in Montréal. They were selected by
their teacher for their fluency in FCSL. The second receiver group
consisted of eight ASL subjects. Six of these were deaf students at the
Keefe Regional Vocational High School in Framingham, Massachusetts. The other two subjects were normally hearing, ASL–English
interpreters living in the same area (one was a native ASL signer). The
examiner considered all of the ASL subjects to be fluent in ASL. The

(a)   (b)

(c)   (d)

Figure 15.1. One of the picture sets used in the experiment. Here alternative "C" is the target picture. From L. Lee, *The Northwestern Syntax Screening Test*. Evanston, Illinois: Northwestern University Press, 1969, Reprinted by permission.

third group of subjects consisted of eight normally hearing students at McGill University. None of these subjects had any prior experience with any sign language. Four of the subjects were monolingual speakers of English; four subjects were bilingual speakers of English and French.

Procedure

All of the subjects were tested in their respective schools in groups ranging from one to four subjects. The examiner or interpreter told the subjects in their respective languages that they would see 84 sign language utterances and that each utterance described one picture on each of the 84 picture pages before them. The subjects were instructed first to glance at the four pictures, then to watch the videotaped utterance, and then finally to decide which picture was being described. The subjects were told that they could see an utterance a second time on request, but that they could not see an utterance more than twice. The subjects were not told that the utterances were from FCSL (although the FCSL subjects knew immediately). Nor were the subjects told that the 84 utterances described the same 21 target pictures.

Method of Analysis

The subjects' responses (correct or incorrect) were analyzed with a four-way analysis of variance to determine differences among the three receiver groups, the four senders, and the 84 utterances. Utterances were crossed with senders, and subjects were crossed with language groups. In addition, t tests were performed on the appropriate means to determine the following: first, if the FCSL subjects' performance differed significantly from a perfect level ($N = 84$); second, if the naïve subjects' performance differed significantly from a chance level ($N = \frac{1}{4} \times 84 = 21$); third, if the naïve bilingual subjects' performance differed significantly from the naïve monolingual subjects' performance; and fourth, if any of the receiver groups' performance improved with practice (first 42 items versus last 42 items).

Results

Table 15.1 shows the range, mean, and percentage correct performance for the three receiver groups. Table 15.2 shows the results of the four-way analysis of variance. The analysis of variance yielded significant main effects for the receiver groups ($F = 19.39$, $df = 2, 21$, $p < .01$), the senders ($F = 27.07$, $df = 3, 63$, $p < .01$), and the

TABLE 15.1

Range, Mean, and Mean Percentage Correct Performances of the Three
Receiver Groups

	FCSL	ASL	Naïve
Range ($T = 84$)	67–59	63–32	55–33
Mean	62.63	49.63	42.00
Mean Percentage Correct	77	61	52

TABLE 15.2

Analysis of Variance for FCSL Senders, Receiver Groups, and FCSL Utterances

Source	Mean square	df	F
A—Senders	357.05	3	27.07**
B—Groups	905.26	2	19.39**
C—Utterances	233.58	20	17.78**
S(B)—Subjects	46.66	21	—
AB	16.29	6	1.24 n.s.
AC	73.46	60	6.17**
BC	41.89	40	3.19**
AS(B)	13.19	63	—
SC(B)	13.19	420	—
ABC	20.64	120	1.73**
ASC(B)	11.91	1260	—

$**p < .01$

utterances ($F = 17.78$, $df = 20, 420$, $p < .01$). In addition, the analysis
yielded the following significant interactions: Senders × utterances
($F = 6.17$, $df = 60, 1260$, $p < .01$); receiver groups × utterances ($F =
3.19$, $df = 40, 420$, $p < .01$); and senders × receiver groups × utter-
ances ($F = 1.73$, $df = 120, 1260$, p < .01). Figure 15.2 shows the
receiver groups × utterances interaction.

A Scheffé test of multiple comparisons performed on the receiver
groups' performance means yielded significant differences between
the FCSL and ASL subjects' performance ($F = 15.59$, $p < .01 = 11.56$),
the FCSL and naïve subjects' performance ($F = 46.70$, $p < .01 =
11.56$), and the ASL and naïve subjects' performance ($F = 8.33$, $p <
.05 = 6.94$).

The first t test yielded a significant difference between the FCSL
subjects' performance and a perfect performance ($t = 11.61$, $df = 14$, p

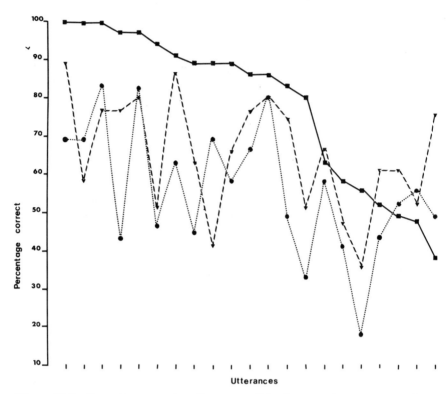

Figure 15.2. Percentage correct performances of the three receiver groups as a function of the FCSL utterances describing the 21 target pictures. The performances are arranged as a function of the FCSL subjects' most to least accurate performance. (Key: ■ = FCSL; ▼ = ASL; ● = naïve.)

< .01). The second t test also yielded a significant difference between the naïve subjects' performance and the chance level ($t = 8.44$, $df = 14$, $p < .01$). The third t test yielded no significant difference in the performance of the naïve bilingual and naïve monolingual subjects ($t = 1.44$, $df = 6$, n.s.). The last series of t tests yielded no significant differences between all the subjects' performance on the first 42 utterances and the last 42 utterances (FCSL: $t = 1.88$, $df = 14$, n.s.; ASL: $t = 0.12$, df = 14, n.s.; naïve: $t = 0.12$, df = 14, n.s.).

Discussion

The ASL subjects comprehended some but not all FCSL utterances ($\bar{x} = 61\%$ correct). These results tend to support the gathered FCSL history, namely, that both ASL and French Sign Language exerted some influence on FCSL development. Thus FCSL should probably be classified with the group of sign languages associated with old French Sign Language (Stokoe, 1974). However, the results' interpretation is complicated by the naïve subjects' performance. The naïve subjects also comprehended some but not all FCSL utterances ($\bar{x}$ = 52% correct). Given this performance, should one also conclude that both ASL and French Sign Language exerted some influence on the development of the naïve subjects' sign language? Of course not. The naïve subjects had no prior experience with any sign language. Conversely, given the naïve subjects' performance, do the results suggest that FCSL is a close approximation to a universal sign language for signers and nonsigners alike? This could only be concluded if performance on multiple choice, picture identification tasks is highly predictive of comprehension in real-life, running conversation, which is highly doubtful. The results are more easily interpreted in conjunction with FCSL and ASL structural similarities and differences as revealed through an examination of the stimuli utterances.

FCSL Phonology

FCSL and ASL phonology appear to be very similar. Within the stimuli sample there were neither movement nor place cheremes that do not also occur in ASL. All the FCSL handshape cheremes in the sample were common to ASL except one. Figure 15.3 shows the FCSL sign TRAIN which uses a "bent-three" handshape. This particular handshape is not among the 19 ASL handshapes described in *A Dictionary of American Sign Language* (Stokoe *et al.*, 1965). This hand-

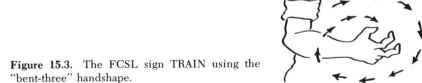

Figure 15.3. The FCSL sign TRAIN using the "bent-three" handshape.

shape does occur in a variation of the ASL sign THREE-HUNDRED, where the "bent-three" replaces the citation form's "C" handshape. The "bent-three" handshape appears to occur with greater frequency in FCSL than in ASL. Because the FCSL sample is limited, it is impossible to determine whether this is the only phonological varia- tion between FCSL and ASL. Casual observation of FCSL also suggests a strong phonological similarity between FCSL and ASL. When an ASL signer observes FCSL for the first time, there is indeed a sense of "seeing something familiar" rather than the striking phone- tic unfamiliarity of, for example, Swedish Sign Language.

FCSL Vocabulary

Sixty-eight percent of the FCSL vocabulary included within the experimental sample was common to ASL vocabulary. Of course, it is impossible to say whether this figure reflects the actual vocabulary correspondence between FCSL and ASL. However, it is interesting to compare this figure with the ASL subjects' mean performance of 61% correct. Some researchers of inter-spoken language comprehension have suggested that vocabulary correspondence in general is a good predictor of inter-spoken language comprehension (Bender & Cooper, 1971). Since the author is unfamiliar with French Sign Language, it is not possible to estimate the vocabulary correspondence between FCSL and French Sign Language.[2]

FCSL Syntax

The FCSL stimuli utterances frequently followed a subject–verb– object word order, which ASL has also been noted to follow (Fischer, 1975). Simultaneity and directionality were syntactic devices that occurred frequently in the FCSL utterances. These syntactic devices are common to ASL (Bellugi & Fischer, 1973) and are surely devices specific to manual–visual languages. Figure 15.4 shows a FCSL utter- ance in which both simultaneity and directionality express syntactic relations. In this utterance (which is one description of the target picture in Figure 15.1), CHAT and REBORD are signed simultane- ously, one with each hand, establishing the relation between the two. Then REBORD is maintained with one hand while the other hand

---

[2] N. Frishberg (1976, personal communication) noted that the FCSL sign ANGLAIS is identical to the French Sign Language sign ANGLAIS, both of which are different from the ASL sign ENGLISH.

Figure 15.4. The FCSL utterance GARÇON CHAT REBORD REGARDE. CHAT and REBORD are signed simultaneously; then REBORD is maintained while RE-GARDE is signed as a directional verb.

signs REGARDE; the sign's direction of movement expressing the relation between the subject GARÇON and the object CHAT. Future research with other sign languages should reveal whether such manual–visual syntactic phenomena are unique to sign languages of the old French Sign Language group or are common to all sign languages.

Thus it appears that FCSL and ASL have many phonetic, semantic, and syntactic similarities. These structural similarities strongly suggest that ASL and French Sign Language exerted some influence on FCSL's development. These structural similarities also support the collected FCSL history. Both the structural similarities and developmental history are supported by the ASL subjects' performance on the FCSL comprehension task. Naturally the question arises as to whether FCSL should be considered a dialect of ASL or a separate sign language. Clearly this study does not answer the question, but does suggest that the differences between the two sign languages are sufficient to prevent ASL signers from complete FCSL comprehension.

This study raises as many questions as it answers, especially regarding research designed to explore inter-sign language comprehension. For example, since the FCSL subjects were observing utterances from their own sign language, why was their performance significantly less than perfect? Why did the naïve subjects perform as well as they did? More important, how should the naïve subjects' performance be interpreted, both in isolation and in conjunction with the FCSL and ASL subjects' performance?

Suggestions for Future Research

Stimuli Generation

Examining the FCSL subjects' performance pattern in Figure 15.2, one might conclude that both the ASL and naïve subjects comprehended some FCSL utterances better than the FCSL subjects did. This does not make much sense. The performance pattern in Figure 15.2 shows that the FCSL subjects were also able to comprehend some FCSL utterances with 100% accuracy. Simply, the FCSL stimuli utterances that the FCSL subjects did not comprehend were often ambiguous in terms of the target picture and alternatives. Hence an experimenter is at some risk when working with a foreign sign language. Only after the data were gathered and the FCSL utterances transcribed was it apparent that some FCSL picture descriptions were so very imaginative and verbose that they were not target specific. In other instances, FCSL senders generated two descriptions, the first being of an alternative rather than target picture. Clearly such utterances were ambiguous for the FSCL receivers, which was reflected in their performance.

There are a number of potential solutions to the problem of stimuli ambiguity. One is to have receivers present and responding during the utterance videotaping. As in the paradigm used by Jordan and Battison (1976), only utterances that result in receivers' accurate picture selection are then used in the experiment.[3] Alternatively, if an appropriate interpreter can be located, ambiguous utterances (in the opinions of the interpreter and experimenter) can be eliminated prior to experimentation. However, too many extraneous variables are perhaps involved in experimental paradigms using target picture description and selection. For example, the receivers' accurate picture selection is clearly as much a function of the senders' ability to perceive and convey distinctions among pictures as it is of inter-sign language comprehension. In addition, picture-generated utterances allow for the possibility that receivers, whether native, foreign, or naïve subjects, can correctly select the target picture without completely comprehending the utterance. This was a problem for some picture descriptions in this experiment. These problems lead directly to the question of transparency in sign language and its effect on inter-sign language comprehension.

The naïve subjects were included in this study as an FCSL transpa-

---

[3] The Jordan and Battison (1976) study was not published at the time this experiment was carried out.

rency measure for the experimental task. Obviously the inclusion of naïve subject performance is a measurement refinement or hindrance, depending upon the particular question asked. For example, in this study the naïve subjects performed with a surprising 52% accuracy level. Does this then suggest that 52% of the ASL subjects' performance can be attributed to FCSL transparency alone and not to inter-sign language structural similarities? The next question is whether transparency in signs is the same for signers and nonsigners. Yet without the naïve subjects' performance as an available yardstick, it would be easy to overestimate the significance of the ASL subjects' performance.

Signers conceivably use both linguistic and nonlinguistic (in this case transparency) cues when attempting to comprehend foreign sign languages. For example, Figure 15.5 shows the FCSL sign LAIT. When naïve subjects were confronted with this sign, a picture of milk, and pictures without milk, the sign was transparent and they selected the correct picture. However, the FCSL sign LAIT is also the ASL sign COW. When ASL subjects were confronted with this sign and the above alternatives, they were at a loss as to which picture to select. Likewise, Figure 15.6 shows the FCSL sign OISEAU, which is the ASL sign BUTTERFLY. In instances such as these, naïve subjects perform as well if not better than signers fluent in a foreign sign language. If the experimenter plans to assess inter-sign language comprehension on the basis of subject performance–comprehension accuracy, perhaps picture identification should not be the sole dependent variable. Transparency in signs is a complicating factor in such

Figure 15.5. The FCSL sign LAIT, which is the ASL sign COW.

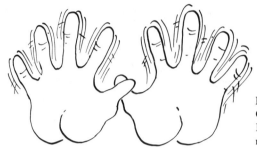

Figure 15.6. The FCSL sign OISEAU, which is the ASL sign BUTTERFLY. This sign is made at midchest level.

tasks. When transparency in signs does become an experimental factor, then it is necessary to answer the following question: If signers are able to comprehend utterances on the basis of transparency alone, should this be considered a part of or apart from inter-sign language comprehension and the linguistic similarities and differences between two sign languages?

There may be a way to assess inter-sign language comprehension that circumvents the entire question of transparency. Shadowing, repeating everything seen (heard), has been shown to be a viable and useful subject response for sign language research. McIntyre and Yamada (1976) successfully used shadowing to measure response latencies in ASL for comparison with response latencies in spoken English. Likewise, Mayberry (1977) has shown that shadowing under varying conditions of signal integrity distinguishes between native and nonnative ASL signers both in terms of overall shadowing accuracy and types of errors. Subjects who are completely unfamiliar with ASL are completely unable to shadow ASL, transparent signs included.

Not only might shadowing circumvent the problem of transparency in signs, shadowing may also allow for stimuli more reflective of real life communication, since any utterances can be potentially shadowed regardless of generation method. However, whether signers would be as inept at shadowing a sign language foreign to them as nonsigners are at shadowing a sign language needs to be investigated. At the same time, some measure of transparency is very useful. For example, is there some measurable phenomenon as "transparency in sign languages," and if so, is the level or degree of transparency useful as a means of classifying sign languages' relationships? No doubt a combination of picture identification and shadowing responses are useful subject–response measures for inter-sign language comprehension.

Sender and Receiver Characteristics

In this study the naïve subjects consisted of bilingual French–English and monolingual English speakers. Casual observation of FCSL revealed that most FCSL signers seemed to accompany their signing with a great deal of French "mouthing." Thus it was hypothesized that the bilingual naïve subjects would perform better than the monolingual naïve subjects on the basis of speechreading alone. This turned out not to be the case. Speechreading may have been a factor in the naïve subjects' performance. Although the bilingual subjects noted that they were able to speechread several signs on the basis of accompanying oral movements, such as the signs CHAPEAU and LAIT, they also reported that such speechreading seemed to be of little help, since the speechread signs–words were often appropriate for all the alternative pictures. Ideally, the monolingual (English) naïve subjects should have provided a control for such speechreading. However, the monolingual naïve subjects reported that they learned to associate some oral movements with pictures over the course of the experiment. This may account for the lack of a significant difference between the two groups' performance.

An important question for inter-sign language comprehension is the role of any oral movements accompanying a sign language. In this experiment, many ASL subjects complained that the oral movements accompanying the FCSL utterances confused and complicated their picture selection. For example, the FCSL sign CHAPEAU is identical to the ASL sign HAT. Here the ASL subjects should have had no problem identifying this FCSL sign. However, the oral movements for "chapeau" and "hat" are quite different. Hence the ASL subjects were confused by the unfamiliar oral movements accompanying the FCSL sign CHAPEAU. Whether oral movements that accompany signing are linguistically optional or mandatory for a given sign language is difficult to determine. This distinction clearly makes a difference in terms of inter-sign language comprehension. For example, in this study one suspects that the FCSL oral movements aided the naïve subjects' overall performance and simultaneously hampered the ASL subjects' overall performance. If these oral movements are linguistically mandatory in FCSL, then the ASL subjects' performance reflects inter-sign language comprehension. On the other hand, if these oral movements are linguistically optional in FCSL, then the ASL subjects' performance probably is not an accurate reflection of inter-sign language comprehension.

There may be a way to attack all these questions at once. Simultaneous recordings can be made of sign language utterances both with and without oral movements using a Chromakey videotape technique (Mayberry, 1977). This then allows for a comparison of sign language comprehension with and without oral movements for (a) native sign language subjects; (b) foreign sign language subjects; and (c) naïve subjects fluent in the surrounding spoken languages of the sign languages under investigation. These comparisons in conjunction with (a) shadowing; (b) picture identification; and (c) structural analysis should yield a wealth of information concerning the relationship of two sign languages in terms of oral movements' contribution to a sign language's comprehension by native, foreign, and naïve subjects and the degree and effect of transparency for foreign and naïve subjects. Both transparency and oral movements are confounding and interrelated factors in inter-sign language comprehension.

Thus far no mention has been made of senders' characteristics and their potential effect on measures of inter-sign language comprehension. In this study four senders were used to determine whether there would be significant performance differences as a function of senders. There were. Figure 15.7 shows the mean percentage correct performances of the three receiver groups as a function of the four senders. Three senders were similar in terms of the subjects' performance. Curiously, sender A's signing resulted in an improved performance for the naïve subjects as well as the signing subjects. Sender A's utterances seemed to be briefer and more "to the point" than those of the other senders. But this alone does not account for the improvement in the naïve subjects' performance. Sender A also signed at a somewhat slower rate than the other senders. Presentation rate may be an influencing factor in such tasks for all subjects. However, it is impossible to say whether presentation rate is the key factor here. The question of sender selection is clearly an important one. Until more is learned about senders' characteristics as they affect sign language comprehension, research designed to assess inter-sign language comprehension should probably utilize a number of different senders.

Although the above factors are all important for experimentation in inter-sign language comprehension, one might legitimately ask about the relationship between inter-sign language comprehension in the experimental setting and in real life communication.

Face-to-Face Communication

Earlier it was pointed out that there are many contradictory opinions regarding inter-sign language comprehension both in the litera-

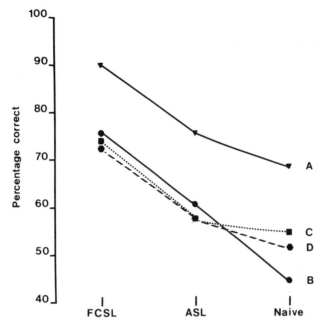

Figure 15.7. The three receiver groups' mean percentage correct performance as a function of the FCSL senders (*A*, *B*, *C*, and *D*).

ture and among signers. Such differences of opinion could be a function of saliency and overgeneralization: The glass is half full and half empty; half the utterances are comprehensible and half the utterances are incomprehensible. Perhaps the actual problem is a lack of distinction between language and nonlanguage communication.

When speakers of two different languages communicate, there is a shift from language to nonlanguage, which also involves a shift from auditory–oral to visual–manual modalities. The modality shift is striking, and the speakers as well as any observers are well aware of this shift. When signers of two different sign languages communicate, there is a language to nonlanguage shift, but there is no modality shift. Some signers are aware of this shift, others are not. At the same time, when speakers of two foreign languages communicate, they typically use both language and gesture. Likewise, signers of two foreign sign languages also use both sign language and gesture. The result is sign language and non-sign language utterances occurring at the same time within the same modalities. Because many gestures can look like signs, signers can easily conclude that the gestures they comprehend are actual utterances from the foreign sign language. This overestimation is heightened by the fact that signers probably use nonlanguage, gestural communication to a far greater extent than speakers of spoken languages: Many signers rely heavily on gesture to communicate with the nonsigners surrounding them. In effect, signers communicate across language boundaries as a part of their daily lives, which probably means that they are very adept at cross-language communication, whether the boundary is one of both modality and language or only language.

Hence, inter-sign language comprehension in the experimental setting may be a measure that has very little predictive value for cross-sign language communication in face-to-face situations. So although sign languages may not be universally understood by signers, signers probably come closest to being the group of individuals who can make themselves universally understood.

CONCLUSION

Research designed to explore inter-sign language comprehension is complex. In fact, the questions raised by this study are probably only the tip of the iceberg. Inter-sign language comprehension involves a number of factors and variables that rarely, if ever, confront the spoken language researcher. Stimuli utterances, subject response, and sender characteristics are factors common to all language research. Questions of transparency, surrounding spoken languages, and oral movements are all factors of prime importance specific to sign language research.

Due to this complexity, definitive statements regarding the relationship of FCSL to ASL are not possible to make. This study suggests that the two sign languages are related and share many structural features. This study also suggests that there are systematic differences between the two sign languages sufficient to impede full inter-sign language comprehension.

ACKNOWLEDGMENTS

The author wishes to thank Julie Roy for her excellent FCSL–English interpreting services, Father Le Boeuf for his help in uncovering bits and pieces of FCSL history, and Martha Cousineau for her help in collecting the data. Special thanks are due to Richard Tucker and the students of his psycholinguistic research seminar for their insightful suggestions and criticisms. The FCSL illustrations were drawn by Jim Siergy.

REFERENCES

Battison, R., & Jordan, I. K. Cross-cultural communication with foreign signers: Fact and fancy. *Sign Language Studies*, 1976, *10*, 53–68.

Bellugi, U., & Klima, E. Aspects of sign language and its structure. In J. Kavanagh & J. Cutting (Eds.), *The Role of Speech in Language*. Cambridge, Massachusetts: MIT Press, 1975.

Bellugi, U., and Fischer, S. A comparison of sign language and spoken language. *Cognition*, 1973, *1*, 173–200.

Bender, M. L., & Cooper, R. L. Mutual intelligibility within Sidamo. *Lingua*, 1971, *27*, 32–52.

Bode, L. Communication of agent, object, and indirect object in signed and spoken languages. *Perceptual and Motor Skills*, 1974, *39*, 1151–1158.

Bornstein, H., and Hamilton, L. B. Recent national dictionaries of signs. *Sign Language Studies*, 1972, *1*, 42–63.

Carmel, S. J. *International hand alphabet charts*. Rockville, Maryland: Published by the author, 1975.

Fischer, S. D. Sign language and linguistic universals. In C. Roher & N. Rewet (Eds.), *Acts du colloque Franco-Allemand de grammaire transformationelle*, Vol. 2. Tuingen: Niemeyer, 1974.

Hansen, B. Varieties in Danish Sign Language and grammatical features of the original sign language. *Sign Language Studies*, 1975, *8*, 250–256.

Hockett, C. *A course in modern linguistics*. New York: Macmillan. (As cited in Bender & Cooper, 1971), 1958.

Jordan, I. K. A referential communication study of signers and speakers using realistic referents. *Sign Language Studies*, 1975, *6*, 65–101.

Jordan, I. K., & Battison, R. A referential communication experiment with foreign sign languages. *Sign Language Studies*, 1976, *8*, 69–101.

Kuschel, R. The silent inventor: The creation of a sign language by the only deaf-mute on a Polynesian Island. *Sign Language Studies*, 1973, *3*, 1–27.

Lane, H. *The wild boy of Aveyron*. Cambridge, Massachusetts: Harvard Univ. Press, 1976.

Lee, L. *The Northwestern syntax screening text*. Evanston, Illinois: Northwestern Univ. Press, 1969.

Mayberry, R. If a chimp can learn sign language, surely my nonverbal client can too. *Asha*, 1976, *18*, 223–228.

Mayberry, R. *Facial expression, noise, and shadowing in American Sign Language*. Paper presented at the National Symposium on Sign Language Research and Teaching, Chicago, Illinois, 1977.

Mayberry, R. Manual communication. In H. Davis & S. R. Silverman (Eds.), *Hearing and deafness*. New York: Holt, Rinehart and Winston, 4e, 1978.

McIntire, M., & Yamada, J. E. *Visual shadowing: An experiment in American Sign Language*. Paper presented at the Winter Meeting of the Linguistic Society of America, Philadelphia, Pennsylvania, 1976.

Peng, F. Kinship signs in Japanese Sign Language. *Sign Language Studies*, 1974, *5*, 31–47.

Sallagoity, P. The sign language of southern France. *Sign Language Studies*, 1975, *7*, 181–202.

Schlesinger, I. M. The grammar of sign languages and the problems of linguistic universals. In J. Morton (Ed.), *Biological and social factors in psycholinguistics*. London: Logos Press, 1971.

Sørensen, R. K. Indications of regular syntax in deaf Danish school children's sign language. *Sign Language Studies*, 1975, *8*, 257–263.

Stokoe, W. C., Casterline, D., & Croneberg, C. *A dictionary of American Sign Language on linguistic principles*. Washington, D.C.: Gallaudet College Press, 1965.

Stokoe, W. C. *Semiotics and human sign languages*. The Hague: Mouton, 1972.

Stokoe, W. C. Classification and description of sign languages. *Current Trends in Linguistics*, 1974, *12*, 345–371.

Wilbur, R. B. Linguistics of manual languages and manual systems. In L. Lloyd (Ed.), *Communication assessment and intervention strategies*. Baltimore: Univ. Park Press, 1976.

World Federation of the Deaf. *Second contribution to the international dictionary of sign language*. Rome: L'Ecole Professionnelle de L'E.N.S, 1971.

Wundt, W. *The language of gestures*. The Hague: Mouton, 1973.

Index